A Brilliant Commodity

A Brilliant Commodity
Diamonds and Jews in a Modern Setting

Saskia Coenen Snyder

OXFORD
UNIVERSITY PRESS

Oxford University Press is a department of the University of Oxford. It furthers
the University's objective of excellence in research, scholarship, and education
by publishing worldwide. Oxford is a registered trade mark of Oxford University
Press in the UK and certain other countries.

Published in the United States of America by Oxford University Press
198 Madison Avenue, New York, NY 10016, United States of America.

© Oxford University Press 2023

All rights reserved. No part of this publication may be reproduced, stored in
a retrieval system, or transmitted, in any form or by any means, without the
prior permission in writing of Oxford University Press, or as expressly permitted
by law, by license, or under terms agreed with the appropriate reproduction
rights organization. Inquiries concerning reproduction outside the scope of the
above should be sent to the Rights Department, Oxford University Press, at the
address above.

You must not circulate this work in any other form
and you must impose this same condition on any acquirer.

Library of Congress Control Number: 2022943910

ISBN 978-0-19-761047-3

DOI: 10.1093/oso/9780197610473.001.0001

9 8 7 6 5 4 3 2 1

Printed by Sheridan Books, Inc., United States of America

To Dashiell Finn,
whose light shines brighter than any diamond in this world

"To us . . . a diamond stood for the making of history, for Empire, and for unbounded wealth. We knew that wars had been waged for the possession of such gems, that neither blackest crime nor oceans of blood could dim their piercing luster. We felt that every celebrated stone, whether shining on the breast of a lovely woman or blazing in the scepter of a king, was a symbol of power, a nucleus of tragedy, a focus of human passion."

—W. C. Scully, *Reminiscences of a South African Pioneer* (1913)

CONTENTS

Preface ix

   Introduction: Clarity, Cut, Carat, and Color 1
1. "Like Dewdrops in the Waving Grass": Diamonds in South Africa 27
2. An Empire Made Portable: London 69
3. "As Long As It Sparkles!": Amsterdam 95
4. "Luxuries Have Now Become Necessities": New York 121
5. Jews and Diamonds in the Popular Imagination 159
   Conclusion 185

Acknowledgments 201
Notes 205
Bibliography 261
Index 277

PREFACE

On a visit to the Amsterdam diamond museum in 2014, in the shadow of the glitter emanating from the Dutch crown jewels, and from a gorilla skull studded with 17,000 brilliants, a modest black and white photograph piqued my interest (Figure P.1). It was a snapshot of Jewish diamond polishers at work in one of nearly seventy diamond factories operating in the Dutch capital at the end of the nineteenth century. Sitting on long wooden benches in front of spinning mills, several men stared into the camera, while others remained focused on the work at hand. They all wore long-sleeved shirts, aprons, and drooping mustaches. Their tired eyes locked with mine. Who were they? How did these *Jodenfabrieken*, or "Jewish factories," come into being?

When I started digging for information, I was stunned to find a wealth of material exposing the weight of diamonds in Dutch-Jewish life and the capital's position as the epicenter of global gem manufacturing. By the late 1890s, roughly 60,000 Jews, or one-tenth of the city population—a proportion that would stay steady until the Holocaust—lived in Amsterdam *diamantstad* ("diamond city"), half of whom relied economically on the stone. The sounds of 7,500 steam-powered polishing mills resonated through the urban landscape for fourteen hours a day. Newspaper boys delivered weeklies of the Diamond Workers' Labor Union to thousands of Jewish families, the majority of whom were working-class people living in the *Jodenbuurt*, the old Jewish neighborhood. Diamond cleaving, cutting, and polishing skills were passed down from one generation to the next, with boys as young as twelve starting apprenticeships. Henri Polak, a Jewish polisher turned labor leader, would eventually secure for this proletarian workforce, by means of large-scale strikes and hard negotiations, a minimum wage and an eight-hour workday—a first in the economies of the Western world. If fin-de-siècle Paris and Berlin laid bare the poles of France and Germany—bourgeois and bohemian, authoritarian and liberal, Catholic and anticlerical—the close of the nineteenth century in

Figure P.1 Diamond Polishers Amsterdam, ca. 1900–1920. International Institute of Social History, Amsterdam: BG A23/56.

Amsterdam was no less fraught with the struggle for dominance in an economy anchored in an extractive industry in Africa, and with a product brought to market by a new Jewish working class that was clawing to get into society.

My explorations deepened with a research trip to South Africa, where I followed the passage of hundreds of thousands of carats moving from hand-dug mines in remote Kimberley to London company offices. Rough stones arrived in mailbags, sent across the South African heartland and the Atlantic Ocean to the capital of the British Empire. Cape Colony records charted the explosive growth of mineral exports. In 1869, as miners discovered massive deposits underneath their pitched tents, 16,542 carats, valued at £24,813—or about £2.5 million by today's values—reached London. Twenty years later, that number had increased to nearly forty million carats at a value of £46,031,190—1/100 of the value today and a full third of the total exports of the entire Cape Colony. Jews were a vital part of this scene. Newspapers from the early 1870s frequently pointed to Jewish *diamantkoopers* (diamond buyers) in the fields, as well as to Jewish auctioneers, and merchant entrepreneurs who set up shop in the emerging "city of canvas." They came from surrounding towns and coastal cities, from London and Lithuania. Touched by diamond fever, Jewish immigrants joined the thousands of people gravitating toward the northern Cape. Barney Barnato, a self-made diamond magnate, first crossed the 750 miles from Cape Town to Kimberley by foot, walking next to an oxcart to a new future.

My quest to learn more about Jews and gems in an age of imperial expansion brought to light transatlantic connections and the formation of a lasting commodity chain. Goods and capital moved at greater speed and in greater quantities from and to previously isolated territories. Jewish diasporic networks linked families and companies in faraway places, positioning Jews at the forefront of the international trade in South African stones. Records at the New York City Public Library disclosed how these diamond networks extended into America, the largest consumer of ornamental gems. New cutting and polishing factories in New York City ran on machinery imported from Holland, as were the workers manning them. Factory owners lured Jewish expert lapidaries across the sea, promising steady paychecks and new adventures. As I searched, map in hand, for old addresses on Nassau Street and Maiden Lane, some façades still featured the outsized glass windows that maximized natural light coming into the workshops, making it easier to work the small stones.

The story that unfolded showed Jews in Africa, Europe, and North America playing crucial roles in every segment of the commodity chain, as immigrant pioneers of the diamond fields and merchant buyers of rough stones, as cutters and polishers in Amsterdam factories and New York city jewelers. Their presence in the industry was sufficiently striking that Jews and diamonds became firmly linked in nineteenth-century popular imagination, a marriage that has persisted to this day.

The archives divulged patterns of economic mobility, as well as of hardship and misfortune. While being Jewish in the diamond business came with certain advantages, it did not guarantee success. There were many failures along the way, and contention between commercial partners was common. Jews in New York threatened the expulsion of immigrant lapidaries jeopardizing the status quo; in Amsterdam, Jewish union leaders fought bitterly with Jewish factory owners; and in Kimberley, Jewish merchants testified in court against their own brethren accused of illegal diamond dealing. Thus Jewish involvement in the industry, fostered by a background in mercantile trade, extensive contacts across oceans, and access to investment capital, did not preclude strife. Ethnic cooperation was practical and sometimes the only option; it was not ideological or always entirely conscious. What mattered most was the extraordinary historical moment when discovery and supply met soaring demand, accelerated by technological advancement, print culture, and the prevailing ethos of enterprise.

Diamonds, Wilkie Collins quipped in his 1868 novel *The Moonstone*, were "carbon, mere carbon." He was mistaken. For Jews, gemstones provided economic sustenance and unprecedented opportunity. The intense, skilled labor that went into preparing rough stones for markets galvanized unions fighting for improved working conditions in factories and workshops. Precious stones drove immigration, not merely to southern Africa and North America, but across borders in Europe as well. They kindled desire among elites to belong and to display new wealth. But seeing Jews bedecked with diamonds raised anxieties over ostentation, charges the non-Jewish public made with ease and regularity.

Stepping out of the diamond museum that day in 2014 and strolling through the city, I was taken aback by how little of this once flourishing industry remains. A few former factories serve as tourist sites while others, razed in postwar redevelopment projects, have disappeared from the urban landscape altogether. The families of the Jewish men in the photograph fell victim to the Nazis in the 1940s. Very few returned from the concentration and death camps. The commodity chain that revolutionized the nineteenth century mineral industry, with Amsterdam as an indispensable link, has decentralized and spread to manufacturers in India, North America, Belgium, Russia, and Israel. Today diamonds are excavated on every continent except Europe, and lapidaries of Jewish, Muslim, Hindu, and Christian descent finish stones for a multi-billion-dollar market. The foundations for this global enterprise, I discovered, lay with Jewish pioneers, *diamantairs*, and merchant entrepreneurs who contributed at every turn to the global economic connectedness that accelerated in the twentieth century.

Facets added to a diamond function like tiny mirrors, refracting incoming light into a multitude of directions, enhancing its sparkle. Placed in its historical setting, the gem performs in similar fashion, illuminating various dimensions of nineteenth-century Jewish life in different parts of the world. As I followed the stone across oceans and hemispheres, I shared in the experiences of the people extracting diamond rich soil in buckets and trolleys, transporting parcels across dangerous, inhospitable terrain in mail carts to seaports, and repositioning gems during the polishing process on cacophonous factory floors. Jewish immigrants and laborers, at work on the African diamond fields, in the Amsterdam *Jodenbuurt*, or on New York's 47th Street, came out of the shadows, and their handiwork shone at the heart of the modern imperial project.

A Brilliant Commodity

Introduction

Clarity, Cut, Carat, and Color

Strolling through the Dutch Impressionism wing of the Rijksmuseum in Amsterdam, visitors may notice that a disproportionate number of oil paintings originate from the art collection of Andries van Wezel (1856–1921). Eduard Karsen's moody scenes of Dutch villages and farmhouses, George Hendrik Breitner's street scenes, Menso Kamerlingh Onnes's flowery still lifes, and Isaac Israëls's colorful portraits of young women adorn the walls, all gifts of this collector. Van Wezel, an affluent businessman and art patron of Jewish descent, born and raised in one of Amsterdam's poorest neighborhoods, had befriended most of the contemporary painters of the Amsterdam Impressionist School. He bequeathed his art collection, consisting of more than one hundred fifty pieces, to the city's largest museum. He wished for the public to marvel, as he had once done, at the artistic talent that portrayed fin-de-siècle life and culture in such fleetingly beautiful ways.

Van Wezel had made his money in diamonds. Born in 1856 to Salomon Levie van Wezel and Judith Levie Ansel, he first set foot in A. E. Daniels & Zoon diamond factory at the age of thirteen. For years he would leave early in the mornings and walk from his home on Lazarus Alley, in the middle of the Jewish neighborhood, to the nearby Daniels factory. Twelve hours later, he returned home to his parents, his older brother Juda (also a diamond polisher apprentice), and his younger brothers Hartog, Marcus, and Joachim. Years earlier, his father had entered *het vak*—the profession, as

Figure I.1 "The South African Diamond Fields," *Harper's Weekly* 14: 725 (November 19, 1870).

the diamond business was known in Dutch circles. Salomon van Wezel, like many other Jewish parents in nineteenth-century Amsterdam, considered diamond manufacturing a sensible career path and subsequently arranged apprenticeships for all of his sons. Not only was it wise to learn a trade but also diamond manufacturing was a line of work that could, when times were good, generate substantial earnings. Fortunately for the van Wezel family, in 1869, the year Andries began his training, the discovery of large diamond deposits in southern Africa injected the local diamond industry with energy, productivity, and revenue, the likes of which Amsterdam had not seen since the Golden Age of the early modern era.

As weekly incomes of skilled diamond workers increased sharply in the 1870s, the van Wezels quickly accumulated capital. Salomon moved up the ranks to manage the Daniels factory. He bought a house on a respectable street and relocated his family. Nearly seventy factories, up from four companies a decade earlier, became operational in Amsterdam over the course of the 1880s.[1] Andries, too, thrived. He invested his savings, and by the age of twenty-six he owned his own firm, purchased a residence on the reputable Prinsengracht (Prince's Canal), and belonged to the privileged male elite with voting rights. Diamonds had changed their lives.

The van Wezels prospered in the transatlantic commodity chain in diamonds that developed in the last quarter of the nineteenth century, connecting people, goods, and technology across continents. West and

East India Company ships had brought diamonds to Europe since the early 1600s, but in small quantities affordable only to European royalty and the aristocracy.[2] These gems came exclusively from India and Brazil, where workers stood knee-deep in riverbeds, sieving muddy debris by hand, unaided by the industrial machinery and mechanization that enabled modern, deep-level mining. Still rare, diamonds were cleaved, cut, and polished by lapidaries in home-based workshops. By the time Andries van Wezel opened his first factory in Amsterdam, all this had changed dramatically. Over two million carats of rough stones arrived annually from an unexpected location deep in the southern African interior; diamond mining companies floated shares and bonds on the European money market to attract foreign investments in the Cape Colony; factories used steam rather than horses to power the mills that metamorphosed rough stones into sparkling brilliants; and tens of thousands of European Jews engaged in the business of buying, manufacturing, and selling diamonds to a growing clientele with regal social ambitions. Van Wezel's success, his factory, the sheer scale of operation, and his professional networks were manifestations of fundamental changes taking place during an age of empire, transforming both the diamond industry and urban Jewish communities.

Focusing on this industry, this book probes the role of Jews in imperial history and, vice versa, the significance of imperialism in Jewish history. Historians have rarely explored the complex Jewish interactions with nineteenth- and twentieth-century overseas empires.[3] It was instead within the political confines of the nation-state that scholars examined Jewish acculturation and integration, a rather narrow lens, considering the geographic mobility and trans-hemispheric commercial networks that were shaping modern Jewish life.[4] *A Brilliant Commodity* hopes to show the permanent footprints that Andries van Wezel and Jewish entrepreneurs like him left on multiple continents—pioneer merchants like Adolf Mosenthal, who, before being drawn to minerals, introduced merino sheep from France and Angora goats from Turkey to South Africa, galvanizing international wool exports; the Lilienfeld brothers; former prize fighter and vaudeville entertainer Barney Barnato, Sammy Marks, known for his salty humor, and the self-effacing Alfred Beit, a master of figures and "exceptional being to rise amid the dust of Kimberley."[5] Their experiences, and those of their families, may not have been the norm for most European Jews, few of whom achieved comparable levels of affluence, yet how they made their living had a profound impact on the lives of countless people in Africa, Europe, and America. Their enterprise and intrigues, their alliances and fallings-out in the development of mining, manufacturing, and trade of diamonds were felt in employment, labor relations, and unionization on the economic front, in public perceptions of Jews, and in patterns of migration and the growth of cities. By 1875, less than ten years after the discovery of diamonds in Kimberley, the diggers' settlement had grown into the second-largest town in South Africa. Seven years later, it was the first town in the entire Southern Hemisphere to integrate electric street lighting. Its nearly 50,000 inhabitants included several hundred Jews, making it the second-largest Jewish community in the Cape Colony. When Barnato, Beit, Marks, and other men from the diamond fields threw themselves into gold mining in the 1880s, applying the expertise and capital resources accumulated in the Northern Cape to the Witwatersrand, they were extending the British Empire's reach into the African interior.[6] As "Randlords," their imprint on local and transatlantic economies, positive as well as negative, deepened.[7]

If these changing realities signaled a revitalized Jewish presence in world affairs within the realms of empire, why have historians paid so little attention to it? Inserting colonialism into that assessment has proven difficult, particularly in Anglo-Jewish history, which has long overlooked the colonial connections that undergirded the *embourgeoisement* of Jews in Great Britain.[8] The identification of colonialism with Jewish finance may have caused the topic to be unpopular, not to mention the ever-present polemics over Zionism and the State of Israel, which makes colonialism "a veritable mine field for Jewish studies scholars."[9] But the lacuna echoes beyond the field of Anglo-Jewish history. Catherine Hall surmised that the discipline of Anglo history as a whole worked for decades under the assumption that "Britain could be understood in itself, without reference to other histories." Only more recently, she admitted, has a consensus formed that "in order to understand the specificity of the national formation, we have to look outside it."[10]

New imperial histories have subsequently tested the premise that "colony" and "metropole" were terms that could be understood only in relation to each other, although in these studies, too, Jews have remained largely anonymous. Their small numbers in imperial settings may have been a factor, as well as their ambiguous social standing and legal status, which took on different meanings as they moved between the physical spaces of the center and periphery. Jews were "white but not quite," and they often fell in-between the categories of "us" and "them."[11] Indeed, "if ever there was a people that lived at the borders between cultures and civilizations it is the Jews," stated Ivan Kalmar and Derek Penslar.[12] The difficulty of neatly placing Jews in familiar categories—they could be both orientalist and orientalized, the colonist and the colonized—frequently resulted in their omission from the literature altogether. It is precisely this hybridity that exposes the lapses of established classifications and the complexities of the imperial project, two useful starting points in the recalibrations of Jewish economic history.

Close examination of the diamond and its trajectory through imperial channels tells the story of the people who mined, traded, cut, polished, wore, sold, and desired these gems in local and transatlantic contexts. It brings to life hopeful diamond diggers in the Northern Cape, factory workers in Amsterdam, and diamond dealers in New York City, all connected through the fluctuations of supply and demand. A material culture approach to the diamond underscores how empire facilitated the movement of diamonds and people, determining their routes and destinations, and how the object itself molded the contours of empire. The stone's economic potential pulled industrial and urban development into the South African heartland, propelling large numbers of people across continents. Extracting diamonds from the earth required water pumps, steam-powered engines, explosives, conveyors, mining locomotives, boilers, and other heavy equipment to be hauled from London to Kimberley, first by boat across the Atlantic and then by cart and wagon, hundreds of miles inland. The diamond's reputation as the rarest, purest, and most precious stone validated the European claim to colonial wealth, justifying imperial rule of the "dark continent," the seizure of land, and the exploitation of black labor. "Diamonds," as one observer of the mineral display at the Paris exhibition exclaimed, really do "sparkle with meaning!"[13]

◆ ◆ ◆

Husband: "I don't believe you heard a word of the sermon today. You were looking the whole time at the diamonds that woman in front of us wore."

Wife: "Well, there are sermons in stone, you know."
—*Puck* 52: 1334 (September 1902)

To acquire rough stones for his factory, Andries van Wezel traveled to London several times a month to meet with suppliers who had received shipments directly from the Cape Colony. The British port was the entry point of diamonds exported from Africa, and consequently it became the exclusive hub for distribution. Weekly trade magazines kept continental factory owners up to date about steamboats carrying Cape stones. Van Wezel consulted the *Diamant Handelsblad* to find the times, dates, and quantities of "rough" scheduled to arrive in London, and with these reports in hand he planned his trips. He first boarded the train to Ostende, stepped on the boat to Dover, and finally took the South-Eastern railroad to London, where he checked into the Grand Hotel Holborn Viaduct. The next day, he met with suppliers at Hatton Garden and paid in cash, after which he returned to Amsterdam with rough gems in his luggage, and allocated the newly acquired goods to his factories, where workers cleaved, cut, and polished rough diamonds into brilliant gems and prepared them for the international retail market. Van Wezel would sell the finished diamonds to clients, most coming from France, Russia, and the United States. Everyone knew the highest quality diamonds were manufactured on Dutch mills, and van Wezel could count on having international buyers travel to him to make their next purchase.

The ambitious van Wezel invested heavily in city property. He purchased residences along the Amsterdam canals, on the elegant Sarphatistraat—named after the Dutch-Jewish physician and philanthropist Samuel Sarphati—and on the Weteringschans. These addresses instantly announced his status and commercial success; only the well-to-do could afford to live in these neighborhoods. Around the turn of the century, he took his business abroad. Leaving the Amsterdam company in the hands of his younger brothers Hartog, Marcus, and Joachim, he moved south to Belgium, where wages were lower and labor unions less powerful. The diamond union succeeded so spectacularly in Amsterdam that it encouraged factory owners to migrate elsewhere, primarily to Antwerp, where the industry soon surpassed that of its northern counterpart, both in size and production. Unionization efforts in Belgium were not nearly as effective as in the Netherlands, where the *Algemeene Nederlandse Diamantbewerkersbond* (General Dutch Diamond Workers Union or ANDB) had played hardball with employers to secure higher wages and a shorter work week.

Van Wezel joined a small exodus of factory owners who circumvented the growing power of the proletariat by relocating across the border.[14] The family business added a transatlantic component when Marcus and Joachim opened firms in New York at the end of the 1890s.[15] America, with its growing appetite for luxury commodities, had become the largest consumer of ornamental diamonds—brilliants cut and polished almost exclusively in Amsterdam. Changes in American import duties, however, made New York an increasingly attractive alternative to the Dutch city. To protect American industries from foreign competition, Congress, in 1894, passed the Wilson-Gorman Tariff Act, tripling duties on imported, finished stones while leaving the tariff for rough stones unchanged at 10 percent. Anticipating a blow to their export sales of polished goods, Marcus and Joachim set up shop in New York, transferring manufacture, technology, and manpower into the territory of the industry's premier customer. The van Wezels opened a factory on the corner of Bleecker Street and the Bowery and established a trade school where American apprentices could learn *het vak*.[16] Most of their factory workers and skilled craftsmen were Dutch-Jewish emigrés who had sought new job opportunities in America after wearying of the recession that had forced mills in Amsterdam to a grinding halt in the early nineties. Attuned to economic barometers, and with a family business to fall back on, the van Wezel brothers adapted. To attract experts, they offered master cutters and polishers an advance on the boat fare from Amsterdam to New York, to be repaid in weekly installments after starting work in the factory. This happened to be a form of indentured labor in violation of US labor laws and led to the deportation of numerous Dutch-Jewish diamond workers in the mid-1890s.[17] By the time the "Bros. van Wezel" mills started production, however, some three hundred Jewish diamond workers from Amsterdam were making a living in New York, congregating around Maiden Lane, John Street, and Nassau Street (currently the Financial District).[18] Most worked for Dutch-Jewish entrepreneurs, such as J. H. Groen, P. De Bruyn, and Van Moppes & Son—all born in Amsterdam—who had established diamond polishing workshops a few years before the van Wezel brothers.[19] Andries followed his brothers to New York in 1909, where he again expanded the family business by opening a firm on Walker Street. In what historian Robert P. Swierenga called "a major technology transfer," the van Wezel family and their contemporaries helped develop the diamond industry on American soil and solidified New York's position in the transatlantic commodity chain.[20]

Andries van Wezel owed his success in part to opportunities generated by the geopolitics of the late nineteenth century. He made his career in an age marked by European imperial expansion, by technological advances, including industrial diamond mining and faster, more reliable transportation, and by the dramatic rise of bourgeois consumer markets. Van Wezel found himself at a turning point that revolutionized the transatlantic gem industry. Timing mattered. The seemingly unlimited supply of minerals discovered in the South African interior, for example, could only be extracted from deep below the surface with the help of innovative mining technology and capital investments provided by European banking families and commercial companies, who understood the economic potential of untapped diamond deposits. Rough stones could reach Europe on a regular basis thanks to Britain's postal services, carrying parcels and mailbags first from mining towns to coastal Cape Town by horse-drawn carriages, and then across the Atlantic Ocean on steamships.[21] Furthermore, with new steam-driven equipment, Amsterdam mills could spin in overtime, boosting production and the burgeoning middle class's unprecedented purchasing power. Once the prerogative of monarchies and aristocracies, diamonds were now available to the *nouveaux riches* to flaunt their affluence and to display their white privilege and geopolitical dominance.[22] The appetite for jewelry, in turn, intensified as advertising in illustrated newspapers and magazines effectively linked sparkling gems to prestige and good taste and, in the early twentieth century, to everlasting love. While husbands did not always last, diamonds would, and no engagement could be genuine without both.

The van Wezels, and other Jewish families like them, functioned as the "software of empire."[23] Jews in the diamond trade could often turn to parents, siblings, uncles, and cousins living on different continents to assist in business transactions, establish transatlantic commercial ties, and secure financial investments and exchange information, functions that reflected the lopsided participation of Jews in the industry. These networks played a crucial role in every segment of the commodity chain, from the moment of extracting rough stones from South African soil to retailing in metropolitan markets across the Atlantic. Van Wezel and his contemporaries operated within a commercial system, imperial and modern, whose infrastructure and outreach expedited a flourishing gem industry. Van Wezel was both an entrepreneur working within empire and an agent of empire, his commercial activities integral to the expansion of nineteenth-century consumer culture. Aided by modernization, van Wezel simultaneously personified it.

Often described in histories of Jewish economic activity as intermediaries operating at the margins of innovation and commercial activity, Jews in actuality were central agents of early globalization.[24] Through commerce in precious stones, Jews fashioned the economic connectedness that characterized the twentieth century. By following the diamond from mine to market, *A Brilliant Commodity* illuminates Jewish pioneers steering the international exchange of a luxury commodity, connecting African sites of supply, European manufacturing centers, and Western consumers. It aims for a fresh understanding of the flow of goods and capital across the globe, as well as a greater appreciation for Jewish contributions to the making of the modern world.

◆ ◆ ◆

"Diamonds here are all the rage, and one hears from morning till night of nothing else."
—A Port Elizabeth correspondent for *The Jewish Chronicle* (April 15, 1870)

While diamonds have a long history, it was the unforeseen boom in diamond mining operations and long-distance trade that ignited the industry. Up to the 1860s, diamonds had been found in so-called alluvial deposits, that is, in the soil of riverbeds where, over millions of years, gemstones were pushed to the surface by means of volcanic pressure and dispersed by the flow of rivers. To extract them from the soil, workers used sieves and water, an excruciatingly labor-intensive process that produced comparatively small yields. The famous diamonds of the pre-modern period, such as the Hope Diamond, the Orlov, and the Kohinoor ("Mountain of Light"), were found in the Golconda region of India, known for producing unusually large stones. For over two hundred years, the majority of Indian diamonds traveled on East India Company ships to London, which by the 1670s had become the most important market for the trade in minerals. Sephardic merchants, adept in transnational commerce, shipped rough stones from the Goa region on the east coast of the Indian subcontinent to London, and from there they distributed yields to European port cities, primarily Antwerp and Amsterdam, for cutting and polishing. Since these two cities had no gem polishing guilds restricting access to Christians, Jews living in the Low Countries encountered few obstacles to finding work in the industry, and many Jewish men and women consequently specialized in the arts of diamond cutting, sawing, cleaving, and polishing.[25]

The discovery of rich deposits in the Brazilian districts of Minas Gerais and Bahia spurred imports. Brazil, then under Portuguese control, soon eclipsed India and remained the largest supplier of diamonds until the 1850s, averaging an annual output of some 200,000 carats.[26] South Africa, meanwhile, was not on any diamond prospector's map. Before 1850, the Cape Colony and its main port in Cape Town had functioned chiefly as staging posts for British commercial ships en route to India. The Cape of Good Hope connected the mother country to fertile imperial territories in the East but lacked potential of its own. While Cape Town had attracted a cosmopolitan populace, the colony appeared to have few natural resources and negligible industries, and consequently it received little consideration from London-based administrators. By the 1860s the Cape Colony was running a deficit of nearly a million British pounds, only worsened by the destabilizing effect of the American Civil War, and by long stretches of drought damaging wine and wool production. Much of the attention the Cape received was therefore negative.[27] British and Boer farmers had trekked inland to eke out an agrarian subsistence, but their numbers were modest, and they certainly were not the solution to the colony's glaring financial distress. There were two railway lines, one running sixty-three miles between Cape Town and Wellington, the other connecting Durban to the Indian Ocean coast in Natal, a mere seven miles. Railway-building had ground to a halt for lack of money, leaving the ox-wagon as the primary means of transportation for people and freight. Telegraph lines did not yet reach beyond port cities, hindering efficient communication. The agricultural Cape colony, living in the shadow of the bountiful East Indies, gained a reputation as one of the most troublesome and expensive possessions of the British Empire.

The first stones were found in the Northern Cape, near the confluence of the Vaal and Orange rivers, some 700 miles northeast of Cape Town. In 1866, a teenager named Erasmus Jacobs picked up an unusually shiny "pebble" on his father's farm, located near a frontier village called Hopetown. The stone exchanged hands numerous times, until months later it arrived by postal mail on the desk of Dr. William Guybon Atherstone, a naturalist and geologist in Grahamstown, who identified the *blink klippe* (bright stone) as a diamond.

Captivated by this unusual find, the governor of the Cape Colony, Sir Philip Wodehouse, bought the gem and, in 1878, sent it to the Paris

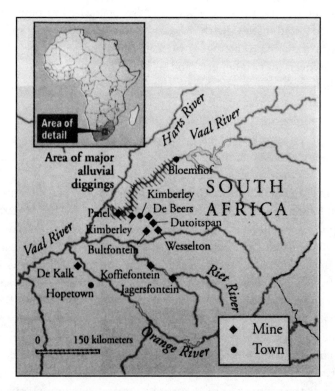

Figure I.2 Map of Diamond Fields. From A. J. A. Janse, "A History of Diamond Sources in Africa, Part I," *Gems and Gemology* 31: 4 (Winter 1995), 232.

Exhibition, where visitors could see with their own eyes that Cape soil produced more than just grapes. Reports in the British press piqued the interest of London-based diamond merchant Harry Emanuel. Emanuel was connected by marriage to the Coster family that owned a large diamond-cutting firm in Amsterdam. To verify the diamond find, Emanuel dispatched mineralogist James R. Gregory to the Northern Cape. Upon his return, Gregory stated in *Geological Magazine* that he "made a very careful and lengthened [sic] examination of the district where diamonds were said to have been found, but he saw no indications whatsoever that warranted the expectation of the findings of diamonds, or of diamond-bearing deposits, at any of the localities." He spoke with such conviction of "the whole diamond discovery in South Africa [being] an imposture, a bubble scheme," that contemporaries often spoke of "Gregories" in cases of mistaken identification of gemstones in subsequent years.[28] Emanuel's interest lapsed. His 1867 *Diamonds and Precious Stones: Their History, Value and Distinguishing Characteristics, with Simple Tests for Their Identification* focused on Brazil. South Africa, he assured readers, held no promise. Doubts about the authenticity of the Jacobs boy's stone originated in part from geographical bias. Everyone knew high-quality diamonds came from India, Borneo, and Brazil, not from the "savage" African interior. For a full year, commented the editor of *Diamond News*, "the wiseacres of England [were] pooh-poohing and ridiculing the reported diamond discovery [because] diamonds at the Cape—or anything good to come from Capeward—was too absurd for an Englishman born on British soil, and especially a Londoner, to swallow."[29]

The British public accepted the reputation of South Africa's backwardness and fights over land between Boer farmers and black African natives. It was less inclined to acknowledge "that there should be any natural formation in the Cape that contained diamonds of the first water." That was "a story to tell the marines—not Englishmen."[30] The enlightened British were not so gullible as to believe that "the dark continent" produced exquisite white diamonds.[31] "[I]t was too much to expect," wrote Victorian novelist Anthony Trollope, "that from a spot so insignificant as this corner of the Orange and Vaal rivers should be found a rival to the time-honoured glories of Brazil and India. It was too good to believe, or to some perhaps too bad, that there should suddenly come a plethora of diamonds from among the Hottentots."[32] Besides, any well-informed reader understood that diamonds were exclusively unearthed near water sources, in alluvial deposits, so whatever stone had been picked up by the farmer's son "must have been carried there inside the gizzards of ostriches from some far-distant region" and deposited on the Jacobs family's property.[33] Thus, while the discovery of a South African diamond was widely covered in daily newspapers and scientific journals, "it did not at first cause any great sensation." Gardner F. Williams, the future general manager of the De Beers Mining Company, noted that its existence was "flatly denied by pretentious examiners who came from England to report on the Hopetown Field."[34]

How mistaken these early observers were. In 1869, a local farmer, Schalk van Niekerk, stepped into a country store in Hopetown carrying a superb 83½ carat diamond. He had bought it from a Griqua shepherd named Swartboy, who had found it and sold it to him for five hundred sheep, ten oxen, and a horse, the equivalent of £400.[35] Van Niekerk had taken the stone to the store, owned by German-Jewish cousins Gustav and Martin Lilienfeld, because he knew they traded in diamonds and could have it appraised. The Lilienfelds had commercial and family connections to the Mosenthal family in Port Elizabeth, whose import and export firm had shipped two diamonds worth £800 on the RMS Briton to London just a month earlier.[36] Gustav and Martin invited lapidary Louis Hond, a Dutch-Jewish émigré to South Africa, to assess the gem. It proved to be one of the largest diamonds ever found. With the financial support and guarantee of Adolph Mosenthal & Co., the Lilienfelds purchased the Star of Africa for £11,200 and sent it to Port Elizabeth. Mosenthal displayed the diamond in his store for two days in late May, charging a small fee to support the local Ladies' Benevolent Society. The company then shipped it, insured for £300, to the Mosenthal parent firm in London. They sold it to the jewelers Hunt and Roskell. By the time the Earl of Dudley purchased the Star of Africa for £25,000, James Gregory's reputation had tarnished and the diamond rush to the Northern Cape had begun.

Into the valley of the Vaal River rode a motley crowd of fortune hunters who hastily established mining camps. First were Pniel and Hebron on the southern and northern banks of the Vaal respectively, and Klipdrift, soon renamed Barkly, twenty-five miles upstream. Still convinced that diamonds required a water source, early diggers gravitated toward the muddy riverbeds. Many had come from small towns and farms in the Orange Free State. They were soon joined by black Africans, including the Tlhaping, Kora, and Griqua peoples, by hopefuls from the southern British colonies, and by newly arrived immigrants. By October 1870, upward of 5,000 diggers had set up tents and were sifting soil. These were men, observed historian Robert Turrell, "of every pursuit and profession"—butchers, bakers, sailors, tailors, lawyers, blacksmiths, masons, doctors, carpenters, clerks, tradesmen, and laborers—"jumbled together in queerer association than the comrades in the march to Finchley," a famous Hogarth painting of disorganized troops.[37] In their feverish attempt to find minerals, they applied techniques similar to those practiced in India and Brazil, that is, standing knee-deep in the soft gravel, tediously washing and sieving debris.

Much to the bewilderment of the first diggers, diamonds cropped up in unexpected "dry" locations, without any clear pattern, challenging long-held alluvial-based theories on diamond extraction. Prospectors found stones on a farm called Vooruitzicht ("Foresight"), some twenty miles from Pniel and the Vaal river, belonging to the brothers Johannes Nikolaas and Diederik Arnoldus de Beer. Two adjacent farms, Bultfontein and Dorstfontein, yielded stones as well. Within a few months, a multitude of diggers and prospectors descended on these properties with their horses and oxen, wagons, tents, tools, and sometimes their families. Clinking and clanging noises resounded in the previously tranquil landscape, sounds that gave way at night to the crackling of countless small fires that burned to keep wild animals at bay. By 1872, wrote one observer, "the glory of Pniel ha[d] fled" and in its stead the so-called dry diggings had produced permanent settlements, including New Rush (the future town of Kimberley), Dutoitspan, and Bultfontein, all located within a four miles radius.[38] Until recently "a howling wilderness," the Northern Cape had become "a glittering Golconda" when diggers discovered underground, funnel-shaped diamond pipes.[39] Water had served to disperse stones but the real treasures, diggers learned, were hiding in large concentrations below the very ground on which they had pitched their tents. Four of these obscure sites would collectively supply millions of carats to global consumers over the course of the next century: the Colesberg Kopje (Kimberley), De Beers, Dutoitspan, and Bultfontein mines.

Johannes and Diederik de Beers sold their farm long before anyone realized the extent of the riches beneath the surface. Overwhelmed by an army of diggers equipped with shovels and pickaxes, they accepted the offer of £6,000 made by merchant speculators and fled. Cornelis Hendrik du Plooi, who owned the 14,457-acre Bultfontein farm, did the same. Already in November 1869, Leopold Lilienfeld, who had examined the Star of Africa in his country store only months before, together with Henry Barlow Webb and Louis Hond purchased the Bultfontein farm for £2,000 and leased the nearby 6,579-acre Dutoitspan farm for ten years. Again with financial support from the Mosenthal family firm, the trio founded a company on the diamond fields, the Hopetown Company.

The first African diamonds to reach Europe arrived by steamship as part of the larger export inventory of companies trading between Port Elizabeth and London. Adolph Mosenthal & Co., for example, received purchases from the Lilienfelds in Hopetown and sent rough stones in its regular cargo containing wool and wine to its London-based branch, Joseph Mosenthal

& Co. During the first two years after the Star of Africa display, the firm exported to England a total of 2,893 diamonds valued at £56,025 to Britain. The Mosenthals carved out the initial trajectory of what would become one of the most lucrative maritime routes in history. Cape Colony records chart the explosive growth of diamond exports as a growing number of mining companies extracted stones. 16,542 carats, valued at £24,813, reached London in 1869; ten years later the annual output topped 2,110,000 carats, worth more than two and a half million British pounds. By the late 1880s, nearly forty million carats had been shipped to London at a value of £46,031,190—a full third of the total exports of the entire Cape Colony.[40]

Jewish diggers, adventurers, buyers, sellers, and entrepreneurs on three continents became key players through close commercial networks and family connections, creating a successful commodity chain between Cape Town, London, Amsterdam, and New York. Examining diamonds and the routes they traveled and the people who mined, processed, and sold them places Jews at the heart of the industry. Similarly, it acknowledges the diamond's significance to Jewish social and economic mobility. The stones' journey—from the ground to the pockets of itinerant traders to polite society's *décolleté*—projects in fascinating ways the mechanics of Jewish modernization.

◆ ◆ ◆

"By the better and more rapid intercommunication of peoples, by the further development of industry and navigation, nations have become wealthy, and luxuries have now become necessities."

—*The Jewish Messenger* (May 19, 1871)

Chapter 1 describes the role of Jewish traders, merchants, and companies in the unfolding of the South African mining industry, their motivations, and the importance of kinship branches in Europe to Jewish commercial connections. Already proficient in local and long-distance trade, Jews in the Northern Cape performed in what literary theorist Mary Louise Pratt termed a contact zone, "a space of colonial encounters [where] people geographically and historically separate come into contact with each other and establish ongoing relations."[41] South African as well as Anglo-German and Lithuanian Jews interacted every day with Boer farmers, non-Jewish immigrants from a host of different countries, and native Africans, all flocking to the diamond fields and making it an arena for imperial encounters. The Koranna, for example, a Khoisan group situated in the northern regions of the Cape Colony, visited the region regularly, supplying budding mining communities with milk, whereas the Tlhaping

VALUE OF ROUGH DIAMONDS EXPORTED FROM THE CAPE COLONY IN THE YEARS 1867 TO 1892 INCLUSIVE. OBTAINED BY COMPARING ALL AVAILABLE SOURCES OF INFORMATION.

Year.	Weight in Carats.	Rate per Carat.	Annual Value.	Value for Five Years.
		£ s. d.	£	£
1867 }	200	,,	650	
1868 }				
1869	16,550	1 10 0	24,818	
1870	102,500	1 10 0	153,160	
1871	269,000	1 10 0	403,319	
1872	1,069,000	1 10 0	1,618,076	
				2,200,343
1873	1,100,000	1 10 0	1,648,451	
1874	1,313,500	1 0 0	1,313,334	
1875	1,380,000	1 2 0	1,548,634	
1876	1,513,000	1 0 0	1,513,107	
1877	1,765,000	0 19 6	1,723,145	
				7,746,671
1878	1,920,000	1 2 6	2,159,208	
1879	2,110,000	1 4 0	2,570,850	
1880	2,140,000	1 1 6	3,367,897	
1881	3,090,000	1 7 0	4,176,202	
1882	2,680,000	1 10 0	3,892,602	
				16,276,758
1883	2,410,000	1 2 9	2,742,476	
1884	2,263,734	1 4 9	2,807,329	
1885	2,489,631	1 0 5	2,480,659	
1886	3,185,061	1 2 4	3,504,756	
1887	3,596,930	1 3 7	4,212,470	
				15,786,684
1888	3,841,937	1 1 0	4,022,379	
1889	2,961,973	1 9 8	4,325,137	
1890	2,504,726	1 13 3	4,162,010	
1891	3,255,545	1 5 6	4,174,208	
1892	3,039,002	1 5 8	3,906,992	
				20,590,726
Totals:	50,910,854	1 4 8	62,600,187	

N.B.—Previous to 1883, the weights and rates per carat can only be taken as approximate. The values of exports from 1872 to 1892, are those given by the collector of customs, Cape Town.
See also remarks on p. 72.

Figure I.3 "Cape Exports," *Cape Almanac* (1893). National Library of South Africa, Cape Town.

sold timber and vegetables. Boer farmers traveled to rapidly growing towns such as Kimberley to market meat—beef and lamb, but also reebok and antelope—although they sometimes sold their provisions to the Mpondo first, who then traveled to the diamond fields to trade their purchases. Merchants from Cape Town, too, sensed economic opportunity and arrived with thousands of single-barreled firearms, items in high demand. Between

1872 and 1877, an estimated 150,000 firearms were brought into the Cape port; half were sent directly to Kimberley while another 3,000 came from Natal.[42] Jews from villages and coastal towns made their way to the diamond fields with wagons full of general merchandise likely to be in demand among diggers and prospectors, such as shovels, buckets, rope, clothing, boots, pots and pans, canvas, and tent poles. They joined the diverse and multilingual community of hopefuls who streamed in growing numbers to the Northern Cape. The excavation and movement of diamonds, and the sustenance of the population immersed in the operation, was contingent on other goods and labor: fuel, food, building materials, machinery, alcohol, guns, and, later, coal and dynamite—all of which had to be hauled hundreds of miles inland, mainly by ox-wagon. The diamond fields therefore operated as a contact zone bringing together people of different nationalities, ethnicities, and faiths, as well as various consumer needs that linked local, regional, and coastal economies in South Africa to already functioning transatlantic commodity chains.

Jewish merchants thrived in this milieu. While the number of Jews in the digging community was small, they were heavily represented among traders and merchants. It was chiefly private Jewish firms that first invested in South African mining technology and were major players in the consolidation of claims, forming joint-stock mining companies at a time when the focus of non-Jewish European banking and investment firms

Figure I.4 "Sorting Diamonds on a Sorting Table, 1872." Kimberley Africana Library #N7964.14.

lay elsewhere, primarily the Far East. In the early 1870s, the immediate sources of capital and initiative lay within South Africa more than overseas, in the periphery rather than in London, and were headed by local Jewish mercantile firms with close commercial and family connections to European port cities. Many Jewish merchants thus benefited from having access to entrepreneurial firms and commercial families in Europe, especially in London and Paris, that might look favorably on investments in mining claims and companies at a time when those opportunities were not as easily within reach, or considered too risky, to non-Jews. One of the chief characteristics of this specialized network in the 1870s and 1880s was the rapid movement of mercantile and private banking capital into the South African centers of operation, leading to investment in the mines and the expansion of wholesale and manufacturing for a flourishing retail market in Europe and the United States. Particularly in the 1880s, when industrial mining required substantial investment capital, commercial connections, and fortitude, Jewish merchants moved from the margins of the mineral trade to the center of the industry.

Chapter 2 follows the diamond from South Africa to London, the global trading hub for rough stones. The Indian and Brazilian trades of the eighteenth and nineteenth centuries had already created the foundations of London's market in rough—*Kelly's Post Office Directory* listed 57 diamond merchants in 1865, several years before the discovery of South African deposits[43]—but the ascendancy of Britain's Cape Colony cemented London as the distribution center of the industry. Diamond dealers clustered in Hatton Garden, a district between Clerkenwell and the Thames that remains the city's best-known jewelry district. Those Jewish merchants who had been successful in South Africa established new firms in London to facilitate international trade. Anton Dünkelsbühler, for example, who had started out as an agent for Mosenthal in 1872, founded his own import business in Hatton Garden in 1875, as did Martin Lilienfeld. Harry Mosenthal, based in Port Elizabeth, opened the London branch Joseph Mosenthal & Co., and installed three cousins to run it. Barney Barnato established a London office in 1880, following in the footsteps of Joseph Bros, and Lewis & Marks Sr., Jewish merchants who shared practical knowledge of the diamond trade. As Chapter 2 demonstrates, most directors of the main diamond importing companies in London had hands-on experience on the Northern Cape's mineral fields and, with the financial support of Jewish investors, became principal actors in the consolidation of claims and companies.

By the early 1890s, largely as the result of company amalgamation and centralization, the De Beers Consolidated Diamond Mines Company came to control over 90 percent of South Africa's production, turning out three million carats per year. De Beers sold its entire yield to the newly established Diamond Syndicate, made up of ten London-based Jewish firms whose company directors had first made careers on the South African diamond fields and became leading diamond merchants at Holborn Viaduct and Hatton Garden. All these firms, including Mosenthal & Co., Barnato Brothers, Werner, Beit & Co., and A. Dünkelsbühler, were linked by marriage and owned sister branches in the Cape Colony. Members of the Diamond Syndicate held monthly viewings for their continental clients, such as Andries van Wezel, who traveled to London to purchase rough stones. Van Wezel would remain on the list of select clients as long as he complied with Syndicate rules that required buyers to accept pre-arranged assortments of mixed quality stones. They knew better than to refuse orders or complain about market pricing. Having gained the exclusive right to sell South African rough, the Syndicate had the authority, in collaboration with De Beers, to regulate the production, sale, and value of diamonds.[44]

The majority of rough stones then left Great Britain for what one contemporary called "hospitable little Holland."[45] In Amsterdam, the focus of Chapter 3, stones were cut, polished, and prepared for the retail market. Diamond manufacturing expanded exponentially after the discovery of South African mines. In 1896, Amsterdam counted 7,500 mills, up tenfold from the early 1850s, and the diamond industry had become the third-largest labor sector after construction and dock work. Remarkably, over 50 percent of the Amsterdam Jewish population, which reached 60,000 people in the 1890s, made its living from the stone—as cutters, polishers, setters, apprentices, tradesmen, factory supervisors, *diamantairs*, or dependents.[46] Contrary to their Jewish brethren across the English Channel, the majority of Jews in the diamond business were working class people who lived modest lives. They most likely never saw the final piece of jewelry that contained "their" diamonds; they never set foot in the retail stores that sold the rings, tiaras, brooches, and pins so desirable to men and women of a social class wholly different from their own. Nevertheless, as this chapter illustrates, Amsterdam Jews proved indispensable to the success of the commodity chain. The millions of carats mined on the South African diamond fields could only find their way to affluent necklines after master cutters and polishers transformed rough stones into sparkling brilliants, pendeloques, roses, pear-, and tear-shaped jewels. While Europe counted various smaller centers of diamond manufacturing, including Geneva, Hesse, Berlin, and Antwerp—the latter would surpass Amsterdam after World War I—Amsterdam in the nineteenth century was its principal home.

The importance of the stone was not merely economic. Unregulated labor conditions and the unpredictability of a supply of stones dependent on the dictates of De Beers and the London Syndicate politicized the proletariat, leading to massive strikes and, in 1894, to the country's first organized diamond workers' labor union. As improved mining technology in South Africa increased supply, threatening to lower the price for rough stones and depress wages, De Beers and the London Syndicate moved to regulate the distribution of rough available to Dutch cutters and polishers and to standardize their compensation. What van Wezel paid in London to purchase new inventory determined the number of workers he could hire to prepare the product for retailers. Developments in South African mines and decisions made in London offices redounded on factory floors in Amsterdam. While each segment of the commodity chain was anchored to a different part of the globe, from extraction in South Africa to distribution in Great Britain, manufacturing in Holland and Belgium, and retail in the United States, segments were conjoined and mutually dependent.

Chapter 4 turns to the United States, where an insatiable American appetite kept demand high, encouraging businessmen to establish, expand, and supply jewelry stores in major US cities with polished stones. Dutch trade magazines wrote reassuringly that wealthy New York ladies, such as "Mrs. Frederick van der Bilt," poised in their status as American royalty, attended opera performances wearing diamond crowns modeled after that of the Queen of England.[47] By the time they reached America, the ornamental gems had traveled thousands of miles, had been touched, cut, polished, studied, appraised, and passed on by numerous hands.

In America, too, external conditions reverberated locally. The Dutch labor strikes of the mid-1890s and the astonishing success of the Diamond Workers' Union (ANDB), headed by the Jewish labor leader Henri Polak, led to the founding of union locals elsewhere, including the United Diamond Workers of Brooklyn, which met for the first time on May 1, 1895.[48] With statutes written in Dutch, the organization aimed to improve the work conditions of lapidaries in New York, the majority of whom had emigrated recently from Holland.

As the establishment of the London Diamond Syndicate had resulted in strictly regulated output, driving unemployment in continental centers of manufacturing, and as the ANDB forced factory owners to abide by new labor laws, Amsterdam-Jewish entrepreneurs branched out to more attractive venues such as New York City. By the late 1890s, they had convinced hundreds of Jewish master cutters and polishers to cross the Atlantic and start new careers. "One hears Dutch almost exclusively when walking through Nassau Street and John Street," reported one newspaper, "as ninety percent of the diamond workers there come from Holland."[49] Chapter 4 examines the effort to establish a polishing industry on American soil.

The involvement of Jews in all segments of the diamond industry had profound cultural ramifications. The final chapter reiterates that this book is not a classic economic or financial history, but a multifaceted account of an extraordinary period. Chapter 5 considers late nineteenth-century representations that associated Jews with diamonds, particularly in the English-language press, political cartoons, and popular fiction. When news about the discovery of diamonds in South Africa first circulated through scientific journals, Jews were largely absent from these narratives. Reporting on the initial Cape finds, *Geological Magazine* and *The English Mechanic and World of Science* focused on geology and the mineralogical properties that determined a diamond's shape and color, rather than on the social origins of the prospector. *Scientific American: A Weekly Journal of Practical Information, Art, Science, Mechanics, Chemistry, and Manufacturers* described the manufacturing process and contained detailed illustrations of the tools, mills, and techniques used by cutters and polishers. That most of these experts were Jewish was not a concern. Sometimes authors mentioned, as a matter of fact, that diamond manufacturing was largely in the hands of "Hebrews," "Israelites," or "Dutch-Jewish masters," but there was no elaboration of this point.[50] Interest in South African diamonds soon spilled over to the popular press and there, too, early references to Jews involved in trade and manufacturing were benign. *The Illustrated London News* and *Harper's Weekly* featured articles and illustrations of the diamond fields, showing readers the physical landscape of the Northern Cape, where diggers hovered over sieves washing diamondiferous debris. They celebrated Amsterdam as the global center of diamond cutting, but also covered the World Fairs and International Colonial Exhibitions in Amsterdam, London, Paris, and Chicago, where visitors gawked at Cape diamonds on display and observed the process of excavation, production, and manufacturing at staged diamond exhibitions.[51] From *The Illustrated London News* to the Dutch *De Diamant Adamas* to America's *Vanity Fair*, the press reported widely on these events, but references to Jews appeared mostly in the margins of this commentary.

The association of Jews and diamonds received explicit attention in Victorian fiction, pulp and highbrow, contemporary travel journals, and political cartoons—literary and artistic mediums—which appropriated long-held stereotypes about the Jew's innate business acumen, untrustworthiness, and thirst for power. In stories by T. W. Eady and George Chatwynd Griffith, for example, central Jewish characters dramatized

IDB (illegal diamond buying), while Yiddish-speaking Jews operated as stock-villains infiltrating London high society.[52] Travelogs, too, chronicling a gentleman's adventures abroad, included accounts of the diamond fields, identifying Jews as members of "the diamond-buying fraternity," as overdetermined "Leviathans" or as "gentlemen of the Hebrew persuasion hailing from Petticoat Lane."[53] Dr. Josiah Wright Matthews, coming across Jewish peddlers on the diamond fields, reminisced that "London sen[t] from Whitechapel and Petticoat Lane her quota of fried-fish dealers, old clo' men, quondam fruit merchants, and 'vill you buy a vatch' gentry, speedily [bringing] their home experience into profitable use." He described Jews as "debased," yet in possession of "business training, quick wit, and racial genius for trade," traits that could turn poor peddlers into wealthy capitalists. The growing monopoly of the London Diamond Syndicate in the 1890s, whose company directors were almost all Jewish, and the fabulous fortunes amassed by a small number of diamond dealers only strengthened stereotypes, feeding popular views of Jewish obsessions with profit and economic control. In an era when racial antisemitism was gaining ground and when eastern European Jewish emigration to England, the United States, and South Africa peaked, Jewish success in the international diamond trade stirred up nativist anxieties that found expression in the literary press.

While diamonds in the long run empowered many Jews, their prominence in the industry worked against them as well. As Jews became "insiders" through their newly attained mobility, acculturation, and political activism, they also remained "outsiders." Jewish commercial success, while admirable and envied, remained suspect in its origins, development, and goals. Political cartoons mocked Jewish affluence by showing opulent, diamond-decked caricatures parading their status in front of others, or by portraying poor peddlers who were secretly wealthy and therefore dishonest. While it was acceptable for Jews to work in the manufacture and trade of diamonds, non-Jews appeared less comfortable seeing them wear such exclusive gems. The highest quality stones, "Cape whites," asserted one popular print, belonged to WASP elites, not to ethnic or racial inferiors. The four C's—clarity, cut, carat, and color—that classified diamonds from highest to lowest grade, from pure white to "boart," a diamond powder used for polishing, aligned with prevailing racial classifications. Attempts by Jews to join the ranks of "Cape white" were met with envy, admiration, and derision—an ambivalence that lies at the very heart of modernity.[54] The dichotomous potency of the diamond exposed the limits to full Jewish integration and acceptance, leaving Jews vulnerable as political realities changed.

"It's dark there, but full of diamonds."

—Arthur Miller, *Death of a Salesman*

Wary of reinforcing stereotypes about Jewish power, scholars of Jewish history and culture have been hesitant to link Jews to global markets in luxury goods or to the growth of capitalism in imperial contexts. Lest Jews appear to be predisposed to capitalist enterprise, maximizing profits, and having their hands on the levers of economic control, most research veered predominantly toward topics within national frameworks such as political integration, religious reform, and antisemitism. The ascendancy of cultural history further pushed questions concerning Jewish commercial activity to the sidelines, though that has changed. In the last two decades, scholarly interests and trends in the field of Jewish Studies have shifted considerably, reflecting the multidisciplinary potential of women's and gender studies, transnationalism, foodways, commodity and consumer cultures, and nonwestern diaspora communities. An awakening curiosity in Jewish economic history has been part of this widening paradigm. In the last few years alone, thoughtful studies have appeared on the relationship between Jews, imperial trade, and the rise of modern capitalism, marking an

Figure I.5 "Diamonds." Uncataloged Card, National Library of South Africa, Cape Town, South Africa.

economic turn in a field that seeks to normalize Jewish contributions to the making of the modern world.[55]

Long experience in commercial and mercantile trades, geographic mobility, and economic need, as well as the inestimable value of access to ethnic and familial networks gave Jews advantages, whether they were prospectors on the South African diamond fields, polishers in Dutch factories, brokers in London, or retailers in New York City. Jews were geographically well-situated and in many cases actively resituated themselves to play instrumental roles at a historically opportune time. This is not to say that the industry ever consisted exclusively of Jews or that they were always successful in their endeavors; the large majority did not become fabulously wealthy. The point is that diamonds affected Jewish lives in Europe, South Africa, and America to such a degree that it is fair to argue that Jewish entrepreneurs, *diamantairs*, brokers, retailers, and manufacturers acted not as intermediaries on the periphery, but as dynamic agents of imperial capitalism.

Ethnic networks and ties of kinship remained important in modern market societies, as Jews in the diamond industry demonstrate. Ethnic ties did not, as classic economic theory predicted, succumb inevitably to the force of individualism, to anonymous or impersonal, rational markets of exchange so characteristic of the industrial age.[56] Trade itself, rather than the religion or ethnicity of participants, became the main explanatory factor of global economic growth. These days, more attention is given to the power of networks—familial, ethnic, religious, financial, commercial, or informational—signaling one of the most significant developments in business history.[57] This book aims to recover the faces and families behind the production and exchange of a luxury commodity and to build on this literature. In the modern, transatlantic diamond trade, Jews mattered.

The study of diasporic activity and transatlantic commercial networks in the realm of Jewish history most often has been confined to the early modern period, when overcoming the difficulties of long-distance travel and communication called for heavy reliance on dependable family.[58] Trust and reputation reduced risk, thereby strengthening transnational mercantile networks. The diasporic nature of Jewish settlement lent itself particularly well to the creation of such personal webs. This has continued in modern times. Jewish adaptation to modernity did not lead to a decline of familial relationships and ethnic cooperation, regardless of whether Jews traded in ostrich feathers, cotton, ready-made garments, or diamonds.[59] Andries van Wezel became an apprentice through his father's connections to the Daniels & Sons diamond factory in Amsterdam. He expanded his business in Antwerp with the help of his brothers, purchased rough materials from Jewish-owned companies affiliated with the London Diamond Syndicate, and established polishing branches in New York City with the aid of his sons.

Acknowledging ethnicity as a factor does not mean that the diamond industry was exclusively Jewish or that its actors worked solely within Jewish networks from a deliberate strategy of ethnic solidarity.[60] The primary objective of diamond workers was to make a living and, when fortunate enough, accumulate capital for investment. These goals could be achieved more easily by cooperating with people within one's own family and milieu, especially at a time when doing business in challenging frontier markets, such as the African interior, carried extraordinary risks. Anglo-Jewish writer and political activist Israel Zangwill astutely observed that it was "not what the anti-Semite vainly imagines, a solidarity of the whole race, but merely a solidarity of private families" that accounted for Jewish economic success.[61] For South African peddlers, Dutch cutters and polishers, British and American entrepreneurs alike, ethnic ties eased entry into and movement within the transatlantic diamond trade.

An 1895 editorial in the *Jewish Chronicle* suggests that Anglo-Jews were well aware of their imperial role. It announced rather loftily that "the great and prosperous [British] empire which is in the making in South Africa will have been largely built up by Jewish effort." While acknowledging the presence and activities of "capitalists from every country of enterprising men," the writer emphasized that "those who owe their energy and faithfulness to Hebrew birth and training have been among the foremost in the beneficent task of converting the temperate regions of the dark continent from barren Veldt into smiling pastures or opulent mines." His hyperbole echoed the prevailing imperial ethos of nineteenth-century European elites, a conviction that superior, educated white men were bringing civilization and prosperity to Africa. Anglo Jews, the *Chronicle* implied, should be recognized as notable actors on the British imperial scene. "What a romantic history will be," he mused, "when the historian relates how the wandering minstrel founded a great industry, and inscribes Jewish names among the earliest and steadiest adherents of the far-sighted Englishman [Cecil Rhodes] who went out the Cape a young Oxonian travelling for health, and returned a few weeks ago the chosen Minister of a great nation of English and Dutch descent, the President of a great Company."[62] The "minstrel" he referred to was Barnett Isaacs, better known as Barney Barnato. Born into a poor Jewish family in London's Whitechapel district, Barnato followed his brother to Cape Town in the early 1870s with a few cents in his pocket. He walked nearly seven hundred miles to the diamond fields, where he started peddling. By the mid-1890s, before throwing himself to his death into the

Atlantic Ocean while traveling to London, Barnato owned the Kimberley mine, secured a lifetime board membership of the De Beers Company, and had become one of the wealthiest diamond magnates in South Africa.

His story, however, was not a romantic one. An imperialist in his thinking and practice, Barnato claimed South African land that wasn't his. He exploited black labor and believed he had every right to maximize profits by all means. How deeply Jewish commercial activity was entwined in nineteenth-century transatlantic markets was clear-cut in the diamond trade. As agents of an imperial project, Jewish men and women built commercial economies step by step. Operating within already functioning imperial geographies ensured their success. An investigation of precious stones—fresh out of the ground, sealed in envelopes en route to London, or dangling from a socialite's ear—reveals how Jews cut and polished a path for themselves in the modern world.

Figure 1.1 "Cape Diamond." Cigarette Card, "Famous Gems of the World" Series, ca. 1890. New York Public Library Digital Collections: Image #1554869.

CHAPTER 1

"Like Dewdrops in the Waving Grass"

Diamonds in South Africa

Bad luck, however, cannot last,
A turn must come some day;
A ninety-carat would change the past,
And make the future gay;
May every digger's luck be this,
Who to these Fields has come;
And take back health, and wealth, and bliss,
To those he's left at home.
—"Digger's Song," in Charles A. Payton, *The Diamond Diggings of South Africa* (1872)

Journeying in the wobbly horse-drawn coach of the Inland Transport Company, connecting the 750 miles between Cape Town and New Rush (Kimberley), Charles Chapman was struck by the diversity of his fellow travel companions. It was June 1871—winter in the Southern Hemisphere—and Chapman, a self-described "traveling agent of the British *Shipping and Mercantile Gazette*," was en route to the recently discovered diamond fields in the Northern Cape.[1] He sat in a box-shaped, open-sided coach that offered seats to fourteen passengers. In front of him, next to the driver and his "bastard Hottentot holding the whip," sat a "stout, red-headed, navvy-looking fellow with a wooden pipe in his mouth." Having received several hundred British pounds from entrepreneurial friends, he intended to find diamonds and make them all a fortune. This lad alone, observed Chapman, constituted "the lock, stock and barrel of a company." A second row of seats was occupied by two merchants and a Scotsman, while the third row included "a gentleman of the Jewish persuasion . . . [perhaps] a dealer in garments," as well as a hotel-keeper and an "officer out of one of the steamers." The officer had impulsively bought a claim at New Rush from a merchant aboard a steamboat between Southampton and Cape Town. Infected by diamond fever, the officer had exchanged a career at sea for a risky venture in the South African heartland. Behind Chapman sat a young gentleman from England with "just enough money to take him [to the diamond fields]," aspiring to join the ranks of the diamond merchant adjacent to him, a London mercantile company representative.

British travel writer Frederick Boyle made the long trek to the diamond fields a few months later and depicted a similarly diverse group of passengers sharing a cramped Inland Transport Company coach for seven full days before reaching "the promised land."[2] His companions included two barristers, a mineralogist, "a woman traveling to rejoin her husband, three fellows [who were] going to dig, one veteran returning from a spree in Cape Town," and two merchants. At an average speed of six miles per hour, the fully loaded coach, drawn by eight horses, was pulled over rocks, tree roots, ant heaps, mud holes, and—most awful of all, according to Boyle—pebbles. In addition to the painful path, the stifling heat, dust, and near constant flies caused such agony for the British gentleman that he felt subjected to "the utmost Beëlzebub could do against [him]."[3]

These coach travelers constituted a microcosm of the early diamond field population. Penniless pioneers and manual laborers as well as educated lawyers, forty-niners from California, and well-to-do merchants; white Capetonians as well as black Africans; Europeans, Asians, and Americans of various religious backgrounds—Christians, Jews, Muslims, Hindus—all were drawn there by the dream of riches. They gravitated to a region that by 1870 newspapers around the world propitiously labeled, in capital letters, "The Diamond Fields" on the African continent and beyond. As news of diamond discoveries spread, stirring popular imaginations and heightening expectations, thousands of diggers, dealers, laborers, and speculators flocked to the areas near the confluence of the Orange and Vaal Rivers and set up camp. By the end of 1870, over 5,000 people had settled in the vicinity, many of them Boer farmers from the Orange Free State and the South African Republic (Transvaal), as well as recently arrived immigrants.[4] They lived in a sea of canvas tents and galvanized-iron shacks around the main excavation sites. Nineteen-year-old George Beet described the scene as "a roaring camp . . . the hullabaloo [of which] would make any California mining camp sound like the twittering of a dove cot."[5]

Contemporary travel correspondents repeatedly commented on the presence of Jews or "Hebrews" in the Babel of early digging communities. In New Rush, Dutoitspan, and Bultfontein, they reported seeing "a marvelous motley assemblage" of diggers, speculators, traders, saloon-keepers, professional gamblers, barristers, indeed "faces of every conceivable cast and colour of the human race, [from] the shores of the Mediterranean, the Black Sea, the White Sea, the Red Sea . . . [from] the shores of the China Seas, the Pacific Ocean . . . Jews and Gentiles . . . Xhosa, Malays, Zulu, Pedi, Englishmen, Dutchmen, Germans, Frenchmen, Turks, Greeks, Swedes and Yankees . . . even a Laplander!"[6] Chapman observed "a smattering of people from every nation on the face of the earth—digging, sifting, and sorting from morning till night, day after day, month after month."[7] Jews thus belonged to a colorful community that descended in large numbers—50,000 by 1872—on the once isolated farmland of Boer settlers.

Of the many Jewish immigrants on the scene, comparatively few were engaged in digging and prospecting. Jewish names appeared periodically in the newly established *Diamond News* and *The Diamond Fields Advertiser* that announced successful finds on a weekly basis. Diamond-digger-turned-editor of the *Diamond News* Ikey Sonnenberg reported that a "Mr. David" as well as a "Mr. Rothschild" found stones at Dutoitspan on May 26, 1871, but the fifty-odd other listed individuals were most likely of non-Jewish descent.[8] "Messr. Heppell and Harley found another pretty diamond" in mid-July, as did Messrs. Giddy and Van Gelder, Murray, McIntire, and Heathcote.[9] The *Diamond Fields Advertiser*, in a section titled "The Finds," mentioned a Fitzpatrick, Kennedy, Clark, and Cox; at the end of August two diggers named Hyman and Moses found stones. In addition to the Fitzpatricks and Kennedys, presumably white, there were large numbers of black Africans with picks and shovels. One Christian missionary remarked that these men were "not servants [but] quite well educated diggers or merchants."[10] In fact, 120 out of 135 registered claim holders at the 1874 Bultfontein encampment were black.[11] Mfengu, Ngqika, Natal Zulu, Xhosa, and Griquas responded to the diamond rush and owned claims before discriminatory mining legislation introduced in the mid-1870s made black claim holding illegal—the first in a series of measures to exclude Africans from mine ownership and steal their livelihood.[12]

In South Africa, as elsewhere, Jews were a minority population. That the number of Jews among those digging, sieving, and sorting remained modest is not surprising. Although exact demographic data for the early settlements in the Northern Cape are unknown, the 1875 census counted

538 Jews in the entire Cape Colony, a mere 0.23 percent of its population of European descent, most of whom lived in Cape Town.[13] Moreover, consistent with their professional experiences and economic profiles, Jews—established South African Jews as well as recent immigrants—concentrated on commercial enterprises to provide growing populations with goods and services.[14] A small number of Jews worked with pick-axes, buckets, and shovels, but a greater number were engaged in getting such tools to the diamond fields in the first place.

In the late 1860s and early 1870s, Jewish involvement thus centered primarily on the trade of general merchandise, outfitting the diggers and their camps, and offering commercial services in the currency for settlement in the Northern Cape. The sudden concentration of human activity in an area of four square miles on a semibarren plateau, remote from coastal centers of commerce and manufacturing, created a high demand for middlemen and provisioners. Having limited access to financial credit, diggers and prospectors relied on long-distance exchange complicated by slow communication and wagon-based transportation. Jewish merchants built a niche. Since networks of produce and labor supplies for the diamond fields were not yet integrated into regional economies, Jewish entrepreneurs sensed an opportunity to service the booming market for commodities and accrue the benefits that could be attained through long-distance networks.[15] The Inland Transport Company that took Charles Chapman and Frederick Boyle to the diamond fields, for example, had been founded by a Jewish immigrant from Polzin in German Pomerania, Adolf Arnholz. He owned a store in Ceres in the Cape Colony—a village named after the Roman goddess of Agriculture—approximately eighty miles northeast of Cape Town. As the original route to the diamond diggings passed through Ceres, Arnholz conceived the idea of running the first regular passenger service between the Northern Cape settlements and the coast, an enterprise that turned into a successful company. Similarly, Joel Myers from Port Elizabeth "brought a portable iron store with him, packed with goods (some four or five loads). He had not opened for more than two or three days ere he ran short of many articles of which he brought a large supply."[16] Meyers had stocked up on goods in Port Elizabeth and relocated, by means of wagons and oxen, not merely the merchandise, but also the materials to build a small store nearly five hundred miles inland. After he arrived in Klipdrift, he set up shop, "keeping the best and cheapest supply of everything for diggers and farmers."[17] The first edition of the *Diamond Field* reported that "both Klipdrift and Pniel are becoming places of considerable trade. . . . Mr. Joel Myer's new store is conspicuous for its size and excellence, between fifty and sixty feet long and thirty wide." In addition to Myers, "Mr.

Figure 1.2 "The Hope Town Establishment." Dolores Fleisher and Angela Caccia, *Merchant Pioneers: The House of Mosenthal* (Johannesburg: J. Ball, 1983).

Schiffman is putting up a store; auctioneers have their regular sales . . . and Mr. Isaac Sonnenberg's stores are crowded with wagons and thronged with customers [and] he has placed a boat on the Modder River."[18] In other pioneer settlements, such as Dutoitspan, David Levy, from the small town of Bethulie, as well as David Seeligsohn opened businesses "selling general merchandise of all kind."[19]

Well-established South African Jewish commercial firms, too, such as the Mosenthal Bros. and Lilienfeld Bros. of Cape Town and Port Elizabeth sent storekeepers to the vicinity to meet the new demand for supplies, contributing to the expansion of an economic infrastructure that connected the South African interior to coastal towns. Adolph and Joseph Mosenthal, who had left Kassel, Germany, in the 1840s, had established trading posts that provided Boer farmers with luxuries and essentials imported from Europe, such as ready-made men's clothing, boots, hosiery, clay and "Dutch farmer pipes," brandy, tea kettles, buttons, furniture, bed feathers, saddlery, cheese, and "pickles and mustard."[20] Their younger brother Julius Mosenthal ran the English side of the South African venture. From London, he selected and ordered English goods, arranged the details of shipping, and sent large consignments of cargo on the *Mazeppa*, the *St. Helena*, the *Horwood*, the *Port Fleetwood*, and the *Mountain Maid* to Cape Town and Port Elizabeth. By 1856 Mosenthal Bros. had opened five country stores in the Cape region besides those on the coast (including Cape Town). As a leading merino wool merchant in the Colony, the company exported twenty-three million pounds of merino wool to Great Britain in 1860, worth nearly one and a half million British pounds sterling. Joseph Mosenthal's niece,

Bertha, married Abraham Lilienfeld, whose brothers Martin and Gustav in turn married Bertha's sisters Minna and Sara Gers, firmly linking the two families. Their entrepreneurial fathers, brothers, and uncles in London and continental Europe established offices to expand their trading network. Hermann Mosenthal, Adolph and Joseph's cousin, managed a South African branch in Murraysburg, a small village some sixty miles northwest of Graaff-Reinet. Nathaniel Adler, Julius's brother-in-law, took the reins of the Cape Town establishment. Martin and Gustav Lilienfeld joined the commercial enterprise by opening a shop in the frontier village of Hopetown in 1861. By the 1870s they were dealing in hides, mohair, wool, and ostrich feathers. It was in the Hopetown branch, located on the border of the Orange River, that the first diamonds found in alluvial deposits were traded and sent via Port Elizabeth across the Atlantic to Europe.

The Mosenthal and Lilienfeld families were prominent names, but other Jewish merchants with coastal interests in the Northern Cape similarly extended the borders of colonial commerce in the late 1860s and early 1870s. The brothers Kossuth, Krauss, and Henry Hart, all from Cape Town, began transporting goods to the mushrooming mining towns of New Rush, Dutoitspan, Pniel, and Bultfontein.[21] One contributor to the *Cape Argus* daily newspaper found it "but natural and in the regular course of things that the most active seaport and trading places in the Colony should have its business branches everywhere, [that] generally speaking, [coastal] Bay men monopolize the trade of the Fields."[22] Documenting "Life at the Diggings" in a weekly series, the author noted rather nonchalantly that "at Klipdrift, you meet Isidore Gordon, Joel Myers, Wilhelm Schultz . . . and many more. [N]early all the Port Elizabeth firms are directly represented on the Fields—Mosenthal & Co., Dunell, Ebden & Co., Hyam Benjamin, Lippert & Co. etc. etc." Jews may not have been very visible among the early diggers, but they were certainly well represented among the dealers and traders who supplied digging communities with whatever they needed to work a claim.

Newly arrived Jewish immigrants, too, engaged in commerce. Isaac Lewis and his cousin Samuel (Sammy) Marks, born in Neustadt-Sugind, Lithuania, arrived in South Africa, via London, in the late 1860s, making their way to the diamond fields with wagons full of provisions for hungry prospectors. Starting out as peddlers, they were dealing in diamonds before long, especially as diggers working claims often bartered diamonds for daily necessities.[23] Rough stones served as currency, and it soon became apparent that the diamond trade alone was sufficiently lucrative to climb the economic ladder. Lewis and Marks assumed an occupation that contemporaries almost exclusively associated with Jews, namely *kopje-walloping*, Afrikaans-English for peddling on the small hillock ("kopje") that topped a kimberlite pipe.[24] They, as well as other Jewish immigrants, such as Leopold and George Albu (originally from Berlin), and Barnett and Harry Isaacs and their cousin David Harris, made daily rounds from claim to claim, buying rough stones directly from diggers either in their tents or at the sorting table.[25] With a set of small scales, a magnifying glass, and cash in their pockets, they asked if workers had any stones to sell. Cash-starved diggers were glad to exchange their finds for money, which they needed for water, food, firewood, liquor, and licenses. When diggers found a stone, they typically sold it that very day for the best price so that their small-scale enterprise could continue to function. *Kopjewallopers* then sold these stones for a profit directly to *diamantkoopers*, or diamond buyers, in the nearest township. They performed a useful service by moving the freshly unearthed gems to buyers, often local representatives from Cape Town or Port Elizabeth commercial firms or, after 1870, from European diamond merchants. As intermediaries, *kopje-wallopers* acted as the first link in a transatlantic commodity chain in diamonds.

It is not unusual to find nostalgic descriptions of Jewish *kopje-wallopers* in the historical literature of the South African diamond fields. Wearing long boots and carrying a courier bag of cash, the itinerant trader, often on horseback, roamed the fields, seeking imminent wealth and pioneering autonomy.[26] That *kopje-wallopers* were a temporary phenomenon, soon replaced by professional agents representing colonial mercantile companies, only enhanced their exoticism. So did the occasional case that lends truth to legend. Sammy Marks, son of an itinerant tailor, made a meager living as a peddler in jewelry. Expanding their sights, he and his cousin bought a horse and cart and traveled from farm to farm, and town to town, selling their wares. Responding to first reports of diamond discoveries, they loaded a wagon full of supplies and made their way to the diamond fields, where they "were eagerly welcomed," reminisced the *Jewish Chronicle*, "for there was not even such a thing as a woolen shirt to be bought for love or diamonds—money there was not yet."[27]

Marks soon entered into a partnership with Louis Cohen, another recently arrived *kopje-walloper*. "These two young Hebrews," recorded one contemporary in his journal, "picked out a shanty to their liking for an office . . . a little tin shed, 8 by 6 feet, owned by an Irishman who offered it for rent at a guinea a day," and started a diamond-buying business next to Maloney's Bar on Dutoitspan's Main Road.[28] They invested their small profits in purchasing individual claims which—after deep-level mining a few years later revealed the abundance of concentrated diamonds deposits—grew into the ownership of the most lucrative real estate in the

Figure 1.3 Barney Barnato and Friend C. Moses, 1875.

world. For Marks and Cohen, their brothers (for whom they sent later), and numerous other Jewish immigrants, peddling had been less a career than a starting point; it served as a business apprenticeship to future success.[29]

Barney Barnato, born Barnett Isaacs in 1852 in Whitechapel, London, shared these humble beginnings. He was the second son of shopkeeper Isaac and Leah Isaacs and grandson of the rabbi of the Aldgate synagogue. For most of his early life Barnato lived over the shop with his older brother, Harry, and three sisters, and attended, together with his cousin David Harris, the Jews' Free School in Spitalfields. As a teenager, Barnato worked in his father's business and, with Harry, performed amateur stage turns as conjurors to earn extra income. Their acts, introduced as "Harry and Barney, too!" led him to assume the stage name of Barnato, a surname that stuck for the remainder of his life. In 1872, the brothers were drawn to the Kimberley diamond fields by the tales of adventure and riches recounted by David Harris, who had gone there at age fourteen. Allegedly toting forty boxes of cigars and a few coins in his pockets, Barnato followed his brother to South Africa in the summer of 1873. It took him nearly two months to reach the Northern Cape by bullock wagon—the slowest and cheapest form of transportation—a time he described as "one of the jolliest times [he] ever had. The accommodation consisted of permission to walk alongside the wagon when it moved, and to sleep under it when it stopped."[30] Once he reached Kimberley, Harris introduced him to the basics of diamond dealing. Initially he peddled notebooks and pencils to diggers, quickly making a name for himself, by participating in amateur boxing and theatrical performances at Kimberley's Theatre Royal.

Barnato, Harris, Marks, and Cohen established themselves as *diamantkoopers* with "offices" in wooden shacks in the center of the local township, relying on *kopje-wallopers* to bring them daily yields. For the first few months following the 1869 diamond discoveries—before the great diamond merchants of Europe sent their scouts to Kimberley to open buying firms—Barnato bought directly from peddlers. He and other *diamantkoopers* then sold the diamonds at public auctions in Kimberley, Dutoitspan, or Cape Town to commercial agents affiliated with coastal businesses, such as Mosenthal Bros., Lilienfeld Bros., and Leopold Lippert & Co. Thus the trade in diamonds was folded into already functioning long-distance import- and export operations. Alfred Augustus Rothschild, for example, promoting himself as an "auctioneer, commissions and general

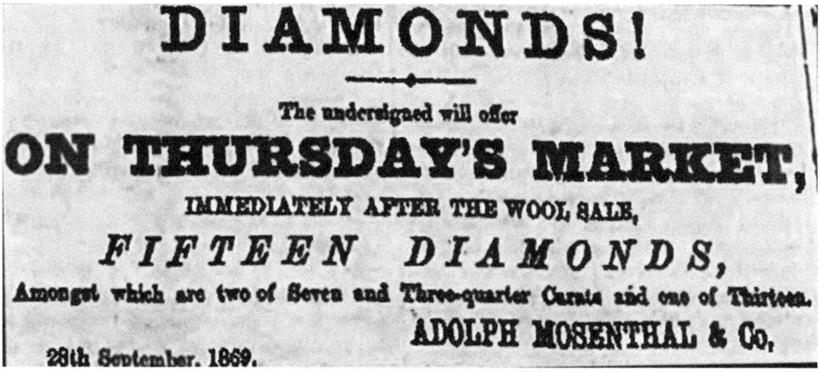

DIAMONDS!

The undersigned will offer

ON THURSDAY'S MARKET,

IMMEDIATELY AFTER THE WOOL SALE,

FIFTEEN DIAMONDS,

Amongst which are two of Seven and Three-quarter Carats and one of Thirteen.

ADOLPH MOSENTHAL & Co,

28th September. 1869.

Figure 1.4 *Eastern Province Herald* (1869).

agent," was a well-known figure on the diamond fields. He presided over biweekly auctions, where diamonds as well as a host of other merchandise were bought and sold.[31] Starting out in a capacious tent that carried a canvas sign "Auction Mart and General Agent," Rothschild's auctions quickly became "a recognized institution on the Fields" and a central place for diamonds to change hands once again.[32]

Early advertising in Cape Colony periodicals confirm that when mineral fever hit, South African commercial firms moved in swiftly and absorbed diamonds into existing circulations of imported and exported goods. Adolph Mosenthal advertised in September 1869 that "immediately after the wool sale, fifteen diamonds, amongst which are two of seven and three-quarter carats and one of thirteen," would be offered "on Thursday's market."[33] As supplies increased, Mosenthal began to offer advances on diamonds, sending them in small boxes to the Port Elizabeth branch that subsequently shipped them to Joseph Mosenthal & Co. in London. An 1870 customs report estimated that the firm had shipped £4,500 worth of diamonds, together with other merchandise such as mohair and ostrich feathers, to Europe.[34] By the end of 1871, it had sent a total of 2,893 diamonds, valued at £56,025 to London. But there were competitors, too. The *Diamond News and Vaal Advertiser* announced that "Mr. Wilhelm Schultz of the firm Lippert & Co. in Port Elizabeth, begged to inform the public that he had opened a wholesale buying office" on the diamond fields. With sister offices in Hamburg, Germany, Schultz "venture[d] to say that he will be able to DEFY ALL COMPETITION . . . [and make] liberal advances on Diamonds."[35] Ikey Sonnenberg publicized that he "paid high prices for diamonds, ostrich feathers, ivory, wool or any other produce" and offered in return direct imports of London manufactures, preserved provisions, and miners' tools."[36] For many of these firms—Lippert & Co., Mosenthal & Co., Lilienfeld Bros., D. Blaine & Co., A. C. Stewart & Co.—diamonds would soon become the most valuable asset in their trading portfolios.

Several merchants exhibited the foresight of buying the land that proved rich in diamondiferous soil. They could purchase the property, rent out claims for a monthly fee, and secure the rough stones excavated by diggers. Understanding the economic potential of the area, they approached Boer farmers with proposals that many could not resist. The *Cape Almanac* asserted that farmers had initially issued "briefjes" or licenses to individual diggers at a small charge, but when "the growing number of diggers soon proved too great for their pastoral tastes," they sold their property and relocated.[37] The Hopetown merchant Leopold Lilienfeld, together with Henry Barlow Webb and the Dutch-Jewish lapidary Louis Hond, "the apostle of the diamond fields," bought the 14,457-acre Bultfontein farm from Cornelis Hendrik du Plooy for £2,000 and leased the nearby 6,579-acre Dutoitspan farm for ten years.[38] With financial support from Adolph Mosenthal & Co., the trio founded the Hopetown Company, the first corporation on the diamond fields. In July 1870, the Port Elizabeth branch of Mosenthal & Co. sent 310 diamonds to its London office on behalf of the Hopetown firm.[39] Using his European connections, Adolph attracted the interest of the Posno family, owners of numerous diamond cutting factories in Amsterdam, and the Ochs Brothers, London diamond merchants, to promote a new company for speculation in South African landed property and diamonds. This resulted in the London and South African Exploration Company, founded in November 1870 with starting capital of £20,000. Adolph and Joseph Mosenthal, Joseph and Charles Posno, Sigmund and L. Ochs, and Charles Martin served as directors. The company absorbed the Hopetown firm, making its original founders major shareholders. No one knew at this point about the enormous diamond pipes beneath their feet. One of the Exploration Company's first purchases was the Dutoitspan farm, bought from the Boer farmer van Wyk for £2,600.[40] Jewish as well as non-Jewish firms participated in this land-purchasing frenzy. In 1871 Alfred Ebden, partner in Dunnell, Ebden & Co., a Port Elizabeth firm of merchants, acquired the farm Vooruitzigt from Johannes de Beers for £6,000. De Beers's property bordered the Dutoitspan and Bultfontein farms to the north and would become the future site of Kimberley's Big Hole.

Merchants were men of influence during South Africa's budding mineral revolution, so much so that the *Diamond News* concluded in 1874 that merchant capital "regulates almost everything."[41] Often supported by coastal firms, merchants sold supplies and daily necessities to the bulging mining population; they also dabbled in land speculation and ownership, enabling them to reap an income by issuing licensing fees to diggers to work a claim. Moreover, their international connections encouraged private banking families and European firms anchored in long-distance trade to invest in deep-level mining and claim consolidation. For example, having access to capital of 500,000 British pounds in early 1870, Adolph Mosenthal—together with his brothers Joseph and Julius—began speculating in diamonds and property, again via their cousins' Lilienfeld firm in Hopetown as a geographically convenient location to conduct business. Adolph's sons Harry, George, and William opened up a London branch to accommodate the import of rough stones to be sold to European diamond manufacturing firms.

It was primarily Jewish diamond merchants—professionals such as Adolph Mosenthal, Leopold Lilienfeld, and L. Lippert, but also newcomers such as Barney Barnato, Alfred Beit, and Anton Dünkelsbühler—who helped lay the foundations for the modern diamond industry of the late nineteenth and twentieth centuries. When European capital markets and banks were reluctant to invest in a commercial enterprise seen in the early 1870s as speculative and precarious, Jewish investors expanded the orbit of long-distance commercial networks to include a commodity increasingly desired by bourgeois consumers. Having already established trade between South African port towns and European companies in wool, wine, hides, mohair, and copper, they added diamonds to their accounts. The immediate sources of capital lay within South Africa, particularly with local Jewish mercantile firms and diamond merchants investing in land purchases and buying up claims. A number of these companies established themselves as major importers in London, where they opened offices with direct links to Hatton Garden diamond dealers. Anton Dünkelsbühler, for example, started out as an agent for Mosenthal in 1872 and founded his own firm in London in 1875, the same year Martin Lilienfeld established an import agency at Hatton Garden. Harry Mosenthal's London branch opened as Joseph Mosenthal & Co., run by Adolph's three sons. Barnato Bros. established a London office at Austin Friars in 1880 and followed in the footsteps of Joseph Bros, and Lewis & Marks Sr.—all Jewish merchants formerly based in South Africa, boasting diamond industry expertise and practical knowledge in mercantile trade. In fact, most directors of the main diamond-importing companies in London had hands-on experience as *kopje-wallopers*, diamond sorters, and *diamantkoopers* on the Northern Cape's mineral fields. Once established in the British capital, they were then able to attract the interest of European finance houses to help finance expansive operations at Kimberley and push through company takeovers. The Rothschild, Hirsch, and Porgès families, among others, became major investors in costly, deep-level diamond mining and company consolidation in the 1880s, securing seats on boards of directors. The primary banking houses implicated in De Beers Mining Company stock, which would dominate diamond production by the end of the 1880s, included Nathan M. Rothschild & Sons, Mosenthal Sons & Co., Jules Porgès & Co., Hardy Nathan & Son, R. Raphael & Sons, T. Henry Schroder & Co., and Kleinwort. The expansion and promise of nineteenth-century industrial markets—producing large revenues and ever-increasing demand—combined with an enterprising economic ethos, made Jewish merchant creditors likely investors in frontier diamond mining.

Jewish participation in the transatlantic diamond trade intensified in the 1880s. At a time when most banks found "Diamondville" too risky, South African and London-based Jewish merchants found a willingness among European Jewish families to invest capital abroad. Compared to other ventures, South African mining attracted remarkably little investment from the London or Continental capital markets in the 1870s, giving the small number of merchant importers more than fifteen years to claim a large share of the market.[42] "We have been neglected," wrote the *Cape Monthly Magazine* in 1873, "by those whose enterprise and capital are always seeking for safe outlets and employment. Even the bulk of well-to-do colonists knew but little of the real capacities of the soil beyond their own immediate districts . . . hitherto public [interest] has always been intensely local."[43] Considering that the structural foundations for an industry in which Jews partook heavily had already been laid—London and Amsterdam were established centers of diamond trading and manufacturing in the late seventeenth and eighteenth centuries—explains the attraction of this economic niche. The Lilienfelds, Mosenthals, Dünkelsbühlers, and others became big players in the industry because their ready access to investment capital, vast commercial experience, and international contacts made diamonds a highly promising professional opportunity.

In the last decades of the nineteenth century Jews moved from the periphery to the center of the international diamond industry, in the Northern Cape and in Amsterdam, London, and, in the twentieth century, in Antwerp and New York. They benefited from the growth in supply and demand, working within imperial infrastructures that promoted economic developments deemed deeply problematic by progressives, such as company consolidation and monopolization, the maximization of profit, unchecked expansion, and the creation of powerful cartels. Individual Jewish businessmen and their companies operated in parallel to non-Jewish merchants trading in different commodities and industries. Jewish diamond merchants and investors were decidedly modern and acculturated, partaking in the imperial project with the same degree of eagerness and possibility as their non-Jewish peers.

◆ ◆ ◆

"Ho! Ho! for the Diamond-Fields!"

—*Cape Argus* (May 26, 1870)

For European adventurers who wished "to do South Africa" in the late 1860s and early 1870s, the journey to the Northern Cape might start in Southampton or London.[44] Every tenth and twenty-fifth of the month a Union Steamship Company's vessel—which "carried Her Majesty's Mails"—left for Cape Town, while a Donald Curry & Company's London Mail Line, known as "the Currie," sailed on the fourth and the twentieth.[45]

To maximize business, the "Blue Cross" Line of regular clipper ships, which dispatched at regular intervals for Cape Town, Algoa Bay, East London, and Port Natal, advertised in the 1875 *Silver & Co.'s Handbook Advertiser* that it was "worthy of notice that the Cape Colonies are rapidly rising in importance, and at present a most favourable opening for intending emigrants." For thirty-one pounds first class, or twenty-one pounds second class, passengers arrived in South Africa after four to five weeks at sea, with a quick stop in Madeira to restock.[46]

Disembarking in Table Bay, travelers found a bustling scene. With a population of over 30,000, Cape Town had all the characteristics of a small-sized colonial city.[47] It was ethnically diverse, primarily driven by international trade, and home to a growing number of private joint-stock companies, imperial and private commercial banks, and a stock exchange. Conveniently located en route to Asia—before the opening of the Suez Canal—Cape Town had long served as an outpost to replenish provisions. Over the course of the nineteenth century, ships anchored in Table Bay to sell their cargo of goods—timber, tobacco, cinnamon, and tiles—and to buy in return local products, such as Cape wine, wool, and dried fruit for the European market. As the British Empire expanded in the East, and as the volume of merchandise transported between the colonies and Europe grew, Cape Town became a destination in and of itself. The Cape Colony

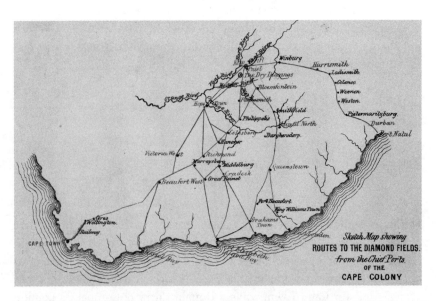

Figure 1.5 Journey to the Diamond Fields. Charles A. Payton, *The Diamond Diggings of South Africa: A Personal and Practical Account* (London: H. Cox, 1872).

may have functioned at a deficit, but its capital port city prospered from the boom of colonial produce.

Travelers could leave for the northern Cape either by ox-wagon or by passenger coach. The Inland Transport Company, which charged twelve British pounds for a one-way journey, took clients through dusty towns and agricultural centers: Wellington, Ceres, Beaufort West, Victoria West, Hopetown and, finally, Pniel, a small mining village located on the Vaal River. A fare covered the 58-mile-trip by train from Cape Town to Wellington, after which travelers took seats in horse-drawn coaches. The Diamond Fields Transport Company took a slightly different route and went through Murraysburg, Richmond, Colesberg, Fauresmith, and Jacobsdal, arriving at Dutoitspan, "the metropolis of the dry diggings," at roughly the same time.[48] Neither company provided food or drink along the way, so passengers packed provisions such as water, bread, brandy, potted meats, and sardines. Some lodgings offered meals, but one had to be prepared for disruptions. Frederick Boyle, whose stomach had growled along the way, "most strongly recommend[ed] the traveller to take with him two or three hams from England . . . remind[ing] him that hams require boiling."[49] Those coming from Port Elizabeth on the Eastern Cape typically boarded a coach run by the Diamond Fields Conveyance Company, which "ha[d] been formed to meet the increased demand for the transport of goods to the Fields to Algoa Bay."[50] At an average of eight miles an hour, coaches stopped every thirty to forty miles at appointed stations to replace the horses and drivers. The road itself, wrote Chapman, "was lined with wagons, some of which were loaded with cases and casks of drinkables, bags of rice, tents, wooden houses, and galvanised iron stores."[51] When this train of humanity finally arrived at the banks of the Orange and Vaal Rivers, ferries took wagons and coaches across. Traffic bottlenecked at times, so heavy was the voluntary migration.

It must have been quite a sight to behold. Hundreds of horses, mules, and oxen pulling loaded wagons, numerous transport coaches carrying disheveled passengers, farmers' wagons hauling entire households, private hire-wagons, "the almighty American spiders and the most useful Scotchcart," post-carts, people on horseback and on foot—all accumulated at the river crossing, waiting for ferries and cooperative water levels to carry them to the other side.[52] Once it was confirmed that the stones found in South African soil were, indeed, diamonds, mineral fever spread quickly. Eight hundred prospectors were digging in July 1870. A few months later five thousand had pitched tents, a number that doubled by 1872, when some ten thousand men and women were digging, shoveling, and sorting diamondiferous ground.[53] Most of these hopefuls soon left the earliest alluvial digging sites along the rivers—such as Hebron, Pniel, and Klipdrift—for the more promising dry digging encampments of Dutoitspan and Colesberg Kopje (renamed Kimberley).[54] In these canvas towns, "the flotsam and jetsam of humanity mingled with the sons of titled British parents."[55] To the mining engineer Gardner F. Williams, who would become the first general manager of the De Beers Consolidated Mines Company, it seemed as if Europe, Asia, Africa, and America "had boiled over into a hotch-potch splashed on a diamond bed in the heart of South Africa." The majority of the arrivals, he observed, were "ordinary men and workmen, toilers and schemers—some working for daily bread and others in pursuit of fortunes."[56]

So many young men succumbed to the siren call of the diamond fields that local newspapers expressed concern about declining local populations. In Grahamstown in the Eastern Province of the Cape two-thirds of its cathedral choir vanished, as did its organist. "We fully expect," stated a desperate Grahamstown resident in a letter to *The Times*, "to be soon reduced to merely sopranos."[57] The author lamented that the "unholy passion for Mammon" unleashed at the diamond fields had "nearly startled the Cape Colony out of its senses." Neighboring people also responded to the centripetal pull toward new centers of trade, selling firewood, game, dried venison, mutton, and maize mealies [sweetcorn bread] at the local market.[58] In the Colony everybody talked of going, recalled newspaper editor Richard W. Murray. As news of diamond finds spread, "[m]erchants, lawyers, clerks, Civil Servants, counter-jumpers, boatmen, tradesmen, and mechanics wanted to be off on the instant. They saw in their lively imaginings diamond fields glittering with diamonds like dewdrops in the waving grass."[59]

Upon arrival, those eager to try their luck typically purchased a license from Boer farmers. Having unabashedly claimed land in previous decades, farmers allotted claims of 31 × 31 square feet to individual diggers, marking off working patches rather haphazardly as there was "nothing on the surface to guide you as to where to dig." Impatient newcomers broke up the soil and shoveled it into a heap. Some set stout windlasses in the surface ground near the edge of their claims and hoisted heavy buckets up to the work levels. Those further along in the digging process carried tubs and rawhide sacks to the surface, climbing ladders resting on successive terraces. Or they mounted flights of steps cut in the rock or trundled wheelbarrows up plank inclines. Around the edge of the excavation carts, barrows, and carriers gathered to take quarried ground to depositing places, where it was dried, pounded, and sifted. The soil was then rinsed in a cradle with two different sieves, one with holes about half an inch in diameter, the other with smaller holes that would prevent any half-carat diamond or more

Figure 1.6 *The Diamond Fields Advertiser* 2 (July 22, 1871), 1.

from passing through. After completing the washings, diggers emptied the remaining gravel onto a table and carefully examined and sorted the heap. The sorting, admitted one digger in 1870, was "the most tedious work of all" as it required sitting still for a long time "with feet on the damp gravel," staring intently at little dark piles to identify the rough diamonds.[60] The backbreaking labor was all done by hand and there were no guarantees that it would yield results. Weeks might pass without finding any diamonds, whereas other times a digger might come across *blink klippe* (bright stones) multiple times a day. "Finding diamonds," observed one down-to-earth local, "is just simply a matter of chance and good luck."[61]

Most diggers who found diamonds, particularly in the early days of the river and dry diggings, sold them to *kopje-wallopers* making daily rounds. *Scribner's Monthly* reported that "[d]iamonds, as they come from the mine, are sold on the spot, i.e., in the same town, like fruit from a garden."[62] Louis Hond was one of the *kopje-wallopers*. An immigrant lapidary from Amsterdam, Hond had become a local authority on diamonds after the 1867 discovery of the 21.25-carat brownish-yellow diamond known as the Eureka. A "Letter from the Fields: A Thousand Diggers at Work," dated July 1870, stated that "Mr. Hond purchase[d] many, and perhaps the most, of the diamonds turned up."[63] In only three days, added a newspaper editorial from Klipdrift, "Mr. Hond purchased 120 diamonds, and of these there were two of eighteen carats."[64] Hond bought from everyone on the fields. He sold these rough stones to representatives of Dutch and German diamond manufacturers in Hopetown and Cape Town. He was soon joined by the Anglo-Jewish immigrant Moritz Unger, hailed by contemporaries as *"the diamond buyer of the day."*[65] Local advertisements regularly announced that he paid, "as usual, ready cash for your diamonds . . . from sunrise till sunset."[66] Unger reminded the reading public that Klipdrift was closer than London and that diggers need not travel far to get within 5 percent of European market value. "One bird in the hand is worth ten in the bush!," exclaimed the ad, assuring diggers that he constituted the most useful link between them, their stones, and the European market. Moritz Unger, diamond merchant, was there to satisfy all parties.[67] The 1870 *Natal Mercury* added that Unger had an office in Klipdrift, where clients interested in "consignments of diamonds for realization in the European market" could do business and receive a proper account sale.[68]

In August 1870, Unger got into a quarrel with a Reverend Kallenberg, a German representative of the Berlin Missionary Society, which operated a mission station along the Vaal River, near Pniel. When prospectors started digging on land claimed by the Berlin Missionary Society in 1845, the latter began to issue digging licenses, stipulating that diggers owed the Society 25 percent of the value of all diamonds found on Pniel lands.[69] Unger, who made his living as a *kopje-walloper*, visited the Pniel diggings to make business inquiries when Kallenberg approached him and forbade him access. They argued in German, but when Unger noticed a curious crowd gathering, he told Kallenberg to speak English, so that those around could understand the nature of their disagreement. Unger contended that the German Reverend "had no right whatsoever to attempt to stop him from exercising his business as a diamond merchant—that he might as well try to stop the course of the Vaal River. This was a free country and not Germany." Since Kallenberg had been sent to South Africa to teach the gospel, he was not to interfere with Unger's legitimate work. Indeed, continued Unger loudly, Kallenberg had no right whatsoever to deal in diamonds. He was, reckoned the diamond dealer, "certainly the representative of the Berlin Missionary Society, and to that [Unger] raised his hat respectfully, but he doubted very much whether he held credentials from Berlin empowering him to order him off the ground." Reminding the Reverend that the Cape Colony was not Prussia, where Jews had yet to receive legal emancipation, and that he had no power over a Jewish subject here, Unger turned the tables and questioned why a religious man of the cloth was engaged in a money-making enterprise in the first place. Especially one, he added, that "lay[s] the exorbitant charge of twenty-five percent on all diamonds, which were found only by hard and persevering labor, and at great expense of the searchers." If he were to dig here, Unger declared, he would first ask Mr. Kallenberg to produce the credentials that empowered him to charge the fearful rate of 25 percent on all diamonds found. "If a Jew in London was to charge such a rate of interest for cash lent," Unger continued, "he would be hunted as a cheat and a villain." Here was a Jewish merchant publicly accusing a Christian reverend of usury and of exploiting the working people while being "loudly cheered [on] by the whole of the diggers." Unaccustomed to being on the losing end of an argument, a silenced Kallenberg "withdrew in confusion," after which Unger went about his business.[70]

From the earliest days on the fields, Jews were widely associated with buying rough diamonds. Hond and Unger were household names in the late 1860s and were joined by other *kopje-wallopers*, most of Jewish descent. Itinerant Jewish traders gravitated toward the Northern Cape from small villages and trading stations sprinkled throughout the Colony, where they had supplied Afrikaner farming communities with agricultural tools, patented medicine, clothing, copper, canvas, oleographs, cigars, and other sundries. To make a living, they loaded up an ox-wagon at a merchant store—including at the various Mosenthal establishments that carried European imports—and ventured into the South African interior. The traveling trader, referred to in local parlance as a *smous*, visited farms, where he bartered his goods for cash or cattle. Sometimes he sold cattle to Africans in exchange for ivory, skins, or exotic feathers, which he would again sell. "With their store in a pack," Jewish peddlers carried the commodities of coastal town to remote parts of the colony, extending the borders of colonial commerce and aiding in its development.[71] *Kopje-walloping* in diamonds was, for these *smouses*, merely a change in inventory and a narrowing of their operational territory.

In the early 1870s, diamonds passed from these *kopje-wallopers*' hands onto the desks of diamond buyers conducting business in canvas tents.

Portable offices steadily gave way to corrugated iron shacks and to brick buildings. Louis Cohen, born in Liverpool, recalled his first impression of Dutoitspan's Main Street, noting that "the signs outside these tented offices displayed that Abraham, Isaac, and Jacob had recovered from their long celestial sleep, and gone in for earthly diamond buying." He admitted to feeling "a real glow of hope as [he] inwardly ejaculated, 'Thank the Lord I'm with my own people—and it's *not* Jerusalem.'" Cohen, a resident of South Africa since age seventeen, expressed amusement at the sight of so many Jewish-owned establishments, whose proprietors "looked as if they had come from the Sublime East—of London."[72] Who were these people if not Jews in the midst of creating a global commodity, a new town, and modern trade? In neighboring New Rush, soon renamed Kimberley, the scene was not much different. In addition to E. R. Moses's dental practice and Adolpus Cohen's wine shop, Main Street touted numerous diamond buying offices, including those of Morris Marcus, Benjamin Hart, Lowenthal & Goldsmith, and J. M. Posno. To attract potential buyers, Posno presented *Diamond Field* readers with an "Enigma: Two O's; one N; an S and a P; Look for your Diamonds and bring them to ME."[73] Gem dealing attracted such high concentrations of Jews that the English adventurer and writer Charles Payton concluded in 1872, "First and foremost amongst the ranks of diamond buyers on the South African Fields must certainly be placed the Jews."[74]

Once buyers had purchased rough stones, they could dispose of them in a variety of ways. First was public auction. In Dutoitspan, Alfred Abrahams presided over one every evening at the Nutzorn's Hotel, where "miscellaneous articles" were sold, including minerals. Other auctioneers—Joseph Levy, Louis Goldschmidt, Alfred Augustus Rothschild, alias "the Baron," and Alexander Levy—opened their own auction marts on Main Street, where the public would congregate to make bids on used merchandise, from claims and horses to rickety bedsteads and Cape-carts. Rothschild, "the Diamondiferous Auctioneer who possessed a marvelous sparkle, verve, and energy," announced evening sales in local newspapers, claiming that "to listen to the beat of his hammer [was] the only pleasant way of passing the time on the Diamond Fields after dark."[75] Adolph Mosenthal & Co. had opened a branch in New Rush and advertised that it offered stones on Thursday's market.[76] There was an element of social entertainment to these events, particularly at evening auctions, when clients were feted with free drinks. Rothschild, having first started out in a capacious tent with a canvas sign that read "Auction Mart and General Agent," would mount a chair and tease the crowd with comments about the second-hand wares up for sale—spades that had unearthed magnificent diamonds the week before.[77] Auctioneers such as Rothschild, as one commentator explained, were themselves diamond buyers during the day, selling their purchases during the biweekly evening auctions over which they presided.[78] The Baron and others like him wore multiple hats.

The diamond auctions that became, in Charles Payton's words, "a recognized institution on the Fields," were modest compared to those held in Cape Town, where biweekly sales at the Commercial Exchange attracted "Cape Town merchants, who dabble a little in diamonds, and have correspondents in London, Amsterdam, or Hamburg."[79] Before departing for Great Britain in November 1871, Payton attended several auctions. At the time of his visit rough diamond exports from the Cape Colony had increased a thousandfold, from 200 carats in 1868 to 269,000 carats; they would top one million carats by the end of 1872. Interested buyers could inspect differently numbered assortments of rough stones prior to sale and record their impressions on the size, shape, and quality of the stones in a printed catalog. The owners had placed a reserve price on their stones and, if buyers met or exceeded his amount, the diamonds were sold. During one of these auctions, Payton reported that 4,512 carats yielded £20,189, "a very small proportion of the diamonds weekly sent away from the South African fields." After the conclusion of the Cape Town auction, the lot would be sent by mail steamer to importers in London, who put up stones again for auction. Debenham, Storr, and Sons at King Street, in Covent Garden, reported *The Times* in 1872, held "the largest sale by auction of these gems known in this country" and "attracted a good many buyers from the provinces and the Continent."[80] Selling diamonds at public sales—on the fields, in Cape Town, and in London—a common practice in the first fifteen years following the diamond discoveries, disappeared once company consolidation centralized production and distribution and thereafter organized tightly regulated "sights" for continental buyers.

Diamond buyers in Kimberley and Dutoitspan, employed by European firms, sent stones directly to London, bypassing the Cape Town auctions. Once they had amassed a few thousand carats, they inspected and sorted the stones, placed them in square paper parcels lined with tissue, and fit four to five parcels in a small box, which then was enclosed in an ordinary paper envelope. Each parcel contained between fifty and two hundred stones. They were registered and sent as part of the regular mail by postal carts to Cape Town, which took approximately six days and six nights. The English novelist Anthony Trollope, recording impressions of Kimberley in his travel narrative *South Africa*, expressed astonishment at this "primitive" practice. "The cart travels day and night along desolate roads," he penned, and "for four-fifths of the way without any guard, very frequently with no one on the mail cart except the black boy who drives it!"[81] Frederick Boyle called it reckless for "twenty, or fifty, or a hundred thousand pounds' worth of gems to be carried fortnightly in an open cart, driven by a wild Hottentot, over mountain and river, seven hundred miles, without a policeman or a soldier to protect it."[82] Both writers cited reports of robberies and lost mail bags. In February 1872, after twenty thousand pounds' worth of stones disappeared from a postal cart, "500 Pound Reward" placards appeared "on every tree and stump between [New Rush] and Klipdrift."[83] An honest passing traveler found the bag alongside the road near Hopetown and took it to the post office. On a different occasion, a driver had left his postal cart unattended during a lunch break and found part of its cargo gone upon his return. Those "lost" mailbags were not returned.

Once in Cape Town, drivers delivered their loads at the post office, where they were stored until the next cargo ship took them to London. In Cape Town, too, the parcels—low in weight and volume, but high in value—were vulnerable. One thief spotted mail bags placed carelessly in front of a post office window and found the prospect of instant wealth too tempting. He broke the window, snatched the bags, and took off, confessing later that he had planned to deposit them in a London bank after returning home from Cape Town.[84] Hearing the news, the Colonial Secretary exclaimed that "there was no reason why *both* the postmaster *and* his assistant should have gone to dinner at the same time!" He issued a serious reprimand for the postmaster's "negligence and want of caution, which will lead to his dismissal from office, if repeated." He proposed securing the building by means of barred windows and fire-proof safes, ordered from England for this purpose.[85] Local diamond merchants, Anton Dünkelsbühler and Charles Mège among them, convened a meeting to "adopt measures for the safe conveyance of diamonds from the Diamond Fields to Cape Town and Port Elizabeth." They appointed a delegation "to ascertain whether the Government would be willing to allow an armed escort to accompany the mail cart."[86] For many years, inertia prevailed and the global supply of rough diamonds, with an annual market value of over a million pounds, continued to travel unprotected in paper envelopes from across the South African interior and the Atlantic to London.

To minimize risk, small-scale buyers commonly sold stones to larger buyers, taking the square paper parcels and offering the content to the highest bidder. A broker, wrote the physician William J. Morton, "may be seen at all hours of the day, hurrying from office to office with a little square pocket case under his arm, containing 'parcels' of diamonds of every variety." Morton recognized that "[t]o 'broke' is the popular mode of beginning life, if one does not go into digging, or has not capital or experience enough to buy. [It] is the training school of the independent dealer."[87] Once a broker had delivered his parcel, the potential buyer would take the stones, examine them one by one, weigh and measure them, and assess their value according to color, clarity, and carat, after which he appraised the entire parcel. Remarkably, there was no standard of value per carat by which to regulate transactions and no direct contact with London to calculate market prices. Rates varied. An interested buyer would fold the tissue-lined parcel containing the stones inside an envelope, seal it, and "mark the face of it with a few strokes of a pen, together with the price offered."[88] The broker returned the stones to the seller, who could either accept or refuse. If rejected, he would break the seal and request his broker take the parcel to another client—a practice that is still common in diamond districts.[89]

Three months after the initial excitement had begun, New Rush had become a center of diamond extraction, an encampment first characterized by white canvas, sand mounds, and "little square tents where diamond buyers sit with their scales before them trying to make the best of bargains." Tents steadily gave way to corrugated iron and brick stores, squares, regularly laid-out streets, and residential homes.[90] By the end of 1871 Main Street included Moss's general store, Squire's shoemaking shop, Harmworth's and the Royal Oak Hotel, a bakery and confectioner's shop, several butchers, billiard rooms, saloons, numerous liquor stores, apothecaries, and diamond merchants' offices. Canteens fed everyone—The Old Cock, First and Last, Hard Times, and The Perfect Cure, to name a few. "The marvel of the whole sight," lectured William Morton to a New York audience in 1878, "is that every piece of timber, every sheet of iron and tent-cloth to build these houses, as well as their contents, of furniture, piano, billiard table and utensils, and more, much of the daily food has been dragged on ox-wagons from the sea-coast up over the weary desert." This mining town, renamed after the Colonial Secretary Lord Kimberley, appeared as if "dropped in the desert at random, as it were, from the clouds, so detached does it all seem from the ordinary surroundings of civilized communities."[91]

◆ ◆ ◆

Here lies a digger, all his "chips" departed,
A "splint" of Nature, bright and ne'er downhearted;
He worked in many "claims," but now, though "stumped,"
He's got a claim above that can't be "jumped."
May he turn out a pure and spotless wight
When the great Judge shall sift the wrong from right,

> And may his soul, released from this low Babel,
> Be found a gem on God's great "sorting-table."
> —William J. Morton, *Scribner's Monthly* 16 (1878)

A few thousand people had migrated to the Diamond Fields by 1870, clustering in tents and iron shanties around the dry diggings in New Rush, Dutoitspan, and Bultfontein. Three years later the area was unrecognizable. What had begun as a compilation of small individual claims of thirty-one square feet coalesced into vast, open-cast excavation pits into which thousands of hired workers descended on a daily basis to collect soil. The Kimberley mine, ten acres in size and divided into hundreds of claims, proved particularly rich in deposits, enticing diggers to reach ever greater depths. Josiah Wright Matthews, a surgeon who arrived in the Northern Cape's "great canvas city" in 1871, compared the enterprise to a "hive of busy human bees, bustling and elbowing, creeping and climbing, shoveling and sieving to gather, if possible, honey from each opening flower." He estimated that no less than 15,000 workers—10,000 black Africans and 5,000 whites—were at work in the Kimberley mine alone.[92] In 1872, the number of Europeans in Kimberley increased to 13,000 out of a population that varied—due to fluctuating numbers of African migrant labor—between 30,000 and 50,000 inhabitants.[93]

Digging was done by men who did not own claims as owners contracted with so-called share-workers, intermediaries who hired diggers to work a claim in return for a percentage of the yield. While the owner paid the license fee and mining taxes, share-workers employed laborers—Pedi people from the Transvaal, Tsonga from north of the Limpopo River, Zulus from Natal and South Sotho. These intermediaries also bought tools, planned production, and sold diamonds to *diamantkoopers*: M. Rossettenstein on Main Street in Dutoitspan, S. Isaacs, "the oldest diamond buyer in Dutoitspan, certified to give the highest prices for all classes of diamonds," J. E. Abrahams on Church Street in Kimberley, and H. B. Hart, who "shipped directly to the European markets."[94] In 1874 nearly 1,500 licenses were issued for the Kimberley mine, which held 470 claims, a number reduced greatly in the 1880s, as private and joint stock companies purchased and consolidated claims, creating mining monopolies that placed nearly the entire South African diamond production in the hands of a few company owners.

Just as excavation became more complex, so did structural labor divisions in the mines. Deep-level mining spawned a whole set of challenges, including the collapse of the dangerously narrow roads between claims. Flooding and landslides following summer storms sent carts crashing down unsupported pathways. Moreover, as diggers went deeper, the friable yellow topsoil gave way to hard, compact "blue ground" that was difficult to penetrate, haul to the surface, and disintegrate to extract carbon stones. Working at unprecedented depths in the earth required ingenuity, recollected Anglo-Jewish mine owner Lionel Phillips: "New methods of extraction and many innovations were invented on the spot."[95] To enable mining at one hundred feet below the ground, workers constructed a succession of timber staging platforms around the margin of the mine that were supported by containing walls called reefs. Each platform carried the one above it, allowing workers to communicate and move between different levels. These platforms also guided the stationary ropes anchored to the bottom of the claim to the top of the mine. The hauling ropes were attached to windlasses and grooved guide-wheels that took swinging buckets made of ox hide (more durable than iron) up and down the mine.[96] Initially workers operated this aerial tramway system of wire ropes and pulleys by hand, but horse-driven whims—windlasses—replaced this component of manual labor in 1874. "The din and rattle of these thousands of wheels," observed one contemporary, "and the twang of the buckets along the ropes were something deafening, while the mine itself seemed almost darkened by the thick cobweb of ropes, so numerous as to appear almost touching one another."[97]

Once buckets filled with lumps of blue ground reached the surface they were emptied via narrow shoots into bags and transported to depositing floors, stretching for miles around Kimberley and creating an artificial landscape of ploughed fields. There the soil decomposed through a natural process of weathering that took several months, after which the softened ground was washed multiple times through sieves. This labor-intensive system of dry-sorting by hand altered with the introduction in 1875 of rotary washing machines that vigorously churned debris in water, allowing heavy particles to sink to the bottom and smaller stones to be filtered out. After a final rinse, the residuum was "placed on the tables before the sorter [who] rapidly passed his metal scrapers over the heap and with sharp points pick out the diamonds from their associated minerals, quartz crystals, iron pyrites, ilmenite or carbon olivine, and garnets."[98] As deep-level mining called for costly mechanization, it became increasingly difficult for share-workers and claim owners to cover the costs of excavation. In the early days of mining independent diggers got by with a tent, a mattress, a pick and shovel, sieves, rope, buckets, and crowbars. Their monthly expenses, including a claim license, food, water, and the like, averaged about eighteen British pounds.[99] These costs could be defrayed as long as diggers found low-carat diamonds on a regular basis or high-carat ones sporadically. By the mid-1870s, however, indispensable mining equipment, such as washing machines and steam-driven water pumps to drain the ground water from the mine—all of which had to be hauled from the South African coast on ox carts—as well as spiking labor costs, increased expenses exponentially. Now, explained William J. Morton in the *Journal of the American Geographical Society of New York* in 1878, a claim holder needs "his outfit of digging tools, washing machines, etc. [that] will cost say $1,000. He requires a gang of twenty Kaffirs, which will cost him $5 each per week or $100. One overseer beside himself $25 per week. Then expenses of carting and taxes will make his total outlay at least $200 per week or over $10,000 a year, excluding his own expenses of living. . . . The rub is to dare to begin and to dare to fail."[100] Many failed or cut their losses and sold their claims, realizing that deep-level operations required capital far exceeding the immediate returns of diamond sales. Individual diggers were "squeezed out" as they simply could not provide the capital it took to find diamonds more than one hundred feet below the ground.[101] Work was often interrupted by collapsing reefs and heavy summer rains, increasing labor costs but closing off revenue. In such times of crisis, concluded the *Diamond Field*, the "system was simply pernicious" to diggers.[102]

Local commercial banks would not loan to diggers who lacked cash reserves or collateral. The largest imperial bank in the Cape Colony, the Standard Bank, viewed diggers as "needy, unmoneyed customers" whose entrepreneurial skills fostered little faith.[103] Conservative in their business practices, Cape banks steered clear of mining claims as a sphere of investment and confined themselves to advancing money against diamonds on confirmed credit only—a practice that helped diamond merchants but not diggers.[104] Negative press did not help matters either. *The Mining Magazine*,

Figure 1.7 Diamond Buyer's Office, Main Street, Dutoitspan, 1876.

among others, took a very poor view of the diamond fields as an object of speculation, citing the Northern Cape as unreliable and stories circulating about the fields "overpuffed." It urged readers to be conscious "of the reality which runs side by side with the romance," disappointing yields, stones of inferior quality, and long arduous days that often ended in deep disillusionment.[105] Others warned British readers of the terrible conditions on the diamond fields and advised those hopefuls considering a transatlantic move not to come and expose themselves to cholera, poor diets, and dust storms. "Diamondville" may have been the buzz of the town but it was an uncertain magnet for investment. In the early 1870s, many considered the Northern Cape a vulnerable producer of a single marketable good in a colonial trade that was still dominated by wool, wheat, wine, hides, copper, and ostrich feathers. Merchants who absorbed diamonds into their trading portfolio and established financial affiliations with local banks stood a much better chance of finding investment capital than diggers. The first companies represented on the diamond fields thus came from Port Elizabeth: Louis Dreyfus & Co., Lilienfeld & Co., Mosenthal & Co., Dunnell, Ebden & Co, and Blaine & Co.[106]

For diggers, the lack of available financing at a time when the expanded scale of operations required tremendous capital investments forced many to fold their tents. Already in 1874 the *Cape Almanac* reported that Dutoitspan was "gradually falling in the hands of companies" and questioned how much longer "the scene of individual enterprise [would] be able to continue."[107] At an 1878 meeting of the American Geographical Society, William Morton lectured that "the great bugbear of the digger is the word 'company' [and that] the next phase of mining operations must undoubtedly be that of several large and competing companies, or perhaps a single one controlling the whole mine." Then, predicted Morton, "the individual romance of diamond-hunting will be over."[108] The steady differentiation between claim holders with steam-driven machinery and those with less-efficient horse-driven gear resulted in the consolidation of claim ownership and the emergence of a mining industry. Out of this process of competitive amalgamation developed a disproportionate Jewish presence in diamond production, primarily as family merchant and limited liability companies acquired clusters of claims.

Diamond merchants understood the intricacies of the market and, with the help first of local sources of investment and later of European merchant banks, they were able to secure credit and investment capital. "It is they," stated the *Diamond News*, "who bring the capital to the Fields, which keeps the mines working and without [them] . . . the mines must soon collapse."[109] Many of the commercial men came from Jewish families. For example, the firm of Adolph Mosenthal and Co., worth £500,000 in the early 1870s, appointed Anton Dünkelsbühler as their primary agent in Kimberley in 1872. Dünkelsbühler had extensive experience as a London diamond merchant. He recognized the potential of industrial mining in the northern Cape and subsequently founded his own diamond buying firm on a return trip to London in 1875. Both Dünkelsbühler and Adolph Mosenthal, codirector of the London and South African Exploration Company, financed claim consolidation with capital accumulated in the sphere of exchange. Mosenthal & Co., in particular, was a big client of the Standard Bank of South Africa and Prescott Bank in London and enjoyed access to substantial banking privileges, including large overdrafts without proof of collateral.[110] While the Whitechapel brothers Barney and Harry (Isaacs) Barnato did not have such a reliable network, they applied the same principle of ploughing all revenue back into expanding the number of claims, in their case a carbon-rich section of the Kimberley mine. Having started as *kopje-wallopers*, they turned to diamond buying and invested their considerable profits into claims and production. They drew on family members to branch out and expand the business. While Harry took care of a new office set up in London, their nephews Isaac (Jack), Woolf, and Solomon (Solly) Joel relocated to South Africa to—in Barney's words—"come within the fold."[111]

Similarly, the diamond merchant Alfred Beit, from a middle-class Jewish family in Hamburg, arrived in Kimberley in 1875 to work for his uncle's company, Lippert & Co., which successfully imported wool from Africa. The owners of the firm were Beit's uncles. His mother's oldest sister, aunt Rosa, had married the Mecklenburg businessman Adolph (Israel) Arnold, the first partner of Lippert & Co, while his aunt Adele had married David Lippert, who made up the other half of the company. Lippert had sent three of his sons to South Africa—Alfred's cousins Ludwig, Eduard, and Wilhelm—to set up sister branches in Port Elizabeth, Cape Town, and Durban.[112] In 1870, when the diamond rush was in full swing in the Northern Cape, seventeen-year-old Alfred was still in Germany, apprenticing at Lippert & Co. The Port Elizabeth branch had already begun to ship small parcels of diamonds to Europe. After a short stint in the German army to complete his required military service, Beit left for Amsterdam to join the workforce at Jules Porgès & Co., a firm owned by the Parisian-Jewish diamond dealer Jules (Yehuda) Porgès. A few years later, young Beit followed his Lippert cousins to South Africa and became a clerk to Max Gammius, the representative of Lippert & Co. in Kimberley, but he left the company in 1879 to become an independent diamond buyer. His time in Amsterdam had served him well. "When I reached Kimberley," Beit stated, "I found that very few people knew anything about diamonds: they bought and sold haphazard." Beit sensed opportunity: "I saw at once that some of the Cape stones were as good as any in the world; and I saw, too, that the buyers protected themselves against their own ignorance by offering one-tenth part of what each stone was worth in Europe. It was plain that if one had a little money there was a fortune to be made."[113] Where could that money come from? Beit wrote long letters to his father, selling him on Kimberley. He related how incredibly rich the ground was, how easy it was to make money with a little capital, promising him "to return whatever money he lent with good interest within a year." Beit invested his first earnings and his father's loan in Kimberley property. Attuned to the fast development of this mining town, he purchased undeveloped sites in the center, erected a dozen corrugated iron huts, and rented these to fellow businessmen. With a monthly rental income of £1,800 secure, he bought and sold diamonds and speculated on a small scale in diamond shares and claims. He reconnected with Porgès & Co. when he partnered with Julius Wernher, Harry Mosenthal's former classmate and representative of the Kimberley company. Beit joined the Porgès team, taking a third share of the profits from the diamonds he shipped to London. In late 1884 he reported that his capital was £35,000, £5,000 of which was invested in fixed property and the remainder in diamonds and diamond shares. With capital from European investors—including from Charles Mège, a Parisian private banker and Porgès's former partner, and from his cousin, a partner in the private bank Ephrussi and Porgès—Beit was able to finance the consolidation of claim holdings and the formation of diamond share syndicates. In 1884, Porgès & Co. merged its claims in the Kimberley mine with those owned by *kopje-wallopers*-turned-diamond-merchants Isaac Lewis and Sammy Marks. Having obtained financial support from Parisian private banker Rudolph Hirsch Kann, they formed the Compagnie Française des Mines Diamants du Cap de Bonne Esperance (the "French Company"), with a capital of £560,000. The formation of the company was possible after Porgès's Kimberley representative, Julius Wernher, wrote "reams of letters to get [his] friends in Paris and London so far as to realize the usefulness of this step."[114] It moved swiftly to control a quarter of the Kimberley Mine. By the following year, Porgès and Wernher had left South Africa to set up a new company headquarters in London, further solidifying the emerging network between the Kimberley mines, London's distribution, Paris financiers, and Amsterdam manufacturing.[115]

Timing mattered here. Improved mining technology and machinery in the mid to late-1870s had significantly increased yields and led to an overproduction of diamonds. With falling prices on the international market and ballooning production costs, small claim owners could balance their budgets only by paying lower wages to their overwhelmingly black labor force. Many workers consequently left the mines. Claim owners, unable to keep their employees, saw no other way out but to sell. Not only did small proprietors lack reserves and collateral, they also suffered from colonial banks' reluctance to invest in what appeared to be an unstable enterprise. The Standard Bank maintained that "at the present moment [1876] the value of money has fallen to a point probably never reached before.... Foreign schemes would appear altogether to be less in favour than when circumstances were altogether different."[116] That London took a wait-and-see approach surprised the correspondent to the *Cape Times* who, in his regular column on "South African Affairs," observed that the Cape may have been "the Cinderella of England's colonies at the [1878] Paris Exhibition," but that it "is certainly not thought so in the City of London."[117] Getting only cold shoulders from colonial banks when they needed increased financing, diamond merchants drew on credit from those who embraced the risk of colonial commerce: local family firms already dealing in diamonds and European-Jewish financiers. All of them committed on the basis of mutual benefit; that is, they would own part of the company and over time receive annual dividends. Small companies were able to grow by purchasing clusters of claims at low prices. Beit, Barnato, and others thus came at the right time, and they drew on a network of relatives and trading partners who were well suited to the challenge of doing business on the South African frontier. Lewis & Marks spent almost £20,000 on purchases in the first quarter of 1877, much of this money a reinvestment of profits made from selling their previous holdings to Jules Porgès. In 1877 Porgès & Co. purchased a 10 percent share in the Kimberley Mine for £70,000. By the end of the year, claim ownership in the Kimberley mine had fallen from 1,600 in 1872 to 300, and less than 20 of these owned half the mine. "It is evident," concluded the *Diamond News*, "that the workings of the Kimberley Mine is passing... into the hands of companies and capitalists," a process of concentrated merchant ownership that would intensify in the years ahead.[118] By 1879, three-quarters of the Kimberley Mine were in the hands of only twelve companies.

To maximize investments, a number of these companies pulled their resources together and purchased larger sections of the four mines, which together covered almost seventy acres. The creation of joint stock companies that issued share certificates brought in coastal and foreign investment capital. In 1879 the first private company to go public, the Cape Diamond Mining Company (DMC), was floated in Port Elizabeth by the diamond merchant firm, Martin Lilienfeld and Co. Lilienfeld ran his firm from London, while his partner, Emil Castens, resided in Port Elizabeth. In 1880 Harry Mosenthal, in association with Charles J. Posno, the Ochs brothers, and H. B. Webb, launched various companies, such as the Bultfontein Homestead Company (with a capital of £35,000), the Central

Mining Company of Dorstfontein (capital £100,000), and the Griqualand West DMC, all of which reinvested profits in additional claims. The next year, Mosenthal established the African, the Adamant, and the Orion Diamond Mining Companies with a total capital of nearly half a million British pounds. His codirectors included Anton Dünkelsbühler, Ernest Mocatta, Charles Posno, Julius Wernher, Elias de Pass (owner of a coastal shipping company that exported guano), and Joseph Sebag-Montefiore.[119] Alfred Beit, with investment capital from Lippert & Co., bought out the largest claim holders in the De Beers Mine, while Barney Barnato floated the Barnato DMC with £75,000 in capital, employing his nephews Woolf and Isaac (Jack) Barnato and Solomon (Solly) Joel in the new business. Between mid-1880 and mid-1881 alone, diamond merchants established joint stock companies valued at seven million British pounds, accelerating claim consolidation and company ownership. One observer noted that there were "no diggers here now in the old sense of the word" and that mines were "rapidly falling into the hands of [joint stock] companies."[120]

By 1882, 103 diamond companies with a nominal capital of 9.5 million pounds had been registered at Kimberley in a dramatic burst of investment. Speculators rushed to buy shares in a new bout of diamond fever that was as intense and hectic as the original diggers' rush of the early 1870s. Josiah Wright Matthews recounted that Ebden Street in Kimberley, where a new stock exchange was established to accommodate the growth in business, "was filled from morning to night with a tumultuous and maddened crowd. The various offices of companies in formation were simply stormed, and those who could not get in at the door from the pressure of the crowd, threw their applications for shares (to which were attached cheques and bank notes) through the windows, trusting to chance that they might be picked up." It was astonishing, recounted Matthews, "how the mania seized on all classes in Kimberley, from the highest to the lowest . . . how everyone, doctors and lawyers, masters and servants, shop-keepers and workmen, men of the pen and men of the sword, magistrates and I.D.B's, Englishmen and foreigners, rushed wildly into the wonderful game of speculation." "Share mania" led to vastly inflated share prices. Diamond mining company stocks in 1881 traded at premiums ranging as high as 300 percent, a situation that proved unsustainable. Eventually the bubble burst, leaving hundreds of minor-league investors in ruins. Shares that had traded at £400 each in March 1881 fell to as low as £25. Bigger companies, which managed to weather the storm, mopped up claims, expanding their hold over the four mines. As competition for shares and company mergers increased, fewer firms owned ever-larger shares of diamond production, and diamond merchants morphed into industrial capitalists.[121]

The crucial role of merchant capital has been neglected in the scholarly literature on the South African mining industry. It was diamond merchants who first floated joint-stock mining ventures, establishing the links between European diamond buyers, private banking houses, and Kimberley companies. Becoming leading investors diversifying in various enterprises, they often served as (co)directors on company boards and as such were instrumental in securing finance for company takeovers. In 1882 seventeen merchants occupied seats on company boards that together owned half (55) of the 103 registered diamond companies.[122] The majority of these merchant directors were Jewish: Jules Porgès, Sammy Marks, Isaac Lewis—like his cousin Sammy born in Neustadt, Lithuania—Martin Lilienfeld, Ludwig Breitmeyer, and Anton Dünkelsbühler, Barney Barnato, M. J. Posno, Harry Mosenthal, the Ochs brothers, V. A. Litkie, J. Walter, Herz, Rosenfeld & Co, Paddon Bros., L. & A. Abrahams, and Joseph Bros.

Of course these companies were not created, funded, and directed only by Jews. Cecil Rhodes, "the Napoleon of the diamond world," whose wealth had its origins in pumping water from diamond mines, established the De Beers DMC in April 1880, while Joseph B. Robinson established the Standard Company with a capital of £225,000. They and other non-Jews became major players in South African mineral mining.[123] Considering the small numbers of Jews in the overall population in the Northern Cape and in London, Jewish merchants and creditors were disproportionately represented in this new phase of company consolidation. Their participation can be explained in part by the prevalence of Jewish diamond merchants with capital to invest and commercial contacts in London, and in part by the willingness of private Jewish financial houses to arrange debt financing for what many still considered a risky venture. Alfred Beit, for example, Cecil Rhodes's right hand in the De Beers Mining Co., crafted a letter of introduction for Rhodes to Nathan Rothschild, who consequently warmed to the proposal to amalgamate several diamond companies and provided credit not just to De Beers but also to the French Company. Rothschild's advisors, having inspected the diamond mines prior to the decision to invest, reported that "those directors who now furnish money to promote consolidation shall ultimately have the handling of the diamonds."[124] South African mining, they counseled, was a promising and lucrative investment. Their predictions were spot-on. By 1886 De Beers's annual dividends had doubled from 12 percent to 25 percent two years later. *The Statist* reported that, while the De Beers DMC excavated 51,682 carats in 1881 and paid £11,600 in dividends to its stockholders, in 1888 it mined 979,732 carats, disbursing £508,042 in dividends. During these eight years alone, the company received £2,636,023 in sales, a number that swelled to £46,170,993 for the 1899–1903 period.[125] The injection of capital into debt financing and mining technology—including steam engines, dynamite, and sophisticated rotary washing machines—combined with the carbon-density of blue ground and lower labor costs to produce astonishing growth. Cape Colony export data indicates that, as the annual output of rough soared, exports of Cape stones ballooned from just over 100,000 carats in 1870 to nearly 4 million in the late 1880s.[126] By the end of the decade, precious stones constituted half of the Cape Colony's total exports.[127]

Twenty shippers exported the majority of these gems from Kimberley to London, with eight firms dominating the market—all of them Jewish-owned. Four of the big eight and seven of the remaining twelve private firms had experience in the diamond trade prior to the Cape discoveries. Only two—Barnato Brothers and Lewis & Marks—were formed in Kimberley. Two others, Mosenthal and Dünkelsbühler, were connected to members of the Salomons family, importers of Indian diamonds since the 1740s.

Jewish participation was equally prominent in what historian Robert Vicat Turrell called the "major five constellations of company promoters" that emerged in the mid-1880s and that moved toward consolidating the dozens of diamond mining firms by drawing capital from local and overseas financiers and investors. The five company owners—Jules Porgès & Co., under whose umbrella fell a group of European diamond merchants; Charles Posno, whose base lay in the Amsterdam diamond cutting industry; Joseph Benjamin Robinson; Barnato Brothers; and Cecil Rhodes—were fully aware that the enormous growth in output threatened to lower the value of diamonds and destabilize market prices, jeopardizing the entire enterprise.[128] They pressed for further centralization and for regulating the production and distribution of diamonds to create the perception of scarcity that would enhance the value of Cape stones. Which companies would sell, merge, and ultimately monopolize the industry depended yet again on access to investment capital, originating primarily in Europe and no longer local. Rhodes, for instance, set sail for London in July 1887, accompanied by Gardner Williams, an American mining engineer and manager of De Beers Mining Company, to meet with overseas financiers. Williams had compiled a detailed report on the diamond industry, highlighting the advantages of amalgamation and debt financing. Having been introduced by Alfred Beit, Rhodes first dined at Nathan Rothschild's home in London, where he requested a loan of one million pounds to purchase the French Company. Rothschild promised to support Rhodes if he could get the agreement of the French Company's directors and shareholders to sell. Rhodes continued his fundraising tour in Paris, where he convened with the directors of the French company, including Jules Porgès. Here, too, Beit had prepared the

TABLE OF STATISTICS

OF THE

DE BEERS MINING COMPANY

Since its formation in 1880 to 1888.

Year ending 31st March.	Number of Loads of "Blue" Hauled.	Number of Loads of "Dead" Ground Hauled.	Number of Loads of "Blue" Washed.	Number of Carats of Diamonds found.	Amount realised by Sale of Diamonds.	Number of Carats per load of "Blue."	Amount realised per Carat sold.	Amount realised per Load.	Balance of "Blue" on Floors at end of Year.	Dividends paid during the Year.	Cost of Production per Load.	Capital of Company during the Year.
					£ s. d.							£
1881	73,642	50,000	73,642	51,682	62,367 17 4	·7	24/1	16/11	Nil.	11,600=5½ p.c.	...	200,000
1882	99,439	96,731	96,439	76,859	104,532 8 8	·797	27/3	21/8	3,000	19,966=3 ,,	13/2	665,550
1883	179,785	143,369	166,136	149,396	158,675 4 3	·895	21/3	19/1¼	16,649	37,714=5⅔ ,,	11/9½	665,550
1884	220,046	204,977	173,666	177,246	198,268 12 9	1·02	22/5	22/10	63,029	52,148=7 ,,	10/	755,120
1885	398,613½	427,215	323,324¾	278,018	237,469 15 7	·859	20/8	17/9	138,318	62,666=7½ ,,	8/1	841,550
1886	391,749¾	569,551	299,407	395,001	323,499 7 2	1·319	16/4½	21/7	230,660¼	121,814=12 ,,	8/3½	1,045,120
1887	589,317	404,387¼	487,295½	560,253¾	517,103 18 4	1·15	18/5½	21/2⅔	288,133½	199,349 4/=16 ,,	8/2 ·15	1,265,620
1888	890,508	6,714	857,906	979,732½	984,035 14 6	1·142	20/1¾	22/11¼	303,405	508,042 10/=25 ,,	9/6½	†2,332,170
Total	2,843,100	1,902,944¼	2,477,816½	2,668,188¼	2,636,022 18 7	1·076	19/9 1/10	21/3⅓	303,405	*1,013,299 10/=71⅔%	9/6½	

* In addition to above dividends, 41 per cent. has been distributed in Bonus Shares. † Exclusive of £177,450 deferred capital.

Figure 1.8 Henry Mitchell, *Diamonds and Gold of South Africa* (London: Mathieson & Son, 1888).

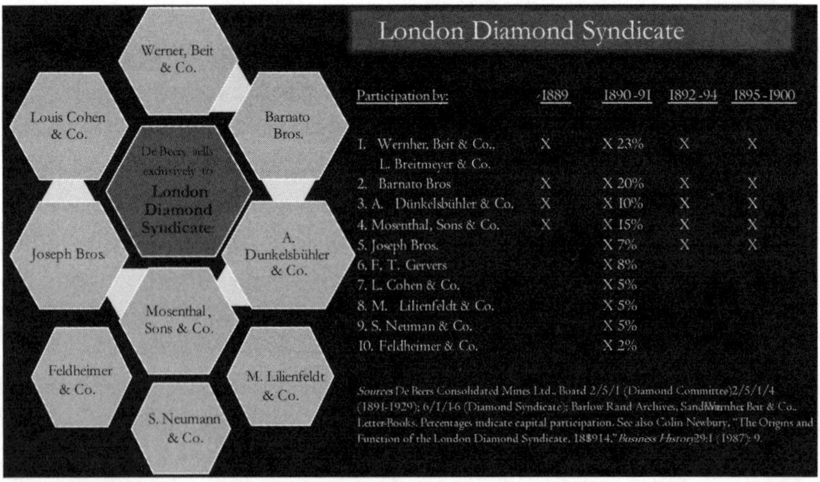

Figure 1.9 London Diamond Syndicate

way, persuading Porgès in advance that amalgamation of the mines was a sound financial objective. They agreed on a price of 1.4 million British pounds, subject to the approval of shareholders at a meeting scheduled for October. Both Porgès and Rothschild would hold large numbers of shares in De Beers and reap steady dividends.[129]

Company amalgamation peaked dramatically when only two companies remained, Rhodes and Beit's De Beers, and Barnato's Kimberley Central DMC. The unfolding of this "battle of titans" has been mythologized with Rhodes, the blue-eyed, Anglican imperial *visionair*, defeating Barnato, the brash, greedy East End Jewish capitalist. Recent and less sensational readings of the events suggest a mutually beneficial agreement that granted Barnato abundant company shares and a life-time governorship in the new De Beers Consolidated Mining Company, rubbing shoulders with Porgès, Rothschild, Dünkelsbühler, Mosenthal, and "little Alfred," Cecil Rhodes's nickname for his 5.3" righthand man, Beit. By 1890, with centralization complete, De Beers achieved a complete monopoly over the four mines, controlling over 90 percent of the world's diamond production. Within a few months, at the initiative of Harry Mosenthal, De Beers agreed to sell its entire production to ten companies—the London Diamond Syndicate—by means of single channel marketing. Such collaboration permitted the regulation of production, sale, and marketing of diamonds as a commodity. At the first annual meeting where Barnato addressed De Beers company shareholders, he asserted triumphantly: "In my humble opinion, in a few years hence, when we have absolute control of the industry, and the world knows we intend only to supply according to the demand, we shall be able to make the price anything we like." Filled with aplomb, Barnato heralded the diamond "a luxury; if you wish to buy, it makes very little difference whether you pay 100 or 150 pounds; it depends more on the price at which the seller deems fit to sell. We shall have the whole of the trade in our hands."[130] "We" and "our" refers to the De Beers company and its stockholders. But the fact that many company directors and board members were Jewish provided ammunition for railing against Jewish power and wealth. Barnato's choice of words and insinuations of making enormous profits at the expense of naïve customers didn't help matters. Wernher, Beit & Co. took 23 percent of De Beers annual production, Barnato Brothers 20 percent, Mosenthal 15 percent, and Dünkelsbühler 10 percent—two-thirds of the entire global diamond production thus fell in the hands of four companies. Six other firms, one of which was Martin Lilienfeld and Co., shared the remainder of the total yield. The London Diamond Syndicate, the forerunner of the Central Selling Organization that oversees today's global diamond market, consisted almost exclusively of Jewish-owned firms, whose managers had started their careers on the diamond fields of South Africa in the early 1870s.[131]

◆ ◆ ◆

The industrialization of mining reduced the number of hands and pockets moving rough stones from one place to the next. Independent diggers made way for companies, *kopje-wallopers* became redundant, and auctioneers no longer lowered their gavel for the highest bid. In the last decade of the nineteenth century, diggers—almost exclusively black contract laborers who lived for months in high-security compounds—used explosives to collect blue ground. After hauling the substance to the surface, a so-called Pulsator separated the stones from the soil, after which the yield was sent under guard to an on-site company office. A hot bath of nitric and sulfuric acid removed any remaining dirt, followed by a rinse with water and alcohol. Once spread out on the table and once any large stones had been removed, the stones were inspected and classified by a diamond sorter according to clarity, color, and carat. A diamond that fell in the "close goods" pile, explained Gardner Williams, was a well-shaped, pure stone of high quality. The next category contained slightly "spotted stones," while broken or discolored gems were grouped under the heading "cleavage." Further down the line of classification one found piles of "flats," "maacles" (deformed granular structure or knot), and the lowest grades, "rubbish" and "boart," which all contained stones with various irregularities and distortions. Once classified, the stones were further subdivided—except the low grades—according to color. The highest grade on the color scale was "blue white," followed by "first cape," "second cape," "first bye," "second bye," "off-color," "light yellow," and "yellow." Williams reported that De Beers employed ten sorters, "all Europeans, two women and eight

Figure 1.10 "Sorting Diamonds." Kimberley Africana Library #P1596.

men . . . [who] determined[d] the quality of diamonds with notable accuracy and speed."[132] After completing the process, Williams reported admiringly, the sorters placed little heaps of diamonds on a long table, covered them with white paper, and placed them into square tin boxes, forty of which fit into what Williams called a "despatch" box. Stored in secured vaults until 50,000 carats had been accumulated, the parcels were delivered to buyers at the De Beers diamond office in Kimberley.

Diamond merchants had previously purchased stones at auctions or from small "diamantkoopers" offices; now they entered company headquarters to view carefully classified stones. They still paid in cash, although De Beers and others also accepted "bills on London, as the company may prefer." Buyers, in turn, resorted their purchases for the London market into hundreds of separate paper parcels, containing descriptions of their contents. They packed these parcels in tin boxes, wrapped them in cloth-lined paper, and "carefully sealed and delivered them to the post-office, which forward[ed] them to Europe as registered mail." The process changed when De Beers, owning 90 percent of South Africa's diamond production, sold its entire yield to the Diamond Syndicate in London. "Composed of the leading diamond merchants of Holborn Viaduct and Hatton Garden," the Syndicate

Figure 1.11 J. E. Middlebrook, "Sorting Diamonds." Kimberley Africana Library #P3186.

held monthly viewings for their clients, who traveled to London to purchase rough stones, most to be cut and polished in Amsterdam diamond factories.

Between 1870 and 1900, over 50 million carats of rough diamonds left the South African continent by steamboat. If piled in a heap, it would form a small pyramid six feet high, with a nine-foot square base weighing ten tons.[133] Together with finds of copper and gold, the discovery of diamonds initiated a mineral revolution that produced lasting benefits—in economic and urban infrastructures, for one—but that also left deep scars. The pursuit of mineral wealth forced company owners to invest in electricity, telegraph posts, roads, railways, and bridges—they spent money to make more money. One contemporary recalled that in 1876 "people were surprised at seeing some heavily-laden transport-wagons crossing the veld" for the construction of new telegraph poles. The telegraph "brought the Diamond Fields one week nearer Europe than before," putting it into hourly communication with Cape centers of trade.[134] This communication had more influence upon the operators of everyday life than could possibly have been calculated by any rule of arithmetic."[135] Soon after planting telegraph poles, Kimberley became the first town in South Africa with electricity. And from the mid-1880s railway construction connected coastal towns to the previously remote interior, supplying a steady stream of men, tools, and equipment to the sites of plenty. Once Griqualand West, which included the diamond fields, became a province of the Cape Colony, and after Rhodes entered politics, new legislation made its way through Cape Parliament to improve infrastructure suiting the needs of mining industrialists. When Rhodes, the owner of De Beers Consolidated Mines, became prime minister of the Cape Colony in 1890, the entanglement between the South African mining industry and imperial politics deepened.

However, the mineral revolution, the discriminatory labor laws, and enclosed mining compounds that accompanied it also contributed to laying the foundation for the system of apartheid that would grip South Africa until the 1990s.[136] Nineteenth-century legislation systematizing racial segregation, controlled and exploited black miners for maximum gain. Already in the 1870s, black workers were required to carry a pass that showed the name of their "baas" (master), their wages, and their period of service; being found without one resulted in fines, flogging, or imprisonment. Employers conducted invasive body searches and established special courts to try offenders without juries. Conditions for black African miners became appalling once legislation for closed compounds passed.[137] In a South African imperial culture where whites were considered superior to black Africans, the discovery, mining, and trade of diamonds scarred a political economy with racial segregation and inequality. What transpired on the ground in Kimberley was a prelude to apartheid, setting the tone and introducing patterns of exclusion—from inherited wealth and economic mobility—for the next century.

◆ ◆ ◆

To find a cousin is better than a mistress in every port.
—Governor Richard Bourke (1834)

Jews were involved in the extraction and commercial dealing of South African rough from the very moment of discovery—the "first" South African diamond coming through the Lilienfeld branch in Hopetown. While some Jewish pioneers joined the community of diggers starting in the late 1860s, most focused on buying and selling—initially general merchandise and digging supplies but soon after, diamonds. Whether as itinerant *kopje-wallopers* towing claims or as *diamantkoopers* occupying corrugated iron offices, Jews moved rough *klippe* from mine to auction, and from auction to the coast, onward to London. Having a commercial infrastructure already in place spurred the growing efficiency with which stones were shipped to Europe. At the edges of empire, Jews were "significant agents of the commercial revolutions that transformed the South African countryside," intermediaries between mines and markets as well as cofounders of a frontier society.[138] Working-class Whitechapel Jews, middle-class German merchants, and Cape-Jewish migrants alike brought skills and ambitions to the diamond fields that launched the modern diamond industry: literacy and numeracy, familiarity with itinerant or long-distance trading, and an openness to commercial endeavor—all together yielding a working knowledge of commodity merchandise, a sensitivity to the wants of the market, and a network of contacts for distribution and credit.

Once deep-level mining boosted yields and enthusiasm, the number of Jewish diamond merchants in "Diamondopolis" grew, along with the population as a whole. Less than 1 percent of South Africa's white population was of Jewish descent.[139] Because historically trade in precious stones had never required guild membership, Jews had been well represented in this profession. South Africa posed no exception. Indeed, Jews were such a presence that the 1881 edition of the *Diamond News* reported that on Yom Kippur, "all the houses of business were closed and the diamond market was deserted, a proof how strong a hold the Jewish people have succeeded in establishing in Kimberley," at the heart of extraction.[140]

Jewish participation in the industry climbed disproportionally over the course of the 1880s and 1890s, during the period of company amalgamation and centralization. A number of structural factors came together: Jewish merchants had access to investment capital, not merely through their own commercial firms but also through Jewish family banks. Beit, Dünkelsbühler, Marks, Barnato, Porgès, Posno, and others relied on contacts and family connections in Europe, who extended resources and functioned at the receiving end of the commodity chain. Absent what Adam Mendelsohn called this "ethnic ecosystem," one that included business networks bridging city and countryside, metropole and colony, their success would most likely have been much more modest.[141] The rise in demand for diamond jewelry was a contributing factor as well. The boom in supply—over three million carats by the early 1890s—coincided with the new wealth generated by industrialization, spawning Western demand for luxury goods by a flood of new consumers. Mining unprecedented quantities of gems could only be sustained if consumers desired and purchased Cape stones. The rapidity and scale of growth of bourgeois commodity cultures, particularly in the United States, sustained a healthy market and created a milieu where Jewish speculators, claim owners, merchants, and investors thrived. A commercial history of dealing in precious stones, combined with economic networks, willing financial investors, and the burgeoning thirst for diamonds repositioned Jews from the mines' edges to the center of the industry.

This is not to say that non-Jews played an inconsequential role in the industry or that an ethnic Jewish ecosystem functioned in isolation. People of different religious and ethnic backgrounds were drawn in as business partners, employees, entrepreneurs, mining engineers, shareholders, and customers. Jews were part of and not separate from the developing diamond world of Griqualand West. Neither did Jews deliberately maintain a faith-based network out of allegiance to their brethren or from a desire to keep the industry within Jewish circles. The ultimate aim was to make a living and be successful. Having access to social contacts and resources facilitated that path, and Jews prospered from working with the commercial mechanisms at their disposal. If Alfred Beit had harbored any aspirations to work exclusively within a Jewish network, he would have introduced Barney Barnato to Nathan Rothschild to finance the amalgamation of diamond mining companies in the 1880s, not the Anglican Cecil Rhodes. To Beit—converted to Protestantism—what mattered was solid investment opportunities and professional expertise.

Working within a Jewish network did not ensure altruistic cooperation and could, at times, be a liability. Barnato found himself in trouble when his nephew Isaac Joel was arrested on a charge of illicit diamond buying in 1884. Fearing for his nephew's future and his company's reputation, Barnato went through great lengths to try to undo the damage and bolster the young man's chances of acquittal. Eventually Joel jumped bail and fled to London, where he assumed the name of Jack Joel and took a job in the London office of Barnato Brothers.[142] The affair damaged Barnato's reputation, already considered dodgy. Members of the Lippert & Co. family firm, which traded between South Africa, London, and Hamburg, had to deal with a problematic family member of their own. The youngest Lippert brother, Wilhelm (Alfred Beit's first cousin), went to Cape Town in the 1860s to establish a Cape branch while his brother Eduard managed the Port Elizabeth establishment. The oldest brother, Ludwig, remained in Germany as head of the company. Wilhelm, however, quit the firm and became a diamond speculator instead, a job for which he was uniquely unfit. After he forged the name of his famous cousin Beit on promissory notes for a hefty sum, besmirching the Lippert name, his brothers strong-armed Wilhelm to return to Europe, promising to support him on the condition that he never come near a diamond again.

Jewish diamond mining company owners—Barnato, Beit, Marks, Dünkelsbühler, Isaac Lewis, and Lionel Phillips, who survived a 300-foot fall down the steep slopes of one of Kimberley's early diamond diggings—were quick to move into the Witwatersrand gold fields in the 1880s and 1890s. They transferred profits and mining experience from Kimberley to the Witwatersrand, nearly 300 miles northeast of Kimberley, where the South African mineral revolution expanded in scope and depth. Dünkelsbühler, for example, founded the Consolidated (Gold) Mines Selection, with Louis Oppenheimer as director, while Barnato set up the Johannesburg Consolidated Investment Company, the Johannesburg Waterworks Company, and the Barnato Bank, Mining, and Estates Company. Beit helped finance Cecil Rhodes's British South Africa Company, founded in 1889, and became one of its directors. After the process of amalgamation in Kimberley, numerous Jewish- and non-Jewish-owned diamond mining companies bought out by De Beers and Barnato also relocated their business activities and mining employees to the Rand, fueling the rapid development of the gold mining industry.[143]

The South African node places Jews at the nerve center of the imperial project. While a demographic minority, South African and European Jews acted like any other pioneer and commercial entrepreneur, taking advantage of opportunities offered by a specific time and place. Moreover, the outcome and impact of Jewish participation suggest that what happened on the frontier is as much part of modern Jewish history as developments in the capitals of Europe and the United States. Sharp distinctions between core and periphery fail to take into account the complexities of Jewish historical narratives.[144] Instead, the experiences of *kopje-wallopers* bartering for diamonds between claims, of a Jewish buyer publicly challenging a Christian missionary, and of Cape-Jewish merchants' prescient investment in land acquisition imply that modernization was occurring in the most remote places of the African interior.

Figure 2.1 "Kohinoor Diamond." Cigarette Card, "Famous Gems of the World" Series, ca. 1890. New York Public Library Digital Collections: Image #1554849.

CHAPTER 2

An Empire Made Portable

London

In 1871, while writing in his journal, the colonial secretary to the government of Griqualand West, John Blades "JB" Currey, recalled the story of a diamond robbery. After a postmaster in New Rush had finished sealing up mail bags, "heaping them against the window to be ready for the cart," a robber "broke the post office window, lifted the sash, and took the mail bags that felt heavy." Planning to hide the loot in his luggage and deposit it in a London Bank, recorded Curry, the thief hurried to Cape Town and boarded a transatlantic liner.[1] Police, on his tail for days, arrested him in the nick of time.

Reports of this kind were not unusual. Letters from the Colonial Office, local newspapers, and travel journals spoke regularly of blatant theft.[2] John William Harding gained notoriety in the press in May 1872, after scouting out the same New Rush post office and, seeing no one inside, had "stuck his arm through the delivery window and removed a six-pound bag from the counter with letters containing 2,381 diamonds."[3] Police detained Harding in a Cape Town hotel three weeks later. A search of his luggage, already aboard the steamship *Syria*, uncovered the missing stones, hidden inside the barrel of a rifle. Harding confessed and was sentenced to five years of hard labor. A few months after his sentencing, "another sensational robbery" shook the Diamond Field community. A postbag full of rough stones, en route to South Africa's primary harbor, "had been dropped—or perhaps thrown—from the mail wagon," but a detective in disguise caught the crook and recovered its contents.[4]

Troubled by the "guaranteed monthly robbery" of diamond "swag" and perturbed by mockery in the press, the Cape governor called for securing post offices by means of window bars and fire-proof safes.[5] Similar to industrial machinery and mining gear, safes arrived from England, hauled across the Atlantic and South Africa's vast semiarid region of the Karoo to safeguard precious stones, collectively worth millions of British pounds as they moved between hemispheres.[6] Indeed, the entire mechanism of the modern mineral trade—on site and in transit—depended on the smooth operation of imperial infrastructures already in place, including Great Britain's postal service, steamships, trade routes, systems of communication, and print media. Everyone with a stake in the business—from diggers, *kopje-wallopers*, and auctioneers to sorters, mine owners, and company shareholders—relied on goods and services connecting metropole and colonies. The diamond industry, and the commercial city of Kimberley that sprouted from it, pulled empire deeper into the South African heartland, casting bright light but also dark shadows onto its permanently changed landscape.

Cape offices of the British postal service soon featured heavy window bars and safes. Colonial Mail was accessible, relatively inexpensive, and, barring the occasional robbery, dependable. Because Europe did not require rough stones to be declared for import duty, mailing boxes and envelopes proved the most practical method for transporting rough stones from the frontier to London for distribution.[7] During the early days of the Diamond Fields, merchants typically traveled hundreds of miles by horse carriage to Cape Town or Port Elizabeth to send gems on their way, but after Kimberley established postal services, they shipped their parcels. As quantities and values swelled, merchants opted to insure their wares, often through a Kimberley or Cape branch of a London bank, such as the Standard Bank, dispatching precious cargo in tin boxes bearing the merchant's seal.[8]

Griqualand West administrators reported that in 1875 postal services handled over 700 pounds of rough stones, valued at 1.4 million British pounds (over £100 million today). This did not take into account "large amounts sent home by shippers through private sources" as part of an export company's cargo—such as Mosenthal & Co.—nor the "very large quantities sent clandestinely," as in the example of the rifle barrel.[9] For 1880, the post office operating on the Fields registered 1,440 pounds of rough, a number that continued to climb.[10] Mail service between Britain and the Cape Colonies was expanded and reinforced to meet soaring

Figure 2.2 Uncatalogued card, National Library of Cape Town.

needs, further cementing London as the primary point of entry for rough diamonds into Europe.

Once stones arrived in the city, they were sold either at public auction or at private "viewings." Debenham's department store on King Street, Covent Garden, held monthly auctions for rough and cut stones. Newspapers announced upcoming auction dates and offered detailed descriptions of the merchandise and sale prices after proceedings had concluded. These events, noted the *Times* in 1872, attracted "a good many buyers from the provinces and the Continent." The *Jeweller and Metalworker* added that "everything possible is done to attract attention, especially to secure the attendance of ladies."[11] Harrods and Edwin Streeter's Bond Street jewelry store displayed replicas of famous diamonds in their windows, tempting passersby to stop and admire the sparkling celebrities. To promote his business and expertise, Edwin Streeter published three popular books—*Precious Stones and Gems* (1877), followed by *Great Diamonds of the World* (1882) and *The Koh-i-Noor Diamond: Its Romance and History* (1895). Well-advertised sales and extensive newspaper coverage about the Diamond Fields' commercial development, along with its scandals and promise of a bright future, brought South African gems to public attention as never before.[12]

As diamond companies consolidated and streamlined the market in the 1880s, public auctions for rough stones waned and distribution occurred increasingly behind closed doors. Having received registered parcels via London banks, diamond importers introduced a new method of selling, namely by arranging "sights" for continental buyers crossing the English Channel to purchase inventory for cutting and polishing factories. Rather than bidding in public, surrounded by an audience, buyers met privately at import company headquarters. These firms clustered in Hatton Garden, a one-square-mile commercial area known as London's primary jewelry quarter and the center of the mineral trade. In the seventeenth and eighteenth centuries Sephardic gem merchants, importers of Indian and Brazilian stones on board East and West India Company ships, had brought the trade to London after settling there themselves.[13] When the South African diamond rush began and parcels stuffed with carbon minerals arrived in London, Hatton Garden was already a nucleus for the commerce in and manufacture of gemstones. When Barney Barnato, feverishly buying up claims in Kimberley in the 1870s, looked to establish an office in the city of his birth to import and distribute diamonds, he gravitated to Hatton Garden, as did fellow Jewish importers with familiar and commercial ties to Europe, among them Sammy Marks, Alfred Beit, Joseph Mosenthal, Anton Dünkelsbühler, and Martin Lilienfeld.[14]

By the early 1890s, each of the ten firms belonging to the London Syndicate managed offices in Kimberley and Hatton Garden, directly linking the sites of production and distribution. Near the famous Big Hole in Kimberley, member company offices stood next to each other in an L-shaped block: Wernher & Beit in one corner, flanked on one side by Dünkelsbühler and L. & A. Abrahams (representing Barnato), and by Mosenthal and some of the smaller firms on the other.[15] Commissioned to purchase De Beers Consolidated Mines' entire annual output, Syndicate managers congregated at Wernher & Beit to divide the yield according to contractual agreements. At De Beers's general office, stones were first boiled in a mixture of nitric and sulfuric acid to remove any dirt, then rinsed in

Figure 2.3 "Sorting Gravel for Diamonds at Kimberley." *Popular Science Monthly* 41 (August 1892).

water and alcohol, and spread out to dry. As soon as roughly 50,000 carats had been collected, sorters—both men and women—classified the stones according to size, color, and quality. Placing the gems in tin dispatch boxes, they carried them, under armed guard, to Wernher & Beit, each firm receiving an allotment: Wernher & Beit and Barnato Brothers each collected 23 percent; Mosenthal & Sons 15 percent; Dünkelsbühler and Joseph Brothers each 10 percent; Neumann, J. Cohen & Co., Lilienfeld & Co., Gervers, and Feldheimer & Co. divided the remainder.[16]

Once fixed quantities had been allocated and paid for, staff reassorted and repackaged the stones in envelopes carrying descriptions of the contents, gathered them in square tin boxes wrapped in cloth-lined packing paper, sealed the parcels, and delivered them to the Kimberley Post Office for dispatch to London.[17] Consignments from De Beers typically numbered 350–400 parcels, each containing up to forty tin boxes. By the end of the century fifty million carats had been excavated from African soil and sent across the Atlantic by steamboat.

◆ ◆ ◆

My father brought me into this business and his father
brought him into diamonds, and his father before him too . . .

But no, my son will not be a diamantaire because in his day,
there will be no diamantaires. There will be only De Beers.
—Antwerp diamond polisher (year unknown)

The official registration of De Beers Consolidated Mines Company in 1888 was the outcome of a decade of company formation and mergers, concentrating management of four deep-level mines under a single board, thereby minimizing internal competition. The expansion and concentration at the production end complemented the rapid growth in Kimberley and London of a network of merchant importers handling the flow of close to 2 million carats a year. Once rough stones arrived by mail in London, Syndicate companies resorted arrivals into a variety of grades, creating so-called series that included a mix of high- and low-quality gems of different colors and carats, shown at weekly sights. Sight holders, rather than selecting only superior stones and dismissing those under par, were required to purchase rough goods in series at fixed prices, allowing Syndicate firms to dispose of their entire stock and pass the cost of handling imperfect stones onto the manufacturer.

Because De Beers and its Syndicate regulated output and prices, making sure to prevent overproduction of a commodity whose desirability depended on artificial scarcity, they enjoyed the power to favor clients willing to accept sales by series without protest. The sales practice placed continental buyers, traveling to London at the behest of cutting and polishing establishments in Amsterdam and Antwerp, in a subordinate position; they could either accept the Syndicate's terms or go home empty-handed, banned from future sights and unable to obtain inventory for their factories.[18] This power imbalance bred widespread discontent among already well-established European manufacturers as well as aspiring entrepreneurs, whose exclusion from the buyers' list or refusal to pay for entire series crippled efforts to start new businesses.

Henri Polak, the Jewish socialist leader of the Dutch Diamond Workers' Union (ANDB) in Amsterdam, bemoaned the Syndicate's monopolization. Recognizing that the livelihoods of more than 10,000 lapidaries depended on rough goods coming in from London, he opposed restrictions on distribution and controlled price increases. He understood that the interlocking interests of De Beers and the Syndicate, with directors sharing a seat at each other's table, had the workers by the throat. "Anyone on this earth in need of rough diamonds," he complained bitterly, "has to turn to [them]."[19] As the union leader, he had witnessed close-up the ripple effects of decisions made across the English Channel. To prevent the circulation of too many diamonds and a free-fall in value, the Syndicate in 1890 drastically curtailed output, more than doubling the price of rough goods and lowering the number of carats in need of cutting and polishing. As a result, Amsterdam's mills came to a standstill, causing debilitating unemployment and uncertainty about the future. Polak held "bandits" and "mountebank arch-millionaires like Rhodes and Barnato" directly responsible for the misery of the diamond proletariat.[20]

In 1894, amid widespread strikes, Polak penned a letter to the Syndicate, explaining ongoing hardships in the Dutch capital. To absorb the exorbitant prices of rough, factory managers had slashed salaries and cut thousands of jobs, prompting Polak to request subsidies from London to support strikers. If the Syndicate wished to keep diamond manufacturing alive, he inferred, it should extend a hand in resolving conflicts between employers and employees. Wernher & Beit took time to reply, thanking the union leader for so graphically portraying the plight of the Amsterdam diamond workers. London's company owners had dutifully presented Polak's appeal to various Syndicate members, and while they wished to "express their full sympathy," hoping for a quick resolution to the strike, they held that both parties—employers and employees—would "be best served if the Syndicate remain in a neutral position." Regretfully they could not (and would not) "hold out on the promise of a monetary contribution to [Polak's] Union."[21] Indifferent to the plight of lapidaries abroad and averse to getting involved in labor disputes, Syndicate firms washed their hands off the Dutch plight.

In New York City, too, manufacturers seethed over London's monopoly. The manager of Chester Billings & Sons, operating offices at Maiden Lane in New York, Tulip Street in Amsterdam, and Holborn Circus in London, concluded that "one thing is certain . . . [t]he diamond trade is in the absolute control of the Syndicate; it can do what it pleases, and the dealers and the public must submit to its dictation." The rigidity of sights and series, the lack of bargaining power on the part of manufacturers, let alone the workers, and the futility of protest were all owing to the Syndicate's absolute control. "You can buy or not," the manager proclaimed indignantly, "but if you don't buy, where are you going to get any goods?"[22] To keep cutting factories in operation, buyers had no choice but "to take the lot exactly as it is offered and pay the price in cash on the spot" to the "Lordly Lords of Diamonds."[23] The American Jewish entrepreneur Leopold Stern, operating a diamond cutting factory with his brother, Isidore, at Maiden Lane, agreed. New York buyers invited for a sight were to present themselves in person in London at a date and time determined by the Syndicate. Packages of diamonds could be accepted or refused, "but refusal is unknown, as it would result in his not getting another sight of the rough gems for some time."[24] De Beers, in close and unyielding partnership with the Syndicate, determined every detail, from price, weight, and scheduled sights to series and buyers' lists. "The world [was] at its mercy."[25]

While Syndicate company ownership consisted almost exclusively of Jews, there was nothing particularly "Jewish" about their positions of authority—Gentile company owners in different industries, such as iron and steel, conducted business in similar fashion, displaying little empathy for the proletariat's struggles, prioritizing profit at all times. All ten firms were Jewish-owned, feeding existing prejudices. It would be incorrect to say that ethnic distinctiveness was consciously wrought. Rather, the Syndicate was the apex and outcome of a long history of Jewish commerce in gems, concentrated further by expanding ethnic and imperial networks, access to investment capital, and *chutzpah*, central ingredients in fulfilling the commercial potential of the nineteenth century.

A brief look into one of the Syndicate company owners, Anton Dünkelsbühler, illustrates how much familial and ethnic relationships mattered. Dünkelsbühler, nicknamed Dunkels, was a veteran of the earliest days on the diamond fields. Like many young adventurers, he had traveled from Europe to South Africa in the early 1870s to make his fortune. Born in 1846 and raised in Bavaria, he journeyed to the Northern Cape and found employment at Mosenthal & Co., where he did increasingly well for himself. In 1876 he returned to Europe to start his own rough diamond import business. Before leaving Kimberley, Dünkelsbühler invested all his resources in buying up stocks to sell in London. He used the profits to establish A. Dünkelsbühler & and Co., managing one office in Hatton Garden and another in Kimberley. He hired a relative of his wife's, an assistant buyer named Bernard Oppenheimer, eldest son of an affluent Jewish cigar merchant in Friedberg, near Frankfurt.

The network widened. Bernard's younger sibling, Louis, followed in his brother's footsteps, arriving in Kimberley in 1886 at the age of sixteen. By this time Bernard had become Dünkelsbühler's chief representative. When Cecil Rhodes bought out Barney Barnato's Kimberley Central Diamond Mining Co., effectively creating a De Beers Consolidated Mines Co. monopoly, Bernard was one of the signatories to the first contract between De Beers and the newly established Syndicate. Having become prominent in the orbit of diamond company owners, he taught his brother the ropes and introduced him to people he needed to know to succeed. Within a few years, Louis took over the Kimberley office, while Bernard relocated to the Witwatersrand to develop gold mining interests on Dünkelsbühler's behalf. Louis subsequently arranged a job for a third Oppenheimer sibling, Ernest, who arrived in England on his sixteenth birthday in 1896. Finding employment as a diamond sorter at Dünkelsbühler's London branch, Ernest graded the packages of precious stones arriving from Kimberley in preparation for sights. With a starting salary of one pound per week, he spent 17 shillings on rent for an upstairs room at 10 North Villas, Camden Town. It came with breakfast and supper.

After testing the London end of the commodity chain, Ernest left for South Africa to learn more about production and sorting. He resided in Kimberley with his mother's cousin, Fritz Hirschhorn, the primary representative of Wernher & Beit and future board member and director of De Beers. Hirschhorn had already hosted Bernard and Louis, and now Ernest arrived with a suitcase and fifty pounds in his pocket. Hirschhorn mentored Ernest, introducing him to "the men who made Kimberley tick," including David Harris, Barney Barnato's cousin.[26] From time to time Hirschhorn invited Ernest to take minutes during meetings of De Beers directors. Here the young man cultivated the mores of the corporate world of Rhodes, Barnato, Beit, and other pioneers. He made a name for himself at one of these meetings. During a visit from London, Solomon "Solly" Barnato Joel, Barney's flamboyant nephew and director of Barnato Brothers, passed around a large stone found in one of the river diggings. While making the rounds for inspection, each attendee gave an estimate. Ernest remained silent. When Solly Joel asked the rookie about its value, Ernest replied that it was mere glass and worthless, accepting a hefty £50 bet to prove he was right. Proper assessment revealed the stone was indeed glass, having fooled even the most seasoned merchant in the room.

Starting as a junior clerk, Ernest was put in charge of Dünkelsbühler's staff in the Kimberley office. Staff was tasked with preparing parcels for dispatch to London. After three years, Ernest returned to England to work for the Syndicate, of which Dünkelsbühler had become a member firm. He married Mary Lina "May" Pollack, whose sister Charlotte had married his brother Louis. May's father, Joseph Pollack, was a stockbroker and the past president of the London Stock Exchange. By the early 1900s, there were Dünkelsbühlers, Oppenheimers, and Hirschhorns in Kimberley, the Witwatersrand, Frankfurt, and London, many connected through marriage.

Similar patterns can be observed with other Jewish families in the diamond trade. Alfred Beit, responsible for introducing Cecil Rhodes to Nathan Rothschild in an effort to obtain financing, joined his cousin's firm, Lippert & Co., well known for its expertise in importing and exporting British and South African products, including gems. The Lipperts, related by marriage to the Mosenthal family, were international traders and diamond speculators. After partnering with Julius Wernher to represent Jules Porgès & Co., leading diamond buyers in Paris, Alfred Beit established a direct line to Jules (Yehuda) Porgès's cousin, Théodore Porgès, head of the family bank, Ephrussi & Porgès. Alfred Beit and Harry Mosenthal were the first merchant directors elected to De Beers's board of directors. What made men like Beit, the Oppenheimer brothers, Mosenthal, and Dünkelsbühler so influential was their position as mining company owners as well as Syndicate associates, which put them in the driver's seat of South African production as well as London distribution. As board members, they regulated volume and prices for the international market and had first dibs in purchasing rough to supply their own London companies.

Having a cluster of family businesses on different continents meant that adolescent relatives could easily be placed somewhere to learn the ropes, whether in London, on the European continent, or in frontier colonies. Many of these kindred mercantile families with experience in transatlantic trade and investment banking had enjoyed long-distance partnerships for generations.[27] The promising field of Cape diamonds, awash with professional opportunities, drew Jewish men to follow in the footsteps of their brothers, fathers, and uncles. Many were young—in their late teens and early twenties—and they benefited from support systems: a rent-free room with a relative, a loan to buy a few promising claims, a mentor with commercial know-how, and connections to markets.

Ernest Oppenheimer did precisely that. Soon he was packaging rough diamonds in tin boxes at Dünkelsbühler's Big Hole office, preparing merchandise for Syndicate sights in London. By the time Ernest came on the scene, the relatively open system of the 1870s and 1880s, with individual claim owners digging for stones that eventually made their way to public auctions, had narrowed to a single sales organization. Vertically integrated, De Beers and the Syndicate were nearly inseparable, having grown into "the most impregnable monopoly in the world" by the turn of the century.[28] The diamond trade had effectively become a closed guild.

◆ ◆ ◆

"The diamond is in truth the very essence of property. . . . A diamond is an empire made portable, with which he might purchase a better kingdom and mount a prouder throne."
—Sir David Brewster, "The Diamond—Its History, Properties, and Origins," *North British Review* (1852)

The German sociologist Georg Simmel, in *The Philosophy of Money*, maintained that the value of an object does not lie with its inherent properties but, rather, in its social significance. When objects are craved by large segments of the population, demand and value are enhanced. Value is therefore a social judgment made about an object, translated into monetary terms.[29]

The desirability of gemstones fits Simmel's description. Once exotic and rare, diamonds were flaunted by those who could afford them and admired, from a distance, by those less fortunate. However, unlike other luxury commodities that entered the mainstream, the social weight of gems mounted as supplies surged and availability eased. Massive deposits in South Africa injected millions of carats into the supply chain, but their exclusivity and allure only intensified. Abundance did not translate into lower value. Instead, diamonds gained in status as signifiers of prestige, power, and wealth. The meaning evoked by diamonds was not new—they had long been associated with regal sophistication—but having access to this social currency was. The growth in purchasing power of the middle class during the nineteenth century democratized ownership of gems and, combined with created illusions of scarcity and effective marketing, catapulted the diamond to one of the most desirable material objects in the world.[30]

In Victorian Britain the social and cultural significance of diamonds took shape within the context of empire. In a variety of different spatial and literary settings, Victorians infused public perceptions of gems with connotations of conquest, economic expansion, and white civilization. Diamonds featured prominently at exhibitions and world fairs, in department store windows and museum vitrines, as well as in commercial advertising, detective novels, and travel journals, feeding the imperial imagination of consumers.[31] Jews often served as props to the narratives being conveyed in these spaces. They were either recognized as master artisans essential to the process of preparing diamonds for others or—primarily in detective stories—portrayed as untrustworthy dealers engaged in illegal activities. Jews were employed as stereotypical characters in visual and narrative texts that paid primary attention to the "Oriental" Other.

International exhibitions were a prominent means for staging imperial goods, including diamonds, and peoples. Built on an enormous scale, they amassed the flora and fauna, natural resources, and merchandise of foreign territories, literally and figuratively parading the fruits of empire. African minerals and "natives" became staple features at these events, intended to enlighten metropolitan audiences about the provenance of diamonds and digging methods. Geological maps and scenic photographs, machinery, working models of mines, specimens, and lectures "explained how diamonds occur in the earth and how they are extracted from their matrix."[32] Organized in numerous European and American capitals, world fairs attracted hundreds of thousands of visitors, from affluent socialites to blue-collar workers, marveling at the technological innovations and colonial commodities on display. Lasting for months, these carefully planned undertakings publicly endorsed claims to colonial wealth by Western nation-states, presenting industrial progress as benevolent and just. Highly performative in execution, exhibitions showed objects to stir the imagination and to assert power.[33]

The 1851 Great Exhibition, held at the purpose-built, 990,000 square feet Crystal Palace in London's Hyde Park, set the bar for organizing committees in subsequent decades. Initiated by Prince Albert and members of the Royal Society for the Encouragement of Arts, Manufactures, and Commerce, the Great Exhibition celebrated modern industrial technology, showcasing Great Britain's dominance on the world stage. Other nations soon followed, hosting *Expositions Universelles*, Colonial and Indian Exhibitions, World's Fairs, and Centennials in such cities as Paris, Amsterdam, London, Cape Town, and Chicago. The local press carried stories about designated sites and major themes featured at the exhibition. During the months of operation, newspapers and illustrated magazines published daily programs and reviews, highlighting exposés not to be missed. Together with widespread media coverage on the African Diamond Fields, frequent advertisements of jewelry, and announcements of public auctions, exhibitions contributed to creating a shared discourse on diamonds.

Surprisingly, the spectacular 186-carat Kohinoor ("Mountain of Light") failed to dazzle audiences at the Great Exhibition. The famous Indian diamond, displayed for the first time as Queen Victoria's possession, had been seized by British forces from the ten-year-old Punjabi maharajah Duleep Singh in 1849. So much had been written about the gem that "curiosity . . . had swelled to a fever pitch by the time the exhibition began."[34] The "exotic" provenance and "dramatic" history of the Kohinoor, recalled one contemporary, was something that "most people [would already] know."[35] Spectators thronged the south-central gallery of the Crystal Palace, eagerly awaiting a chance to catch a glimpse of this artifact of conquest. The antic nonetheless flopped.[36] Encased in a gilded cage surmounted by a royal crown, visitors found it dull and ungraceful, mocking it as "the diamond that won't shine. The satirical magazine *Punch* referred to the Kohinoor as the "Mountain of Darkness" that radiated "as much light as the sun in England."[37] Metal reflectors, inserted in the cage to magnify its sparkle, proved futile, providing additional fodder for ridicule. Chagrinned, Prince Albert ordered the "Oriental" stone with its mythical origins recut "according to European taste."[38] He invited the best lapidaries in the field to take on the task: Dutch-Jewish masters Meijer Coster (son of Mozes Elias Coster, founder of the Coster diamond manufacturing firm) and his most gifted employee, Levie Benjamin Voorzanger.[39]

Coster and Voorzanger traveled to London to inspect the precious gem and, after weeks of examination and planning, started the cutting process using a steam-powered mill specifically built for the job at Robert Garrard & Co. in Haymarket. The operation took thirty-eight days. Under the watchful eye of Prince Albert and the Duke of Wellington, and under the technical direction of the queen's mineralogist, James Tennant, Voorzanger reduced the Kohinoor's weight from 186 to 105.6 carats. The egg-shaped stone, similar in overall appearance to other Mughal era diamonds, had initially contained 169 triangular and rectangular facets with a high-dome and a flat base. This "Oriental cutting had caused its apparent dullness" and failure to impress, making the stone an imperfect jewel to grace the body of Britain's monarch. Coster and Voorzanger, with the aid of Western science and machinery, received instructions to refashion and civilize the Kohinoor "upon the improved principles of modern art."[40]

An illustration in *Punch* reflected the civilizing mission. The Kohinoor, depicted as an ailing patient dressed in a long robe and supported by the Duke of Wellington, is guided to the operating table, a polishing mill. "Eminent Scientific Men" stand behind the "requisite machinery," while "the Dutch artists," Coster and Voorzanger, are gearing up to cure him. "Ah," exclaims a woman in the background, "He ain't never bin altogether bright—so to speak—since he made that exhibition of himself in Igh Park," referring to the Kohinoor's disappointing performance. The patient, however, could presumably be healed after treatment. Undergoing an aesthetic and religious conversion, the Indian stone would be domesticated upon transformation into a white, Anglo-Saxon, and rational gem.

Punch and the *Illustrated London News*, as well as other popular news media, refrained from drawing attention to Coster and Voorzanger's Jewishness. They spoke of "Dutch artists" and "gentlemen from Amsterdam," but their Jewish identity was either presumed or not worth mentioning. The Other was the objectified "Oriental." Jews, despite their ethnic and religious distinctiveness, appeared to be squarely in the European camp. Voorzanger's somewhat scruffy appearance—contrary to that of Coster, his boss and owner of the Amsterdam diamond factory—is complemented by the portrayal of the woman, whose dress and accent reveal her working-class background. Uncaricatured and described as "practical," Jewish artisans appeared to assist in westernizing the diamond, preparing it to reflect the brilliance of the British Empire.[41] Satisfied with the result, Victoria, during her state visit to Paris in 1852, awed crowds wearing "her" diamond, mounted in a honeysuckle brooch.

After the discovery of South African deposits, international exhibitions expanded diamond exposés, staging not merely the artifact but also the processes of mining and manufacturing. In the 1880s and 1890s, mounting diamonds in an imperial setting both exoticized and domesticated African

Figure 2.4 "The Poor Old Koh-i-noor Again!" *Punch Magazine* 23 (August 1852), 54.

gems. Rough stones, unearthed from the bowels of the "dark continent," were washed, then cut and polished during live demonstrations into sparkling brilliants befitting the necklines of civilized white women. Exhibitions enabled this cultural sanitation to be seen by the public from beginning to end. They allowed visitors to interact with precious stones—touching them, hearing the sounds of washing and manufacturing, and eyeing the final product in glass cases—all the while gaining knowledge about diamonds as possessions and celebrations of empire. Diamonds, symbolizing the empire's civilizing mission, threw a public, positive light on imperial conquest.

The Colonial and Indian Exhibition, held in South Kensington in 1886, offers an example. There African diamonds were turned into commodities for metropolitan consumption. As visitors arrived at the Queen's Gate entrance, they were led directly into the Cape Court, where the mounted head of an African elephant heralded "this portion of the Queen's dominions."[42] Wall panels with meticulous classifications, official catalogs, and public lectures broadcast the message that Great Britain's technological expertise and economic drive tamed the "wild" and promoted the welfare of all subjects of the Crown.[43] Upon entering, spectators saw numerous large maps and wall panels describing the Cape's physical and geological features, natural resources, rainfall, railways and telegraphs, and statistical data on the import and export of wine, wool, and minerals. Maps and photographs, "scrutinised by those who have relatives and friends settled at the Cape," familiarized viewers with colonial landscapes, "bringing home the vast progress which [has] been made there in civilization since . . . General Sir David Baird conquered it from the Dutch in 1806."[44] By complementing the visual imagery of foreign places and peoples with detailed statistical information, Cape Commissioners presented the Colony as both exotic and controlled.

Once past the introductory illustrations and charts, visitors encountered the main attraction of the Cape Court, the minerals exhibit. The entire commodity chain was on display, from digging up blue ground and washing debris to polishing and setting a diamond in jewelry, fulfilling the Royal Commission's request to show the "raw product in connection with the manufactured article."[45] The highlight of the exhibit was a complete working model of a diamond mine. The Cape Commission, in collaboration with a Subcommittee for Minerals in Kimberley, built the model based on the design of the Bultfontein mine at the center of the Court to demonstrate the process and methods used to excavate rough stones. Various mining companies at Kimberley, De Beer's, Du Toit's Pan, and Bultfontein had provided the Commission with diamondiferous soil, hauled nearly 8,000 miles across the Karoo and the Atlantic to South Kensington.[46] The subcommittee, responsible for collecting indigenous living subjects and artifacts to populate the Cape Court, hired African laborers, "Kaffirs," to work the mine, promising payments of cattle upon their return from London.[47]

The working model included a depositing floor, state-of-the-art aerial hauling gear employed for deep-level mining, horse-whims, and washing machines with pulsators, surrounded by collections of mineralogical specimens, photographs of Kimberley and its diamond mining companies, and charts itemizing monthly yields. The elaborate display afforded "a practical demonstration of the wealth and industrial development of the outlying portions of the British Empire."[48] By including visual images and descriptions of the Diamond Fields' early days, the exhibit took on a didactic role, underscoring that British technology and innovation had served as the primary ingredients to realize the industry's progress and Kimberley's urban development. Those inspired to partake in the adventure could visit the emigration office at the South Promenade near the Colonial Market.[49] Promoting the mineral rich Cape colony as an extension of Britain, exhibition organizers offered prospective settlers information and advice. The success of Empire could be theirs, too.

Visitors were especially drawn to live demonstrations of diamond washing and sorting, scheduled between 3:00 and 4:00 PM, attracting "thousands daily."[50] "The operations of washing the blue ground," wrote H. Trueman Wood for the Society of the Arts, "sifting the gravel and picking out the diamonds, were carried on daily before an intently gazing crowd. No exhibit excited more general interest or more closely riveted the attention of the public than this actual process of diamond-washing on a large scale."[51] A detailed etching of the demonstration in the *Illustrated London News* portrayed bare-chested black workers wearing long necklaces, rinsing soil while a white supervisor showed the findings to curious spectators. Children in the front row gawked at the scene, as their well-clad parents stood behind them. The secretary to the Cape Commission reported to the Cape governor that "Kaffirs and Bushmen, utilised in connection with the washing machine, were generally well conducted, and had great interest taken in them by the British public." Moreover, he stated with relief, "[i]t was by the exhibit of the diamond washing and cutting . . . that such enormous crowds were attracted to the Cape Court, and had it not been for such attractions I am afraid that the wool, mohair, cereals, minerals and other valuable products would have remained unnoticed."[52] The colonies supplied British consumers with an abundance of foreign goods, but none magnetized the public like diamonds—not only because they had been rare for so long, but also because spectators witnessed how they were made. They could see with their own eyes how rough stones, washed by "uncultured" black hands, were cut and polished into civilized brilliants. By including both in exhibit displays, jewelers emphasized the transformative effects of their craft.

A uniquely exciting performance occurred during the sorting process. "Ladies," presumed more trustworthy than gentlemen, were allowed to sit a sorting table under the guidance of the manager, Lewis Atkinson, and search the washed debris for rough stones. "With their hands and a tin scraper pushing about the blue pebbles," women became participants in the process of "diamond hunting," crossing the glass boundary dividing producers and consumers. When these "fair sorters" believed to have found a gem, Atkinson, in dramatic fashion, "placed it under the scraper and with one blow smash[ed] it," proving, much to the disappointment of the crowd, that the promising find was only a pebble.[53] By taking a seat at the sorting table and placing themselves within the commodity chain, Victorian women gave their consent to colonial practices, taking riches from African soil when they could.

Occasionally sorters spotted genuine diamonds. On the day of Queen Victoria's visit, professional sorters found a small, off-colored stone

Figure 2.5 "Colonial and Indian Exhibition." *Illustrated London News* (October 16, 1886), 414.

offered—perhaps out of a sense of obligation—to the guest of honor. Victoria requested it cut, polished, and set in an original design. The result was a brooch in the shape of an anchor, symbolizing the Cape of Good Hope (see fig. 2.5), mounted and displayed at the exhibition stall of Ford & Wright's Diamond Cutting and Polishing Works.

In addition to depicting washing and sorting, the *Illustrated London News* image showed a diamond polisher being scrutinized by visitors while working on a stone. "The [polishing benches] run round three sides of a roomy stall," noted one observer, where "white-aproned craftsmen were busy all day long cutting and polishing the hard gems." International exhibits and world fairs staged live cutting and polishing demonstrations performed by experienced lapidaries from Amsterdam, at the time the diamond manufacturing mecca of the world.[54] The Dutch-Jewish family firm M. E. Coster became regular contributors throughout the 1860s, '70s, and '80s, although they were conspicuously absent at the 1886 Colonial and Indian Exhibit in London.[55] The Cape Commission, intent on highlighting British achievements, invited a London firm instead: Ford and Wright's Diamond Cutting and Polishing Works of Clerkenwell Green, near Hatton Garden. When starting his business in the early 1870s Ford had employed

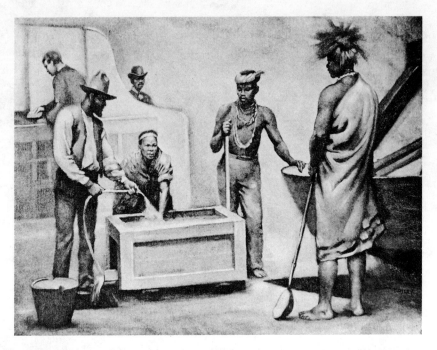

Figure 2.6 "Diamond Washing." Frank Cundall, *Reminiscences of the Colonial and Indian Exhibition* (London: William Clowes and Sons, 1886), 87.

Dutch lapidaries, "whom he paid exorbitant wages until he had mastered the task himself," and then hired only English artisans—whether they were of Jewish descent remains unclear. Ford maintained that since "nine-tenths of the diamonds in the whole world come from the Cape," it was "only right that diamond cutting should be conducted by English workmen." Ford was commended for his defiant stance on outsourcing labor and for bringing to England the art of diamond cutting, whose "secrets" Dutch masters had kept to themselves for too long.[56] Diamond manufacturing remained solidly in Dutch hands for the entirety of the nineteenth century, yet the Exhibit organizers welcomed the opportunity to show off British inroads into Dutch territorial expertise. Ford must have beamed when the Prince of Wales drew Queen Victoria's attention to his diamond cutters, remarking "that her subjects were for the first time in public engaged in diamond polishing." The British flag, he implied, flew over every segment of gem production. National pride swelled when Princesses Louise, Beatrice, and Mary of Teck, and the Duchess of Albany, guided by Ford, "each cut the first facet on a diamond," adding a royal touch to the proceedings.[57]

Neither the popular press nor official Exhibit catalogs drew attention to Jewish preponderance in the mineral trade. Jewish company names appeared on wall panels, but Jewish identity was largely absent from the narrative, in part because company amalgamation and centralization through the London Syndicate took place in the years immediately following the London Exhibit. In the domain of diamonds, the exotic Other was not Jewish but African. Displaying the "Kaffir" as serviceable labor for colonial industry carried the message of British imperial dominance and power.[58] Over the course of six months, five and a half million visitors watched black laborers work washing debris within the model mine in the Cape Court, while their white supervisor, Atkinson, smashed stones in front of oohing and aahing audiences. Flaunting the importance of the trade between Great Britain and its colonies, the Commissioners promoted the Cape as a producer territory, justifying its annexation as part of the imperial project. That Jews participating in this endeavor did not seem noteworthy.

The Kimberley subcommittee had initially proposed constructing a spectacular diamond pyramid, made of wood and covered with crystals.[59] But it was deemed too passive, showing only the end product rather than the intricacies of the production process. Favoring a fully functioning model mine, the commissioners shelved the proposal. A different version of the idea materialized at the *Exposition Universelle* three years later. "Scarcely on any occasion have so many diamonds been collected and exhibited as at the Paris exhibition," marveled the *Scientific American* in 1889.[60] A nearly three-and-a-half-foot-tall model of the Eiffel Tower, made entirely of diamonds, was a tour de force and such a crowd-pleaser that it was "going off to America" to be displayed at the 1893 Chicago World's Fair. In Paris, Dutch-Jewish cutters and polishers returned to the scene. Lapidaries from Boas & Co. performed live demonstrations in front of glass cases displaying finished stones in a pavilion near the South African wing, where organizers had again recreated the working model of the Bultfontein diamond mine.[61]

Illustrations circulating in the 1880 and 1890s purport to show what "white" diamonds turned into once the manufacturing process was completed. The front cover of the Colonial and Indian Exhibition Program featured an eclectic group of people, each representing a different colony in the British Empire. Resembling a Roman Emperor and holding a laurel wreath symbolizing victory, Britannia stands behind a shield of armor bearing the British flag. She is flanked by a sensual white woman, her right arm draped over her head, wearing a head band that reads "Cape Colony." Her diamond earrings, necklace, and ring shine. Her seminudity and multilayered skirt render the woman exotic, an impression intensified by the maned lion, yet she is white and given Roman features. The image corresponds with the popular card linking diamond powder (boart) and

Figure 2.7 Front Cover of *Colonial and Indian Exhibition Daily Programme* (London: William Clowes & Sons, 1887).

unpolished stones to people of color, and finished brilliants to affluent white ladies (Figure I.5). Raw, unpolished and "uncivilized," diamonds, like "natives," required western ingenuity to elevate them. Whiteness, in racial and mineralogical terms, reigned supreme.

London jewelers capitalized on these presumptions. Edwin Streeter's New Bond Street jewelry house, in its marketing of diamond jewelry to middle class customers, touted "Gems and Pearls From the Ends of the Earth." In *The Times* and the *Illustrated London News*, Britannia, seated on top of the world, holds an imperial orb, indicating the vast geographies under her control, including India's Golconda and South Africa's Northern Cape. Angelic women, symbolizing the daughters of Empire, ascend with trays of rubies, emeralds, sapphires, and diamonds—tributes for their global ruler.[62] Marketing itself as uniquely positioned to offer clients the spoils of empire, the ad guaranteed that "the Brilliants are white and properly cut," never "off-colored" or inferior. African miners and Jewish lapidaries disappeared from the scene once diamonds were ready for retail. Together with international exhibitions, feature stories in illustrated newspapers and magazines, and "every jeweller's shop ablaze with

Figure 2.8 Streeter's Advertising. *Illustrated London News* (October 1886), 65.

diamonds," Streeter's ads encoded the coveted stones and gems with ideas about provenance, social and racial hierarchy, empire, and consumption.[63]

◆ ◆ ◆

There is no danger of the diamond ever becoming common.
—*A Short Sketch of the African Diamond Mines* (1881)

If London exhibitions and media coverage refrained from drawing attention to the extent of Jewish representation in the diamond commodity chain, Anglo-Jews felt no qualms about doing so among themselves. The *Jewish Chronicle*, the most widely read Jewish newspaper in Great Britain, regularly published pieces on Jews in the gem trade, boasting that "[t]hey were amongst the earliest pioneers of the Diamond Fields and helped in no little measure to prospect and develop the great gold fields." That Jews were "gaining wealth and renown in South Africa goes without saying."[64] Proud of Jewish achievements in the Cape Colony, newspaper correspondents noted their brethren's "commercial supremacy that has remained unchallenged to the present day" and credited merchant entrepreneurs for "lifting this end of South Africa from its old insignificance."[65] Like their non-Jewish contemporaries, they were convinced that an imperial presence in

Africa was morally just, advancing industry and civilization where none allegedly existed. Keen to be part of it, they did not question the system of imperialism.

In addition to learning about Cape diamonds in the press, London Jews attended lectures on the subject at local synagogues, often designed to encourage young working-class men to take advantage of professional opportunities abroad. In 1871, Jonas Bergtheil, a founding member of the Anglo-Jewish Association, delivered a talk on "The Diamond Fields of the Cape and Life in South Africa" at the Spanish and Portuguese School at Heneage Lane, near Aldgate.[66] In the presence of Dr. Hermann Adler, head of the Bayswater congregation and future chief rabbi of the United Hebrew Congregations of the British Empire, Bergtheil addressed a small crowd of "Jewish working men," although there were also "several ladies and gentlemen among the audience."[67] After describing the African landscape, Bergtheil explained the process of diamond digging, circulating objects used by pioneers as he spoke: wooden spoons, mugs, snuff boxes, even a "wooden head pillows (like a small trestle) which the Kaffirs use." Touching and passing artifacts around while listening to the lecture, Bergtheil interspersed his remarks with advice for potential emigrants, cautioning that diamond hunting carried risks and offered no guarantees. He closed, however, with an animated account of a spectacular find, a "goose-egg-sized diamond," leaving listeners with the impression that they, too, could become heroes in a diamond story and that South Africa offered adventures beyond their wildest dreams.

London Jews continued their support of the British Empire and their role in it during the 1880s, when the hype over the Colonial and Indian Exhibition as well as Queen Victoria's upcoming Golden Jubilee peaked.[68] Celebrating Victoria's rule over an empire on which the sun never set, the *Jewish Chronicle* reflected on the position of Jews under the British crown. "The last fifty years," it exulted, "have constituted the golden age of Anglo-Jewish history."[69] Jewish notables must have been heartened by the festive mood, because in May 1886, two weeks after the opening of the Colonial Exhibition, leading community members met at the residence of the philanthropist Frederic David Mocatta, to plan an Anglo-Jewish Historical Exhibition of their own. Rabbis Hermann Adler, Morris Joseph, and Albert Löwy, as well as journalist Lucien Wolf, civil engineer Isidore Spielmann, lawyer and vice-president of the Numismatic Society of London Hyman Montagu, and directors of several archeological and anthropological societies attended.[70] The aim of the meeting and, ultimately, of the exhibition was twofold: to determine the extent of existing Jewish ritual and cultural resources available in the community and the feasibility, through public display, of promoting deeper knowledge of Anglo-Jewish life.

The executive committee drafted a circular addressed to presidents of provincial Jewish congregations, members of metropolitan synagogues, and leading Jewish members of literary and scientific societies. They wrote to Anglo-Jewish institutions abroad, including South Africa, to request temporary loans of objects. Prompted by the Colonial Exhibition model, the committee set up the display in Royal Albert Hall, presenting maps of the United Kingdom and the British Empire, statistical data on Anglo-Jewish emigration, and ecclesiastical art and antiques. Inundated with artifacts, the committee added a fourth foyer and arranged for concurrent exhibits at the South Kensington Museum, the Public Records Office, and the King's Library at the British Museum, whose collections of Hebrew manuscripts, engravings, printed books, and documents pertaining to Anglo-Jewish history were put on display in glass cases.

The Anglo-Jewish Historical Exhibition was a great success in terms of its outreach to British Jews and the intensity of responses. Musical recitals and a series of lectures on Jewish history delivered by German scholar Heinrich Graetz contributed to a sense of momentousness. Graetz's address on "Historic Parallels in Jewish History," reprinted in the *Jewish Chronicle*, exhorted the community to establish an academy for the promotion of Jewish science and research similar to the German *Wissenschaft des Judentums*.[71] The exhibit, open on Saturdays, offered free admission in June "so as to render it accessible to those Jewish visitors who were only disengaged on their Sabbath."[72] Children from London Jewish Schools taking field trips saw photos of the "Kimberley Diamond-Fields Synagogue" and engravings of its interior during an 1881 Yom Kippur service.[73] While diamonds were not the main theme, representations of Jewish life on the diamond fields exposed the interwoven histories of Anglo Jews and the British Empire. Lasting for three months and drawing an estimated 12,000 visitors, the exhibit allowed Jewish elites to insert themselves into imperial narratives in ways that the Colonial Exhibition had not. Integrating objects from communities across Britain's territories, including South Africa, communicated a message of Jewish pride and belonging—they had helped build a collective British nation and global presence. It was a tough message to sell outside of the Jewish community. On the continent, leading German antisemites had launched a petition campaign to demand that Jews' legal emancipation be rescinded. Massive demographic shifts, triggered by the 1881 assassination of the Russian tsar and by debilitating poverty, pushed East-European Jews to the West, permanently changing the profile of Jewish communities, including London's. The swelling presence of destitute, Yiddish-speaking *Ostjuden*, as well as the legitimization of racial and political antisemitism challenged narratives of Jewish belonging so eagerly put on display in libraries and museums. Diamonds shone brightly on the British Empire, but Jewish contributions, perpetually suspect, lingered in the shadows.

◆ ◆ ◆

> Every civilized lady, and a multitude of civilized men, expect to possess a few diamonds for their personal adornment.... [Diamonds] are no longer unattainable except for the very rich or the very extravagant.
> —*The Times* (April 20, 1885)

Diamond displays at international exhibitions, combined with heightened media attention and effective advertising, boosted demand for a luxury item that evoked affluence and privilege. Being able to purchase and wear diamond jewelry proclaimed more than an elevated place in the social hierarchy; it associated wearers with whiteness and authority. In Victorian Britain, empire found its way into the fabric of everyday life via a constant and dynamic flow of objects and images. Contemporaries in Great Britain wore calico cotton from India and embroidered silk robes from China; they enjoyed Indian tea, Sri Lankan cinnamon, and South African grapes; they decorated home interiors with carved blackwood furniture and ceramic inspired by non-Western themes—all available at the "Oriental Department" in fashionable stores like Liberty, Debenhams, and Freebody in London's West End and Bayswater.[74] Department stores and their richly illustrated catalogs offered men and women images and goods of empire, whether they bought something or not. Magazines, museums, theaters, and music halls, too, transported sights and sounds from distant places that fascinated audiences, so much so that empire itself became a commodity for consumption.[75] In this cornucopia of imperial merchandise, diamonds stood out. Diamond jewelry, formerly a royal and aristocratic prerogative, descended to the reach of the middle class. Consumers could wear the epitome of cultural sophistication on their bodies. The hardest material on earth could be tamed to embellish the softest white skin.

The trade publication *Jeweller and Metalworker* soldered the connection between jewelry and social advancement by declaring "the art of personal adornment" as having "played a great part in the civilisation and progress of races." A country's ideal of beauty, it maintained, could be measured by its production of gold, silver, and gems designed into "beautiful forms of ornamentation."[76] The jewelry trade, exulted a self-congratulatory editorial, was "a product of a certain state of civilisation [that] ministered not to actual wants, but to taste for luxuries inherent in human nature." Whereas "the savage tattoos his body, fashions his anklets and armlets, strings his necklaces of beads and wampum," the white European had allegedly advanced aesthetically to brilliant tiaras, chokers, and pendants.[77] The global supply of Cape diamonds—adding more than fifty million carats into circulation by the turn of the century—adorned Victorian necklines with valuable social currency, endowing those who held the keys with an aura of superiority.[78]

Associating diamonds with celebrities was a way to raise the profile of both. The South Kensington Museum featured an exhibition of jewelry worn by prominent Victorians at balls and operas, while their wax replicas drew crowds at Madame Tussaud's in Marylebone.[79] Debenham's department store catalogs advertised public auctions of jewelry worn by the rich and famous at a time when the British Museum and the Natural History Museum were showing glass models of the Kohinoor and other renowned gemstones. Bond Street, the center of high-end shopping in London's West End, awed passersby with a "mass of diamonds," the splendor of which "owe[d] much of its magnificence to Kimberley wares."[80] Large plate glass windows and electric lighting—new technologies—enchanted shoppers by literally shedding light on the many tempting products for sale.[81] Lavish descriptions of diamond jewelry worn at high society weddings or offered as wedding gifts filled the pages of fashion magazines.[82] In other words, Victorian streets and media were studded with diamonds, persuading viewers to fantasize about their origins and meaning. Regardless of whether shoppers acquired actual gems, diamonds were integral to the imperial narratives they consumed.

Victorians seemed comfortable depicting Jews as cutters and polishers, but the final product, pure and white, was meant for customers whose ethnic, religious, and social identifications were not bifurcated or questioned. Assumptions about Jews' personalities, business acumen, and morality—traits both admired and despised—were becoming decidedly more disparaging around the turn of the century, when large-scale East-European-Jewish immigration and the Boer War in South Africa fueled racial and ethnic anxieties. Jews in Victorian Britain may have inserted themselves into the imperial narrative, but times of conflict or demographic change exposed underlying tensions in the close link between gems and Jews, suggesting that full acceptance, even in cosmopolitan London, remained incomplete.

Figure 3.1 "Blue Diamond." Cigarette Card, "Famous Gems of the World" Series, ca. 1890. New York Public Library Digital Collections: Image #1554871.

CHAPTER 3

"As Long as It Sparkles!"

Amsterdam

And a plucky people are those Hollanders; bold, sturdy, independent, and invincible. But they make so much noise for a State so unsubstantial on the earth's surface; there, however, the superficiality ends; for Holland is rich and becoming wealthier every season; and Holland beats the world for steady industry, scrupulously honest merchants, neatness, conservatism, diamonds, dahlias, and dykes.

—*Jewish Messenger* (December 13, 1867)

One weekday in 1863, Salomon Levie Tas and Betje Hijman Content entered the Amsterdam town hall to be married. Marriage ceremonies were free outside weekends for those unable to pay, and Salomon and Betje sought a quick and efficient affair. After the ceremony, they returned to their small, dilapidated dwelling on Uilenburgerstraat, in the city's poorest Jewish slum. Only a few months earlier, Salomon's first wife had died after giving birth to their third child. At twenty-nine years of age, Salomon, making a meager living as a porter, urgently needed a wife and a mother for his children. He found both in Betje, a maidservant from a poor Ashkenazi background.

Municipal tax records indicate that the Tas family's socioeconomic status improved considerably in subsequent years. An 1874 entry discloses that Salomon had entered "het vak," *the* profession, as Dutch contemporaries referred to the diamond industry, first by becoming a polisher and later a "slijpersbaas," the manager of a diamond processing factory. In 1884, his annual tax payment (127 guilders) granted Salomon the right to vote, a privilege enjoyed by only 14 percent of adult males who constituted the economic elite in the Dutch capital. He invested in real estate, moved his family of six children from the old Jewish district to Plantage, a middle- to upper-middle-class neighborhood. The Tas family fared so well that, by the mid-1880s, they could afford to hire a servant.[1]

Jacques Metz, one of Salomon Tas's contemporaries, experienced a similar rise in wealth and status. The son of a Jewish diamond cutter, he grew up in the business and became a cleaver in the early 1870s. Together with his father-in-law, Barend Roelof Citroen, he opened a factory at Rapenburgerstraat no. 53-61. Over the next decade, his taxable income increased fivefold. Whereas he paid close to 100 guilders in taxes (including property tax, the so-called patent tax, and personal tax) in 1874, Metz owed nearly 700 guilders a decade later.[2] He soon moved to a new residence facing the respectable Nieuwe Herengracht canal, an extension of the highly prestigious Herengracht (Patricians' Canal) that had constituted one of the main concentric belts around the city since the Golden Age.

Solomon Tas and Jacques Metz were two of the many thousands of Jews employed in the Amsterdam diamond industry. By 1890, at least 6,500 Jews made their livings in the profession, as buyers or sellers; as cleavers, cutters, and polishers; as jewelers, dealers, and managers of diamond mills; or as apprentices. Assuming an average family of five, then an estimated 30,000 to 35,000 Jews—a solid 50 percent of the total Jewish population in the Dutch capital—depended quite directly on the diamond.[3] Tas and Metz both typify the ascendance of late nineteenth- and early twentieth-century Dutch Jewry. The large majority were working-class into the 1890s and lived in the densely populated *Jodenbuurt* (Jewish neighborhood). Often dependent on communal support—over half received welfare—by the 1910s many Jews were living in more humane circumstances. The diamond and the gem industry more broadly were to a large extent responsible for transforming Amsterdam Jewry from a predominantly poor *lumpenproletariat*, engaged mostly in street vending and market trading, to an acculturated, middle-class.

Fluctuating fortunes affected Jewish and non-Jewish lives far beyond local factories. First, as gem cleaving, cutting, and polishing matured from a "primitive domestic industry and *kleinbetrieb*," where men and women processed stones in small attics, to a large-scale capitalist enterprise, Amsterdam solidified its position as the unrivaled center of the diamond manufacturing business.[4] Especially after 1869, when the discovery of abundant deposits in Kimberley saturated the Dutch market with unprecedented supplies of rough stones, Jewish entrepreneurs created an economic infrastructure linking Kimberley, Amsterdam, London, and New York in a lucrative transatlantic trading network. Second, the diamond industry caused Jewish and non-Jewish laborers to organize politically and professionally. Putting the benefits of unionization over ethnic and religious differences, factory workers from different backgrounds cooperated in founding the nonconfessional *Algemene Nederlandse Diamantbewerkers Bond* (the General Dutch Diamond Workers Union, or ANDB) in 1894. In contrast to other European cities, such as London, Paris, and Antwerp, where labor movements rarely crossed ethnic or religious divides, and where Jewish unions typically sprang from immigrant initiatives, in Amsterdam Jewish and non-Jewish "natives" collaborated and achieved spectacular successes.[5] Led by Henri Polak—son of diamond polisher Moses Polak and Marianna Smit—the ANDB organized strikes, improved conditions in the factories considerably, and cultivated a new political consciousness among Jewish and Christian workers alike. Their union, for a long time the largest labor organization in the country, formed the basis of the Dutch Federation of Unions (FNV), a national organization that still

Figure 3.2 "Diamond Workers," Engelien Reitsma-Valença. Jewish Historical Museum, Amsterdam. Object Number M012679.

exists. Precious stones not only sustained the Amsterdam Jewish community in the late nineteenth and early twentieth centuries but also directly shaped Dutch political discourse for the next century.

Furthermore, Amsterdam Jews played a prominent role in preparing diamonds for markets in the metropole and beyond, entrenching the public connection between Jews and gems. The purchasing power of an expanding middle class, especially visible in Great Britain and the United States, created an unparalleled demand for diamond jewelry. Consumers were assured that "their" stones were cut and polished by Jewish masters in Amsterdam, whose expertise was unrivaled.[6] To own and wear Cape diamonds prepared by Dutch-Jewish artisans became a means for the *nouveaux riches* to flaunt affluence and success and to display, perhaps incidentally, "emblems of empire," white privilege, and geopolitical dominance.[7]

◆ ◆ ◆

> A Jew in Holland could be anything he wanted to be—a cigarmaker or a diamond cutter.
>
> —Dutch diamond polisher, quoted in Renée Rose Shield, *Diamond Stories: Enduring Change on 47th Street* (2002)

When Salomon Tas first entered a diamond factory in the late 1860s, almost nothing of the local or international significance of the stone, let alone its political potential, was apparent to him or his fellow workers. Tas faced a twelve-hour shift without a lunch break, during which he sat bent over his mill in a badly ventilated space. It was dusty and loud. Dozens of steam-run mills were spinning at full speed and his coworkers had to yell in order to be heard. Before the mechanization of polishing in the 1840s by means of steam, horses had powered the mills. They had replaced women pushing and pulling wooden wheels for hours on end, enabling mills to rotate. Substituting horses for women in the 1820s had relocated manufacturing from home attics to more spacious shops, where gem cutters and horses shared the same room, called a *manège* (merry-go-round).[8] One jeweler named Meijer opened a diamond manufacturing workshop in 1826 with twenty-two mills operating on horsepower. Nearby, I. M. Posno managed thirty-one mills.[9] Steam power proved cheaper than horses, in no small part due to high grain prices in the 1840s, driven by the Irish famine and the 1848 revolutions. When Jewish owners Hesselmeijer, Marchand, Rosen, and Hont introduced the first steam-driven mills in their Rapenburgerstraat factory, they permanently altered what had been, for hundreds of years, a predominantly domestic vocation into a mechanized, factory-based industry. Dutch diamond manufacturing therefore partook in the international industrial transformations of the mid-nineteenth century that revolutionized production of textiles and steel. The modernization of gem cutting and polishing by means of steam intensified speed and efficiency, but it also produced high levels of noise and debilitating dust filled with fine metal particles.

As a polisher, Tas made approximately fifty Dutch guilders per week (fl. 50 or US $12), although incomes fluctuated greatly from year to year. Because he rented a mill, Tas owed his boss a fee, plus payment for the use

Figure 3.3 Diamond Factory Coster, Amsterdam, 1875. International Institute for Social History, Amsterdam: #BG B14/301.

of so-called boart, diamond powder that is used in the polishing process. Mixed with oil, boart allowed polishers to sculpt carbon stones and add dozens of facets to maximize brilliance. Chamber of Commerce records indicate that the average polisher paid fl. 30 in expenses, leaving Tas with some fl. 20 to live on. These earnings were not meager. But taking into account seasonal swings and irregularities in the volume of stones, most factory employees did not work throughout the year. Men like Tas averaged about fl. 11 per week over the course of twelve months.[10] In dry periods, factory workers occasionally drew lottery tickets in local cafés to "win" employment for a day—tickets that factory owners had distributed to the pub-keeper, who sold them for five cents apiece.[11]

At a higher rung of the occupational hierarchy, jewelers, that is, merchants of unpolished stones who purchased rough diamonds from London suppliers, hired local professionals to process them and sold the finished product to buyers who visited Amsterdam on a regular basis.[12] Jewelers subsequently employed cleavers to perform the delicate job of splitting an imperfect stone into one or more usable parts. Cleavers were regarded as aristocrats in the business, since their specialty required years of apprenticeship, and they consequently earned a higher salary. They worked in a jeweler's atelier rather than a factory floor and were thus separated from other workers.[13] Once this job was done, jewelers outsourced split stones to a *slijpersbaas*—the manager of a factory, like Salomon Tas later in his career—who then hired cutters and polishers.

Hierarchical divisions continued within factory walls. Diamond cutters gave cleaved stones their basic shape. These specialists were divided into *briljantsnijders*, who prepared larger, more expensive stones, and so-called *roosjessnijders*, who cut remnants into small "roses" for much smaller compensation. Many rose cutters, in fact, were Jewish women working from home. Finally, polishers, the largest group within the industry, were responsible for adding the angled facets to the stone's surface to perfect its reflection and luminosity. The density of carbon slows down light passing through, splitting the color spectrum into different shades. Light interacts with multiple facets that act like a series of tiny mirrors, refracting the beam and causing sparkles when finally liberated.[14] Polishers engineered the stone's most desirable potential. Securing the diamond in a small copper cup attached to a narrow pole, they polished it on a rotating, horizontal disk into the desired shape, most often into the popular fifty-eight facet brilliance cut or into crescents, briolettes, pendeloques, emeraudes, or baguettes. It took skill to achieve perfect, angular symmetry; asymmetry in surface angles led to "false spacing," decreasing the value of a stone.[15] Polishers, as well as cutters, typically had assistants who set, tightened, and detached precious stones dozens of times during the process. These men and women, at the bottom of the ladder in terms of wages and esteem, earned a mere seven or eight guilders a week.[16] All of these people—cleavers, cutters, polishers, and their helpers—were independent workers compensated for piece work.

With the exception of M. E. Coster—whose family went back generations in the diamond trade—and B. & L. Arons, every diamond firm in Amsterdam was a member and shareholder of the *Diamantslijperij-Maatschappij*, or Diamond Polishing Company, founded by prominent Jewish families in 1845, after large Brazilian deposits came on the market. The newly established company bought up existing, horse-powered workshops and initiated large-scale production in a steam-powered factory on the Nieuwe Achtergracht canal, where diamond cutters and polishers rented mills. In the early 1850s, the company already owned 520 of the city's 700 mills, a monopoly that would only increase in subsequent years.[17] The *Maatschappij* mandated that prices of supplies sold to factory managers be fixed, that annual dividends be invested in structural and operational expansion, and that rough stones be processed only in their own workshops.[18] In an attempt to bind employees to the factory, they were required to contribute to a communal fund that paid benefits to those suffering illness, disability, and old age. Cutters and polishers renting mills at factories unaffiliated with the *Maatschappij* would promptly lose these benefits. Initially the *Diamantslijperij-Maatschappij* umbrella included 51 jewelers, 44 of them Jewish. Its board of directors included well-known locals such as Jacob Joseph Posno, J. E. Dresden, Josephus Jitta, B. du Moulin, Leon Marchand, L. J. Posno (living in Paris), and E. Zadok Dresden (in London). The boom in supply, caused by the Kimberley finds, encouraged cutters and polishers—like Jacques Metz—to break loose and start their own businesses, undermining the dominance of the mother company.

After his shift at the factory, diamond polisher Salomon Tas returned to the old Jewish district, home to the majority of Amsterdam's 30,000 Jews. A little over 11 percent of the city population, most residents were working class and lived modest lives.[19] A report from the Ashkenazi committee for the poor found that in the 1860s, 52.6 percent of the community received charity in the form of bread, peat, medical care, and short-term loans. For the Sephardic community this percentage was over 60 percent.[20] While these numbers decreased by the turn of the century, in large part due to gem manufacturing, the Amsterdam Jewish proletariat remained comparatively large and poor throughout the nineteenth century. Tas's Uilenburgerstraat address, in one of the most dilapidated sections of the Jewish neighborhood, indicates that his family most likely lived in one of

Figure 3.4 P. Ferat, "Het Diamantslijpen," ca. 1870–1900. Joods Historisch Museum, Amsterdam. Object Number: M006765.

5,000 dwellings deemed unacceptable for human habitation "due to dampness, snails, and mold" by the city's Health Commission.[21] Population density in the *Jodenbuurt* was seven times higher than anywhere else in Amsterdam, concluded the commission, and contagious diseases, such as measles and scarlet fever, as well as death rates, were exponentially higher. These numbers worsened in the last decade of the century, when the Jewish population doubled to nearly 60,000.[22]

Living in poverty, Tas belonged to what one Dutch historian described as "a group of ghetto-Jews despised for their primitive morals and values."[23] Most entered the business as thirteen- or fourteen-year-old apprentices, receiving their general education on the factory floor.[24] Regarded as an uncultured and rough bunch, their appearance and manners seemed strangely at odds with the regal qualities associated with diamonds—brilliance and transparency, esteem and status. It would be one of union leader Henri Polak's primary ambitions to alter public perceptions of Jews and Dutch laborers at large. Indeed, to Polak the ANDB functioned not merely as a means to organize the masses, but a way to elevate them materially and culturally into well-informed and respectable citizens.[25] He was more successful than anyone anticipated.

◆ ◆ ◆

Amsterdam and diamonds are two inseparate things: diamonds have set their mark on the old city on the Amstel and there were times when the economic life of the capital stood or fell with the diamond industry, which in its turn reacted minutely to the general state of affairs in Amsterdam.

—J. K. Smit & Sons (1938)

The discovery of vast diamond deposits in South Africa in 1869 inaugurated a new phase in the industry. Dutch factory workers cleaved, cut, and polished nearly 100,000 carats in the late 1860s. A decade later they processed close to two million carats.[26] South African mines produced 3,140,000 carats of rough stones in 1880, a remarkable number that did not include rampant illegal exports. The Dutch historian Henri Heertje calculated that South African mines generated three times as many diamonds in twenty years than Brazilian mines in the previous century and a half. Most of the stones ended up on Dutch mills.[27] The spectacular increase in supply caused such an intense demand for specialized labor that salaries reached record heights for those willing to work long hours. Wages surged to 150 to 200 guilders per week for polishers, some twenty times the income of factory workers in the cigar-making and textile industries.[28] Cutters and cleavers, ranking higher on the professional ladder, saw their incomes rise to fl. 750 to fl. 1,000. By comparison, typesetters at the time earned six to eight guilders per week.[29]

The first shipments from South Africa arrived in Amsterdam, via London, in the winter of 1870, mostly inside suitcases of jewelers returning from Hatton Garden. Andries van Wezel traveled to the Grand Hotel at Holborn Viaduct in London to acquire stones on a regular basis. Van Wezel, whose father, Salomon Levie, was a diamond cutter, had started out as an apprentice in the diamond factory Daniels & Zoon in the Jewish district, but he had ventured out on his own. Times were good. With cash in his pockets, van Wezel would travel to Ostende, where he would take the boat to Dover, and from there he rode the South-Eastern Railway to the Grand Hotel. It was a short walk to Hatton Garden to purchase supplies. The weekly trade magazines *Diamant Handelsblad* and *Algemeen Handelsblad* informed gem merchants of South African shipments coming into London, so he could easily time his arrival. After staying the night, he then returned to Amsterdam to begin, after distribution, the process of manufacturing stones.[30] One of the workers in van Wezel's diamond factory was a young man named Henri Polak.

The sharp rise in the supply of South African rough met the strong demand for polished stones by American and European markets. The end of the American Civil War and the Franco-Prussian War restored consumer spending. Particularly in the United States, the growth of railroad and steel industries produced moneyed elites eager to display their prosperity and status. As a result, diamond consumption rose sharply. The Dutch periodical *De Diamant* reported that US imports of finished stones rose from $2,917,216 in 1873 to $8,320,315 in 1881. By the late 1880s, the estimated value of legally declared imported gems topped twelve million dollars, a figure that would double again by the end of the century, making the United States by far the largest client on the global market.[31] The German historian Wilhelm Treue contends that widespread economic expansion in western capitalist societies brought forth the "democratization of luxury"; the indulgence of material comfort was no longer the prerogative of aristocratic elites but a possibility for broader segments of the population.[32] Diamonds were "no longer the appendage of great families," observed one contemporary, "but of great fortunes. A skillful deal on the Stock Exchange, a successful 'corner' at Chicago, a lucky hit in railways, are celebrated by the prompt purchase of many-faceted crystals."[33]

While sudden wealth stimulated the desire for and production of many forms of material display, this was especially true of precious stones, as wearing them in earrings, necklaces, and brooches visually announced that affluence and cultural refinement had been achieved. Oil paintings, professionalization. Café trading culture slowly disappeared, particularly after the establishment of the Association for the Diamond Exchange on September 17, 1890. Approved by royal decree six days before King William III's death, the Exchange concentrated the international trade in polished diamonds in one location, the *Sociëteitsgebouw Casino*, at Zwanenburgerstraat, in the center of the Jewish district.[42] Clandestine transactions continued in the cafés De Poort van Weesp and Het Hooischip, and another small association called the Diamant Club set up shop across the street in the Concordia building—disdainfully dubbed *kinnesinnebeursie* or "little exchange of envy"—yet most transactions occurred "in an orderly fashion" in rented quarters at the Casino.[43] Open for business from Sunday morning through Friday early afternoon, the building provided a trading hall for jewelers to receive clients, as well as upstairs workplaces for cleavers and their employers. Functioning in Jewish time, Amsterdam diamond manufacturers and their international agents—clean-shaven, secular Jews from Paris and New York as well as Orthodox buyers from Antwerp—congregated in a shared commercial venue endorsed by the state for conducting business. The Dutch writer Siegfried van Praag, who spent a lot of time at the Exchange as a boy, recalled seeing "religious and fashionable gentlemen from Antwerp during the week, returning to Antwerp in the weekend. . . . There were men of the world such as the Gurwirts and Aronsons, to whom I looked up. Amsterdammers weren't as chic, there was nothing cosmopolitan about them." These buyers, van Praag reminisced, "used to have a room upstairs in the Exchange where they would say mincha, the afternoon prayers."[44] Accommodating the needs of Jews from different backgrounds, the Diamond Exchange integrated commercial, religious, and later also social functions; its future location included a kosher restaurant, billiard room, and library. All 1,300 members, reported the *Jewish Chronicle*, "with few ever-dwindling exceptions, are Jews."[45]

The Cape Era witnessed an extraordinary expansion of Amsterdam diamond manufacturing, precisely at a time when international consumer demand rose sharply.[46] Businesses boomed, salaries reached new highs, and quantities of rough South African stones seemed infinitely abundant. Times were exceptionally busy early in the New Year and in August and September as foreign buyers prepared for the upcoming Easter and Christmas seasons, when jewelry sales spiked. Many clients took up lodgings at the reputable Les Pays-Bas Hotel in the Doelenstraat, the Mille Colonnes on Rembrandtplein, and the grand Amstel Hotel, the construction of which had been financed by Jewish urban developer Samuel Sarphati. The gem industry therefore sustained not merely those directly involved by means of manufacturing and exchange, but also those engaged in local hotel and restaurant businesses catering to the needs of a steadfast clientele. The Dutch capital truly became *Amsterdam Diamantstad*, city of diamonds.[47] After five fat years, however, an international economic crisis reduced consumer demand for precious stones, leaving a substantial work force frequently unemployed. Over the next few decades, the industry recovered in fits and starts, but it would never again experience such heights of abundance and prosperity.

◆ ◆ ◆

Woe is me, woe is me,
so many woes in the diamond industry!"
—Herman Heijermans, *Amsterdam Diamantstad* (1904)

Many Dutch-Jewish diamond dealers owed their success, at least in part, to what economists have called "ethnic capital." Amsterdam-Jewish bankers, including Wertheim & Gompertz, Becker & Fuld, Lippmann & Rosenthal—a name the Nazis would appropriate to loot Dutch Jews of their possessions— and Hollander & Lehren supplied credit needed by entrepreneurs to establish new companies or to secure international clients. Frederik Salomon van Nierop, one of the cofounders and directors of the *Amsterdamsche Bank* (founded in 1871), offered financial support to a number of Jewish diamond firms, smoothing the way for business with foreign buyers who demanded credit lines for valuable purchases.[48] The proliferation of American agents in the 1880s, demanding high-volume transactions and large sums of money, necessitated the assets, expertise, and reassurance of a third-party financial firm. While most banks considered the risks too high, the Amsterdam Bank, an active investor in industrial companies at home and abroad, became closely involved in "the profession." It offered loans to jewelers in need of capital to obtain rough stones in London and bonds to private investors eager to capitalize on industrial expansion.[49] The Amsterdam Bank was the only financial institution to extend "diamantwissels," or bills of exchange— the forerunner of the modern check—to Jewish diamond dealers, a practice that required a level of trust often gained through close social and economic ties.[50] Jewish bankers consulted with their clients to acquire intimate knowledge about the status of a firm.[51] They curried favor with company directors and shareholders. *Diamantslijperij Maatschappij* company director Josephus Jitta was a client and personal friend of Abraham Carel Wertheim, indisputably the most successful Jewish banker and philanthropist in nineteenth-century Holland.[52] Wertheim, meeting regularly with Jitta and fellow banker van Nierop, became a commissioner of the *Amsterdamsche Diamantslijperij*, a diamond finishing company built in 1873 for fl. 140,000 (or 28 shares of fl. 5,000 each). Wertheim & Gompertz financed the new firm.[53] Concurrently, he was serving on the supervisory board of the Amsterdam Bank. The alliance of Jewish bankers and diamond factory entrepreneurs thrived in a recovering economy.[54]

Dutch historians agree that the application of the so-called *crédit-mobilier* principle by Jewish banking firms, forging stable coalitions between *haute finance* and industry by means of capital investments, revitalized Amsterdam after 1850.[55] Whereas banks had long engaged in currency and stock exchanges and offered financial services to business clients, they typically did not initiate private, high-risk industrial investments. Following French and German examples, Dutch-Jewish banking firms such as Lippmann, Wertheim & Gompertz, and De Hirsch & Bisschoffsheim broke this taboo by injecting substantial credit into promising companies. Although not always successful, this type of industrial finance contributed to a new economic dynamism, one that reverberated in the diamond business.[56] It was no coincidence that the Amsterdam Bank established a branch office in the basement of the Diamond Exchange building to facilitate transactions between local diamond firms and international clients.

For Jews, the partnership between the diamond business and the Amsterdam financial world offered clear economic advantages. The expansion of the industry brought profits that launched many entrepreneurs into the upper middle class and into the city's electorate.[57] The success of a new diamond elite can be measured by the money they put into philanthropic initiatives.[58] The resources of the *Handwerkers Vriendenkring* (Craftsmen Circle of Friends), for example, a mutual aid society founded to improve the living conditions of Jews by means of education, healthcare, small business loans, and scholarships, grew substantially in the last quarter of the nineteenth century as more and more affluent patrons shared their wealth. *Vriendenkring* recipients, many of whom were diamond factory workers, benefited from a new health insurance fund, the first in Amsterdam, called "Ziekenzorg" or sick care, designed to reduce dependency on charity.[59] The aid society eventually established a building fund to provide affordable homes for working-class Jews. Additional support organizations arose to meet perceived needs in the Jewish community, such as the Society for Child Nourishment, which provided 200,000 meals to poor Jewish and non-Jewish schoolchildren every three months, and the Society for Public Housing, whose donors were new industrial leaders and helped pull Amsterdam Jewry out of poverty.[60]

By the 1870s, Amsterdam had become the unchallenged center of manufacturing precious stones for global retail, yet this status did not translate into power or influence. Most jewelers were utterly at the mercy of their suppliers, clients, and customers. The entire enterprise depended on rough stones from South Africa, whose extraction, transportation, and distribution were solidly in British hands, namely that of De Beers, which assumed full control of diamond extraction by the late 1880s. The establishment of the London Syndicate, in turn, determined the distribution of raw materials to continental buyers and manufacturers, all of whom were required to secure membership to access the London office.[61] To avoid flooding the market with stones, lowering prices and revenue, the Syndicate, consisting of less than a dozen dealers with exclusive rights to sell rough, tightly regulated quantities and output so as to keep supplies low and prices high. When independent entrepreneurs with small businesses replaced the *Diamantslijperij Maatschappij* monopoly, Dutch jewelers had no choice but to accept Syndicate terms. A report of the Chamber of Commerce stated soberly that most Amsterdam jewelers "had no leverage whatsoever" when facing London magnates.[62] Even Andries van Wezel, a powerhouse among Amsterdam diamond traders and regular customer of the "one-headed monster," could either agree to London terms or return empty-handed.[63] Even he was obliged to purchase fixed assortments of stones of various sizes, carats, and quality. "The practice of negotiating and bidding," lamented the *Hollandsche Revue*, a basic practice in buying and selling commodities, "is really non-existent among Syndicate dealers, who sell not what jewelers *need*, but what the almighty Syndicate itself *wants*. . . . All powerful, it tells jewelers: take it or leave it! The Syndicate has complete power over them."[64]

Spending more for their raw materials, Van Wezel and other merchants like him could minimize damage to the bottom line by slashing manufacturing costs, which meant hiring fewer cleavers, cutters, and polishers to process stones. When De Beers cut output by 40 percent in 1889, nearly doubling the price of rough from fl. 18 to fl. 35 per carat, Amsterdam mills slashed their staff and unemployment soared.[65] The British Consul in the Dutch capital confirmed the devastating economic implications in Holland as a result of decisions made in London and Kimberley. "The resolution of a well-known company to reduce production," he reported, "at once sent up the market prices of raw diamonds in Holland 100 percent," forcing "a great number of men with their families, by falling off in the demand from their labour, to absolute destitution."[66]

Dutch jewelers, unable to purchase inventory at grossly inflated prices, stayed home, and consequently so did their employees. The London cartel, in what one editorialist called "a "masterstroke of financial policy and trade manipulation," regulated the level of employment and wages in Amsterdam.[67] London's monopolization and centralization of diamond distribution left Dutch jewelers with comparatively little influence.[68] Amsterdam constituted a crucial link in the overall commercial diamond chain, yet its position in international wholesale remained weak.

antiques, and country homes could be purchased, but not worn physically and brandished at all times to a status-sensitive audience. Diamonds adorning the body drew the gaze of admirers. German sociologist Georg Simmel recognized a kind of "radioactivity" around a woman wearing diamond jewelry, creating an extension of her personality and inviting envious looks. The very nature and function of adornment, he observed, claims the eye of others, elevating the ego of the wearer and heightening the jewel's aura. For women parading their status, diamonds were a form of social capital shaping interactions.[34] One had one "arrived" when bejeweled.

During this five-year period, known in Dutch history as the *Kaapse Tijd*, or Cape Era, Salomon Tas began his social and economic ascent. His polishing skills were in high demand. That he was relatively inexperienced, particularly compared to his colleagues, did not really matter. "Als't maar glimt!" (as long as it sparkles) became the prevailing motto.[35] The high salaries earned during these years allowed Jacques Metz and Barend Roelof Citroen to open a factory and become so-called *eigenwerkmakers*, or self-employed entrepreneurs. Circumventing the established infrastructure created by the *Diamantslijperij Maatschappij*, dozens of ambitious polishers and cleavers started their own firms. They invested in new factories, imported their own rough, outsourced their product to diamond workers leasing their mills, then sold polished brilliants to buyers from Antwerp, Paris, London, and St. Petersburg, congregating in cafés around the Rembrandtplein. "Hands enough cannot be found for the work to be done," remarked an American newspaper, the *Jewish Messenger*, in its Foreign News column, having discerned the "striking amelioration in the condition of the middle classes of Israelites in Amsterdam within the last few months."[36]

Indeed, an impressive proportion of Amsterdam's annual retail sales took place not in tidy company offices, but in dimly-lit, smoky pubs. In contrast to jewelers affiliated with the *Diamantslijperij* company receiving their clientele in the established trading center Het Vosje at Rokin square, "eigenwerkmakers" did not have a shared space.[37] They bought and sold diamonds predominantly in social establishments, among them Café Rembrandt, Het Hooischip, and Café Wien, all located in the Jewish neighborhood. One contemporary recalled that at café De Poort van Weesp, also a trading hub for diamond dealers, "cigar smoke escaped in clouds" whenever the door opened.[38] An 1889 almanac from an Amsterdam student society described the ritual of stones changing owners. "Every afternoon," it reported, "a diamond exchange is held here in this café on Rembrandtplein."

> [N]ot only in this café but in almost all the cafés of this area, be they large or small. And also in the beer parlours around Rembrandtplein.... A heavy, sweet cloud of tobacco smoke hangs midway between floor and ceiling.... [One hears] incomprehensible babble—German Hebrew?—haggling over prices, and when the deal is clinched the whole troop gathers around a table. The buyer and seller sit down and one of the others opens a jacket pocket and produces a mahogany box out of which he draws a set of scales. It is a small model with two copper weighing pans, each one suspended from three green silken cords. The scales are placed on the table and the pans are gently raised until they are the correct height and the balance needle is in the correct position.... The serious business can begin. Stones of different size, glittering and delicate, are cast onto the scale. The tiny weights are placed on the scales using a pair of tweezers. Now the stone has a label: so many carats. Calculations are made independently by both buyer and seller, naturally before long there is disagreement over prices. The seller asks too high a price, the buyer one too low. One of the bystanders pulls a crumpled piece of envelope out of his waistcoat pocked and the stub of a pencil. He asks the seller, "How much are you due?" The man does a calculation and announces the result—somewhere between the two amounts. Then the buyer pulls out a wad of bank notes from his inside pocket and lays bills worth 25, 40, and 60 guilders on the table.[39]

The author, unfamiliar with Yiddish, witnessed a key moment in the commercial chain, namely the transition of diamond manufacturing in Dutch hands to retail and consumption abroad.

The growth and success of *eigenwerkmakers*' independent dealings threatened the monopoly of the *Diamantslijperij* company. Newcomers lacked substantial capital and could not afford to postpone a sale of polished stones in the event of price fluctuations. The Dutch painter Salomon "Sal" Meijer, born into a family of diamond workers, recounted watching French, American, and Russian buyers "patiently wait in their hotels until the dealers in Café Wien reached such dire financial straits that prices of polished goods inevitably declined." Having no reserves, independents often negotiated forced sales, even at a loss, in order to obtain the capital to purchase rough and keep the manufacturing process going. The *Diamantslijperij* Company suffered from this kind of aggressive competition that favored quantity over quality and by the mid-1870s it had lost most of its power.[40] By the end of the century, the majority of its prosperous founding families had left the industry altogether. Most businesses that survived the economic recession of the late 1870s and 1880s had their roots in the Cape years and grew out of the Jewish working class.[41]

The group of self-employed entrepreneurs that made it through the Cape Era and subsequent economic malaise underwent a period of

American Federation of Labor, serving as its first president. At the time of filing the affidavit against Stern, Gompers's brother Jacob, a diamond worker, had only recently arrived in New York City.[5]

Gompers and Vriesland accused Stern Bros. & Co. of violating American labor laws, exploiting immigrant workers, and keeping wages low. New York diamond workers averaged about $25 a week, but Stern paid his Dutch employees only $15, an amount, he conceded, that "wasn't much, but [that] had to be considered in light of his factory being operational year-round," a benefit that most Amsterdam factories could not offer.[6] Appalled by this practice, Gompers and Vriesland notified the authorities about the imminent arrival of the Kalf brothers.

Once Joseph and David Kalf were released from detention, Leopold Stern swiftly hired them. The brothers joined the modest but growing Amsterdam-Jewish labor force in New York City—some 300 men and their families by 1893—employed by Stern and other entrepreneurial factory owners, most of whom were recent Dutch-Jewish immigrants themselves.[7] Disappointed but not deterred by the judgment and fearful that "foreign artisans would displace American workmen," Gompers and Vriesland decided to investigate the matter further. They claimed that "more than a score of diamond polishers and cutters have come to this city from Holland within the past few months, and that all of them were under contract to work for Messrs. Stern & Co."[8] It was only a matter of time before someone made a mistake and could prove the employers were violating the law.

Eighteen months later, the local New York press reported that "another batch of diamond workers [had] come to these shores."[9] In November 1894, immigration authorities detained twenty-six passengers on the transatlantic Red Star steamer *Friesland*, who allegedly were coming to New York "under contract to work for diamond cutting concerns in the U.S." This time they had received information from the US Consul at Amsterdam, Edward Downes, after he spotted an advertisement in the Dutch trade newspaper, *Algemeen Handelsblad*, addressed to diamond cutters and polishers. Those interested in emigrating to America, promised the ad, could expect steady work and good wages. Two New York addresses were provided where workers could apply for employment. Downes sent a translation to the Treasury Department in Washington, DC, which in turn contacted newly appointed Immigration Commissioner Dr. Joseph H. Senner. Senner learned that two diamond cutters, Solomon and J. A. Hudmacher, were in charge of the operation. On board the *Friesland*, inspectors found the Hudmacher brothers in one cabin and the others—some with families—in another. All were held at Ellis Island. "Comfortably clad and [carrying] some money," they denied being contract laborers.[10] Owing to the stagnation of their trade in Amsterdam, they had emigrated to America, they said, hoping to find "remunerative employment." Skeptical that twenty-six diamond manufacturers just happened to book passage on the same steamer headed for New York, Senner ordered a Special Board of Inquiry to investigate.

J. A. Hudmacher, it turned out, had owned a small factory in Amsterdam and sold it, turning his possessions into cash and planning to start over in New York. He figured his chances were better in a country whose population consumed the largest global share of ornamental diamonds. He swore under oath that none of the detained workers were under contract to him or anyone else. His brother, Solomon, in turn, professed that he had formerly made good wages as a diamond polisher, but had been unemployed for some time and had come to America to find work. He also denied being under contract. Neither of the Hudmacher brothers could adequately explain, though, why so many workers with a shared expertise boarded the *Friesland* on the same day. Accumulating more information, the Special Board of Inquiry took testimony from four diamond importers operating in New York City, including Stern Brothers & Co. "One man was brought to this country under contract for the purpose of testing the law," the company admitted, but this worker was not directly connected to the Hudmacher case. Stern's legal counsel Samuel Greenbaum argued that the company had not broken the law at all since "the man was brought here to work in a *new* industry in this country, diamond cutting, for which it was, at the time of its establishment, impossible to get labor here." Greenbaum had found a loophole. The fate of the Dutch émigrés hinged on the question of whether the diamond cutting industry in the US constituted a new or an established trade. American legislation allowed alien contract labor in cases where immigrant skills helped promote an industry that did not yet exist, with the expectation that employment opportunities for American citizens would follow. Diamond cutting, argued Greenbaum, was just such a case. This argument unleashed a year-long debate that reached all the way to the US House of Representatives. In the meantime, the Board could find no reason to hold the diamond workers any longer and all twenty-six were released.[11] Had investigators seen the private letters sent by Dutch-Jewish diamond cutters in Brooklyn to Henri Polak, head of the ANDB in Amsterdam, relating in detail the aggressive recruitment efforts in Holland and the blacklisting of immigrant workers who threatened to report broken promises and illegal activities, they might have reached a different conclusion.[12]

Pushed by the crisis in the Dutch diamond industry and pulled by the allure of opportunities in America, hundreds of Amsterdam-Jewish diamond workers arrived in New York City in 1893 and 1894. These immigrants were almost exclusively Jewish; their Christian co-workers tended to stay in Holland. Christian lapidaries cut and polished smaller diamonds while their Jewish colleagues manufactured larger stones, earning them a higher salary. Smaller stones being in greater demand, Jewish cutters and polishers were the first to be let go during downturns, especially those with fewer years of experience. International trade pressures further incentivized relocation, encouraging the development of diamond manufacturing outside Europe. The US Congress passed protective tariffs directly affecting the transatlantic diamond trade. The 1890 McKinley Tariff and the 1894 Wilson-Gorman Act both sharply increased import duties on finished stones—first from 10 to 25 percent, then to 30 percent—thereby discouraging imports from Amsterdam and promoting the relocation of workshops to America. Dutch diamond manufacturers were priced out of the market. At this very time, the van Wezel brothers moved to New York and opened a factory on Bleecker Street. Adaptation, they realized, was the only response to American protectionism. They had the resources and family networks to transfer technology and craftsmen overseas.[13] Joachim and Marcus van Wezel, whose firm would become the largest diamond company in New York by the 1920s, joined many other dreamers of Dutch-Jewish descent in starting manufacturing firms and initiating the American diamond cutting and polishing industry: Zilver Bros., Eduard van Dam, Kryn & Wouters Bros., Sanders & Bruhl Manufacturing Co., D. S. Granaat, D. De Sola Mendes & Co., J. Hoedenmakers, Konijn & Frank, H. A. Groen & Bros., and others.[14]

The import numbers of rough stones are an indicator of how effective the new tariffs were in stimulating diamond manufacturing in America. Valued at $78,033 in 1877, imports reached $1,109,429 by 1892.[15] By 1906, they topped $10 million.[16] The value of imported finished stones, on the other hand, plummeted from $12,429,395 in 1890 to a mere $2,987,487 five years later, a decline aggravated by the Panic of 1893. The recession that hit America that year slashed consumer spending on luxury goods, further damaging the already ailing Amsterdam manufacturing industry, whose largest customer was the American market.[17] Yet, the economic difficulties afflicting the United States between 1893 and 1897 did not deter Dutch-Jewish diamond workers and entrepreneurs from setting up new businesses in Brooklyn and Manhattan.

The influx of lapidaries and factory entrepreneurs pulled New York firmly into the orbit of diamond manufacturing. "Until a few months ago the cutting of diamonds was an industry of little magnitude in America," observed the *American Economist* in 1894, but now "no other movement that has transpired in the jewelry trade has possessed greater significance than the expansion of the diamond cutting industry."[18] For cutters and polishers, low wages in America were better than no wages at all. And for factory owners like the van Wezel brothers, Eduard van Dam, and Arie Zilver, who had their commercial infrastructure in place and purchased rough "directly from their brokers in London," low labor costs and zero import duties made New York an ideal place to expand their operations. While American purchasing power may have been dealt a temporary blow, the well-to-do still bought their gems for ornamental as well as investment purposes.

By 1913, Manhattan and Brooklyn counted thirty-six factories and 811 employees, with Dutch-Jewish diamond workers dominating the industry.[19] Those interested in hearing Dutch spoken, recommended one newspaper correspondent, only had to visit the corner of Nassau and John Street, and they would "soon hear the weal and woe of diamond workers in [their] mother tongue."[20] Dutch mills had started spinning in America.

◆ ◆ ◆

[T]he diamond remains a thing to be explained, with fire, light, and fever.
—"Something about Diamonds," *Flag of Our Union* (January 25, 1868)

The first workshop in North America opened in Boston in 1858. The business started after Aaron Keizer, a Jewish fruit peddler, entered a jewelry store and, in conversation with the owner, Henry D. Morse, mentioned that he used to be a diamond cutter in Holland before the sinking economy induced him to emigrate and start over. One of Keizer's friends, also residing in Boston, had been a "bruter" in Amsterdam (*bruting* or girdling is the technique of sculpting a cleaved diamond into a round shape).[21] Intrigued by the idea of cutting his own diamonds, Morse ordered the necessary tools and machinery from Holland and hired Keizer to set up "a workshop in the style of the old country."[22] He would pay Keizer $60 a week, a whopping salary for the time. Morse, a partner in the jewelry firm Morse, Crosby & Foss, started this operation before the discovery of South African diamonds. He purchased his inventory through Amsterdam and London, when Brazil was still the primary supplier of rough stones, although its mineral resources had been depleted by midcentury.[23]

Aaron Keizer became the first cutter at the new workshop. He was soon joined by other émigrés, including two polishers, G. van Herpen and J. de Boer, both Amsterdam natives. Keizer, in turn, hired two setters named Wiener and Streep, and two more polishers, van Volen and Cohenno, all Hollanders. Morse ambitiously set out to improve upon "the antiquated methods employed in Holland," introducing steam-powered equipment around the same time this new technology was revolutionizing Dutch polishing mills. His American business partners, recounted Morse later, were firmly of the old school and "deeply prejudiced against every innovation," an attitude that eventually caused them to part ways. Morse's workshop thrived, however, and produced several important diamonds, including a 77-carat stone for Tiffany & Co., proudly displayed at the 1889 Paris exposition.

Around the same time that Morse opened his workshop in Boston, Amsterdam-Jewish immigrants were pioneering small businesses in New York. Polishers J. H. Groen and P. de Bruyn set up shop in October 1860, importing the necessary specialized tools from Europe. The *Jewish Messenger* applauded the "new commercial enterprises of our coreligionists" in New York, "wish[ing] the beginners every success, of which we feel assured when we consider that the art is now almost exclusively in the hands of the Israelites of Amsterdam."[24] The editors evidently found it reassuring that the entrepreneurs were both Jewish and Dutch, a pedigree that intimated experience in diamond manufacturing. The city's first cutter, Isaac Hermann, worked in Manhattan during the 1860s and, in 1871, founded the New York Diamond Company: Importers, Cutters, and Polishers, located at 36 John Street, near Maiden Lane. "One of the first recipients of diamonds from the newly discovered fields of South Africa," Hermann trained several apprentices, including Sadie Battles, the first woman employed as a diamond cutter in the country.[25] Described as "a brunette of about twenty-five years who has been in Mr. Hermann's employ for eleven years," she apparently "dresse[d] plainly and modestly" and was "a lady in every particular."

Since Cape discoveries fueled an abundance of work and astronomical salaries for craftsmen in Amsterdam, most of the Dutch diamond workers in New York and Boston were lured back to Holland, stalling the nascent industry in America. While jewelry retail stores, centered predominantly around Nassau Street, Maiden Lane, and John Street, flourished, manufacturing could not compete with Amsterdam. In 1880, the *Washington Post* fretted that "there are only 16 polishers who can be considered expert mechanics in this country and they are about equally divided between New York and Boston."[26]

Lean times for cutters and polishers persisted into the early 1890s. Monopolization by De Beers and the London Syndicate made it tough for novice entrepreneurs in America to obtain rough diamonds, hindering the manufacturing industry from taking root. The Syndicate invited only a select number of clients for monthly "sights" to purchase inventory. "The difficulty in establishing a diamond cutting industry in this country," explained

American mineralogist George Kunz in 1896, "is the inability of dealers to obtain rough stones at first hand, and the fact that the diamond cutting is [already] an established industry." The tricontinental commodity chain seemed to be set in stone: Kimberley supplied rough; London was the epicenter of distribution; Amsterdam cleaved, cut, and polished; and New York specialized in retail. In the early 1880s, Kunz continued, "a number of American jewelers opened diamond cutting workshops, but the cutting has not been profitably carried on in this country on a scale large enough to justify branch houses in London, the great market for rough diamonds."[27] Establishing American branch houses in London would allow direct access to sights and lower expenses, but this reality remained out of reach. The Syndicate was not the only obstacle. American importers had for decades purchased finished stones from reputable Dutch companies and were not motivated to switch loyalties to small-scale American manufacturers who lacked the distinction enjoyed by Dutch masters. Furthermore, American banks, unlike their Dutch counterparts, would not give loans to obtain an inventory of uncut diamonds, making the initial investment difficult to fund.[28]

This equilibrium was shaken by the McKinley and Wilson-Gorman tariff acts. Import duties for finished diamonds sharply increased, making European brilliants much more expensive to American importers. At the same time, rough stones became duty-free, almost instantly stimulating interest in relocating manufacturing from Amsterdam to New York. During the first six months of tariff-free roughs, 150 diamond workers and their families boarded transatlantic liners. Among them was cutter Emanuel Pais, who arrived in 1894 and took up residence at 64 East 88th Street. His wife, Sophia and their six children, two of whom, Abraham and Jesaya, were also cutters, followed a year later. Polisher Solomon van Duyn came with his wife Flora, daughter Lena, and his sister Minnie, wife of polisher Eliaz van Kollem. All resided at 15 East 79th Street. Benjamin Voorzanger and his son Heiman, both cutters, arrived in 1894. Benjamin took in his cousin Gerrit Speyer, a cutter, his niece Bertha, and, in 1899, his nephew Jacob Weening, a cutter as well. Meyer van Rijn decided to settle at 388 Garfield Place, near the Zilver Bros. diamond factory in Brooklyn, founded by the Dutch-Jewish cleaver Arie Zilver. Van Rijn came with his wife, daughter, and brother-in-law Daniel Coffee, a polisher.[29] The apartment next door, at number 386, housed Samuel Italiaander, a diamond worker, who had arrived in 1894 with his wife and three children. Dutch-Jewish lapidaries were leaving Amsterdam, taking their families and skills with them, and this time they were here to stay.

Their employers relocated, too. Eduard van Dam owned a large factory in Amsterdam when he first set foot in New York City in 1894.[30] Van Dam had entered *het vak* in 1873, at the height of the Cape Era, when he was only twelve years old and became a successful cleaver and entrepreneur. Diamond merchants Joachim and Marcus van Wezel took up residence in Manhattan's Upper West Side, Joachim and his wife Katherine at 151 Central Park West and Marcus, his wife Louisa, and their young son Salomon at 276 West 82nd Street. Diamond company owner Arie Zilver and his three sons, "foreseeing that the new U.S. tariff . . . would materially injure their American trade, remove[d] their works to this country." The *Jewelers' Circular* reported that "about four weeks ago they carried this plan into execution. [They] are now comfortably located in one of the upper floors in the large factory building of the Geo. W. Shiebler Co., at St. Marks and Underhill Avenues, Brooklyn, NY." In an editorial boldly titled "An Amsterdam Industry Transferred to New York," the trade journal reported that "many of their 50 operators were employed by the firm in Amsterdam and followed Zilver Bros. to this country," legally by all assurances and "on their own responsibility."[31]

The proposed tariff changes on cut diamonds "raised a storm of disapproval" among established importers in the United States.[32] Higher import duties on finished goods, they warned, would encourage smuggling and prove detrimental to American importing as well as to the government. Taxed too highly, the number of brilliants entering the country illegally, tucked away in coat pockets, sewn into corsets, or pressed in the sole of a boot rather than properly reported, was certain to skyrocket.[33] The temptation to evade high import duties on a luxury item that could be so easily hidden as it crossed oceans and borders was simply too great, fostering an illegal market that jeopardized the business of law-abiding importers. Not only did the diamond tariff "offer an inducement to corrupt people to smuggle," declared a representative of Tiffany & Co., "it [also] sends rich people abroad to buy their gems and prevents a man of moderate means from buying." In short, consumers would either buy less or buy elsewhere. Diamond importers therefore denounced the tariffs as counterproductive and posing a threat to all parties involved. Under the new law, decried one commentator, diamond importing "would degenerate into a contraband trade" that "put a premium on dishonesty" and that hurt honorable businessmen, as they could not compete with illegal activities.[34]

To make their voices heard, fifty-two diamond importers from New York formed the Diamond Importers Committee, chaired by A. J. G. Hodenpyl, whose company at 170 Broadway had been acquiring precious stones from Amsterdam since the 1860s. The committee petitioned Congress to scale down import duties. "We, the undersigned," stated their appeal to the Chairman of the Ways and Means Committee, "respectfully submit to you our reasons of the inadvisability of the proposed changes." Signers included Oppenheimer Bros. & Veith, Tiffany & Co., Henry Dreyfus & Co., Ludwig Nissen & Co., Herzog, Goldsmith & Frank, Leopold Stern, and Meyer D. Rothschild. Hodenpyl traveled to Washington to personally lobby against the hike in import duties and met with the US Representative from New York, William Bourke Cockran, a member of the Ways and Means Committee.

Diamond tariffs were discussed on the floor of the House of Representatives a few weeks later, in early 1894. While precise rates were being negotiated, Hodenpyl sent Cockran a note, thanking him for his "personal interest [to prevent] a serious loss to the diamond importers of New York."[35] Cockran was heavily criticized for returning a telegram to Hodenpyl and the Diamond Importers Committee confirming that their "suggestion [to lower the rate on cut diamonds to 10 percent] has been adopted" when in fact the issue was not at all settled. Amos J. Cummings, Democrat from New York, reproached Cockran for having made a promise he could not keep. Cockran's behavior was particularly egregious because he had also met with delegates from the Association of Diamond Workers of New York, promising them the very opposite, namely a higher import tax on finished stones to protect and stimulate employment in American diamond manufacturing. Caught red-handed catering to competing loyalties, Cockran appeared unfazed. Not only had American diamond workers and importers effectively organized their constituencies, but politicians were using diamonds and tariffs as tools for their own agendas.

Representative Andrew J. Hunter of Illinois made the debate over diamond tariffs one about class, "insisting that it was a shame to tax the poor eighty-six percent on their clothing and twenty percent on the roofs that covered them, while the rich were taxed but ten percent on their diamonds." The job of the Democratic party was to correct these inequalities. Together with his colleague from Indiana, William Steele Holman, Hunter motioned to increase the tariff to a whopping 30 percent. "If there was anything in this world that ought to be taxed high," they maintained, "it was diamonds.... What becomes of all our arguments if we leave a low duty on diamonds?"

Maine Representative Thomas Reed responded drily that "the proposition to put a thirty percent tax on diamonds made by certain Democrats was not for the purpose of raising revenue, but of raising the value of certain democratic speeches." Holman supported the motion, he cried, "just as he had supported a proposition to appropriate $100,000,000 for pensions, because he knew it would not carry." House Members, Reed alleged, were conveniently advocating the highest rate to make a political point. Amos Cummings, in a less hostile but firm voice, agreed Democrats had always advocated levying taxes on luxuries, not on necessities, and that demanding a high import duty on finished diamonds fell in line with party principles. "I am astonished," he boomed, "that any Democratic Committee on Ways and Means would leave a higher tariff on necessaries than on diamonds. I don't care whether you make the tariff 15 or 25 or 30 percent, but it certainly ought to be higher than 10. I want it to be fixed where it will bring the most revenue, and at the same time will afford protection to the diamond workers.... [We] should listen to the request of the poor and not of the rich."

Representative Cockran publicly defended the case for low import duties, insisting that the Ways and Means Committee "tried honestly to fix the rates that would bring the best revenue to the Government.... The treasury officials told us that 10 percent on diamonds was the duty that would yield the most revenue. We took their judgment as experts. Whether it was to affect the rich or the poor, or how, we did not stop to consider." Complicit in increasing tensions between diamond workers and importers, between blue-collar cutters and polishers and white-collar importers by promising both an import tariff that best served their interests, Cockran audaciously warned his colleagues: "[W]hen class hostility is introduced into the framing of a bill of this sort it will be time to pronounce the doom of our system of constitutional government."[36]

Members of the Diamond Importers Committee were fuming over the empty promise made by their New York Representative and of the growing consensus that lowering the tariff "was a reversal of [Democratic party] doctrine."[37] In an open letter addressed to Representative Cummings, import company owner Meyer D. Rothschild accused Congress of "running amuck on the Tariff Bill." If a 30 percent duty on cut diamonds passed, his customers would "cease to buy diamonds and other gems in this country, and upon their annual visits to Europe will buy their jewels in London and Paris and will bring them to the US without paying any duty at all." The impact of the tariff, he warned, "would be fatal to many an old established business" in America.[38] The *Jewelers' Circular*, in the pocket of the jewelry firms, published Rothschild's letter, the minutes of the House of Representative debates, and commentary by business owners, brooding over the looming implications of the Tariff Act. The journal interviewed members of the Diamond Importers Committee, printing their individual responses in full.

The proposed bill aroused fierce opposition in distant South Africa. Cries against the tariff mounted after the news reached industry leaders there.

Exorbitant American import duties would translate into higher consumer prices and less demand, closing mines and decimating local employment. It was therefore only natural, commented one correspondent, that "the Kimberley and Jagersfontein diamond industry should seek refuge with the legislature, asking them to protect by intervention, if possible, one of our most important South African industries from . . . certain ruin."[39] Kimberley locals described the situation as "grave." Threatening a trade war, they reminded the US government that the Cape Colony had become a large consumer of American products, with many American goods coming through South African ports. The business community must do its utmost to prevent "an *international* impost," a measure that would "certainly cause damage to the friendly and reciprocal trade relations between the US and the Cape Colony." De Beers showed its teeth, too, sending a telegram protesting the proposed increases, threatening "Cape Colony reprisals were the measures to pass." Cecil Rhodes, it reminded members of Congress, the Colony's prime minister, was director of De Beers and a stalwart in the London Syndicate.[40]

After months of deliberations, Congress passed the Wilson-Gorman Act in August 1894. The bill lowered tariffs on such necessities as iron, coal, and wool, and increased rates on cut diamonds from 10 to 25 percent. Cut and set diamonds were taxed at 30 percent.[41] Needless to say, members of the Diamond Importers Committee, initially hopeful that their visit to Washington would bear fruit, felt defeated. The industry was but "little understood by those not engaged in it."[42] American legislators considered diamonds purely a luxury, ignoring the economic complexities jewelers faced to produce and market them.

As soon as September, the American Consul to the Netherlands, Edward Downes, informed the State Department that the heightened tariff had "produced a depressing effect on the Amsterdam market" and that the outlook for local manufacturers "is worse than at any time during the past year."[43] Many cutters and polishers, he wrote, were leaving for New York as Dutch exports plummeted and mills ground to a halt. Monroe Engelsman, an American diamond buyer living and working in Amsterdam, wrote a scathing letter to the editor of the *Jewelers' Circular*, observing that by passing "this ridiculous law . . . the American government unintentionally created a new industry."[44] Dutch lapidaries were taking their work ethic and expertise to the Hudson shores, diversifying the local New York economy with a specialization it did not yet have at any scale. These people, touted Engelsman, were independent, moral, and thrifty craftsmen and would do well in America. They posed no threat to the existing labor force. The newcomers set up their own workshops or found employment with "some of the diamond importers [who have] opened cutting and polishing establishment in New York and Brooklyn, anticipating the advance of the duty."[45] If import tariffs caused the fortuitous sprouting of diamond manufacturing in America and "the transfer of the diamond cutting industry from Amsterdam to New York," the wisest response would be "to welcome these men without restrictions."[46]

◆ ◆ ◆

Keep the Diamond Cutters Out

—*The World* (March 19, 1895)

The Special Board of Inquiry, set up by Immigration Commissioner Joseph Senner to investigate alleged violations of contract labor law by Dutch-Jewish lapidaries and their employers, met for a hearing at Ellis Island in December 1894. Attorney Samuel P. Greenbaum represented recently detained immigrants and New York cutting firms, including Zilver Bros. & Co., Sanders & Bruhl Mfg. Co., Arnstein Bros, Stern Bros, Herman Levy, Mendes Cutting Works, and Wallach & Schiele. Greenbaum had called a meeting at the office of Bruhl Bros. & Co. at 21 Maiden Lane a week earlier to prepare for the hearing. The attendees "decided that [they] should act together in fighting the attempt to stop the importation of foreign workers."[47] Aiming to employ experienced craftsmen in their workshops for low wages, local factory owners joined forces to fight immigration restrictions. Defining diamond manufacturing as a new industry, Greenbaum believed, was the most promising strategy. He cited Session 5 of the Alien Contract Labor law, which permitted corporations to "engage, under contract or agreement, skilled workmen in foreign countries to perform labor in the U.S. in or upon any new industry not at present established in the U.S., provided that skilled labor for that purpose cannot be otherwise obtained in the U.S."[48]

Opponents to this scheme included the US Immigration Authorities, the Diamond Polishers Protective Union of America (DPPU), and the Diamond Cutters' Association of New York (DCA), the last two belonging to the American Federation of Labor and regularly organizing drives in the 1890s and early 1900s. Cutters and polishers had been inspired by their Jewish brethren in Amsterdam to form labor unions in New York, but Jewish unions organized in many industries, from garment makers and typesetters to cigar makers and butchers.[49] Unlike Amsterdam, New York diamond workers formed separate unions based on their specialty. Cutters and polishers did not unite to fight for improved working conditions but remained small, fragmented, and geographically separated between

Manhattan and Brooklyn. At the immigration hearing, representatives from both organizations spoke in favor of enforcing the Alien Contract Labor Law, contending that diamond manufacturing was, in fact, an established domestic industry and urging that all lapidaries detained on suspicion of entering the country under contract be deported. If ever there was a moment that challenges popular stereotypes of ethnic solidarity among Jews in the diamond industry, this was it: Jewish diamond workers rejecting the entry of other Jews into the country and advocating for their immediate expulsion.[50]

The diamond workers pleaded wages, not ethnic prejudice. As long as immigrants willing to toil for low pay kept coming to New York, they maintained, wages dropped and, with it, workers' standard of living.[51] Likewise, factory owners appeared unmotivated by ethnic solidarity. They wanted Dutch lapidaries to come to America not because they were fellow Jews, but because they were highly trained and experienced specialists who would work for lower pay than their American coreligionists. For owners and workers on different sides of the question, economic factors took precedence over religious ones.

At the hearing, Leopold Stern, who only weeks before had rushed to Ellis Island to file an affidavit in the Hudmacher brothers' detention case, was called as a witness, as were Solomon Bass (of Bruhl Bros.), Henry Fera, E. Arnstein, and others. The hearings, which began on Friday morning, continued on Saturday (Shabbat) and into the following week. The Board focused on the case of Abraham Hoed, a polisher who had boarded the steamship *Obdam* in Amsterdam and had been detained at Ellis Island since November 30. Hoed did not help his own cause when he admitted to "having come to this country under contract to perform labor in the U.S. as a diamond polisher." The Board voted unanimously to bar Hoed and ordered his deportation. Greenbaum appealed and his client was granted a rehearing. The attorney must have made a more convincing case the second time around because three of the four Board members reversed their vote, freeing the polisher to stay in the country. Lawrence P. Lee cast the dissenting vote. He was so perturbed by the Board's reversal in its ruling that he sent the complete transcript records and testimonies to the Office of the Commissioner-General of Immigration at the Treasury Department, headed by H. Stump and Acting-Secretary Charles S. Hamlin.[52] The *New York Times*, *Washington Post*, and *The World* covered the story, reporting that "the question of the right to come to this country under contract" had been taken to Washington, where Greenbaum as well as members of Immigration Bureau presented arguments.[53] The final decision, warned the *Post*, "will involve probably 5,000 diamond cutters from Holland, who desire to come to this country to engage in this industry." Hamlin announced that "the case was so important in its bearings that he and Supt. Stump would hold a session in New York [the following] week, at which further testimony would be adduced and further hearings accorded to interested parties."[54]

Meanwhile, more diamond workers were crossing the Atlantic. The *Brooklyn Daily Eagle* proclaimed on its front page that "Diamonds and Street Bands Are Keeping the Immigration Commissioner Hustling."[55] *The Sun* and the *New York Times* reported that ninety diamond workers and their families would be arriving within the next two weeks. This time the men were coming from Antwerp, "engaged to work in a new shop which is being fitted up at the building at 164 to 172 Seventh Street, Brooklyn, although the name of the firm which engaged them is not known."[56] This new cutting factory belonged to Jacques and Henry Kryn and Wouters Bros., Jewish immigrants to the United States who owned firms in Antwerp and Amsterdam respectively. Following the Wilson-Gorman tariff, they shipped equipment and labor to Brooklyn, installing 250 mills in the newly leased building on the corner of Seventh Street and Third Avenue, "more than their combined factories in [Europe] contain." All they needed was manpower. In an interview with the *Jewelers' Circular*, the firm's representative charged that the alien contract labor charge against them was completely fabricated: "There is no truth in it. . . . There may be many of our employees in Antwerp among [the ninety immigrants]," he continued vaguely, "or there may be none." While it was certainly true that "the 25 percent tax had made it necessary to have a factory here" and that for the past months diamond workers in Amsterdam and Antwerp had been out of work, their firm "had made no arrangements whatever to bring in even one workman." "That the houses of Kryn and Wouters Bros," he continued, "the two largest and most reputable cutting firms in the world, would stoop to smuggle a few workmen—for I call it nothing less than smuggling—is simply preposterous."[57] Jacques Kryn himself was unable to speak to the reporter because he was in Europe recruiting workers, a detail left unmentioned.

The same week, *The World* reported that an additional 120 polishers were bound to arrive on board *The Majestic*.[58] One reader, claiming to be well acquainted with Flemish and Dutch diamond workers, penned an angry letter to the editor, asking: "Is there no way to prevent the landing of the 120 diamond polishers who have sailed on *The Majestic* for this city?" The author, "A. Samuels," purported to be "certain [that] they would never come to this country unless knowing beforehand the name of the firm and salary they will receive. Is our Contract Labor Law only a farce," he asked rhetorically, setting up his true sentiment, "that is, given over to the manufacturers' own sweet will?"[59] Samuels received a reply a few days later. A letter titled "To Keep the Diamond Cutters Out" reassured him that Brooklyn's Immigration Restriction League would "lay the matter before the Ellis Island authorities and, if possible, to have the immigrants sent back."[60]

As further arrivals were announced in the press, the Commission of Immigration at the Treasury Department studied the papers and testimonies submitted by the Board of Special Inquiry at Ellis Island. For two days, lawyers representing the two sides made their cases before Assistant Secretary Hamlin. After the deliberations, Commissioner-General Stump ruled that diamond cutting in the United States did not constitute a new industry, reversing the previous decision of the Board and directing the "deport[ation of] the said Abraham Hoed to the country whence he came at the expense of the steamship company bringing him to the U.S. in conformity with the law."[61] The Dutch trade newspaper, *Algemeen Handelsblad*, whose foreign correspondents had been following the story, took heart. "Dutch diamond workers are now warned. The American government will apply their alien labor law as strictly as possible. . . . The plans to establish new factories may have to be abandoned."[62]

The 120 diamond workers on *The Majestic*, whose awaited arrival caused "something of a sensation at Ellis Island," disembarked in New York only days after the Treasury Department's ruling and were immediately detained.[63] Immigration Commissioner Senner, emboldened by the decision from Washington, announced to the press that the recruits "were [planning to] go to this new concern in Brooklyn." The evidence against many of them was so conclusive they were at once barred by the authorities. Twenty men were charged with labor violations, while another twenty were deemed paupers and instantly deported. Twenty-five others were allowed entry—only "bright men with money," according to one perceptive reporter—and the remainder, "likely to become a public charge," were held for further investigation.[64] The newspapers reassured readers that, despite being incarcerated behind iron gates guarded by "a gaily buttoned official" and "not given much liberty," the immigrants were "comfortably housed and well fed." They joined the additional thirteen detained diamond workers and their families, "all of them Hollanders," who arrived in New York on the *Westerland* as the Treasury Department was drafting its statement on contract labor in the diamond industry. After questioning they, too, were "to be sent back on the same steamer next Wednesday." The firm responsible for importing the job seekers was liable for a fine of $1,000 for each man.[65]

A delegation from the New York Diamond Cutters' Association attended the investigations of the diamond workers. The group's president, M. H.

Zwart, and vice president, M. Hertse, as well as the other union members in attendance—Jonas Osterman, Jacques Fera, T. Monnikendam, and L. van Gelder—were all former Dutch-Jewish émigrés themselves. If they had any loyalty to or empathy for their fellow lapidaries, they displayed none of it at Ellis Island. Anxious to protect their interests, the union was "as much averse as the Board of Inquiry to the importation of contract labor" and opposed the landing of "foreign" diamond cutters.[66] Union members' attitudes were driven to a great degree by labor tensions in New York. At the same time that cutters and polishers were walking off the job in Amsterdam, diamond workers in Manhattan and Brooklyn went on strike for higher wages and better working conditions. The last thing union leaders needed was an endorsement from the US Immigration Authorities for Amsterdam workers to flood the factories. Surely owners would use them to break the strike. Barring cheap labor put pressure on factory owners to keep their employees and to provide them with a decent living wage. From the American diamond unions' perspective, the solution to labor exploitation and unemployment was not for diamond workers to exchange Amsterdam for New York, but rather for each proletariat to fight capitalist owners in their own city, on their own turf, as Dutch men and as newly minted Americans.[67]

The Board's verdict did not stand. Secretary of the Treasury Charles S. Carlisle reversed the deportation order for several of the diamond cutters a few days later. The *Washington Post* praised him for preventing "the blunder," vilifying the Immigration Bureau (but not Hamlin) for having "little intelligence and discretion" when it detained all the lapidaries. "These diamond cutters came here as part of a move which contemplated the transfer of a most important industry from Amsterdam to New York," lectured the *Post*. "The great diamond houses of that city, attracted by our tariff arrangements . . . were coming here with millions of capital and hundreds of expert workmen to add to our wealth and population and factors of commercial prosperity." Were they "to be sent back to Europe like criminals and paupers"? The decision was "preposterous."[68] Controversy over the immigration of diamond workers did not end in 1895. A story in the *Chicago Daily Tribune* in 1909, headlined "The Diamond Cutters May Enter," suggests ongoing discord and continued arrivals.[69]

• • •

New York as the future diamond market is not a phantasy.
—*Jewelers' Circular* 29: 18 (November 28, 1894)

Those who wanted to come to America still tried to enter, even when sent back on the first try. Numerous polishers who had been deported made second attempts, entering via Philadelphia instead, where scrutiny was less severe. "The impression that America offers a propitious opportunity to foreign cutters and polishers," observed one London reporter, "is now current throughout Holland and Belgium."[70] Advertisements in trade newspapers encouraged workers to apply to New York factories; ANDB weeklies discussed New York as the emerging center of diamond manufacturing. As editor of the ANDB's newspaper, union leader Henri Polak received requests from successful Dutch émigrés to publish their letters and to include *New York Times* clippings on diamond factories in his paper.[71] In May 1895, for example, D. de Sola Mendes, who had started a manufacturing workshop at Maiden Lane after leaving Amsterdam, told Polak he "could use a couple of good polishers [and] a good *versteller* [setter] or two who can do small work . . . only first-class workmen." Emphasizing that he could "make no contract according to the United States law" and could not pay any expenses, he "only [wanted] to let him know that any good *versteller* and one or two polishers . . . can readily get work in our factory at good wages and work the whole year round." After requesting information about the latest wages paid in Amsterdam, he ended his letter by asking Polak "if [he] had such workmen as we require," hoping that the most influential person in the Dutch diamond industry would spread the word. Some owners, Leopold Stern for one, recruited in person, taking the message of labor opportunities in America across the Atlantic. Even after the Wilson-Gorman tariff passed, many left "without a written contract *in optima forma* but always with some kind of understanding" with their future employer.[72]

Maiden Lane—whose original name, *'t Maagde Paatje*, dates back to seventeenth-century Dutch settlers of Manhattan Island—was the heart of New York City's jewelry district and, by the mid-1890s, "the Wall Street of the diamond trade."[73] Already by the 1840s, New York's business directory listed more than two dozen firms selling watches and jewelry on the relatively short street, including Lyon & Behrman at no. 19, Louis & Meir at no. 32, and Neustadt & Barnett at no. 42.[74] Jewish-owned firms proliferated in the 1860s—Dinkelspiel & Oppenheimer; Kahn & Limburger; Hirsh, Oppenheimer & Freund; and Jacob Saltzman & Co, among others, were open for business. Non-Jewish retail companies thrived as well. Jewelry making and retail were not concentrated in Jewish hands, but attracted silversmiths, watchmakers, and salesmen from many ethnic and religious backgrounds. They typically obtained diamonds, pearls, rubies, and other precious stones from European company representatives, who showed and sold stock to New York jewelry firms, or from brokers who brought back inventory acquired in London, Paris, and Amsterdam. Georges Guynet, for example, a well-known dealer of precious stones, traveled on a regular basis between Paris and New York. The Maiden Lane he frequented teemed with retail stores but did not yet accommodate wholesale businesses that dealt strictly with diamonds.

This changed in the 1870s and 1880s, when the South African mineral fields brought millions of carats into circulation, energizing the transatlantic commodity chain. Maiden Lane saw an influx of new importing firms. *Wilson's Business Directory of New York City*, lacking headings on anything diamond in the mid-1860s, introduced new classifications of "Diamond Merchants" and "Diamonds & Other Precious Stones" ten years later.[75] Smith & Hedges, at 1 Maiden Lane, announced that they were merchants who "exclusively imported diamonds and precious stones." Forty names appeared under "Diamonds and Precious Stones," including Henry Fera, Henle Brothers, Isaac Hermann, Eisenmann Brothers, Louis Strasburger & Co., David Bruhl, and Schaffer and Hahn, all congregating around Nassau and John Streets and Maiden Lane. In 1895, the Business Directory listed 216 company names under the same heading, over 200 concentrated on three streets.[76] The majority suggested Jewish ownership—Moses Adler, Richard Cohn, Henry Oppenheimer, Max Nathan, Isaac Weinberg—but certainly not all. Benedict Brothers, James Browne, John Saunders, and James Butler II indicated non-Jewish participation as well. The emergence of various organizations reflected the mixed professionalization of the trade; the Jewelers' Mercantile Agency (1873), the New York Jewelers' Association (1874), the Jewelers' League (1877), the Jewelers' Security Alliance (1883), the Jewelers' Safety Fund Society (1884), and the New York Jewelers' Board of Trade (1885, with headquarters at 41 Maiden Lane) drafted founding constitutions and bylaws. Trade newspapers and journals soon followed suit. The *Jewelers' Circular and Horological Review* had been around since 1870, while the *Jewelers' Weekly* and the *Jewelers' Review* published their first editions in 1885 and 1887, respectively. Diamond merchants, jewelers, and their ancillaries became ensconced in a growing organizational network.

By the early 1890s, the Maiden Lane district consisted almost entirely of businesses specializing in the import and manufacturing of precious stones and the retail of fine jewelry. As in Amsterdam, New York's built environment visually reflected the growing presence and economic significance of the diamond. In 1892, real-estate developers Abraham Boehm and Lewis Coon acquired the property at 14 Maiden Lane and, together with the help of city architect Gilbert A. Schellenger, built a ten-story Diamond Exchange "in the heart of the diamond and jewelry trade, specifically intended for and adapted to the business for which it was intended."[77] The fire-proof building boasted a cast-iron and steel frame, hollow-brick floor arches, large front and side windows, electric lights, double plate glass partitions and quartered oak floors, a mail chute, steam heat, and elevators—all designed to meet the requirements and wish list of diamond merchants and jewelers. The frame and floors were reinforced to accommodate heavy safes and the front bay windows were set out to maximize natural light. Built on a lot only 23.5 feet wide, the Exchange was a narrow yet imposing building that towered over neighboring structures. With construction complete in 1894, every single office, renting for $900 per year, was filled.[78]

Business records reveal the growth of both Jewish and non-Jewish retail professionals. Diamond manufacturing, however, was in Jewish hands, typically manned by Jewish cutters and polishers from Amsterdam and Antwerp. D. L. van Moppes & Co., for example, first located at no. 2 John Street and later at 48-50 Maiden Lane, belonged to diamond manufacturer and entrepreneur David Levie van Moppes, who previously had managed a small factory at the Plantage Middenlaan in Amsterdam. Van Moppes purchased the adjacent building soon after, expanding the business to 393 mills with 400 employees by the mid-1880s.[79] After moving his family to Paris and leaving the Amsterdam firm's management in the hands of his brother, van Moppes opened a New York branch to import finished stones directly from the home firm. His son, Simon, was put in charge of the American office.[80] The family company expanded further with a cutting and polishing factory in Antwerp, managed by David's father Hermanus, and an additional workshop at 81 Nassau Street in New York City.[81] By the mid-1890s, the van Moppes family manufactured and sold diamonds in Amsterdam, London, Antwerp, and New York. A few doors down from their Maiden Lane plant, at nos. 41 and 43, stood Meyer D. Rothschild's firm, whose London office at 15 Holborn Street had easy access to rough stones arriving from South Africa, while across the street at no. 35 the brothers Seligman and August Oppenheimer, together with Gustave and Henry Veith, managed Oppenheimer Bros. & Co. The company dealt closely with the diamond merchant Louis (Levie) Tas, who shared an office in Amsterdam as well as at 35 Maiden Lane. Tas was the nephew of Salomon Levie Tas and Betje Hijman Content, who rose from the Jewish working-class neighborhood of Amsterdam.

Other importers of precious stones and manufacturing jewelers in the Maiden Lane district included Arnstein Bros. & Co., Sigmund Hirschberg, Henry and M. E. Oppenheimer, Ludwig Nissen & Co., Koch & Dreyfus, Stern Bros. & Co., Henry Fera (who crossed the Atlantic Ocean 108 times over the course of his career), Zilver Bros. & Co., A. J. Groeneman & Co., L. Tannenbaum & Co, D. De Sola Mendes & Co., Wallach & Schiele, H. A.

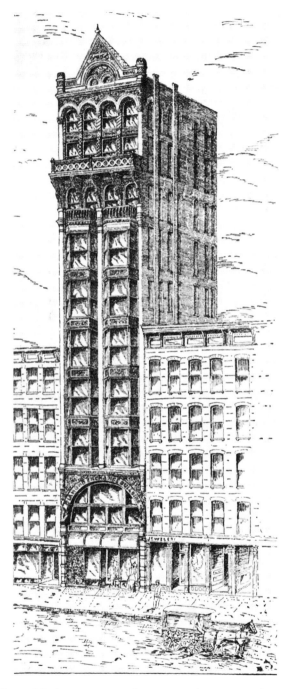

Figure 4.2 Diamond Exchange at 14 Maiden Lane. *Real Estate Record and Builder's Guide* 53: 1366 (May 19, 1894).

Groen & Brother, Goldsmith & Weill, Herman Levy, and John Disselkoen. The majority added cutting and polishing facilities to their already existing companies after the Wilson tariff act passed, creating the need for experienced diamond workers. Henry Fera, in an ad in the *Jewelers' Circular*, "[took] pleasure in announcing that [he] just opened, in addition to the present establishment at 10 Maiden Lane, new diamond cutting and polishing works at No. 60 Fulton Street, fitted up with all modern improvements."[82] Stern Bros & Co, on the corner of John and Nassau Streets, opened a factory with steam-powered mills at 29-31 Gold Street, boasting "the largest and most complete of its kind in this country and rivals the best equipped establishments in Europe." The innovative factory employed some fifty skilled artisans, "all Hollanders of long experience in Amsterdam establishments."[83] The factory was "as complete in every sense as any to be found in Amsterdam . . . [marking] an important epoch in the diamond cutting industry of this country."[84] Similarly, Arnstein Bros & Co., an import firm established in the mid-1880s at 37 Maiden Lane, set up a cutting workshop around the corner at 45 John Street. Zilver Bros. & Co. and Kryn & Wouters opened factories in Brooklyn.[85] L. Tannenbaum, who imported rough via his London office at 25 Hatton Garden, "beg[ged] to notify his customers and the trade in general, that he has largely extended his facilities for cutting and polishing" to the corner of Maiden Lane and Nassau Street. "New York as the future Diamond Market is not a phantasy," he prophesied. "American cutters will be shown an assortment of rough, at prices which will perhaps cause them to believe that this has already been brought about."[86] At the moment he spoke, Tannenbaum was right. Although manufacturing had stagnated elsewhere and the American economy was experiencing hard times, the New York diamond industry kept growing, adding hundreds of polishing mills and employees to newly established workshops over the course of the 1890s. Jewish entrepreneurs with strong commercial relationships and access to diamond distribution centers in Europe led the way. The official census of 1890 counted sixteen firms cutting and polishing diamonds in New York, a tally that reached thirty-six by the 1910s.[87] Leopold Stern owned the largest factory, employing 290 workers, including thirteen children between the ages of fourteen and sixteen.

Dutch dominance in manufacturing is reflected in the adoption of Dutch technical terms into the English language, terminology still used today. "Dop," for example, refers to the lead cup that holds diamonds in place while being cut and polished. It was the primary job of setters to heat the lead to the point when it would be malleable, then solder the stone at the desired angle and cool the dop. The dop was then fixed into a copper holding tool called a "tang." This procedure had to be repeated continuously during the finishing process. The "skive" or "scaif" [schijf] refers to the horizontal grinding table or wheel on which a diamond is polished.[88]

Dutch spilled over from the manufacturing floor into the streets—quite literally to the sidewalk of Dutch Street, soon known in local parlance as "the diamond curb" and "the diamond curb market." Dealers bought and sold ornamental gems on the corners of John and Nassau Streets, John and Dutch Streets, and Maiden Lane. All business done here, wrote the *New York Times*, was "strictly intra-trade" from which regular consumers were excluded because they were unacquainted with the lingua franca of the trade; they were regarded as "strangers."[89] Dealers "negotiated on the curb" in Dutch and English, appearing to be "gossiping, idling away their time, [and] hanging around." In reality they were moving diamonds from the end of the manufacturing phase into the hands of brokers and jewelers. With their "offices inside their coat pockets," they bought and sold stones with a handshake and the verbal expression "mazal u' bracha" [good fortune and a blessing]. One diamond could be bought and sold multiple times at small profits, "circulating about on the curb" for weeks before it ended up in the hands of a jeweler.[90]

Diamond traders were active at jewelry auction salesrooms centered around the Bowery and Canal Street, at the end of the Manhattan Bridge, where diamonds and jewelry pledged for loans at pawnshops were sold. Harry A. Mount, an astute observer of the industry, called these auction rooms a "mecca" not merely for dealers, but also for many diamond setters and workmen in the city's jewelry shops. There lapidaries could find purchasers for stones they bought independently and set at home. Mount depicted the scene:

> A long, dingy hallway leads to the rear of a dingier building where a room is fitted up roughly. There is a show case on casters in which the jewelry to be auctioned is placed, a raised platform with a chair for the auctioneer, a number of high chairs for the bidders and a tall, pulpit-like box for the salesclerk. In addition, in one corner is a cage-like structure in which are built many tiers of little drawers. The auctioneer takes his place on the platform and the bidders, each drawing up a chair, arrange themselves in two long lines, facing each other.

Intrigued by the setting and rituals, hidden from public view, Mount captures the performance:

> The auctioneer's jargon is absolutely unintelligible to the unlearned observer. [With] machine-gun like utterances he announces the buyer's name as he passes

the purchased article through the bars of the cage. It is placed in one of the drawers and the bidder's name is chalked on the front of the drawer . . . and a final settlement is made at the end of the sale. There is absolute quiet in the room, except for the auctioneer's voice. Not a bid is heard from the bidders, nor can one at first see any signs from them. But as the novelty of the situation wears away it appears that Mr. Goldstein, who is buying heavily, occupies the second seat from the end. He announces his raise of a bid to the auctioneer by the slightest possible nod of his head. Mr. Greenberg, who sits beside the other, apparently signals his bids by merely raising a finger. Mr. Cohen, who came in later, pulls a corner of his coat as a signal for his bid. The sale goes on with unbelievable rapidity. For two minutes in succession the auctioneer knocks off an article every ten seconds, and then twenty seconds are required for a sale because the weight of the piece has to be verified. In this time the auctioneer keeps up a steady fire of figures in his monotone and the bidders sit for all the world like a tableful of expert poker players, masking behind an apparently disinterested examination of the goods as it passes along the line.

The author admitted to being captivated by this "mysterious" scene, and while he does not remark on the strong Jewish presence, his references to Goldstein, Greenberg, and Cohen show his awareness of the audience's ethnic make-up. The contrast between the grimy physical space and the precious, sparkling objects sequestered in casters magnified the appeal. The buyers used their poker faces to feign nonchalance while perfectly cognizant of the moment's commercial intricacies. Mount tapped into conventions linking Jews to diamonds—secrecy, control behind the scenes, speaking in code, invisible money—that would harden in the 1890s.

Besides indoor sales in dim-lit auction rooms, outdoor trading at the site of the Bowery and Canal Street created a sidewalk market that rivaled Maiden Lane. Small crowds of traders "hung around the auction rooms," buying and selling stones that had just changed hands at auction and "were brought to the curb."[91] Sidewalk dealing would disappear in both locations as the jewelry district gradually relocated to midtown Manhattan in the 1920s. As finance and insurance companies increasingly concentrated downtown, driving up rental prices, small business owners were forced to move to more affordable neighborhoods. Up-to-date quarters with better lighting, more space, street-level showrooms, and proximity to Grand Central Station incentivized dealers to migrate to new quarters. Real estate developers, eager to fill newly constructed buildings, capitalized on the moment. In 1923 Fenimore C. Goode, a broker, promoted 20 West 47th Street specifically to Maiden Lane firms, tempting them to relocate. The strategy proved successful. A year later, the *New York Times* reported that tenants showed a "marked alacrity" in taking up occupancy in Goode's structure.[92] More projects followed at no. 1, 40, and 66 West 47th, with the prospect that "within the coming year 75 percent of the jewelry business will be centered in this district," a transition confirmed by the Real Estate Record and Guide. The 47th Street block, it declared, "has almost overnight become New York's Maiden Lane."

Over time, 47th Street, between Fifth and Sixth Avenues, did indeed become the nucleus of the new "Diamond Jewelry Way," anchored by the Diamond Dealers Club (and its 500 members), which took up an entire floor at nos. 36-38. By the early 1940s, a contemporary affirmed, "precious stones from all over the world found their way to 47th Street." Refugees fleeing Nazi-occupied Europe, many of whom arrived with experience in the gem industry, reinforced the district's Jewish presence. To this day, deals are made in Yiddish, with handshakes, in front of store windows ablaze with diamonds.

• • •

This may indeed be called the golden age of diamonds, for these jewels have never been distributed so generally throughout the world and particularly in the United States, where their use is so common as to be almost universal.
—Sarah Brentworth, "Diamonds," *The Chautauquan: A Weekly Newsmagazine* (1896)

In New York, polishers constituted the largest group among diamond workers, some 370 out of 500 in 1896.[93] Monitoring developments on the Amsterdam scene and encouraged by the burgeoning American labor movement, lapidaries formed the Diamond Polishers' Protective Union of America (DPPU) with Dutch-Jewish immigrant, Andries Meyer (née Meijer) as president. The roughly fifty cutters organized their own union, the Diamond Cutters Association (DCA). The two groups merged in the early 1900s into the Diamond Workers' Protective Union of America (DWPU), whose mission was "to promote the moral and financial welfare of all workers in the diamond-cutting industry."[94]

The United Diamond Workers of Brooklyn, seeing themselves as a direct sister union of the Amsterdam diamond workers' union, wrote a charter on May 1 (Labor Day), 1894. The statutes were written in Dutch and all members were recent émigrés. But the organization collapsed soon after its founding, as the number of diamond workers employed in Brooklyn proved too modest to be self-sustaining.[95] The DPPU and DCA were more successful. They initiated strikes periodically to secure higher wages. The average wage for polishers ranged from $1.75 to $2 per carat, or approximately $25 per week, but that did not cover "bench expenses" such as boart.[96] Moreover, factory owners hired cutters and polishers fresh off the boat for significantly lower salaries. Stern Bros. allegedly paid its employees only $1.25 per carat for polishing, or $15 a week. When these lapidaries learned of higher wages elsewhere, their discontent grew.

Massive strikes broke out in Amsterdam in November 1894, paralyzing Dutch diamond manufacturing. Ten thousand workers walked away from their mills and protested in the streets, demanding higher wages and decent working conditions. The American press covered these events extensively, interviewing factory owners in Manhattan and Brooklyn about possible implications for local business. The owners appeared rather stoic, even opportunistic, adding that "the boom in the diamond cutting industry in this country offers opportunities to as many striking workers to obtain good wages on this side of the Atlantic as desire to accept it."[97] If lapidaries found Amsterdam lacking, they could always emigrate.

The owners' complacency was shattered when, two weeks later, diamond workers in New York followed suit. In the eyes of the *Jewelers' Circular*, America's infant industry was plagued by the same troubles as its parent in Amsterdam.[98] Thirty-five of the forty employees of Wallach & Schiele at Mott Street put down their tools, followed by colleagues at the Arnstein Bros. & Co.'s factory at John Street. They induced eighty polishers and setters at the Stern Bros. establishment on Gold Street to join the walkout. Their numbers grew when the crews of Herman Levy on Dutch Street and De Sola Mendes & Co. on Maiden Lane silenced their mills. The group of disenchanted workers convened at Bleecker Street, where they proposed the formation of a union and a shared pay scale for setters, cutters, and polishers, including a 50 percent wage increase.

When a *Circular* reporter heard the news and called on Stern's factory, he found the upper floors deserted. The ground floor of the building, however, managed by the former Ellis Island detainees Solomon and J. H. Hudmacher, was still buzzing. Leopold Stern fumed to the reporter that the strike was "the work of foreign socialist agitators." His men were paid good wages, given steady work, and were satisfied, but they "must have been intoxicated by their own prosperity when they thought of joining the movement." Stern had recently agreed to pay his workers $3 instead of $2.75 for piecework and was stunned therefore when, "during a temporary stop of the machinery, the strikers happened to come in and soon induced about 80 of their men to join the movement." At Wallach & Schiele, too, workers had "just walked out at Monday noon." D. de Sola Mendes gathered that his men "must have struck through sympathy" because he could not understand how they could possibly be nursing any grievances.[99] By the end of the week the Stern employees joined the protest, as did workers from Zilver Bros. in Brooklyn, bringing the total to nearly 300 strikers—a percentage comparable to their Dutch compatriots.[100] The majority of diamond workers in both cities took to the streets.

Stern, Levy, de Sola Mendes, Zilver, and other owners collectively refused to negotiate and rejected a compromise advanced by the State Board of Arbitration. The workers declared their decision to unionize, an announcement welcomed by Daniel Harris, a delegate of the Cigar Makers' Union, at a meeting of the Central Labor Union at Clarendon Hall: "These people . . . came here from Europe under contract, thinking conditions were better here," Harris explained. "When they began to mingle with the American workmen in this city and Brooklyn, they found that the money they were earning here had not so much purchasing power as the money they earned in Europe, and that they were actually worse off here." Harris offered his services to the diamond workers, "expecting them soon to join the central body."[101] But fortunes did not favor the workers. Lacking funds and depleted of resources, the lapidaries were forced to concede to their employers and resume work by early December.[102] Contrary to Amsterdam, where the general strike and unionization efforts were a smashing success, in New York diamond workers suffered a crushing defeat.

Almost a year later, in October 1895, they tried again. Frustrations boiled over at the Zilver Bros. factory in Brooklyn, where seventy polishers went on strike "on account of too much enforced idleness."[103] Joseph Zilver, one of the three Zilver brothers who managed the firm, responded from his comfortable residence at Park Place that polishers in New York were paid twice as much as in Holland and Belgium, "from which countries they came last spring." Undeterred, his employees organized a strike committee of the United Diamond Workers of Brooklyn, No. 1, headquartered at 535 Atlantic Avenue in Brooklyn. Their colleagues at Wallach & Schiel soon joined the strike, demanding a 25 percent wage increase after the firm had reduced weekly compensation from $14 to $12.[104] This time, as affiliate members of the American Federation of Labor and the Central Labor Union, diamond workers were able to hold out and the strikes lasted well into November, precariously close to the Christmas holiday season.

Most of these diamond cutters, observed the *New York Herald*, had not been in the country for more than a year. "Imported from Holland and Belgium by Brooklyn and New York diamond polishing firms," they had come with certain expectations and discovered, much to their dismay, that the life of a New York diamond worker did not differ much from Amsterdam; factory owners chased profits at the expense of their employees on both sides of the Atlantic. If conditions failed to improve, threatened the strikers, there was not one reason for them to stay, but plenty of reasons to return "to the old country."[105] Dismissing this warning—it was still October—Joseph Zilver scoffed: "If these men want to go back to Holland, let them. They spend all their money as they make it, and if they did get better pay it would do them no good." Counting on the probability that strikes in Amsterdam and high costs of transatlantic return fares reduced the risk of his employees actually leaving, Zilver stuck to his guns.

As the strike ended its fourth week in late November, Zilver and other employers must have started to worry. Van Dam & Co., at Carmine and Bleecker Street, offered to increase wages, but it was the only firm to do so. All others refused to recognize the union. To break the deadlock, wrote *The World*, the 175 diamond workers still on strike "concluded that the only way to score a victory over their employers is to emigrate again and thus leave them in the lurch."[106] On November 20, thirty polishers sailed back to Holland on the St. Louis, sent off by a Diamond Workers Union delegation.[107] Some fifty other strikers had left the week before. More were to return to Europe, leaving employers, in the words of *The World*, "practically helpless."[108] New York union representatives declared that the remainder of the 350 workers in the city would follow as soon as possible, knowing full well that they could not afford the fare. Union president Jacob [Jacques] Hegt wrote to Henri Polak, chairman of the ANDB in Amsterdam, requesting money to help send diamond workers home. "It is the only way to allow fathers and their families to return to Holland, to weaken and destroy the trade in America.... Without your help, our cause here will be lost and all workers will have to return to their hated patrons and resume work until they starve." Underscoring the transatlantic dimensions of the diamond industry, Hegt used the incendiary language of nineteenth-century labor activists to command Polak's attention. "Our eyes are on you and your fellow countrymen," he declared, "as a last resort to escape this so-called land of the free, to be liberated of its horrendous slavery and tyranny."[109]

Known for his pragmatism, Polak must have raised an eyebrow when he read this dramatic plea. He was concerned enough to send 200 guilders (approximately $80) to the New York contingent. The ANDB set up a commission to raise additional funds and sent inquiries to steam companies about reduced group rates. Its sister organization in England, the London Diamond Workers' Union, also pledged an initial sum of £7 (approximately $30 at the time).[110] Sending Dutch lapidaries home would make it impossible for New York manufacturers to fill work orders, strengthening the workers' negotiating position. Diamond merchants and jewelry companies would be forced to purchase finished stones from Europe, slapped with the new Wilson tariff of 25 percent. In a dangerous power play, New York unionists raised the ante by wagering virtually the entire manufacturing industry to secure decent wages.

It is clear now why New York union leadership balked at helping new immigrants arriving at Ellis Island in 1895, destined for jobs in local diamond factories. Their presence as potential replacement workers and strike breakers undermined local struggles to pressure employers for better pay, especially when the lapidaries came under contract. Supplanting the existing workforce with new cutters and polishers fresh off the boat would guarantee the strikers' defeat. Fearful of losing their jobs, employees at the Zilver factory caved under pressure and resumed work without a pay raise. They could stay on the condition that they refrain from making financial contributions to any union.[111] Those workers who stuck it out to December fared better. In preparation for the holiday trade, most manufacturers had large quantities of rough stones in need of cleaving, cutting, and polishing to go to market. Where striking persisted, factory bosses finally yielded to union demands and granted concessions. The victory was short-lived, however. Small-scale strikes continued well into the early 1900s, at Stern Bros & Co., S. L. van Wezel, Krijn & Wouters, and L. and M. Kahn & Co.[112] Correspondence from diamond workers in New York, addressed to Polak in Amsterdam, mentions ongoing labor tensions and sudden strikes.[113] Pay scales remained an issue—as workers called for a minimum wage as opposed to compensation for piecework—as well as an end to the practice of hiring too many apprentices as cheap labor.

What remained a weakness among diamond workers in the United States was their inability to unite small unions representing different specialties in Brooklyn and (separately) in Manhattan into one substantial labor organization. The Diamond Polishers' Protective Union, the Cutters Association, the United Diamond Workers' Union [aka the United Diamond Workers Bond of America], the United Diamond Polishers' Union, the Diamond Verstellers Union of America, the Machine Diamond Cutters Union of American, and (later) the United Diamond Cutters of America operated independently, with occasional aid from Europe and the American Federation of Labor, but they never gained enough traction to grow and unify. Knowing that the ANDB's newspaper circulated among Dutch-speaking lapidaries in America, Andries Meijer, secretary of the DPPU, pleaded with Polak to promote the benefits of a union merger. Complaining that US workers "were a century behind," Meijer believed an endorsement from an effective union leader would move workers to overlook professional hierarchies and individual aspirations in favor of collective power.[114] This was precisely the strength of the ANDB in Amsterdam, where over ten thousand cleavers, cutters, polishers, and setters, Jewish and Christian, formed one organization, managed by uncommonly strong leadership. New York diamond workers lacked the strength in numbers, funds, and vision to achieve the same level of success. "Having all the diamond workers under one name," wrote the chairman of the newly established United Diamond Cutters of America to Polak, in 1898, "we can't expect that, can we? It would be too good to be true."[115]

After the dust of the mid-1890s immigration and tariff controversies settled, American diamond unions plodded along. One unionist grumbled in 1901 that "there is really no more feeling for the movement."[116] Numerous union organizers aired their frustration in correspondence to Polak, not merely about their inability to stay organized for more than a few months, but also about the popular perception in Europe that "diamond workers in the United States were merely [the ANDB's] stepchildren, careless infants incapable of standing on their own feet." Polak was bitterly reproached for failing to offer guidance and public support and, most of all, for ignoring letters from America. "Not one syllable, not one word of encouragement, nothing from the organization that aims to pull workers from the sludge of Capital! . . . Please answer us and break the silence."[117] Wasn't the labor movement supposed to be international, the union men asked? If so, then why were they not being taken seriously? While New York diamond unions strived to replicate the ANDB, admiring its organizational strength, size, and influence, and wanting to be stronger but independent sister pillars across the Atlantic, union leaders complained about being left to fend for themselves. Polak, knee-deep in his own labor fights and facing significant political uncertainties in Holland, could hardly be held responsible for American labor demographics. Yet union members continued to berate him, in Dutch and in English, to no avail.

Diamond workers in New York faced new challenges in 1897, when the Dingley Act readjusted tariffs on European-cut diamonds from 25 to 10 percent, alleviating heavy taxation and boosting foreign imports. Within days of the act's passage, American importers ordered nearly $2,000,000 worth of finished stones from European firms.[118] Some diamond workers protested the measure, fearing it would strangle domestic industry and throw lapidaries out of work. Cutter J. de Vries called the measure cruel. "We are all Americans," he wrote to *The Sun*, "and have as much right to make a living as the most important importer . . . who was perfectly able to carry on his trade at 25% duty."[119] American manufacturing had flourished with the enactment of Wilson-Gorman tariffs and he saw no reason to jeopardize the status quo. Diamond union representatives again trekked to Washington, defending their cause at the tariff hearing before the Ways and Means Committee. They begged Congress "to take care of our interests, of the interests of our wives and families, by recommending a tariff that shall enable us to work, to earn a livelihood, and that will not compel us to leave [this] land and seek a living in foreign countries."[120] The union reps and de Vries were not overreacting. Several factories shut down operations for months at a time after import duties fell, throwing many diamond workers out of work. The firms of D. S. Granaat, J. Hoedenmaker, and S. Konijn folded during the industry's "spasmodic growth."[121] Yet others remained in business and survived, especially those with parent companies in Europe such as Van Wezel & Co., Eduard van Dam, and Zilver Bros. Owners adjusted to national and international market conditions, keeping factory doors open when profit margins justified production and curtailing production when they did not—always at the cost of their employees.

Dutch diamond workers continued to dominate the industry in New York. In 1908, 80 percent of the work force was still Dutch-born. That same year, Andries Meijer, of Dutch-Jewish descent, became president of the Diamond Workers' Protective Union. By 1919 the industry employed 700 workers, 200 of whom came from Holland, while most of the others had Dutch-born fathers. "It is said that fully 80 percent of the diamond cutters in New York are Hollanders or the sons of Hollanders," stated *Scientific American* in 1926, "and practically all of them are from families in which every male member is a diamond cutter."[122] By then the van Wezel firm was the largest diamond manufacturing company in New York, employing more than 70 workers. The American appetite for diamonds was so voracious that importers bought finished stones from practically any mill, domestic or foreign. Jewelers bought entire inventories from American manufacturers plus an astounding 90 percent of all finished diamonds produced in Europe.[123] Elevated consumer demand kept diamonds moving in the commodity chain, embellishing the *décolletées* and self-image of American customers. Despite fluctuating tariffs, Ways and Means Committee hearings, strikes, immigration and deportation controversies, and struggling labor unions, the New York manufacturing industry persevered, creating over time a niche of its own—namely the finishing of large stones, two carats or more. Small diamonds produced for mass markets continued to be cut and polished in Holland, Belgium, and, in the second half of the twentieth century, in India and Israel; America milled the largest stones for its wealthiest customers.

• • •

I verily believe that at Cape May, Long Branch, Newport and Saratoga I have seen this season enough diamonds to fill a barrel. It is a rare exception to meet a woman who has not diamonds somewhere on her person and the majority have them distributed

wherever it is possible to find a lodging place. I would not be surprised if the next move is to bore holes in their noses to stick them in.... Had it been en règle to come into the room barefooted I make no doubt they would have had diamond rings on their toes.
—"A Barrel of Diamonds," *Washington Post* (1882)

By the late nineteenth-century, the United States had become the chief consumer of polished diamonds, owing to forces that fundamentally and permanently changed American consumer culture. The enormous output of new merchandise and improved transportation networks ushered in commerce that was no longer local and regional but national and global in scope. The expansion of railroads, telephones, and telegraphs accelerated the movement of goods, money, and information, connecting people and markets across great distances. The advent of mail-order houses and department stores, both promoting their wares in newspapers and magazines, fueled consumer demand for the vast array of goods, most unavailable to American households only a few decades before. More and more Americans could afford these items, not merely because mass production had cut costs, but because industrialization had led to rising incomes: between 1869 and 1900 real per capita income rose by 2.1 percent every year. Although the late nineteenth century was punctuated by economic panics (beginning in 1873, 1884, and 1893), the long-term trend was strongly upward in the most sustained expansion that the US economy had thus far experienced.

The new American commodity culture embraced acquisition and conspicuous consumption as the means of achieving happiness. Consumption defined an entire way of life geared to a secular ideology that widely endorsed the display of status and success. Desire for and access to luxury goods underwent a process of democratization: everyone had the right to crave the same durables and to enter the world of comfort and luxury.[124] The revolution in acquisitiveness and display proved a perfect setting for sparkling diamonds. The surge in the supply of ornamental gems from South Africa thus occurred at a time when American consumers were in the best possible position to covet and buy them.

Advertising played a key role in stimulating consumer demand. Diamonds had typically been the prerogative of wealthy elites, unobtainable to the wider public. In the 1890s, however, jewelry firms began marketing "the wonder of precious stones" to a broader clientele that cut across social class and gender, that included both men and women. New mass market magazines of the 1890s, such as *Cosmopolitan*, the *Saturday Evening Post*, the *Ladies' Home Journal*, *Harper's Bazaar*, *Puck*, and *Comfort Magazine* offered a whole new commercial aesthetic of longing and desire. No longer confined to small print and single columns in newspapers, typically without visual illustrations, advertisements filled entire pages of magazines, promoting luxury items in color and with bold headlines, varied typescripts, and distinct images. "What can equal a matchless diamond?," one jeweler asked. "In a small space you carry about with you all the hues of the rainbow. Light a taper and immediately a thousand rays flash forth and delight you with a feeling of power and possession. They are all yours and neither grow old nor fade away."[125]

A new type of retail, the so-called credit jeweler, appeared on the scene. Credit jewelers invited customers to purchase diamonds in installments, making them affordable to the middle class. The firm of Loftis Brothers in Chicago became one of the leading jewelers selling diamonds on credit. The so-called Loftis System, introduced at the turn of the century, allowed "any person of honest intentions, no matter how far away they may live, to open a confidential charge account for a diamond . . . and pay the same in a series of easy monthly installments."[126] The company sent a free catalog, featuring over 1,500 illustrations of diamond rings, pins, brooches, and earrings that varied in price from a few dollars to over a thousand dollars, for customers to make a selection. After they opened an account, agreed to put down a 20 percent deposit and make monthly payments, Loftis would ship their order via registered mail. Buyers could examine their purchase "as leisurely and as carefully as [they] wished," and if they changed their minds, the order could be returned at no cost to the customer. A guarantee certificate accompanied the stone, vouching for Loftis's integrity. The company charged no interest, promoting the idea that "the wealthy man buys on the same terms as the lowest salaried employee. . . . A pen, paper and postage stamp bring to the home an array of all the latest gifts in the jewelry line."[127] Co-owner Samuel T. A. Loftis made it his mission to put diamonds "within reach of the common people."[128]

A 1903 Loftis Bros. ad features a man and a woman raising their arms in worship toward a diamond deity, whose light lights up their faces. Framed as a painting, an angelic woman with flowing hair watches over them, holding diamond rings in each hand, blessing the couple with brilliance. The headline "Diamonds on Credit: There Is Nothing That Would Please Her So Much" sanctions desire and pleasure, while the detailed description below explains step by step how to obtain a commodity previously reserved for the wealthy. Similarly, a *Puck* ad showed a mustachioed gentleman presenting an oversized diamond ring to a woman extending her arm and lifting her ring finger, welcoming the commitment. The ring and the word "credit" are fused and appear between the couple's heads, as if the fiancé is whispering the word to her while he slips the ring on his future wife's finger. "A diamond is the gift of all gifts," read the ad, "it lasts forever, and every day brings to the wearer thoughts of the giver's regard and generosity." Loftis Bros. promised audiences that diamonds were the surest way to a woman's heart.

Before the 1880s, Americans purchased their everyday merchandise at neighborhood shops, pharmacies, and modest-sized dry goods firms whose inventory was regularly stocked by local producers or wholesalers. People of leisure purchased luxury goods at specialty stores. By the end of the century, however, shopping habits were at the cusp of change. Most major cities boasted at least one new department store, concentrating selling power into a single massive building. In New York, Macy's, Lord & Taylor, Siegel-Cooper, and A. T. Stewart opened "pleasure palaces of desire," while Philadelphia and Chicago became home to Gimbels, Marshall Field, the Fair, and Carson's. Together with mail-order businesses and retailing chains, modern department stores soon dominated urban trade, selling everything from ready-made clothing, pianos, and liquor to cheeses, tropical fruits and vegetables (irrespective of season), kosher food, South African diamonds, and even exotic animals.[129] At Marshall Field more than seven thousand employees catered to Chicago's clientele gawking at dazzling window displays. Visitors spent hours shopping in half a million square feet of merchandising space. As many as fifty thousand people a day crowded into this castle of commerce, spending seventeen million dollars annually by the end of the 1900s.

The department store was the place to see and be seen, to fantasize, and to imagine a way of life defined by comfort, beauty, and style. Strolling through Macy's or Gimbels stimulated the senses. Glass window displays and electric lighting visually amplified merchandise, while small orchestras played soothing and seductive chamber music in the background. Pleasant smells of chocolate perfumed the air and the soft fabrics of cashmere shawls and fur coats excited the touch. In this constructed environment, the acquisition of diamonds granted access to affordable decadence. If purchasing diamond jewelry in a department store proved too costly, customers could always admire, select, and mail-order on credit.

An advertising innovation in the form of small, brightly colored cards targeted department store shoppers and theater patrons. A series of diamond cards surfaced in the 1890s, opportunely placed in packets of cigarettes, coupling famous diamonds with women of different national origins. The "Cape Diamond," for example, featured a white, bohemian-looking woman with golden, looped earrings, posing on an African shield, adorned by fur and spears (see fig. 1.1). A cloth head cover decorated with jewels surmounts her flowing hair, suggesting that she is not aristocratic in the Western tradition. Rather, she blends whiteness and exoticism,

Figure 4.3 "Diamonds on Credit" Loftis Bros. & Co. Advertisement. *The Ladies' Home Journal* 21 (December 1903), 55.

conveying white ownership and appropriation of South African diamonds. Similarly, the card titled "Kohinoor" (fig. 2.1) confirmed that the world's largest diamond belonged to the British Empire, positioning it as the heart of British royalty. "The Blue Diamond" (fig. 3.1), portraying a woman wearing a traditional Dutch headdress surrounded by windmills, attested to the importance of the Netherlands in diamond production. Another card simply titled "Diamond" featured a veiled woman of Indian descent, looking directly into the eyes of the viewer through a horse-shoe framed opening of a gold-colored screen (fig. 5.1). These cards popularized and exoticized diamonds at the same time, sculpting the stone's reputation of mystique. People were bombarded by images and promises of diamond gems when reading newspapers and magazines, buying cigarettes, and strolling through department stores.

American buyers responded. Between 1870 and 1910, sales increased more than twentyfold, with imports of rough and polished stones topping $34,000,000.[130] The *Washington Post*, wondering who was buying all

Figure 4.4 "Diamonds on Credit," Loftis Bros. & Co. Advertisement. *Puck* 54: 1395 (November 25, 1903), 13.

these diamonds, found it was "principally persons of moderate means." Recognizing the rise of middle-class purchasing power, the *Post* continued: "Even the least worldly people, the sort of people who once were satisfied with a cameo brooch and plain gold pins and rings, want a few good diamonds these days. They don't hanker after pearls, emeralds, turquoises, and other fancy stones, but they do care for diamond solitaires."[131] Americans bought diamonds as Christmas and birthday presents, and more frequently as an engagement offering. By the early 1900s a new cultural custom had taken hold, popularized in a highly charged consumer environment that kindled purchasing exclusivity on credit—a marriage proposal ought to come with a diamond ring. "[W]e are about the only people," wrote one newspaper correspondent in amazement, "among whom every young man thinks he must give a diamond ring to his sweetheart to seal the promise of marriage. . . . Many prospective grooms are now buying such rings on the installment plan, and there is a regular business of selling them on long time, at so much down and at so much per month, until paid."[132] The power of marketing and the socially sanctioned willingness to go into financial debt turned tiny carbon crystals, extracted from dirt, into universally recognized symbols of love. When the De Beers company launched its triumphant and lasting ad campaign, "A Diamond Is Forever," in the mid-1940s, it built on economic and cultural foundations already in place around the turn of the twentieth century.[133]

"There is a tendency to a lavish display of jewelry and jewels even among those who have only a moderate degree of wealth," observed Sarah Brentworth in an 1896 edition of *The Chautauquan*. "Is it not," she pondered, "a desire to own what others own?"[134] If Mrs. Frederick Van der Bilt wore fashionable diamonds at New York's Metropolitan Opera House, then why couldn't every woman?

Figure 5.1 "Diamond." Cigarette Card, "Famous Gems of the World" Series, ca. 1890. New York Public Library Digital Collections: Image #1554861.

CHAPTER 5

Jews and Diamonds in the Popular Imagination

In early June 1897, 46-year-old Barney Barnato, the poor Jewish lad from Whitechapel who had "made it big" on southern Africa's diamond fields, boarded the steamship *Scot* in Cape Town. Heading for England to attend Queen Victoria's Diamond Jubilee, Barnato, his wife Fanny, and their three young children, Lilly, Jack, and Babe, planned to spend the next few months at their new home on Park Lane, near Hyde Park. On a Sunday afternoon after lunch, as the steamer neared Madeira, Barnato strolled on deck, arm in arm with his nephew, Solly Joel. He asked for the time, and as Joel halted to look at his pocket watch, Barnato unlocked his arm, hoisted himself onto the railing, and jumped into the Atlantic Ocean. Joel, running after him, threw out his hands to catch his uncle, but only caught the back of his trousers. The "Diamond King" was gone.[1]

Stunned and horrified, fellow passengers sounded the alarm. "For God's sake, save him," yelled Joel to an officer of the Union Steamship Company, who took off his coat and leaped overboard in an attempt to rescue Barnato. With lightning speed, the crew lowered a lifeboat to get the two men out of the water. High seas complicated the operation, and as the steamer moved at seventeen knots per hour, they disappeared from sight. By the time the lifeboat reached the spot where the jumpers were last seen, only the exhausted officer could be rescued. They found Barnato minutes later, floating face down.

News about Barnato's death spread quickly. The American, European, and South African press chalked it up to mental instability, blaming the incident on a history of depression. The mineral magnate, explained reporters, had suffered financial losses of late, the severity of which pushed him into a fit of "lunacy." The collapse of gold shares in 1896, together with the botched Jameson Raid—an attempt to overthrow the Transvaal Republic over the 1895–1896 New Year's weekend—had unhinged Barnato, causing him to drink heavily. With moral overtones implying that wealth did not produce happiness, correspondents concluded that a delicate emotional state had caused him to "jump into the sea."

Others were less convinced of "suicide by temporary insanity," the official ruling issued by a British coroner.[2] The *Cape Town Daily Telegraph* maintained that "he fell overboard" rather than jumped. Barnato's own family contested the theory as well, claiming suicide was out of character for a man who had been a pioneer in the rough-and-ready days of the Diamond Fields. That he was buried at Willesden Jewish cemetery in London suggests that United Synagogue officials did not agree that he intended self-harm. Had Barnato

Figure 5.2 "Jumped into the Sea." *Ann Arbor Argus* (June 18, 1897).

taken his own life, in violation of Jewish law, the family would not have received permission to bury him in a Jewish burial ground.

The public had its own take on Barnato's tragic demise. A founding member of the London Diamond Syndicate, Barnato had amassed a fabulous fortune, built a mansion in a fashionable neighborhood, and entered high society, arousing unease that found confirmation in negative stereotypes. The Jewish businessman, so the rumors went, had become a multimillionaire not through hard work, foresight, and perseverance, but because his "racial genius" and cunning predisposed him to success. Barnato exemplified traits many believed to be typical, namely the Jewish instinct for making money at the cost of everyone else. He jumped at a time when East-European Jewish immigration was altering the profile of established, middle-class Jewish communities and racial antisemitism was gaining legitimacy. The sudden death of a Whitechapel Jew turned Diamond King, his obituaries insinuated, "destabilized markets" and "cause[d] a panicky condition in London financial circles," jeopardizing economic stability in Britain and South Africa.[3] Barnato's jump generated myths the non-Jewish public far and wide relied on to explain Jewish success and tragedy. South African diamonds had benefited Jewish entrepreneurs like Barnato, making them "insiders" in commercial, social, and political circles, but ethnic prominence in the industry simultaneously sharpened already existing perceptions of Jews. Barnato was not a diamond magnate; he was and remained a *Jewish* diamond magnate.

Victorian fiction immortalized characters like Barnato and fortified associations between Jews and gems. Novelists and short story writers incorporated diamonds and gem dealers into narratives of discovery, suspense, and crime.[4] There was something exhilarating about a valuable stone's foreign provenance and portability. Readers experienced vicarious pleasure reading about the latest exploits of adventurers in Africa and India, even more so when they involved secret caves, diamond heists, and smuggling. Shrouded in mystery, gemstones could be easily concealed and trafficked across borders, making them tempting characters in their own right. Ancient Indian diamonds, for example, aglow with supernatural properties, maddened the heroine in Anthony Trollope's *The Eustace Diamonds* (1871) and cursed every "presumptuous mortal who laid hands on the sacred gem" in Wilkie Collins's *The Moonstone* (1868).[5] Beautiful but dangerous, diamonds disappear and are never recovered by their owners. The Eustace diamonds eventually end up on the bosom of a Russian princess, while the Moonstone reaches India and is returned to the forehead of a four-armed deity, the God of the Moon. In both novels, the agents moving gemstones across imperial borders, through illicit and invisible channels, are Jews.

It was an easy step to create Jewish personae in plot lines that exploited themes linking Jews to international trade, secret wealth, and immoral practices. Trollope's *Eustace Diamonds*, first serialized in the *Fortnightly Review*, introduced Mr. Benjamin, a jeweler, moneylender, and receiver of stolen property, along with his partner in crime, Mr. Harter. Trollope's *Can You Forgive Her* (1865) and *Mr. Scarborough's Family* (1883) cast equally shady characters, "small and oily, and black haired and beaky-nosed." Scheming and devious, they were "modern Hebrews . . . beginning with nothing, determined to die rich, and likely to achieve [this] purpose."[6] Similarly, in Collins's *Moonstone*, Septimus Luker—*lucre* alluding to money and profit—is a cunning gem dealer and pawnbroker responsible for covertly passing the lost Indian diamond to an accomplice, an act that takes place inside of a bank. Luker was "so vulgar, so ugly, so cringing, and so prosy . . . he didn't stand at the top of the prosperous and ancient profession of usury for nothing!"[7]

For Victorian novelists, Jews and diamonds were inherently intertwined, even when the connection was symbolic. In H. Rider Haggard's bestselling adventure story, *King Solomon's Mines* (1885), three British explorers stumble upon a cave in Africa, where they find diamonds the size of pigeon-eggs and gold pieces with "Hebrew characters stamped upon them."[8] Nearly trapped in a diamond mine named after a biblical patriarch, the men, stuffing their pockets with loot, "shrieked with laughter that the gems were now [theirs], found for *us* thousands of years ago." "Solomon never got them," cries Quatermain, one of the explorers in near ecstasy, "nor David, nor da Silvestra, nor anybody else. *We* had got them." Taking pleasure in undermining Jewish riches, hidden underground for centuries, and reasserting Anglo-Saxon superiority, Haggard created a scene that fused objects, setting, and popular prejudice into one.[9]

Haggard, Trollope, Collins, and others drew on alleged racial tendencies and biases about Jews as well as colonial Others. Indian characters frequently exuded an aura of Hindu mysticism while Africans were "wild" to the point of savage and unintelligent to boot. Giving free reign to colonial racial fantasy, Victorian writers, most of whom had never set foot in Africa or Asia, created a cast of imperial actors for consumption in mainstream British culture. Together with travel narratives, journalism, and poetry, imaginative literature made empire—and Jews and diamonds moving within it—intelligible and seductively sinful to readers.[10]

English-language authors consistently used diamonds in their writings to signify the Jew's avarice, rootlessness, and immorality, qualities transmitted from parents to children and amplified by the capitalist nature of the diamond business. They portrayed Jewish wealth as ubiquitous, its origins suspect. Jews had an alleged racial genius for commercial enterprise devoid of ethics. Diamond Jews were painted as greedy crooks, quick-witted and mercurial, their new prosperity and cosmopolitanism challenging traditional society. Popular detective novels routinely portrayed Yiddish-speaking Jews as illegal diamond buyers who had infiltrated high society undetected. In Britain, W. T. Eady's 1887 *I.D.B. (Illicit Diamond Buying), or the Adventures of Solomon Davis on the Diamond Fields and Elsewhere*, loosely based on the life of Barney Barnato, as well as George Griffith's *Knaves of Diamonds: Being Tales of Mine and Vel'd* venomously linked Jews to diamonds and crime, as did the American author Louise Vescelius-Sheldon's *An I.D.B. in South Africa* (1888) and South African novelist J. R. Couper's *Mixed Humanity: A Story of Camp Life in South Africa* (1892). Alluding to Charles Dickens's notorious Jewish villain, Fagin, Couper described his IDB characters, Mosetenstine and Faganstine as "decidedly Hebraic."[11] Whether protagonists or fleeting characters, the Solomons, Benjamins, and Lukers were unfailingly "Cockney-Hebrew[s] of the lowest type [whose] repulsive fulness of his lips, and the sinister curves at the corners of his mouth, betrayed greediness and cunning of no common intensity."[12]

Political cartoons and caricatures in newspapers and magazines mocked Jewish affluence and its foundation in immorality. Immense wealth, they implied, was hiding behind the façades of crooked merchants who spoke with thick foreign accents. The satirical magazine *Puck* derided the Kohinoor, the fabled "mountain of light," as in reality the "Cohen-oor"—a mountain of money and influence obscured from view by a bespectacled and large-nosed "Popper." Leaning on a modest display case inside the rather shabby-looking jewelry shop "A. Cohen, Watches & Jewelry," the shopkeeper informs his grandson Ikey, as he sweeps the wood floor, that "he ought to have known" the largest diamond in the world belonged to Jews. Not even young Ikey seemed to have been aware of the family secret.

In Great Britain and the Cape Colonies these popular stereotypes turned openly hostile in the late 1890s, when tensions between colonial forces and Boer populations in southern Africa burst into a full-blown war. Jews, already mistrusted for dual loyalties, were denounced for profiteering. Opponents of the Boer War, primarily on the political Left, charged Jewish diamond magnates with deliberately engineering conflict to fill their own coffers and manipulating the British army for economic gain. British Member of Parliament John Burns lamented that the armed forces, "which used to be for all good causes, the Sir Galahad of history, has become the janissary of the Jews. . . . Wherever we examine, there is the financial Jew operating; directing, inspiring the agonies that have led to this war."[13]

The Trade Union Congress agreed. It passed a resolution condemning the conflict, blaming "cosmopolitan Jews, most of whom have no patriotism

HE OUGHT TO HAVE KNOWN.
IKEY—"Popper, vat's der larchest di'munt in der voild?"
IKEY'S POPPER—"Such a iknoramus vat you are! Vy, der 'Cohen-oor' is der larchest, of course!"

Figure 5.3 *Puck* (1902). The Katz Ehrenthal Collection, United States Holocaust Memorial Museum, Accession Number 2016.184.509.

and no country," for aiming to secure the mineral fields of South Africa. The Social Democratic newspaper *Justice* echoed these sentiments, pointing fingers at "unscrupulous Jewish financiers" and the "Semitic-capitalist press."[14] Diamonds shone as the epitome of modern materialism and condensed wealth. Jews, as capitalist enablers, had maneuvered the country into an imperialist war.[15] "Beit, Barnato, and their fellow Jews," bristled Henry Hyndman, founder of the Social Democratic Federation, aimed at nothing less than "the constitution of an Anglo-Hebraic Empire in Africa stretching from Egypt to Cape Colony," primarily to swell their "overgrown fortunes."[16] Anyone could see that Jews, with their hands on the world's diamonds and gold, were directing capitalist exploitation and imperial aggression. Critics on the radical Left drank from the well of antisemitism, calling Jewish businessmen and entrepreneurs "gold-greedy ghouls," "destructive microbes," and "parasites."[17]

Caricatures of the bloated financier entered the popular iconography of South Africa. *The Owl*, a Cape Town anti-Semitic weekly, published malicious cartoons showing obese, diamond-decked Jews carrying bags of money on their way to London, leaving their local (white) neighbors behind, empty-handed and desperate. It accused Jewish upstarts of rapacious exploitation, reaping the benefits of the British Empire yet refusing to share its responsibilities. A white woman in a modest dress representing South Africa, her hands clasped in front of her face, towers over a pleading population. She can't bear to see the cigar-smoking Jewish capitalist robbing her poor children, none of whom appear to be of African descent. A cartoon from 1902, conflating Jews and De Beers, ominously devined that the company "trapped so many people, that it is time the people trapped them."[18] It featured a Jewish parvenu with a large, crooked nose and bulging lips, wearing spectacles and a top hat labeled De Beers, caught in a metal bear-trap. Accusing a Jewish minority of the very greed that for centuries had impelled Christian colonial settlement, the South African media openly exhibited envy and resentment.

Along with biting criticism, the British and South African press expressed fascination with "Park Lane millionaires," described as ambassadors of Jewish wealth, hidden or displayed. Coined "Randlords" by the press, the sobriquet stuck to successful mine owners and financiers on the fields, many of whom were of Jewish background. Maintaining offices in Kimberley and Hatton Garden, Barnato, Beit, Lionel Phillips, and other tycoons often spent time in London, where their lavish lifestyles and socializing in elite

Figure 5.4 *The Owl* (December 1, 1905).

circles attracted attention. Particularly well captured was the popular caricature, Max Hoggenheimer. Drawn with grossly exaggerated features, Hoggenheimer became a stock character in musical comedies and cartoons. The archetypal Randlord, he exploited the working class, indifferent to or even unaware of the misery he caused. The English playwright Owen Hall brought Hoggenheimer to life in his West End musical comedy, *The Girl from Kays*, later revised as *The Belle of Bond Street*. The story revolves around a mix-up between newlyweds on their honeymoon. Hoggenheimer, the loudmouthed Jewish millionaire, plays a supporting character who is unrefined yet ultimately benign. Opening at London's Apollo Theatre in 1902, the musical proved so popular that, after 432 performances, the London Gaiety Club brought it to adoring audiences in the Cape Colonies. Max Hoggenheimer surfaced in political cartoons soon after, making regular appearances in the South African news and becoming, in the words of John X. Merriman, the last prime minister of the Cape Colony, "a classical character."[19] Progressively sinister, Hoggenheimer evolved into a symbol of Jewish imperial avarice, conflating "Jew" and "capitalist" for literate and semiliterate theater-goers.

From the *American Economist* to *Scientific American*, from *Puck* to *Ladies' Home Journal*, the American press produced accounts of the diamond trade and America's love affair with sparkling stones. Many noted the disproportional presence of "Hollanders" or "Dutch Hebrews" in the industry as businessmen and as lapidaries. Yet the weight of that acknowledgment rested more on their foreignness and expertise than on their Jewishness per se. References to Jews occurred as statements of fact, neither positive nor negative, and in the margins of the story. What caught the eye were Jewish *nouveaux riches* making inroads into a class that had been overwhelmingly and unambivalently white and Christian. Socially ambitious, Jews with "new money" challenged the given social order and their entrée triggered harsh responses. "*Toujours les diamants!*, that is their motto," sneered one observer as he described Jewish women in Long Branch, a posh New Jersey seaside town.[20] If the presence of Jews in high-end resorts made some uncomfortable, Jewish women flashing diamonds added insult to injury. It was distasteful, a sign of being too eager to fit in—a view echoed by the American Jewish press. Modesty, they preached, not bling, paved the way to social acceptance.

• • •

IDB was the custom of the country. I have lunched at a restaurant—the London Hotel, kept by Harry Barnato (on Stockdale Street), or Madame Delalee's French Cafe, or the Red Light—and seen diamonds change ownership without the least effort at concealment. Who cared, who bothered?

—Louis Cohen, *Reminiscences of Kimberley* (London: Bennet, 1911)

Illegal diamond buying (IDB) was everywhere on the South African diamond fields. Black and white laborers working claims regularly hid stones from their superiors, selling their finds below market rates to shameless hawkers. They, in turn, passed on stolen goods to receivers, some of whom worked for established diamond buyers in Kimberley and, by extension, London. The loot often exchanged hands in shared social spaces. Pubs, canteens, and "Kaffir eating houses," drawing small crowds and constant traffic, became common sites for illicit dealing.[21] In the early days of the Fields, when currency was still scarce, frequenters of The Old Cock, The Perfect Cure, First and Last, Hard Times, and The Crystal Palace paid for their food and drink with stones that only hours before had been quickly tucked in a sock or sleeve, or placed under the tongue. Referring to "soup diamonds," contemporaries recounted that diggers sometimes left small gems in *pannikin* (small pots) of soup and stews to pay for supper.[22] As Kimberley expanded and currency flowed, IDB flourished and diamonds were increasingly exchanged for cash rather than for soup, quick profits seducing people at all levels in the distribution chain. Women participated in these clandestine transactions as well, hiding stones under petticoats, in bosoms, or "where no man could find [them] without getting sunburnt."[23] Louis Cohen, who at age seventeen traveled with his cousin Lewis Woolf (Barney Barnato's nephew) to the Cape Colony in 1872, recollected that "in the Land of Diamonds" IDB had become "the chief industry of Kimberley, an exhilarating game, taken all round, excitable, profitable, and not so very risky, unless the adventurer went about with his wits in his pockets—then, of course, he would be landed like trout on a bank."[24] Illicit trade went on everywhere, an open secret in both canteen and court room.[25]

In tall tales grounded in truth, smugglers used dogs, chickens, and horses to transport diamonds from the fields to the Transvaal and the Orange Free State, where anti-IDB legislation was less strict or not enforced. Feeding the animals meat or meal balls containing stolen goods, traffickers took them across colony lines and waited for nature to take its course. Sometimes they slaughtered the animal to recover the loot. Ox tails proved useful in hiding stones, too, as did carrier pigeons "requisitioned to fly through the air with the greatest of ease, laden with the brigands' booty."[26]

The association of IDB with Jews was made early and often on the fields. Jewish predominance in buying and selling rough, first as *kopjewallopers* and later as store or company owners, placed them in the lineup of usual suspects. Already in 1873, the governor of the Cape Colony, Henry Barkly, characterized IDB as a Jewish-instigated phenomenon. In a lengthy dispatch, Lord Kimberley, the secretary of state for the Colonies, described an incident that had turned violent in New Rush as having been caused by a "Jew Dealer," who paid for it with his life. Having gotten wind of the story, the *Jewish Chronicle* in London expressed dismay with Barkly for singling out one Jewish delinquent while "forgetting to define the other[s] as Christians." Why had Barkly emphasized the man's Jewishness? "We scarcely expected this mark of intolerance from a man of the education, position and colonial experience of Sir Henry Barkly," the editorial intoned, "who must be well aware . . . how high a position is taken by the Jewish residents of our colonies and how patriotic are the services they render to the Crown."[27] Letters in the *Eastern Province Herald*, published in Port Elizabeth, protested "Barkly's attack on the Jewish race" and his "attempt to vilify a class that has proved itself to be loyal and moral." Barkly should have instead expressed sympathy for the "Jew Dealer," who died "in a savage assault perpetrated by a furious mob . . . who we presume were Christians."[28] Barkly never responded, but the mood had been set.

A decade later, the most widely read newspaper on the Fields, the *Diamond News and Griqualand Gazette*, featured a letter from Sidney Mendelssohn. The author had read a report in the *Diamond Fields Advertiser* about a case involving "Aaron Lyon, a young Jew" suspected of IDB. Unaware of "what the religious persuasion of the man had to do with the case, or why it was thus brought forward," Mendelssohn maintained that "had the prisoner been a Catholic, or a Presbyterian, or a 'Plymouth Brother' . . . we should never have heard of it." He stated that "[i]t is only a small thing, very small, but last week there was another small thing, when only Jewish passengers were searched on the coach."[29] Charging the *Advertiser* with prejudice and drawing attention to bias on the diamond fields, Mendelssohn reminded the public that "Jews are Jews amongst themselves," but that "to the world at large they are English, French or Dutch &c, identifying themselves with the country they live in." While the Northern Cape may have been ethnically and religiously diverse, a potpourri of peoples gravitating around the common goal of getting rich, it was as susceptible to age-old bigotry as any other place. These "small things," to Mendelssohn, were symptomatic of a deeper problem.

Mendelssohn had a point. Cape politicians, bank managers, and medical doctors were quick to link Jews to illegal or dubious business practices, building on ancient prejudices. Lewis Mitchell, the general manager of the Standard Bank, admitted that he would welcome "[t]he departure of hordes of hook-nosed Polish and Lithuanian Jews whose evil countenances now peer from every little shanty." Legend of universal dislike, and "under cover of keeping a *winkel* [shop]," Jews "at present flock[ed] to Kimberley from afar, like *asvogels* [vultures] to a dead ox, and their villainous faces enable one easily to understand the depth of hatred borne to them in Russia and elsewhere."[30] Legitimizing his distaste for Jews, the bank manager used language that everyone understood: hordes of crooks had descended on the Diamond Fields. Well-respected men of the Cape's upper crust perpetuated the myth of Jewish criminality. Josiah Wright Matthews, who traveled to the Cape in the mid-1860s and practiced medicine in Kimberley, described Jews as "haunting the edge of the mine" with satchels full of gold and banknotes, "tempting sorters to steal from the storing table."[31] Matthews moved into politics by representing Kimberley in the Cape Colony's House of Assembly. With a flair for inflammatory language, he denounced both the "Whitechapel old clo' Jew who runs the *klips*" [stones] and "the Hebrew swell who keeps his carriage at the West End"—they were "all as much thieves as the veriest pickpocket of St. Giles."[32]

Some Jews were involved in IDB. Police detained people of different backgrounds for illicit dealing, including Jews, yet ethnicity or religion seldom mattered in the severity of punishment. The newspapers took note, however. For example, Barney Barnato's record was an open book, and the press took every opportunity to remind readers of his Whitechapel "ghetto" background.[33] Rumors had circulated since his earliest years on the fields, when Barney's brother Harry ran the London Hotel, a notorious IDB den on Stockdale Street, across from Mrs. Jardine's Queen Hotel and doctor Leander Star Jameson's office. While Mrs. Jardine allowed no nonsense in her establishment, the London Hotel had a reputation. In March 1884, following years of suspicions, police arrested Isaac Joel, the 21-year-old nephew of Barney and Harry and an employee of Barnato Brothers & Co. at the London Hotel. It was the first prosecution of a dealer under section 34 of the Diamond Trade Act, specifying that stones over ten carats or £100 required separate itemization.[34] Joel's records didn't add up. In the investigation, police detectives noticed that a 16 ½ carat diamond, sold to a dealer named Leopold Herz, was missing from the young man's purchase accounts. In his defense, Joel explained that the diamond's purchase price fell below £100 and that it had subsequently been sold in a mixed parcel. To convince the court that he was lying, the prosecutor invited numerous diamond dealers to take the stand. They stated under oath that a Cape white of that size never sold so cheaply, let alone got mixed into parcels containing low-carat stones. Even Alfred Beit, a major force on the fields by the early 1880s, estimated the value of this "remarkable stone" at £10 to £12 per carat, or between £165 and £198 total.[35] Beit testified against a fellow Jewish gem trader because he believed Joel to be guilty—yet he surely was aware of the reputational damage that such a family scandal would inflict on the Barnato Bros. company. Beit's main competitor, Joel, unable to account for the "perfect octahedron," most likely had swapped the diamond for a low-quality diamond amounting to 16 ½ carats to balance the books.

Joel got off on a technical error in the indictment. The police promptly rearrested him, but he was released on bail set at £4,000. The second the gavel came down, Joel packed his bags and fled to London, where he assumed the name of Jack Joel. His uncles, who had helped smuggle him out of the Cape colony, appointed him company manager of the London office, tending to Barnato Bros.' affairs from the safe sanctuary of Hatton Garden. But the incident tarnished Barney Barnato's name. Compounding the family's bad luck, the *Cape Argus*, the primary newspaper in Cape Town, uncovered details of bribes offered to John Fry, Chief of the Detective Department, to have Joel's second court case dismissed. When the *Cape Argus* accidentally mistook Isaac Joel for Woolf Joel, his brother and a fellow diamond dealer, Barney sued the newspaper for libel.

Suspicions of foul play followed Barnato for remainder of his life. *Scientific American*, reporting on IDB, relied on "one notable instance and that is the case of a Jew, who came to Griqualand some twelve or fifteen years ago, and who, in some mysterious way, has amassed a fortune of nearly a million pounds, upon which he is now living in great magnificence."[36] Alluding to Barnato's astronomical success, the author claimed that "[h]e is known to be an IDB, but he has covered up his transactions with such cleverness that the accusations against him are only whispered." Many IDBers, he inferred, "carry on their trade in a manner so cunning and so secret that they feel secure from justice." Jews, secrecy, and inbred business practices all fell neatly into place.

If Jews were labeled unscrupulous dealers, black "Cape boys" were charged as their subservient accomplices. The corrupting influence of "white sharks" teaching African workers thievery brought "all the cunning of their nature" to the fore.[37] Jews, the accusation went, needed black accomplices to take diamonds out of the mine. "Had it not been for the unscrupulous scoundrels who first introduced illicit diamond buying," declared Josiah Wright Matthews in his travel account, "native laborers would in all probability be still as honest as at the early period, when, except in trivial assault cases, they were very rarely brought before the court."[38] To Matthews, who judged assault a lesser crime than theft, the noble savage turned criminal gem runner used his nostrils, toes, and hair to smuggle stones from mines to canteens, in the employ of treacherous Jews. Mine owners would claim endemic black thievery to justify closing the migrant worker compounds. To control the movement of their workers, they introduced invasive searches of African bodies on a daily basis.[39]

• • •

Horace—Will you be my wife?
Minnie—I can't say.

Figure 5.5 "Plan of Ownerships in Kimberley Mine" (1882). Kimberley Africana Library.

Horace—Don't you know your own mind?
Minnie—Yes, but I don't know what you think of diamonds.
—*Jewelers' Circular* (August 26, 1891)

Arriving dirty in Europe and America, Cape stones underwent a process of whitening before reaching their ultimate market. Once cut and polished in Europe for white Europeans, the flawed aura surrounding the diamond had been purified. Henry Knollys, writing for *Blackwood's Edinburgh Magazine*, graphically described this process. He asked readers to envision "Scene 1: a squalid hut," where he detailed an African laborer is subjected to a humiliating body search to retrieve a "dirty little white stone [that] drops from the poor black carcass," supposedly from his anus. Then, in "Scene 2: Six thousand miles distant, [in] a London ball-room with all accessories of civilized splendour, the stone reappears cut, and in the shape of a brilliant enhancing the charms of some young loveliness, and prompting the instinct which bids us worship and honour her beauty, as though it were something divine."[40] While critical of Western worship of diamonds—they only accentuated "the ugliness of aged hags"—Knollys acknowledged the course of sanitation that diamonds went through on the journey from the Cape Colony to Europe, literally from inside a black body to a white woman's neckline. By launching into a discussion of IDB, Knollys inserted a commentary on Jews. He singled out Barnato, who amassed "a considerable sum by nefarious traffic and who is now flourishing in several public capacities, though, according to the rules of justice, he should be behind the bars of a jail." Knolly referred to Isaac Joel's trial, which had exposed "a

Figure 5.6 Details from previous "Plan of Ownerships in Kimberley Mine" (1882). Kimberley Africana Library.

very hotbed of IDB." Like the cat with nine lives, Barnato Brothers escaped punishment.

More than forty thousand Yiddish-speaking Jews, fleeing poverty and pogroms in the Pale of Settlement, emigrated to southern Africa over the course of three decades, indelibly altering the profile of the Jewish community, including the Cape Colony.[41] This demographic shift happened at a time when company consolidation landed diamond distribution in Jewish hands and mining companies introduced closed compounds for African laborers. As legal restrictions against Jews were lifted in the West, the sentiment that Jews were a separate and dangerous race that could never be assimilated into European society sparked a transnational backlash against Jewish prosperity and social recognition. Despite a palpable rise in anti-Jewish hostility, Jews in South Africa continued to be beneficiaries of a colonial order that counted them as (almost) white. Against the backdrop of British imperial expansion and an increasingly assertive and racist settler class, segregationist labor practices became normal. The consequences for black residents, however, were decidedly different than for their Jewish counterparts.[42] Indigenous Africans and people of mixed descent were consigned to second-class citizenship until well into the 1990s, while Jewish immigrant communities experienced sustained social and economic mobility and became largely middle class over the course of the twentieth century, following patterns comparable to Jews in other frontier societies.[43]

Well-to-do Cape Jews deplored the influx of Jewish immigrants from Britain to South Africa. They wanted to distance themselves from newcomers, blaming them for illicit diamond dealing and for igniting anti-Jewish feeling. Referring to poor Ostjuden, a correspondent for the *Jewish Chronicle* questioned the objectives of the London Emigration Society, sneering that "there ought not to be sent out here a class of individuals, I am sorry to say, [who] are by no means credible to the name of Jew." "In England," he continued, "they are not so conspicuous, they are lost in the multitude, but here [in southern Africa] it is different. It is like living in a small village where everyone knows what his neighbor cooks for dinner; and if a discreditable act is committed by any of them . . . it reflects on the whole community."

Anglo-Jewish societies, keen on moving foreigners along to American or African shores, offered aid with emigration, a policy that the colonial correspondent found troubling. "I think it necessary to be plainspoken," he wrote, "and I say if only *ad honores* keep such at home, at all events there is no chance for them here—in legitimate channels of business." Poverty bred crime, and for East-European Jewish immigrants to the Cape, who lacked economic standing, that often meant IDB. Anxious to maintain Jewish respectability by keeping poor peddlers out, the correspondent urged: "Wash your dirty linen at home."[44]

In an effort to acculturate poor, Yiddish-speaking coreligionists, Jewish organizations offered language training, evening classes, and small-term loans to accelerate economic independence, as paternalistic and self-serving as the aid may have been. The Jewish mercantile establishment in the Cape Colony, who had come over on Dutch and British ships in the early decades of the nineteenth century, feared the repercussions of mass immigration. Nothing good could come of an influx of poor Jews into a race-conscious society that already suspected them of foul play.

⋯

> [I]n the process of cutting, flaws and imperfections are often laid bare, which go much deeper than the appearance of the rough diamond would predict; and, on the other hand, the colour, apparent in the rough stone, is sometimes found to arise from the presence of flaws or specks, which are removed in cutting, thus leaving the stone white.
>
> —Harry Emanuel, *Diamonds and Precious Stones* (1867)

In an era when mineral exhibits enticed hundreds of thousands to visit World Fairs and when a media furor over the Kohinoor diamond prompted Madam Tussaud and London museums to display replicas, diamonds found an equally glittering presence in print culture. Fascination with IDB inspired scores of detective novels and adventure stories, soaked up by a public with an unquenchable thirst for the subject. Newspapers, monthly magazines, and yellowbacks—one-shilling reprints of bestselling books—featured stories about diamonds and crime, both at home and abroad. W.C. Hudson's "The Diamond Button: Whose Was It?," Louise Vesalius Sheldon's *An I.D.B. in South Africa*, and Arthur Griffiths's "Jewel Robberies" in *Mysteries of Police and Crime* added a sensational flair to historical accounts of gems that had titillated society. Harry Emanuel, the skeptic who had dispatched a mineralogist to the Northern Cape Africa in 1867 to verify the discovery story, published *Diamonds and Precious Stones* the same year. Edwin Streeter, jeweler to the London masses, advertised *The Great Diamonds of the World: Their History and Romance*, while Louis Dieulafait published *Diamonds and Precious Stones, a Popular Account of Gems*—both bestsellers in England, France, and the United States.[45] These volumes complemented dramatizations of IDB in the *Illustrated London News*, *The Graphic*, and *Cosmopolitan* as well as local newspapers like the *Glasgow Herald* and the *Aberdeen Weekly*.[46]

Diamonds had performed mightily in fiction before the mid-nineteenth century—in *One Thousand and One Nights* (c. 1706), Sinbad the sailor falls into a valley of diamonds—they became more conspicuous as items of personal wealth and more closely tied to Jews as the mineral revolution in South Africa exploded. Only months after Erasmus Jacobs picked up a shiny "pebble" on his father's farm near Hopetown, initiating the diamond rush, Wilkie Collins penned his novel. Hailed by T.S. Eliot as "the first, the longest, and the best of modern English detective novels," *Moonstone* constructs a story of intrigue around the largest yellow diamond ever found in India.[47] The scintillating stone, imbued with magical properties, has a dubious past. Wrapped in legend, it glittered with danger, temptation, and sin. Having first been set in the forehead of a four-armed Indian God of the Moon, the stolen diamond has since brought on personal trauma and madness to each "presumptuous mortal who laid hands on the sacred gem."[48] Illegally obtained by a British Colonel, John Herncastle, during a military campaign in India, the cursed diamond wound up in the possession of his niece, Lady Julia Verinder. Herncastle suffered social ostracism upon his return from India and behaved as if possessed by the devil in the last years of his life. Julia, too, changed in the presence of the Moonstone, its spiritual provenance and magnificence seducing anyone of sound mind.

Scholars of Victorian literature have shown how Collins, a dear friend of Charles Dickens, made the Moonstone a metonym for India, encoding it with oriental fantasies, superstitions, and romance.[49] The novel validated imagined traditions, embodied by the three Brahmins who follow the diamond across continents in an effort to restore it, at all costs, to the God of the Moon. A similar argument can be made about Collins's portrayal of Jews. His main Jewish character, Septimus Luker. the unsavory gem dealer and moneylender in possession of the lost jewel, "was, in every respect, an inferior creature to the Indian."[50] Luker is the one moving behind the scenes, hiding the stone inside a bank and undertaking "what was (even in *his* line of business) a doubtful and dangerous transaction." An unprincipled Jew with money and connections, he stands between the upper-class British family and the mysterious Brahmins, deciding the fate of the diamond.

Luker understood that a jewel the size of the Moonstone could not be sold. A defect in the very heart of the diamond left it imperfect. Both problems could be fixed, suggests Luker, by secretly sending the diamond to Amsterdam, where "a famous diamond cutter" could cleave and recut it into multiple stones, increasing its value.[51] The scene is starkly reminiscent of *Punch*'s illustration of an ill-stricken Kohinoor in need of a Western cure. Like the Indian gem, the spectacular but flawed Moonstone could be tamed and made perfectly white by redesigning its Oriental appearance, excising its mysticism in order to domesticate it. Here too, Dutch Jews would be the experts in charge of its transformation, securing the "end of its sacred identity as the Moonstone [and] an end of the conspiracy."[52]

Collins's story was serialized in the periodical *All the Year Round*. Intoxicated with suspense, crowds gathered around the publisher's office whenever a new edition was due to come out. People placed bets on how and where the illustrious gem would be recovered.[53] Diamond crime stories held their allure for decades, peaking in the late 1880s and 1890s. T. W. Eady's *IDB* and Dalrymple J. Belgrave's *Luck at the Diamond Fields*, both published in 1887, capitalized on the genre's popularity. Eady relates the story of a poor Jewish lad from London, whose parents managed a fried-fish shop in Petticoat Lane and regularly invited "gentlemen of the Hebrew persuasion from the neighborhood" to a small parlor to indulge in card games. "Most of them," writes Eady as he sets the scene, "aired their black suits and stove-pipe hats in synagogue on the day of atonement, when they howled away the transgressions of the previous twelve months in company with a crowd of temporarily mournful hypocrites like themselves and then straightway went out of there with their monstrous noses elevated to catch scent of the first swindle that might be floating around." The young protagonist escapes this "den of thieves" and, together with his brother Barney, sets off to South Africa to make a career on the diamond fields. The Davis brothers form a "predatory alliance," buying diamonds illicitly and shipping them to a "certain well-known firm in Hatton Garden, who got splendid prices and asked no questions." After Solomon is accused of murder and put on trial, he is released and returns, with his fiancée Fanny, to England—a part of the story that evoked Barnato Bros.' 1884 court case. Once wealthy, Solomon and Fanny change their names to Mr. and Mrs. Montague Vaughan—"as Mr. and Mrs. Solomon Davis [they] would never have made their way in London society." By assuming false identities, and through "lavish expenditure and adroit toadying," they build up a pleasant social position among the inhabitants of Bayswater and Kensington, in London's West End. In Eady's imagination it is the lucrative alliance of diamonds and IDB that enabled Jews to infiltrate London high society.

Judith Walkowitz, in her pathbreaking *City of Dreadful Delight*, observed that Victorian Londoners often juxtaposed the West End, alight with glittering leisure and consumption, to the East End, an area of obscure density, indigence, and crime.[54] Eady, Trollope, and Collins set their stories in these opposite worlds, contrasting the jewelry market and reputable department stores of Bond Street with surreptitious dealings of Jewish gem dealers in Houndsditch's "black slum golcondas."[55] However, the sinister tone of their writings comes from blurring these very lines. The boundaries between Petticoat Lane and Park Lane, between dark and light, become porous as East End Jewish corruption seeps into West End respectability. The veneer of Mr. and Mrs. Montague Vaughan hid the reality that Jews, perpetually aesthetically displeasing, were everywhere. George Griffith's 1899 tale "The King Rose Diamond" magnified this imaginary threat. His central character, the IDB Michael Mosenstein, rises suspiciously fast in London society, given away by his wife's propensity to wear "too many diamonds in public." Mrs. Mosenstein's desperation "to make up for the weakness of her race" drove her to ostentation. Rather than uplifting her status, excessive diamond jewelry instead reveals she did not belong.

Jewish literary characters, and their associations to diamonds and London's East End, turn up in Cape publications, too, in fictional as well as nonfictional guises. They suggest how these stereotypes traveled to places of new settlement. For example, when an English clergyman named Reverend B. B. Keet faced imprisonment for failure to repay a debt owed to Rothschild Brothers, well-known auctioneers in Kimberley, an editorial in the Cape newspaper *Uitenhage Times* evoked the character of Shylock. Responding to a letter from "Afrikander" a few days earlier, defending Keet, the editor declaimed: "We have met many Shylocks in our time of the tribe of Benjamin, and we can fully sympathise with the English clergyman and his Afrikander defender." Reducing all Jews to a common type, he stressed their liability to the colony, their undesirability. He spoke up for the Reverend, whose religious and ethnic pedigree made him trustworthy. "These are the kind of Afrikanders we want in the Colony," he continued, "if we had more 'Afrikander' and few[er] Hebrews of the Rothschild type, the Colony would be better off than it is." Spewing hate, he ranted that "few will be found to state [this fact] publicly," it was "nonetheless true that that the Jewish race has been one of the greatest curses to South Africa."[56]

Setting up British clergy against Jewish diamond field capitalists, the editor even contemplated violence as a viable response. "If a few of those slightly bloodthirsty peasants could be imported with a full cargo of prosecution from South Russia," he brooded, referring to the pogroms raging in the Russian Empire at this very time, "they would have gay times in Kimberley and the neighboring villages—and the Jews wouldn't. All [of] Houndsditch, Petticoat Lane and Seven Dials rolled into one," he averred, "could not produce such an aggregate of knavery and vice as the Hebrew fraternity of the Fields exhibit."[57]

Anti-Jewish hysteria heated up in times of tension, whether in minor, local quarrels or imperial war. The late nineteenth century was marked by profound demographic and economic changes affecting populations in the metropolis as well as in frontier communities. Large-scale immigration, industrialization, and urbanization exacerbated suspicion and loathing toward Others, reflected in anxieties voiced in respectable dailies such as the *Cape Times* or the *New York Times*.[58] Diamonds served as convenient symbols for social dysfunction. They connected Jewish capitalists at the sites of production to poor, dirty peddlers carrying on unregulated trade; the cosmopolitan IDB to the rootless immigrant who taught African runners to smuggle. Such contradictory representations of "the Jew" as both rich and poor, visible and undetectable, acculturated yet tribal, polished but still dirty persisted well into the next century, bequeathing a lexicon that Europe's fascists and murderous anti-Semites readily appropriated for their own purposes.

• • •

"Yer kin talk," said a philosopher of the East Side, "'bout it's bein' vulgar t' wear di'monds, but I notice that them that has 'em wears 'em."
—"The Other Side of Life," *Jeweler's Circular* (January 3, 1894)

Popular representations of Jews and diamonds in the United States were less politically charged. While plenty prejudiced, they eschewed the venom dripping from the pages of the colonial press. Jews and gems showed up in social critiques, primarily of Jewish climbers deemed too eager to display their "arrival" into the American elite. Jews wearing diamonds struck many observers as an indecent display of new money. It was not unusual to come across cartoons that ridiculed Jews for imitating proper American dress and behavior, betraying their inability to become true Americans. Portrayed as dandies, bejeweled Jewish men prance in front of "respectable" members of society, making fools of themselves. Diamonds in these illustrations symbolize wealth and ostentation, but also serve to maximize contrast. The purest gemstone known to man adorns a wannabe desperately trying to become white and refined, an unobtainable goal. A brilliant, so the insinuation went, could not outshine his Jewishness. *Puck* seized on stock images of Jewish men, picturing the obese, bow-legged capitalist with exaggerated features. By the 1890s he wore diamonds.

The American-Jewish suffragist and author Nina Morais raised the issue of stereotyping as early as 1881. The imagined Jew, she wrote, was "an objectionable character, whose shrewdness and questionable dealings in trade enable[d] him to wear large diamonds and flashy clothes." Raising his voice "beyond the fashionable key, in a language execrable to the ears of English-speaking people," he spent money "with an ostentation" that gave away his inelegance. "In a word, he is foreign—outlandish—a Jew . . . the one-all comprehensive charge."[59] Blaming both Christians and Jews for perpetuating the harmful image, Morais counseled less conspicuous conduct to decrease "social banishment."

Jewish women, too, came under fire for wearing diamond jewelry. In 1887, a contributor to the *New York Times* complained of Jewish wives at the oceanside resort of Long Branch, "swollen to almost bursting with self-importance, and armed to the teeth with diamonds," signaling a "sorrowful decline in character" of the local community.[60] The author, dubbing Long Branch the New Jerusalem," grumbled that the "English pure and undefiled

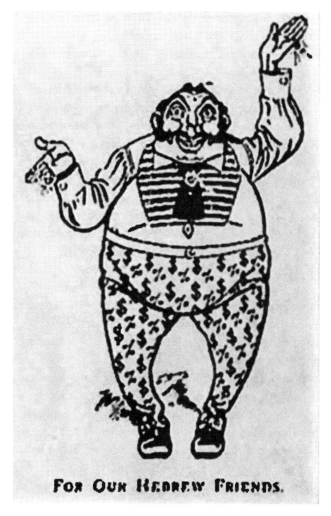

Figure 5.7 T. M. Honning, "Why Not Let the Apparel Proclaim the Man?" *Puck* (February 23, 1898).

has given way to a hideous patois." The editor of the *American Hebrew*, chastising the *Times* for fomenting prejudice in its columns, retorted that these women were "Americans in the same sense as the Presbyterians, Methodists, Episcopalians, and Catholics that live here," yet stigmatized Jews. While "[a]ttention has frequently been called to the ostentatious, frolicsomeness (that will do as a mild term) and the ballet-like bathing attire of ladies at Narragansett and Asbury Park," he continued, "we fail to recall that the newspapers made any reference to the religious persuasion of the sporting damsels." Flamboyance may have been an annoying feature of resort culture, but everyone in Long Branch participated in it, not just Jews. The real vulgarity on display, suggested the editor, was not the bejeweled Jewish woman, but the letter writer and his "pitiful exhibition of narrow-minded prejudice."[61]

Because the diamond served as an indicator of both personal wealth and moral worth, non-Jewish observers had difficulty harmonizing two seemingly opposite conceptions. To many Gentiles, Jews were morally impure and not fully white, so for them to wear the luminous symbol of purity and whiteness on their bodies was improper.[62] Purity was the prerogative of Christians, even in commodified form. As in Victorian Britain, where expert lapidaries "whitened" the Kohinoor, Jews may have been the aristocrats of diamond manufacturing and trade, but once gems were ready for ornamentation and consumption, they were expected to be handed to "refined people."[63]

In America then, too, well-to-do Jewish flashing diamonds risked public rebuke. The stereotype of the bejeweled Jewish parvenu, loud in utterances as well as appearance, came to personify excessive consumption and urban decadence. American Jews emulated the behavioral patterns and social aspirations of their peers. They adapted to abundance, finding new ways to display and cultivate a sense of belonging.[64] Yet accentuating belonging with sparkly gems could produce a counter result. Diamonds functioned differently than other consumer goods, drawing attention to the wearers' Jewishness, inviting envy and suspicion. Rather than reflecting adaptation, diamonds set them apart. Simmel's interpretation of adornment sheds light on such response patterns. Unlike any other object, he theorized, precious stones singled out the wearer, expanding egos and spheres of significance rather than equalizing them. Diamond necklaces, brooches, or earrings, shining brightly in the direction of the viewer, conveyed meanings that Gentiles were reluctant to accept, namely that Jews could belong to America's nobility of wealth.

Jews and diamonds assumed a greater presence in the American cultural imagination at a time of soaring immigration and rapid, hectic growth of cities that were profoundly transforming the nation. Associating Jews with conspicuous consumption gained currency in the years known as the Gilded Age, when Americans fretted over these massive changes. Labeled in the popular mind as urban, non-Christian, itinerant, and commercial, Jews served as receptacles for fears that white, middle-class Americans harbored regarding the rise of industrial capitalism and an ethnically diverse social order, anxieties that American Jewish elites internalized and shared.[65] Bejeweled Jews triggered all kinds of discomfort.

Sensitive to accusations of ostentatious materialism, the American Jewish press, like Nina Morais, urged modesty. As it became crystal clear that Jewish women fancied diamonds just as much as anybody else, the *American Israelite* complained about bedecked ladies out and about in public and advocated restraint to avoid being branded as "intolerably vulgar," tarnishing the image of moderation that American Jews had tried so diligently to cultivate. Internalizing anxiety about public criticism, the journal called on the "mothers and daughters in Israel to discourage" the practice of buying diamond engagement rings and to deposit the money that would otherwise be spent on a gem "in a good savings bank."[66] The *American Hebrew* concurred. In an effort to dissuade conspicuous extravagance, the weekly newspaper printed extracts from a Sunday sermon by Reverend Dr. Talmage on "Costume and Morals," protesting the worship and idolatry of "the goddess of fashion." Talmage portended that "the evil is terrific and overshadowing," blaming profligacy for creating a depraved society. "There are clerks in stores and banks on limited salaries," he thundered, "who in the vain attempt to keep the wardrobe of their family as showy as other folks' wardrobes, are dying of muffs and diamonds and camel's hair shawls and high hat. . . . The country is dressed to death."[67]

The minister's words fell on deaf ears. America's craving for diamond engagement rings, pins, earrings, tie clips, dress studs, and cuff links, worn to convey social class, had a moment of its own. An article titled "A Ladies' Column: The Persistent Diamond Earring" in the *American Israelite* conceded that for women, diamonds conveyed wealth and fashion; they could not resist them. "She *knows* that they are inappropriate," declared the author, "but stronger than mental conviction is the warm, secret feeling that, being expensive, they must be what she designates as 'swell.'" So Jewish women—all women—will "wear diamonds with shirt waists and mourning veils, with bicycle suits, cotton wrappers, and curl papers," on every occasion of life without a thought for fitness."[68] This indulgence, to be sure, was not the fault of women. "A woman would not care a jot for jewelry, were not the fond father or the admiring husband to press upon her gifts of diamonds . . . that she may outshine some other wife, or daughter, on whom luxuries have been heedlessly showered. If a woman dress extravagantly, it is because of man."[69]

• • •

"Mere carbon, my good friend, after all."
—Wilkie Collins, *The Moonstone*

Who but Barney Barnato, also known as "the modern Midas" and "a London street Arab," would so perfectly embody ambiguities toward Jews and diamonds?[70] A rags-to-riches story, Barnato's rise to fortune and fame drew admiration and scorn from contemporaries on three continents. Growing up in London's poorest neighborhood, the "Diamond King" became the poster boy for IDB, a self-interested entrepreneur who achieved success through legal and illegal dealing and by circumventing the law. A Randlord wealthy beyond imagination, Barnato never gained complete acceptance in the social circles in which he moved. Having left Whitechapel at age sixteen, he could not shed the stereotypes of East-European Jewish London. Variously described as scheming and vulgar—the very opposite of his Anglo-Saxon rival, Cecil Rhodes—he secured a seat in Cape Parliament, earning respect from his colleagues but still remaining racially suspect. The press never passed up an opportunity to point out that he was Jewish. In the public eye he remained "a queer character of rather hazy origins [who] acquired wealth as rapidly, almost as did Aladdin. The impress of youth spent in Whitechapel," reported the *Morning News*, "remained with him to the end—he was always Barney Isaacs, born and reared in that historic spot in London . . . always the sidewalk juggler, whose sleight of hand ability stood him in good stead in the manipulations and the 'rigging' of the stock market."[71]

The American mining engineer and future general manager of De Beers Gardner Williams attributed Barnato's success to his "racial genius for trade." The two titans in the diamond world, Barnato and Rhodes, could not be more different: "[t]he little, chunky, bullet-headed, near-sighted, mercurial Hebrew, taking a hand in current sport or traffic, and the tall, thoughtful, young overseer . . . fixing his blue eyes intently on his work." But Barnato had what it takes. "[A]nyone could see [sic] at a glance," said Williams, "that the young Hebrew was unsinkable, and peculiarly fitted to make a good living" on the South African diamond fields.[72] Rhodes, his racial opposite, far surpassed Barnato in ruthlessness, but his Anglican white background permitted a degree of exculpation unavailable to a Jewish Randlord.

Barnato's death was reported around the world. The *New York Times* remembered the "juggler and peddler of old clothes and pickles, who became a millionaire," as the "shrewdest of speculators."[73] The *Philadelphia Inquirer* commented on "his bold and unscrupulous methods, the ease with which he influenced European exchanges and caused them to rise or fall at his simple nod; the cold calculation with which he originated booms and organized companies and caused thousands of men and women to pour their money into his lap by the mere magic of his name." The writer felt obliged to add, "there can be no feeling of regret at his untimely death."[74] The *New York Tribune* and the *Evening Herald* similarly noted "the meteoric career of the South African multi-millionaire speculator," but could not help reminding readers that this "English Jew illustrated in an extraordinary way the financial genius of his race" and had "since 1894 controlled the English bank exchanges."[75]

No matter that he had moved from Petticoat Lane to Park Lane, from grime to glitter, Barnato would always be Eady's Solomon Davis, a shady diamond dealer. *Reynolds's Newspaper* in London featured two articles in the same edition, one paying tribute to "the story of his romantic life from old clothes dealer to millionaire," another vilifying the "swollen corpse of the miserable wretch fished up from the deep [sea]," a "money-grabber" who floated "schemes" and "never created or organized anything." Barnato, they concluded, "was the great typical man of the whole community, a swindler. . . . What a tragedy!"[76] Even the Jewish press was of two minds when telling readers that the man's untimely death had moved the Cape Assembly to adjourn and the stock exchanges in Cape Town and Johannesburg to close. The *Jewish Chronicle* wondered if "perhaps a little more reserve would have contributed to his happiness and peace of mind," suggesting that his swagger and "love of display" had taken a toll, while the *Jewish Messenger* dismissed and recognized him in the same notice, smugly asserting "his self-inflicted death calls for no special notice [as] he was the type of modern gambler in stocks [whose] name will be forgotten save to point to a moral and adorn a tale." Barnato "in his lifetime received no mention in these columns," and the *Jewish Messenger* saw no need to change that after his demise.[77]

Barnato's prominence in southern Africa's mineral revolution, the London Syndicate, and De Beers provided fodder for critics on the political Left even after he had departed the scene. British Marxists reviled the Diamond King and other Jewish financiers like him as examples of individuals bound by ties of race and blood who would stop at nothing, not even war, to maximize profit. That Barnato's single-mindedness was no different from his non-Jewish peers engaged in various industries, each partaking in the imperial project with the same degree of eagerness and go-for-brokeness at a time of profound economic and social change, escaped notice. In stories linking imperialism and "Jewish finance," it was not uncommon to hear the words "diamonds" and "financial serpents" mentioned in the same breath.[78] Cartoonists publishing in the Cape Colony sketched Jews with an uncanny resemblance to Barnato. To *Reynolds's Newspaper* he represented "the whole community," both imperial capitalists and Jews in general—perhaps explaining the Jewish press's inclination to distance itself from this complicated figure.

Figure C.1 *The San Francisco Sunday Call* (March 21, 1909).

Conclusion

> After a stone is set into jewelry, it is almost impossible to decipher who harvested the gem from the river shore, who carried it from the wilderness to the market, who cut it, who polished it, and who made the match between the stone and its setting. Once a diamond becomes a piece of jewelry, the fingerprints of all these people disappear.
> —Alicia Oltuski, *Precious Objects: A Story of Diamonds, Family, and a Way of Life* (2011)

On May 15, 1940, five days after the Nazi invasion of the Netherlands, Henri Polak drove by car to IJmuiden, a coastal town in the northwestern part of the country. He and his wife Milly tried to catch the ferry to England to escape the Nazi onslaught. Their adopted son Hans, a soldier in the Dutch army, had procured boat fares for his parents and wife Mitzi (Maria Polak-Feistl), a non-Jewish woman born in Germany. Once Polak arrived in IJmuiden, he caught glimpses of the last ferry leaving the harbor and carrying Dutch fugitives to safety. They had no choice but to return to Amsterdam.

Still a regular contributor to the *ANDB Weekly*, seventy-two-year-old Polak had sounded the alarm about National Socialism and its threat to democracy. He had scorned British Prime Minister Chamberlain's "peace for our time" declaration after his celebrated return from Munich in 1938. No peace, he warned. The era of fascist rule "had only just begun."[1] Polak confronted contemporaries in popular journals and newspapers speaking favorably of Germany or airing anti-Jewish sentiments. Yet there were signs that his initial panic, culminating in a hurried drive to IJmuiden, eased, especially when the first months of the occupation brought few changes to everyday life for Jews and non-Jews alike—a period Dutch historians refer to as *accommodatie*, adaptation to a new status quo. Hans had urged his parents to flee and Polak had packed his bags, but he also demurred, insisting that the Nazis "won't arrest an old man like me."[2] The former diamond union leader understood the threat of fascism; he did not grasp—could not have grasped—the genocidal violence unfolding in Europe targeting Jews like him, those nearing the end of their natural lives as well as those whose lives were just beginning.

One week after Polak's unsuccessful attempt to catch the ferry, his daughter-in-law committed suicide. In a fit of despair, Mitzi, "Aryan" and a German citizen, entered Polak's home (to which she had a key), opened a gas tap, and ended her life. Their neighbors, Isidore Keesing and his wife, attempted the same, but an alarmed family friend threw a brick through the kitchen window and fetched a doctor, saving their lives. The Jewish couple died three years later from gassing in a Nazi death camp. Having lost his daughter-in-law and unaware of his son's whereabouts, Polak wrote to a friend that he "was surrounded by sadness and mourning."[3]

On July 18, as he sat down for dinner, the doorbell rang. Two Nazi soldiers arrested the ANDB founder, charging him with "inciting hatred against Germany." Taken to the Huis van Bewaring, a detention center in Amsterdam, Polak would spend the next two years in solitary confinement. For a man of the people, whose life work consisted of organizing the proletariat and pushing through labor reform, whose boundless energy and convictions had changed the life of every diamond worker in the country, isolation in a holding cell was especially cruel. To occupy the time, Polak translated into Dutch, without the aid of a dictionary, *Of Men and Music* by the American composer Deems Taylor, as well as Clifford C. Furnas's hopeful American vision, *The Next Hundred Years: The Unfinished Business of Science*. He started writing a book about proper usage of the Dutch language, a lifelong obsession already discernible in his didactic "articles of thunder," published in the ANDB's weekly newspaper decades earlier.

Perhaps Polak, locked in his cell, spent time reflecting on his remarkable accomplishments in the world of diamonds and beyond. Starting out as a polisher in 1890, Polak joined the thousands of lapidaries working steam-powered diamond mills in loud and unhealthy factories. Under his leadership, nascent Socialist sentiments matured into a formidable labor movement, the first of its kind in Holland.[4] The ANDB secured a minimum wage, an eight-hour workday, and humane conditions inside factories, a campaign that left a permanent footprint on Dutch economic and political life.

A leader among trailblazers, Polak had built a labor union that, for many Amsterdam Jews, functioned as a secular alternative to synagogues and other religious institutions. The Dutch Diamond Workers' Union building became a place for members to congregate, listen to lectures, and enjoy companionship on a regular basis. Polak envisioned it as a place for *Bildung*, educating and elevating the working classes to dignified status. The library in Polak's *Burcht* (fortress) contained high literature and newspapers, including the ANDB weekly's long sermons on etiquette that encouraged union members to become more "cultured." The monumental structure, designed by one of Holland's most well-known architects, H. P. Berlage, bespoke rationalism and practicality, but also beauty and refinement. Its interior walls, decorated with a dozen large murals painted by Richard Roland Holst, exalted the accomplishments of labor performed by men and women in the industry. The poet Henriette "Jet" Roland Holst, nicknamed "Red Jet," wrote the accompanying texts. Union halls became places of belonging for Jews as Jews, but also as members of the Dutch labor class, as "native" Amsterdammers. Diamond unions in New York remained small by contrast, lacking the power in numbers that anchored the ANDB in the Dutch community.

In Amsterdam the stone brought together Jewish and Christian lapidaries in the mutual fight for improved working conditions. The ANDB's power came from unifying diamond laborers of all ethnic and religious backgrounds into a formidable political force. Union bylaws were purposefully nondenominational. Yet the union could not help but reflect the prevailing *verzuiling* ("pillarized") structure of Dutch society that separated Catholics, Protestants, Liberals, and Social-Democrats, inhibiting full integration and accommodating religious distinctiveness.[5] Jews worked in *Jodenfabrieken*, Jewish factories that operated on Sundays and closed on Friday evenings and Saturday for Shabbat. Christian factories, located outside of the Jewish neighborhood, kept mills running on Saturdays, but shut down on Sundays. Segregated spatially, Christian lapidaries also received different compensation. They typically cut and polished smaller diamonds while their Jewish colleagues specialized in larger stones. Jews earned higher salaries but were more likely to lose their jobs during economic downturns. Smaller stones being in greater demand, Jewish cutters and polishers were the first to be let go and therefore more amenable to relocating to manufacturing centers outside Europe, such as New York City. The ANDB's success is even more impressive considering the levels of separation—religious, communal, spatial—that demarcated Jewish from Gentile craftsmen. Polak and Jan van Zutphen, his Christian colleague, were able to convince diamond workers that mutual benefit and shared

Figure C.2 Richard Roland Holst, "Carrying Hope in One's Heart Brightens a Dark World" (1900–1907). Mural in ANDB Building, Amsterdam.

ideological solidarity trumped ethnic differences. United, they could prevail. This degree of collaboration was atypical for nineteenth-century Jewish labor movements in Europe and America, organized almost exclusively by Yiddish speakers into ethnically homogeneous organizations.

Perhaps Polak, confined in the city of his birth, marveled over the road that the ANDB had helped pave for Jewish women. Female cutters, inspired by the union's success and seeing themselves as workers, became active in the cause. Betje and Sophie Lazarus, for example, both rose cutters, were dynamos in the drive to unionize their sisters. The Lazarus siblings had shared the progressive views of union men but faced staunch conservatism when insisting the same reforms be applied to lapidaries of the opposite sex. Joining the fight, they founded the Rose Cutters Union (RSSV) in 1896, in the face of aggressive skepticism from men and women alike. In 1900, the RSSV scored a huge victory: a minimum wage for women workers that drew in hundreds of new members.[6] Demanding recognition, the Lazarus sisters affirmed that women were an integral part of the international diamond industry. Women pushed hand-driven polishing mills in the early 1700s, smuggled rough stones in their brassieres and petticoats on the African diamond fields, and organized strikes in Amsterdam, calling for equality.[7]

◆ ◆ ◆

Polak awaited his fate in a cold cell. A diary entry from New Year's Eve describes 1940 as a "disastrous year that brought darkness on the world [and] slavery to my fatherland; it has destroyed everything that is essential for a life worth living: freedom, humanity, and justice."[8]

Sir Ernest Oppenheimer, with whom Polak had corresponded on the matter of diamond manufacturing in South Africa, had no inkling of what was going on at the Huis van Bewaring. Operating in a different hemisphere, Oppenheimer had become chairman of De Beers in 1929. A German-Jewish immigrant, he had started out as a diamond sorter with Dünkelsbühler & Co. at the age of seventeen; now he stood at the helm of a corporation that controlled nearly 95 percent of the global trade in rough diamonds, set prices, and regulated distribution. Oppenheimer had been mayor of Kimberley and founder of the Anglo-American Corporation with £100,000,000 investment from J.P. Morgan & Company of New York to exploit gold reefs in the Witwatersrand. The British Government had knighted him for his contributions to the British way of life. Wildly successful and politically ambitious, Oppenheimer was elected to the House of Assembly as the Member for Kimberley, a seat he held until the late 1930s. While Polak, distressed by the rise of fascism in Europe, penned letters to newspaper editors, Oppenheimer reached the pinnacle of his career, chairing one of the most powerful cartels in modern history.

Unfazed by the clouds darkening over Europe, Oppenheimer had sent his son Harry to New York City to convene with board members of the advertisement agency, N. W. Ayer & Co. Only weeks before Germany marched into Poland, De Beers hired Ayer to start an advertisement campaign aimed at American customers. During the war, when Nazi soldiers rang Polak's doorbell and Jewish lapidaries were under threat of deportation to Nazi concentration camps, De Beers sanctioned the purchase of sparkling gems by launching the "Fighting Diamonds" campaign, joining gemstones to American patriotism and luxury consumerism.[9] Buying diamonds, assured the ad, supported the war effort.

Oppenheimer understood the power of advertising and display. De Beers had familiarized the public with African diamonds for decades, fanning popular demand among those with money to spend. International Exhibitions in the capitals of Europe and America had heightened the allure of the stone by staging intricate replica mines, inviting visitors to participate in the process of washing debris. At the 1893 Chicago World's Columbian Exposition, for example, De Beers put up a large mineral exhibit, a visual spectacle of the commodity chain that showed the evolution of mining. Over the course of six months, twenty-seven million fairgoers had watched industry and empire in action. The mineral exhibit featured deep-level mining and diamond sorting as well as cutting and jewelry making. The commissioner for the Cape Colony had requested no less than 10,000 feet of exhibition space during the planning phase, aiming to mount a fully functioning cross-section of a Kimberley mine to demonstrate the entire excavation process. Two thousand tons of diamondiferous soil, yielding an estimated two carats per ton, would be shipped from the northern Cape to Chicago, to be worked by "native Zulus . . . in the charge of an overseer." While the exhibitions in London and Paris had shown only a handful of "live specimens" of "native labor," the Chicago Exposition promised at least a dozen.[10] The Fair had offered jewelry exhibits, some with multimillion dollar diamonds in glass cases, but "not one of them," reported the *Chicago Daily Tribune*, "is so closely watched as this great pile of dirt." Imported from the African diamond fields, the 1,200 bags of soil had been safeguarded by "three native Zulus who live in the enclosure in a Kaffir hut erected by themselves."[11]

The Cape Colony had overreached with its original proposal and had to reduce the volume of imported soil to 150 tons, valued at $250,000.[12] It proved impossible to dump the massive pile of dirt in the middle of the mining display, so it was housed instead in an enclosure in Jackson Park, some 500 yards from the mining exhibit. Iron buckets attached to an overhead metal wire hauled blue ground from Jackson Park directly into the Mining Building, continuously supplying the replica-mine with "virgin diamondiferous ground." Courting the uninitiated, De Beers knew full well that the exhibition would "draw a great many people who have read all about the production of diamonds but have never had an opportunity of witnessing the operation," and that infatuation translated into demand.[13] Wedged in between displays by Mexico and Brazil, the Cape Colony exhibit proved highly successful, the "center of attention," the *Official Guide* claimed, inviting spectators to observe the mining process and browse through the diamond machinery hall, the mineral room, and the reception room, "where files of South African papers and books of reference are kept for visitors." Behind plate glass, they could watch cutters and polishers "turn rough diamonds into dazzling brilliants." As in London, Jewish predominance in diamond trading and manufacturing went largely unnoticed; official guides and press releases referred to "skilled workmen." It was the African worker, the "gigantic Zulus," who drew attention, adding the aura of a distant foreign country to the whole undertaking.

America's appetite for gems began to soar. One contemporary keenly observed that the 1890s "may indeed be called the golden age of diamonds, for these jewels have never been distributed so generally throughout the world and particularly in the United States, where their use is so common as to be almost universal." It was no surprise, she continued with an air of intoxication, for "what in the long list of precious stones more delights the eye of a lover of jewels than a pure, sparkling gem of the first water, rivaling in splendor and brilliancy the morning dewdrops which tip the tiny blades of grass or the glory of winter's icy down sparkling at the gentle touch of the cold morning sun?"[14] Everyone wanted these carbon dewdrops imbued with elegant mystique, even if it meant going into debt or ordering them through a mail-order catalog.

The U.S. government took note. "In the past twenty years," stated a Secretary of the Interior Report in 1896, "Africa has produced £70,000,000 [$350,000,000] worth of diamonds and the world has absorbed them all."[15] In its most concentrated, portable, and ornamental form, the precious stone built up cities, created industries in southern Africa, Europe, and America, and provided livelihoods to tens of thousands of families. But the stone cast dark shadows in the process. As one of the early sites of modern and unforgiving industrial capitalism, the diamond fields witnessed the introduction of discriminatory legislation that excluded black African ownership and obstructed the shared use of resources. These laws, soon to be replicated on the Witwatersrand's gold fields, would serve as models in South Africa at large for the cruel system of Apartheid, first officially enacted in Kimberley in the 1870s.[16] Diamond manufacturing made a small group of people—like Ernest Oppenheimer—very wealthy and a larger group comfortable, but kept the majority hunched over a mill or deep down in a mine for long hours each day, every day, at wages that precluded savings and transmission of generational wealth. Unemployment in times of economic crisis, often induced by fiscal or political decisions made thousands of miles away, caused widespread misery.[17] Under the diktat of a powerful monopoly, diamond workers at various points of the commodity chain were vulnerable

Figure C.3 "A Diamond Mining Display," in Hubert Howe Bancroft's *The Book of the Fair* (Chicago: The Bancroft Company, 1893).

to exploitation and the first to suffer during disruptions. Black Africans, beholden to low-wage jobs, were subjected to the abuses of imperial capitalism, denied rights and protections, that Jews, perceived as white, did not face.

South African society was not immune to the poison of antisemitism, but the primary Other was black, not Jewish. Racism had produced closed compounds, denied black ownership of mines, and driven segregation—a modus operandi that did not target men like Oppenheimer, even when prejudices about Jews intensified in times of crisis.

In Europe, as hatred toward Jews turned genocidal, De Beers advertised diamonds in 1942 as "precious helpmates" to the war effort, encouraging Americans to splurge at the very moment that Nazis were gathering Jewish gem dealers at the Amsterdam Diamond Exchange and forcing them to hand over their inventories, a total of 71,000 carats.[18] Jewish cutters and polishers, initially exempt from deportation to continue manufacturing, were sent to their deaths at Sobibor and Auschwitz. By 1947, when De Beers launched its most successful advertising campaign, two-thirds of Europe's Jews and four-fifths of Dutch-Jewish lapidaries had been murdered.

The Nazis dealt the final blow to the Amsterdam industry, decimating the Jewish population and leaving *diamantstad*, the city of diamonds, a shadow of its former self. Only a handful of ANDB members returned to silenced factory floors after the war. Henri Polak, "the rebbe of the diamond workers," was dead. He succumbed to pneumonia in 1943, only weeks before his wife was deported to Westerbork, a waystation to Auschwitz.[19] Efforts to revive both industry and union were hopeless. The devastating human losses could not be overcome. Competition from abroad made it difficult to attract investment and professional uncertainties drove away younger generations who did not look back. In 1958 the ANDB ceased to be independent and was subsumed by the Dutch Metal Workers' Union.

◆ ◆ ◆

Few objects have received the degree of scrutiny and appraisal that diamonds have in preparation for life as an accessory, drawing upon many of mankind's capabilities: science, industry, art, commerce, and culture. The journey of a nineteenth-century diamond, from mine to market, spanned continents and involved countless hands—those of miners, appraisers, and mail carriers, as well as cutters, polishers, jewelry makers, retailers, and of course, customers. While they were sometimes left as rough stones to pay for a meal or snagged from a mailbag by a thief, most often they were carefully sorted and wrapped in paper envelopes, sent across the Karoo and the high seas, only to see daylight again on office desks in London. From there, they gained luminosity and sparkle on polishing mills in Amsterdam, the premier diamond manufacturing center of *belle époque* Europe. Thousands of lapidaries spent their days setting individual gems in hot, softened lead to add dozens of facets to the surface—workmanship that depended on "the delicacy and accuracy of eyesight and touch."[20] Lapidary experts knew, in the words of a contemporary cleaver, "the structure of a diamond far more intimately than a physician that of the human body."[21] Some diamonds became famous and spent their existence as the centerpieces in crown jewels or on display in museums, feeding the imagination of authors of criminal detective stories. Many more ended up in engagement rings displayed in jewelry cases and shop windows, awaiting eager buyers in need of an incentive to convince their ladies to say "I do!"

The transatlantic commodity chain in diamonds demonstrates what historians Catherine Hall and Sonya Rose called "connections across empires, the webs and networks operat[ing] between colonies, and the significance of centres of power outside of the metropole."[22] Over the last two decades the traditional binary between center and periphery, between an all-powerful economic nucleus imposing its will on subdued colonies, has shifted to an understanding of multidirectional flows of knowledge, capital, and people. The diamond trade is a case in point. It reveals how social networks operated in building the early transatlantic trade in gems, bringing into contact digging settlements on the Fields of South Africa, port cities, and commodity markets in Europe and America, integrating local, regional, and transnational economies. In fact, the first financial investments in diamond mining came not from London and the mother country, but from local, Cape-based entrepreneurs who saw an opportunity to add a lucrative item to their export and import businesses.

The foundations of the nineteenth-century diamond trade were laid by immigrants in contact with relatives in Europe. Each geographical center shaped the realities of the other. The jobs and income levels of Dutch lapidaries depended on output in Kimberley; the struggles of New York manufacturers were a direct consequence of London Syndicate monopoly practices. Local decision-making and innovation shaped global demand.

Jewish commercial connections, familial or intracommunal, were key. The diamond trade thrived where mercantile relationships had already flourished, allowing diamonds to move through existing imperial channels. When a new opportunity presented itself on the diamond fields in the early 1870s, Jewish merchants already enjoyed close commercial ties across oceans that weren't readily available to others. Starting a business in the interior of southern Africa, not yet integrated into regional, let alone transatlantic, economies was risky—but less so for Jews than for Gentiles. Having a merchant uncle in Port Elizabeth or London willing to invest in deep-level mining, or a cousin managing the family bank in Paris, facilitated loans for Jewish-owned companies and eased the incorporation of precious stones into global commercial channels. Alfred Beit, Sammy Marks, Barney Barnato, Jules Porgès, and the Mosenthals could rely on trustworthy contacts in African port cities and Europe to provide resources and function as receiving ends of the rough gems' journey. This diasporic ethnic system bridged city and countryside, metropole and colony, advancing Europe's imperial presence in Africa. Aided by new technologies—from imported water pumps and pulsators to transatlantic steamboats and registered postal services—Jews helped build "Diamondville," extending empire into the South African heartland while moving its mineral riches to London for distribution.

Jews played formative roles in manufacturing as well, in Europe and in America. European Jewish lapidaries had already found a niche as gem cutters during the early modern period, most notably in bustling urban centers such as Amsterdam and London, home ports for East India ships carrying precious cargo from Brazil and India. Passed on for generations, diamond cutting and polishing became a specialty that produced a desirable accessory in perpetual demand. In tumultuous times, Dutch-Jewish gem experts emigrated to new centers with high consumption to start over—a transfer of craftsmen, skills, and technology from Amsterdam to New York

City, often misconstrued in histories of Jewish commerce as activity on the margins of innovation and business enterprise. In reality, these Jewish workers played formative roles in the early stages of the mineral trade and its growth into a global industry, a development encouraged by popular cravings for luxury goods and a seemingly endless supply of rough stones.

Outside the immediate orbit of commerce, diamonds influenced urban planning, spawned labor movements, manipulated spending habits, colored stereotypes about Jews, and drove patterns of migration. In the span of only a few years, tens of thousands of people from dozens of different nationalities, ethnicities, and tribal affiliations migrated to the Northern Cape, pitching tents far from home in dry and dusty soil. The term "diamond fields" exerted enormous magnetism, enthralling the press and the popular imagination, prompting people near and far to relocate. A steady stream of hopefuls circulated in new contact zones, building a city that literally stood on top of its raison d'être and that served only one purpose: to find precious stones. By 1876 Kimberley had become the largest diamond source for coastal merchants, its yield surpassing in value traditional South African goods, such as wool.[23] Pulsing with diamond fever, Kimberley was the first place in the Southern Hemisphere to introduce electricity because the mineral industry required it. Carbon stones sparked the construction of railroads to expedite the transport of goods and mining equipment arriving in port cities hundreds of miles away. Legions of men quite literally moved the earth to find diamonds—close to twenty million tons of Cape earth had been excavated by the turn of the century, all of it sifted, pulsated, and washed to extract rough stones. Innumerable holes were dug to erect telegraph poles, connecting the Fields to the coast and beyond. When the civil commissioner of Kimberley, R. W. H. Giddy, sent "[c]ordial greetings and best wishes from the Diamond Fields" over the first telegraphic message in 1876, could he have imagined the economic implications of "the link that now unites us"?[24]

Diamonds continued to stimulate urban development in the Northern Cape. Kimberley settlers built schools, theaters, tailor shops, banks, hotels, five churches, and a synagogue. "It is a fact," lectured William Morton at the American Geographical Society of New York in 1878, having just returned from southern Africa, "that the milliners of Capetown, notably a gay city, reserve their best ball dresses, laces, and other goods, for the ladies at the diamond-field market."[25] Where diamonds were found aplenty, new money and energy flowed. Morton had marveled at the sight of Kimberley, a restless town where none had stood a decade earlier, reminding his listeners that every piece of timber, every sheet of iron to build homes, as well as every item of their interiors—furniture, billiard tables, pianos, utensils—had been "dragged on ox-wagons from the sea-coast up over the weary desert."

Already in 1877, on a visit to the diamond fields, Anthony Trollope observed that "[t]he sudden influx of national wealth has come from the capability for consumption created by the new industry." It was "not the wealth found [that] directly enriches the nation," he wrote, "but the trade created by the finding."[26] Cape populations, in constant need of equipment and produce from Europe, North America, and Asia, consumed at ever higher levels. In 1900, the Cape Colony imported over 2.2 million pounds worth of dynamite, 1.2 million pounds of "haberdashery," and over a million gallons of ale—all of it taxed for imperial coffers.[27] As railway lines reached further into the interior, goods could be sent and received at greater speed and in larger volumes. Colonial statistical records indicate substantial revenues from postage, railways, and telegraphs, services the diamond industry had required and propelled. Diamonds transformed the size and potential of the Cape economy, shining, literally and figuratively, as a brilliant asset in the British Empire's crown.

◆ ◆ ◆

"Diamonds Are Forever" and "Diamonds Are A Girl's Best Friend" are iconic slogans to modern consumers. What is a marriage proposal without a diamond ring? The basis for its desirability and charisma, and the conviction that diamonds are rare, are firmly rooted in the nineteenth century. As first-hand accounts of the Kimberley diamond fields flowed into Europe and America along with the stones themselves, and as museums, department store windows, and magazines displayed sparkling minerals, audiences were sold.

In 1911, the American author Wallis Richard Cattelle observed that "in twenty-five years the diamond did more to build a new empire, than the pioneers of the most vigorous and tenacious races the earth has ever known succeeded in doing in over three hundred years." He expressed astonishment at the gem's capacity to kindle engineering skills, scientific research, and commerce. Oblivious to its human and environmental costs, and examining the diamond trade through a racial lens, Cattelle saw only positive outcomes, praising its "civilizing" potential. "By its magic," he maintained, "hitherto almost inaccessible stretches of the earth have been added to the habitable world, thousands of savages are brought to a better understanding of life and made amenable to the laws of civilization, and as the previous pebbles pass from one to another until they bring delight to the final possessor, from the Hottentot laborer in the compound, to the fair hand of plighted troth, they leave in the passing a betterment of conditions to all."[28] His description of rough stones transforming into polished brilliants, progressing from black to fair hands, echoes Victorian exhibition narratives: gems originating from the "dark continent" turned pure white as they traveled through imperial channels to the West.

Unlike his Victorian contemporaries, Cattelle attempted to explain the preponderance of "Hebrews" in the profession, especially in New York City. "Most of the men of whom the Jewish firms are composed, are of foreign birth," he noted, "whose home training and connections had familiarized them with the trade and industry at the source of supply." Their "European training and connections" played a part, but so did Jews' "almost instinctive understanding of the principles of finance," "quick recognition of merit in those who serve him," and enjoyment of a duel. Jews were not in it for money alone, he reckoned, but "to win in the battle of wits."[29] Cattelle's study of gems—he wrote several books on diamonds and pearls—were sincere efforts to understand their provenance and allure. A white man of his time, he credited racial qualities—African "savages" and a Jewish essence—as explanations for what were in reality historical processes. Jews were successful not because they were Jews, but because they were well positioned to take advantage of opportunities they encountered in the 1870s and 1880s. Occupational experience, networks of relatives and trading partners, and access to credit gave them an edge, and the syncing of supply and demand in new markets paid dividends when the mineral frontier opened to anyone who showed up on South African soil. Cooperation with relatives and coreligionists reduced risks when doing business in the far reaches of the British Empire.

It would be erroneous to assume that Jews in the diamond business were always successful. Familial connections came with obligations and carried their own risks. Coming from the same place and worshipping in the same building was no assurance of trustworthiness; a relative's misdeeds could damage reputations.[30] Jewish members of the London Syndicate showed little empathy to unemployed coreligionists across the English Channel; Alfred Beit did not hesitate to testify against his rival's nephew in a court of law during an IDB trial; Henri Polak habitually published blacklists of Dutch-Jewish lapidaries delinquent on union dues, exposing their "irresponsibility." Fostering ethnic solidarity was not the objective in this business, although it could be mutually beneficial at opportune times. Most mineral merchants and lapidaries were unconcerned about religious or ethnic identity. Their Jewishness mattered much more to Christian observers than it ever did to Jews themselves. As far as we know, Barnato, Marks, Beit, and others never discussed it. It was their Gentile contemporaries who drew attention to their backgrounds, marking them as "Other" and folding gems and Jews into already existing popular narratives.

Jews were not the only group to benefit from nineteenth-century frontier commerce, nor was the diamond business ever an exclusively Jewish pursuit. Although distribution moved firmly in Jewish hands in the 1880s, the inclusion of non-Jews in deep-level mining, manufacturing, and retail paints a picture of an ethnically diverse industry. Jews were, however, prominent in the field, especially considering their small numbers in the overall populations of southern Africa, northern Europe, and America. In Jewish communities, established as well as frontier ones, diamonds provided opportunities and sustenance to thousands of families.

Ultimately, Jews in the diamond industry behaved like their compatriots in other commodity trades. Jewish immigrant entrepreneurs in the nineteenth-century textile industry took advantage of ethnic business networks and changing consumer markets.[31] By the turn of the century, the lion's share of American ready-made clothing came from Jewish-owned textile companies. American Jewish immigrants gained a foothold in the business, clearing a path to prosperity for their offspring. Analogous to the experience of American Jews in textiles, the success of Jews in the diamond industry sprouted not from commercial genius or Jewish "essence," but from the confluence of structural forces in the transatlantic market. These included the positioning of Jewish entrepreneurs on the edges and then at the center of the unfolding industry, and by ethnic cooperation to ambitious individuals in the field. Many Jews, whether cutting clothes or gemstones, worked long hours in noisy factories for little pay, enduring periods of unemployment and uncertainty, but collectively and in the long run, they helped build an industry that sustained Jewish families around the world.

Tracing "the work of the Jew" in southern Africa, the *Jewish Chronicle* took pride in "show[ing], upon historical grounds, that he has contributed, powerfully and richly contributed, towards the political, industrial, commercial and economic progress of every portion of the King's dominions in these regions."[32] It was a mutually beneficial relationship: Jews had been good to Great Britain while the empire, in turn, provided unprecedented opportunities for Jews.[33] Diamonds had allied them into a fruitful union. "Kimberley has been mainly built up by Jews," puffed the *Chronicle*, "nor could Rhodes have effected his amalgamation without Beit and Barnato."[34] Even Henri Polak, although sharply critical of mineral magnates, agreed that the diamond business "offered economic pioneers near virgin-like territory to explore," where men and women could become skilled "in all aspects of this most remarkable profession."[35]

Ornamental diamonds, as they so brilliantly demonstrate, do more than unite two lovers in a relationship; they bind us to entire communities of people and to skilled individuals who have left fingerprints along the way. Despite the intimacy we share with a diamond as it touches our skin, radiating promises of eternal love, and despite the financial sacrifices that buyers are willing to make, we rarely ask questions about the stone's long journey. Perhaps we don't always want to know the details of an object of desire, especially if the full story might dim its luster and incandescence. But what if the story might also add to its illustriousness? Carbon gemstones, excavated from great depths in the earth and crossing continents, built labor movements and political parties, inspired consumer revolutions and launched countless marriages, financed and provided philosophical justification for empires, and brought a Jewish proletariat and ownership class onto the world stage. Their facets, complex and radiant, expose where Jewish and imperial histories intersect, each field requiring the attention of the other, and together revealing how the modern world was made.

ACKNOWLEDGMENTS

Writing a work of history is difficult, but acknowledging the many people who have helped me along the way is most certainly not. Mining archives for source materials took me to various cities on three continents, and in each place I enjoyed the assistance and expertise of countless archivists and librarians. Colleagues read chapters and manuscript drafts, providing useful feedback that added weight to arguments and sparkle to prose. Family and friends offered unconditional love and support, even if they didn't always share my infatuation with carbon. Much of this book centers on professional, social, and familial networks. I wouldn't have been able to complete *A Brilliant Commodity* without my own.

Several institutions offered generous support over the years. The University of South Carolina's College of Arts and Sciences awarded a Humanities Grant, as well as an Advanced Support for Innovative Research Excellence (ASPIRE) Grant, making it possible to collect materials in South Africa and the Netherlands. UofSC's Digital Research Services and Collections provided assistance as well. Without Kate Boyd and Rhea Ray's masterful skills, many images in this book would never have seen the light of day. The Hadassah Brandeis Research Award, the Memorial Foundation for Jewish Culture Research Fellowship, and a Franklin Grant from the American Philosophical Society supported various research visits across the globe. The Walker Institute of International and Area Studies at the University of South Carolina provided a Faculty Research Award to spend time at the New York Public Library. I am grateful for their generosity and commitment to historical scholarship.

The Netherlands Institute for Advanced Study (NIAS) in the Humanities and Social Sciences created an intellectual haven for the 2017–18 academic year. Nurturing interdisciplinary research, the NIAS allowed for an extended period of collecting data, reading, and writing. Being a Fellow-in-Residence in the heart of Amsterdam, with an office around the corner from one of the largest (repurposed) diamond factories in the city, was almost too good to be true. I learned a great deal from being in the stimulating company of NIAS scholars. Jeremy Stolow, Preeti Chopra, Remco Raben, Roxane Farmanfarmaian, and Joe Bauman, coming from different fields of expertise, posed challenging questions and offered useful perspectives. Their keen insights, encouragement, and humor kept me going when the topic of diamonds and empire seemed too rich to grasp.

Joe and Robin Bauman opened up their beautiful home in New York City and together we searched for the addresses of former diamond factories in lower Manhattan. Our digging produced mixed results, but roaming the city with an old-fashioned paper map, staring up at façades, was just plain fun. Their excitement made me realize that this book could reach wider audiences intrigued by the connections between diamonds and Jews. I'm grateful for their hospitality and warmth.

I have presented portions of this work in various settings, including the Kaplan Centre for Jewish Studies at the University of Cape Town, the Center for European Studies at Harvard University, the Jewish Genealogical Society at Hebrew College in Boston, the "Contact Day" at the University of Antwerp, and the Yaschik/Arnold Jewish Studies Center at the College of Charleston. These meetings were fruitful, generating lively debate and thoughtful commentary. I thank those who sharpened my focus and shared their family stories.

I have enjoyed working with my editor at Oxford University Press, Susan Ferber, who has been prompt and professional from the moment we were introduced. She believed in this project, in its ambition and scope. After years of archival research and writing—sometimes a lonely enterprise—it was exhilarating to find a good home for this book. I am grateful for her guidance, unreserved enthusiasm, and editorial expertise. Production editor Sarah Green came on board in the last inning and helped prepare the final manuscript for publication.

Colleagues and friends have been invaluable. Kara Brown and Doyle Stevick: your perpetual optimism and smiles are unmatched. Green egg barbeque master David Fuente and Payal Shah: your kindness, boundless energy, and down to earth approach to life are inspirational—I'm so fortunate to have you as friends. Carol Harrison, donut-maker *extraordinaire*, and Tom Brown: I cherish our friendship inside and outside of Gambrell Hall. Bob Cox, Todd Endelman (for his long-standing support and mentorship), Richard Cohen, Gene Avrutin, Lou Fontana and Ginny Williamson, Bre Grace, Josh Grace, Emil Kerenji, Dawn Skorczewski, Allison Marsh, Adam Mendelsohn, Tom Lekan, Andrew Berns, Mark Smith, Karin Hofmeester, Federica Schoeman, and Bob Ellis: thank you all.

My Dutch musketeer buddies, Harriet Luijendijk-Jungerius and Anette van Sandwijk: we've shared a "triangular diary," written in longhand and sent by snail mail across the Atlantic, for more than a decade. *Wie heeft 't schriftje*? Krista van Vleit, thank you for feeding me delicious meals countless times. I owe you gallons of gin. Jenna Weissman Joselit: I'm so grateful for your enthusiasm and brilliance—you asked all the right questions. I hope I've been able to answer some of them! Sheila Rae Morris, Teresa Williams, and your house of sugar: what would Finn and I do without you? Sheri Robinson: our weekly tennis has kept me sane, especially when everything else in the world screamed insanity.

All of you are diamonds of the first water.

I am deeply indebted to my most careful and loyal reader, Ted Rosengarten. This book would be infinitely duller without his astute commentary and careful polishing of my prose. He has taught me invaluable lessons, not merely about writing and history, but about what's important in life. He has shown me my strengths and weaknesses, always encouraging me to have more faith in my own abilities as a scholar. I have also learned how to cast a fishing net (sort of), pick up a blue crab without getting pinched, and spot pods of dolphins in South Carolina's intercoastal waterways. Ted truly is the crown jewel. Dale Rosengarten: you give the best hugs when I walk into your beautiful home. Thank you for your big heart, love, and support.

And finally, my family. My parents, all four of them, showed unfailing support from thousands of miles away. Due to the pandemic we couldn't see each other for nearly two years, even when one of our loved ones spent five weeks on a respirator and in a coma due to Covid-19. I literally stood with my feet in the Atlantic Ocean, staring in the direction of Europe, unable to board a plane. I miss you all dearly and hope to hug you soon. As for David: what to say? I don't really have the words. This book is dedicated to our son, Finn, the light of our life. Always.

NOTES

INTRODUCTION

1. Whereas four companies operated approximately 850 steam-powered polishing mills in 1870, by the late 1880s this number had increased to 70 companies with 7,500 diamond mills. See Rein van der Wiel, *Van Rapenburgerstraat naar Amerika: De levenstijd van diamantbewerker en kunstverzamelaar Andries van Wezel* (Zwolle: Waanders, 2010), 28; Wietske van Agtmaal, "Het Diamantvak in Amsterdam: Van Oudsher een Joodse Negotie," in Hetty Berg, Thera Wijsenbeek, and Eric Fischer, eds., *Venter, fabriqueur, fabrikant: Joodse ondernemers en ondernemingen in Nederland 1796–1940* (Amsterdam: Joods Historisch Museum, 1994), 114–129; Salvador Bloemgarten, *Henri Polak: Sociaal democraat 1868–1943* (The Hague: SDU, 1993).

2. For a history of the diamond trade before the nineteenth-century, see among others Godehard Lenzen, *The History of Diamond Production and the Diamond Trade* (New York: Praeger Publishers, 1970); Gedalia Yogev, *Diamonds and Coral: Anglo-Dutch Jews and Eighteenth-Century Trade* (New York: Holmes & Meier, 1978); Tijl Vanneste, *Global Trade and Commercial Networks: Eighteenth-Century Diamond Merchants* (London: Pickering & Chatto, 2011), 41–66; S. Tolansky, *The History and Use of the Diamond* (London: Shenval Press, 1962); Karin Hofmeester, "Shifting Trajectories of Diamond Processing: From India to Europe and Back, From the Fifteenth Century to the Twentieth," *Journal of Global History* 8: 1 (2013), 25–49; Hofmeester, ed., *Een schitterende erfenis: 125 jaar nalatenschap van de Algemene Nederlandse Diamantbewerkersbond* (Zutphen: Walburg Pers, 2019); Todd Cleveland, *Stones of Contention: A History of Africa's Diamonds* (Athens: Ohio University Press, 2003), 19–38; Marcia Pointon, *Rocks, Ice and Dirty Stones: Diamond Histories* (London: Reaktion Books, 2017). Salomon van Wezel moved to the Oude Zijdse Achterburgwal, a street located in the heart of the city.

3. Ethan Katz, Lisa Moses Leff, and Maud Mandel offer a useful historiographical overview in their thought-provoking book *Colonialism and the Jews* (Bloomington: Indiana University Press, 2017), 1. They pose the questions: "Where are the Jews in colonial history? Where is imperialism in Jewish history?" Their edited volume was the outcome of a workshop centered on "Jewish History after the Imperial Turn: French and Comparative Perspectives," sponsored by Brown University. Ten years ago, David Feldman already lamented that "historians have barely touched on the subject [of Jews and empire]." See David Feldman, "Jews and the British Empire c. 1900," *History Workshop Journal* 63 (2007), 70. Literary scholars have been more successful in showing the presence of empire in representations of Jews: Bryan Cheyette, *Constructions of "the Jew" in*

English Literature 1875–1920 (Cambridge: Cambridge University Press, 1993), 55–94; Adrienne Munich, "Jews and Jewels: A Symbolic Economy on the South African Diamond Fields," in Eitan Bar-Yosef and Nadia Valman, eds., *The Jew in Later Victorian and Edwardian Culture: Between the East End and East Africa* (New York: Palgrave Macmillan, 2009), 28–44.

4. Gary Wilder observed that many of these nation-states were also empires, or as Wilder says, "imperial nation-states." To separate the metropole from the colonies would sever two close ties and create artificial models of analysis. Countries like France, for example, embraced not only universalism but also particularism; not only an ideology of equality but also an ideology of inequality predicated on racial and religious difference; not only liberalism but also, and no less fundamentally, illiberalism. "The paradox of simultaneously embracing two contradictory sets of ideas is not resolved by assigning one set to the empire and the other to the metropolis; in fact, both tendencies within French political culture were present in both settings." A similar point can be made about other imperial nation-states, such as Great Britain and the Netherlands. Gary Wilder, *The French Imperial Nation-State: Negritude and Colonial Humanism between the Two World Wars* (Chicago: University of Chicago Press, 2005).

5. Brian Roberts, *The Diamond Magnates* (London: Hamilton, 1972), 159.

6. Lionel Phillips contributed to the failed Jameson Raid, an attempt to overthrow Paul Kruger's South African (Transvaal) Republic in January 1896. Phillips initially received the death sentence, a punishment commuted to a £25,000 fine, banishment, and public embarrassment. Phillips, sent to London by Kruger to be tried by a Crown court, returned after the Boer War to South Africa, where he rebuilt his career and reputation.

7. Henning Albrecht, *Alfred Beit: The Hamburg Diamond King* (Hamburg: Hamburgische Wissenschaftliche Stiftung, 2012), 67: "No more than 10 companies dominated the development and exploitation of the gold fields of the Eastern Transvaal in the mid-1890s: Barnato Bros, Lewis & Marks, the Rhodes' Group, J. B. Robinson, the Farrar group (Anglo-French Exploration Co.), A. Goerz & Co., Abe Baily, G. & L. Albu and S. Neumann & Co, Wernher, Beit & Co. (the successor of Jules Porges & Co. after 1890). Beit used a similar business model as in the diamond business: he invited selected business partners as investor, who would acquire an interest in a parent company for the mining firms. He would draw on international connections in London and Paris. Became dividend paying. His youngest brother, Otto (1865–1930), had joined Jules Porges & Co. in London in 1888, but he was sent to Kimberley and then to Johannesburg, where he worked at the H. Eckstein company. Ten years later Otto, like Alfred, returned to London and became a partner in the stock-broking firm Ludwig Hirsch & Co. and later a director of the British South Africa Company." See also Raymond E. Dumett, ed., *Mining Tycoons in the Age of Empire, 1870–1945: Entrepreneurship, High Finance, Politics and Territorial Expansion* (London: Ashgate, 2008).

8. David Feldman, "Jews and the British Empire, ca. 1900," *History Workshop Journal* 63: 1 (2007), 70–89; Abigail Green, "The British Empire and the Jews: An Imperialism of Human Rights?," *Past and Present* 199 (May 2008), 175–205.

9. Katz et al., *Colonialism and the Jews*, 2.

10. Catherine Hall, *Civilizing Subjects: Colony and Metropole in the English Imagination, 1830–1867* (Chicago: University of Chicago Press, 2002), 9, 12; Catherine Hall, *Cultures of Empire: A Reader* (London: Routledge, 2000); Kathleen Wilson, ed, *A New Imperial History: Culture, Identity, and Modernity in Britain and the Empire,*

1660–1840 (Cambridge: Cambridge University Press, 2004); Antoinette Burton, ed., *After the Imperial Turn: Thinking with and through the Nation* (Durham, NC: Duke University Press, 2003).

11. The postcolonial critic Homi K. Bhabha explores the concept of "white but not quite" and cultural hybridity in his influential book *The Location of Culture* (New York: Routledge, 1994).
12. Ivan Kalmar and Derek Penslar, *Orientalism and the Jews* (Waltham: Brandeis University Press, 2004), xx.
13. Quoted in Danielle Kinsey, "Imperial Splendor: Diamonds, Commodity Chains, and Consumer Culture in Nineteenth-Century Britain" (PhD Dissertation, University of Illinois, Urbana-Champaign, 2010), 355.
14. Wiel, *Van Rapenburgerstraat naar Amerika*, 159. By 1920, the number of diamond workers in Antwerp ballooned to 14,000, up from 400 in 1896.
15. For a recent history of the Jews in New York, see Deborah Dash Moore's multivolume *City of Promises: A History of the Jews of New York* (New York: New York University Press, 2012). The historian Moses Rischin made an earlier reference to New York as the "city of promise" in his pioneering work *The Promised City: New York's Jews, 1870–1914* (Cambridge, MA: Harvard University Press, 1962).
16. The firm, located at 10–14 Bleecker Street, first employed 20 polishers. After two years, it relocated to the Fox building at 228 Pearl Street. In 1901, the firm expanded and relocated again, this time to 380 Canal Street. By 1915, S. L. van Wezel Inc. had grown to 170 employees. It opened new headquarters at 2 John Street, "with a factory connected in the new building in which it occupied the upper floors." See "Artistic Silver Plaque Presented by the Employes of S. L. van Wezel Inc. Silver Anniversary," *The Jewelers' Circular* 79: 2 (December 31, 1919), 91–93.
17. See, among others, *Weekblad van de ANDB* (December 7, 1895); "Diamond Cutters Coming Here," *Ithaca Morning Herald* (November 21, 1894): 1; "Against the Diamond Polishers: Treasury Department Decides That They Cannot Come Here under Contract," *New York Herald* (March 17, 1895), 5; "To Detain Diamond Cutters," *The Sun* (March 17, 1895), 3. According to an editorial in *Het Nieuws van de Dag* [*The Daily News*], the protective trade policies introduced by the United States "forced hundreds of skilled diamond workers to move to New York." See "Handel, Scheepvaart, en Nijverheid te Amsterdam in 1894," *Het Nieuws van de Dag* (October 2, 1895), 13.
18. Wiel, *Van Rapenburgerstraat naar Amerika*, 164–166.
19. "Mr. D. L. Van Moppes, of Amsterdam, and of 37 Maiden Lane, New York, has just opened in the first named city a large and excellently fitted up diamond cutting and polishing factory, containing 9 workrooms, with 220 mills and one cutting and polishing room. The Dutch newspapers compliment Mr. Van Moppes highly for his industrial zeal in erecting such a well-built factory, specially by having another one already in operation for a length of time." *New Amsterdam Gazette* (1883), 3.
20. Robert P. Swierenga, *The Forerunners: Dutch Jewry in the North American Diaspora* (Detroit: Wayne State University Press, 1994), 114.
21. *Jeweller and Metalworker* reported that in 1880 alone, £2,000,000 worth of diamonds passed through the Cape Post Office in Cape Town. See the *Jeweller and Metalworker* (February 15, 1881), 34.
22. Kinsey, "Imperial Splendor," 2.

23. Gary B. Magee and Andrew S. Thompson, *Empire and Globalization: Networks of People, Goods and Capital in the British World, c. 1850–1914* (Cambridge: Cambridge University Press, 2010), 16.
24. Frank Bovenkerk, for example, in his preface to Dina Siegel's book, referred to Jews as "middlemen minorities." See Dina Siegel, *The Mazzel Ritual: Culture, Customs and Crime in the Diamond Trade* (New York: Springer, 2009), viii.
25. The manufacturing of diamonds in Amsterdam dates back to the late 1500s, when Huguenot refugees from Antwerp brought along their diamond cleaving, cutting, and polishing skills. Sephardic Jews, who settled in the Dutch capital after expulsion from Spain and Portugal, adopted their specialties. As a new branch of industry, diamond manufacturing did not fall under the city's guild system, which rendered it an attractive occupation for Jews. For more on premodern history of the Dutch diamond trade, see among others Henriëtte Boas, "Jews and the Amsterdam Diamond Trade," *Studia Rosenthaliana* 26: 1–2 (1992), 214–223; Vanneste, *Global Trade and Commercial Networks*; van Agtmaal, "Het diamantvak in Amsterdam"; Henri Heertje, *De diamantbewerkers van Amsterdam* (Amsterdam: D. B. Centen, 1936); Hofmeester, "Shifting Trajectories," 25–49; Roelie Meijer and Peter Engelsman, *Vier eeuwen diamant: Amsterdam, Antwerpen London* (Hoorn: Uniepers, 1986); Felix Leviticus and Henri Polak, *Geïllustreerde Encyclopaedie der diamantnijverheid* (Haarlem: De Erven F. Bohn, 1908).
26. The word "carat" comes from Arabic (*qīrāṭ*), in turn borrowed from Greek *kerátion* κεράτιον or "carobseed," used as a unit of weight due to its consistency and uniformity. The carat has been standardized and now equals 200 milligrams, or 5 carats to the gram.
27. As a result of the Civil War, American imports and exports dropped dramatically, causing a depression in the English textile industry, which in turn depressed the South African market for wool. For more on the economic impact of the American Civil War on the nineteenth-century textile industry, see Adam Mendelsohn, *The Rag Race: How Jews Sewed Their Way to Success in America and the British Empire* (New York: New York University Press, 2015); Michael R. Cohen, *Cotton Capitalists: American Jewish Entrepreneurship in the Reconstruction Era* (New York: New York University Press, 2017).
28. For early reports on the discovery of South African diamonds, see among others "Diamonds at the Cape," *The Times* (September 20, 1867), 9; Harry Emanuel, "Diamonds at the Cape Colony," *Journal of the Society of Arts* 16: 83 (1868), 849–850; James R. Gregory, "Diamonds from the Cape of Good Hope," *Geological Magazine* 5: 54 (1868), 558–561 and 6: 61 (1869), 333–334; J. Tennant, "On the Discovery of Diamonds at Hope Town in the Cape Colony," *Proceedings of the Royal Geographic Society* 12: 5 (1868), 322–323; J. Tennant, "South African Diamonds," *Journal of the Society of Arts* 19: 940 (1870), 15–18; W. B. Chalmers, "Diamonds at the Cape Colony," *Journal of the Society of Arts* 17: 747 (1869), 199–200; E. Muskett, "Diamonds at the Cape," *Journal of the Society of Arts* 17: 855 (1869), 379; A. Wilmont, "Diamonds," *South African Magazine* 3 (1869), 570–586; Harry Emanuel, "Diamonds at the Cape," *Journal of the Society of Arts* 17: 861 (1869), 517; William G. Atherstone, "The Discovery of Diamonds at the Cape of Good Hope," *Geological Magazine* 6: 59 (1869), 208–213; "Port Elizabeth, South Africa," *Jewish Chronicle* (April 15, 1870), 4; J. Shaw, "On the Geology of the Diamondiferous Tracts of South Africa," *Cape Monthly Magazine* 1: 3–5 (1870), 129–133, 249–253, 368–372; H. Hall, "The Diamond-Fields of South Africa," *English Mechanic and World of Science* 12: 291 (1870), 99–100; G. S. Higson, "Diamonds and Gold

at the Cape," *Journal of the Society of Arts* 18: 923 (1870), 759–760; "The South African Diamond Fields," *The Graphic* (June 22, 1872), 575; "Port Elizabeth, South Africa," *Jewish Chronicle* (April 15, 1870), 4; *Times* (November 23, 1870), 9; "The South African Diamond Fields," *Harper's Weekly* 14 (November 19, 1870), 740; "The South African Diamond Fields," *The Graphic* (June 22, 1872), 575; For more on Gregory, see Mendel Kaplan, *Jewish Roots in the South African Economy* (Cape Town: Struik Publishers, 1986); Jonathan Green, "Buckets of Diamonds," *The British Empire* 29 (1972), 785–812.

29. Richard W. Murray, *South African Reminiscences* (Cape Town: J. C. Juta & Co., 1894), 113.
30. Oswald Doughty, *Early Diamond Days: The Opening of the Diamond Fields of South Africa* (London: Longmans, 1963), 38. E. B. Biggar wrote that "no one expected any kind of riches from such a dreary region, and few of the South African colonists believed, even after the diamonds were discovered, that anything so valuable could come out of Griqualand." See "The Diamond-Mines of South Africa," *Lippincott's Magazine* (March 1881), 217–231.
31. The explorer Henry M. Stanley first used this term his 1878 book *Through the Dark Continent*, describing a continent largely unknown and mysterious to Europeans.
32. Anthony Trollope, *South Africa, in Two Volumes* (London: Chapman and Hall, 1878), 164.
33. Gardner F. Williams describes the ostrich poop theory in his *The Diamond Mines of South Africa*, Vol. 1 (New York: Buck & Company, 1906), 121–122; "The Diamond Fields," *Cape Almanac* 1871, 354–358; George Beet and Thomas Laurent Terpend, *The Romance and Reality of the Vaal Diamond Diggings* (Kimberley: Diamond Fields Advertiser, 1917), 15.
34. Williams, *The Diamond Mines of South Africa*, 121–122.
35. Chas. V. Allen, *Diamond Mining in the Kimberley Field and the Mechanical Equipment of the Kimberley Diamond Mines* (New York: Dunlap, 1903), 1–2.
36. Dolores Fleischer, *Merchant Pioneers: The House of Mosenthal* (Johannesburg: J. Ball, 1983), 214. Mosenthal & Co., maintains Fleischer, was one of the few firms that could have given the instant financial backing for a purchase such as this. Not only was the volume of their trade enormous but also they had substantial banking facilities both in Port Elizabeth and in London.
37. Robert Vicat Turrell, *Capital and Labour on the Kimberley Diamond Fields, 1871–1890* (Cambridge: Cambridge University Press, 1987), 126. "The March to Finchley" refers to a painting by the English artist William Hogarth (1697–1764), depicting a fictional gathering of troops on their way to northwest London to defend the capital from the second Jacobite rebellion of 1745. It portrays soldiers in a humorous light, emphasizing their lack of discipline and training.
38. Doughty, *Early Diamond Days*, 17.
39. "Among the Diamonds: By One Who Has Visited the Fields," *Cape Monthly Magazine* (1872), 113.
40. "Appendix: Exports and Imports of the Cape Colony Increased by the Export of Diamonds: 1869–1888," in Max Bauer, *Precious Stones* (London: Charles Griffin & Co., 1904), 236. For additional information regarding diamond import and export, see A. Michielsen, *De diamanteconomie: Waarde, prijs en conjunctuur* (Antwerp: Christelijke Belgische Diamantbewerkerscentrale, 1955), 125; *Handbook to South Africa: Including the Cape Colony, Natal, the Diamond Fields, the Transvaal, Orange Free State* (London: S. W. Silver & Co, 1880), 296: Exports for

the year ending December 31, 1879, totaled £7,164,735 pounds (including 3 1/2 million for "unregistered diamonds").

41. Mary Louise Pratt, *Imperial Eyes: Travel Writing and Transculturation* (London: Routledge, 1992), 6. Pratt writes that Jews "lived in 'contact zones': as merchants, translators, or mediators, they employed their linguistic skills and vast commercial ethno-religious networks to advance British financial, strategic, and cultural interests in these areas."

42. For more on economic activity in Kimberley's early days, see William Worger, *South Africa's City of Diamonds: Mine Workers and Monopoly Capitalism in Kimberley, 1867–1895* (New Haven: Yale University Press, 1987); Kinsey, "Imperial Splendor," 178. Firewood was the major fuel in the 1870s and 1880s, until a railroad could be built between Kimberley and the Cape that supplied Welsh coal to the fields beginning in 1885. Gwayi Tyamzashe, writing for the bilingual missionary journal *Kaffir Express/Isigidimi* in 1874, stated that "those coming [to the diamond fields] from far up in the interior, such as the Bakwena, Bamangwatu, Mapeli, Matebele, etc. come with the sole purpose of securing guns." Gwayi Tyamzashe, "Life at the Diamond Fields," article published in the bilingual missionary journal *Kaffir Express/Isigidimi* (August 1874), reprinted in Francis Wilson and Dominique Perrot, eds., *Outlook on a Century: South Africa 1870–1970* (Lovedale, South Africa: Lovedale Press, 1972), 19–21.

43. Robert Turrell, "The 1875 Black Flag Revolt on the Kimberley Diamond Fields," *Journal of Southern African Studies* 7: 2 (1981), 194–235.

44. Raymond Dumett explains that "the terms 'empire-builder' and 'imperial' had not acquired the largely negative and pejorative connotations that they hold today and these names were often worn with pride by companies. It was recognized that capitalism by its very nature was expansionistic." Mining moguls were motivated to expand their business enterprise, to join cartels to control production and prices, to establish and join in syndicates, to take advantage of cheap labor, new sources of supply, and buying out rival firms to establish business monopolies. "Business empires" were proud achievements. See Dumett, *Mining Tycoons in the Age of Empire*, 18–19.

45. "Though many Europeans have become skillful workers at this trade," writes Williams, "the most successful lapidaries have been of Hebrew stock. The Jews had, at one time, the monopoly of the trade in diamonds in Portugal.... But unfortunately for Portugal and for the Jews, religious bigotry kindled the fires of persecution against this ancient people and they were expelled from the kingdom. Hospitable little Holland opened her doors to receive the exiled merchants and lapidaries, and Amsterdam has since become the central mart for the diamond merchant and his comrade, the diamond cutter. Out of 35,000 Jews who reside there, at least a third are engaged in one department or another of the diamond industry." Williams, *The Diamond Mines of South Africa*, 548.

46. *Diamantairs* typically refer to businessmen involved in one of more aspects of the diamond trade.

47. *De Diamant Adamas* 7 (December 19, 1890). American periodicals published widely on diamonds and diamond production. See among others "The Diamond Mines of Kimberley," *Scientific American* 82: 4 (January 27, 1900), 57, "The Great Premier Diamond," *Scientific American* 92: 14 (April 8, 1905), 285; "A Craze for Diamonds," *Washington Post* (September 7, 1881), 4; Frederic J. Haskin, "Diamonds," *Washington Post* (April 29, 1910), 10, "The Art of Cutting Diamonds," *New York Times* (August 7, 1885): 8; "Dear London Diamonds," *New York Times*

(January 12, 1890): 14; "Diamonds," *The Chautauquan: A Weekly Newsmagazine* 15: 2 (May 1892), 252; Sarah Brentworth, "Diamonds," *The Chautauquan* 23: 5 (August, 1896), 629–631; William J. Morton, "To South Africa for Diamonds!," *Scribner's Monthly* 16: 4 (August 1878), 551–562; "Diamond Mining in South Africa," *The Youth's Companion* 61: 50 (December 13, 1888), 638–639; "Diamonds Worth Millions Purchased by Americans," *Atlanta Constitution* (July 10, 1903), 3.

48. "Diamond Workers Go on Strike," *New York Herald* (October 19, 1895), 7; Wiel, *Van Rapenburgerstraat naar Amerika*, 164–165.
49. The *Nieuwe Rotterdamsche Courant* is quoted in Wiel, 171. In 1912 the New York correspondent of the *Nieuwe Rotterdamsche Courant* asked readers, "Do you wish to hear Dutch spoken on Nassau Street? Then go on a Saturday afternoon to the corner of Nassau and John Streets and stand near 'Ye Olde Dutch Shop House' and you will soon hear the weal and woe of diamond workers in your mother tongue." See Jacob van Hinte, *Netherlanders in America: A Study of Emigration and Settlement in the Nineteenth and Twentieth Centuries in the United States of America* (Grand Rapids, MI: Baker Book House, 1985), 83; Alicia Oltuski, *Precious Objects: A Story of Diamonds, Family, and a Way of Life* (New York: Scribner, 2011).
50. "Diamond Cutting," *Scientific American* 29: 14 (October 4, 1873), 207, 215–216.
51. For example, "The South African Diamond Fields," *Illustrated London News* 60 (March 30, 1872), 320–321; "The South African Diamond Fields," *Harper's Weekly* (November 19, 1870), 740.
52. T. W. Eady, *I.D.B. (Illicit Diamond Buying), or the Adventures of Solomon Dairs on the Diamond Fields and Elsewhere* (London: Chapman & Hall, 1887); George Chetwynd Griffith, *Knaves of Diamonds: Being Tales of Mine and Vel'd* (London: C.A. Pearson, 1899).
53. Charles A. Payton, *The Diamond Diggings of South Africa: A Personal and Practical Account* (London: Horace Cox, 1872), 116; Josiah Wright Matthews, *Incwadi Yami, Or, Twenty Years' Personal Experience in South Africa* (New York: Rogers and Sherwood, 1887), 227; Frederick Boyle, *To the Cape for Diamonds: A Story of Digging Experiences in South Africa* (London: Chapman and Hall, 1873), 231; Williams, *The Diamond Mines of South Africa*, 268.
54. Bryan Cheyette, *Constructions of "the Jew" in English Literature and Society: Racial Representations, 1875–1945* (New York: Cambridge University Press, 1993), preface.
55. See, among others, Jonathan Karp and Rebecca Kobrin, eds., *Purchasing Power: The Economics of Modern Jewish History* (Philadelphia: University of Pennsylvania Press, 2015); Mendelsohn, *The Rat Race*; Gideon Reuveni and Sarah Wobick-Segev, eds., *The Economy in Jewish History: New Perspectives on the Interrelationship between Ethnicity and Economic Life* (New York: Berghahn, 2010); Andrew Godley, *Jewish Immigrant Entrepreneurship in New York and London, 1880–1914* (London: Palgrave Macmillan, 2001).
56. The economic historian Stanley Chapman observed that "[e]conomists have traditionally taken only limited interest in entrepreneurship on the grounds that their subject is about rational choices in the production and distribution of goods and services rather than about dimensions of personality. However, there is now an economic theory of the entrepreneur distinct from mainstream neoclassical economics and this recognizes the relevance of culture to the varying performance of firms and of national economies." See Stanley Chapman, *Merchant Enterprise in Britain from the Industrial Revolution to World War I* (New York: Cambridge University Press, 1992), 11.

57. G. Jones and K. E. Sluyterman, "British and Dutch Business History," in F. Amatori and G. Jones, eds., *Business History around the World* (Cambridge: Cambridge University Press, 2003), 111–145.
58. The most common examples are those of the Jewish, Huguenot, Greek, and Armenian diasporas. See, for instance, E. R. Seeman, "Jews in the Early Modern Atlantic: Crossing Boundaries, Keeping Faith," in J. Cañizares-Esguerra and E. R. Seeman, eds., *The Atlantic in Global History, 1500-2000* (Upper Saddle River, NJ: Pearson Prentice Hall, 2007), 39–59; R. L. Kagan and P. D. Morgan, eds., *Atlantic Diasporas: Jews, Conversos, and Crypto Jews in the Age of Mercantilism, 1500–1800* (Baltimore: Johns Hopkins University Press, 2009); I. B. McCabe, G. Harlaftis, and I. P. Minoglou, eds., *Diaspora Entrepreneurial Networks—Four Centuries of History* (Oxford: Berg, 2005); M. Rozen, ed., *Homelands and Diasporas: Greeks, Jews and Their Migrations* (London: I. B. Tauris & Co, 2008); Jonathan Israel, *Diasporas within a Diaspora: Jews, Crypto-Jews and the World Maritime Empires, 1540–1740* (Leiden: Brill, 2002); Jonathan Israel, *European Jewry in the Age of Mercantilism, 1550–1750* (Oxford: Clarendon Press, 1985); Francesca Trivellato, *The Familiarity of Strangers: The Sephardic Diaspora, Livorno, and Cross-Cultural Trade in the Early Modern Period* (New Haven: Yale University Press, 2009); Francesca Trivellato, *The Promise and Peril of Credit: What a Forgotten Legend about Jews and Finance Tells Us about the Making of European Commercial Society* (Princeton: Princeton University Press, 2019); David Cesarani, ed., *Port Jews: Jewish Communities in Cosmopolitan Maritime Trading Centres, 1550–1950* (London: Routledge, 2002).
59. I. Ben-Amos, "Gifts and Favors: Informal Support in Early Modern England," *Journal of Modern History* 75 (2000), 295. See also I. Ben-Amos, "Gifts and Favors: Informal Support in Early Modern England," *Journal of Modern History* 75 (2000), 295–338; Michael R. Cohen, *Cotton Capitalists: American Jewish Entrepreneurship in the Reconstruction Era* (New York: New York University Press, 2017), introduction.
60. Tijl Vanneste maintains that the nineteenth-century international diamond trade was "a branch of business that built upon a relatively high degree of cross-cultural cooperation . . . [it was] not as closed off and mono-cultural as presumed. Intercultural partnerships are found commonly in lists of merchants active in the Indian diamond trade and existing commercial correspondence suggests the importance of non-Jewish diamond merchants." See Vanneste, *Global Trade and Commercial Networks*, 5. Francesca Trivellato studied a cross-cultural diamond network spreading from Lisbon to London and India, demonstrating that other ethnic groups played an equally crucial role in the trade, including Catholics and Protestants. See Trivellato, *The Familiarity of Strangers*; Francesca Trivellato, "From Livorno to Goa and Back: Merchant Networks and the Coral-Diamond Trade in the Early-Eighteenth Century," *Portuguese Studies* 16 (2000), 193–217.
61. Israel Zangwill, "What Hebrews Have Accomplished," *Washington Post* (June 24, 1906), 3.
62. *The Jewish Chronicle* (March 22, 1895), 8. The *American Israelite* picked up the story, maintaining that "it is not possible to exaggerate the share in the awakening of Africa which has been taken by the enterprise, the commercial instinct, the dash and daring of Jews. The halo of romance shines over the whole story." See "Jews and South Africa," *American Israelite* (May 9, 1895), 4; "Additional Notes on Jews in South Africa" (July 18, 1895), 5; Sidney Mendelssohn, "Jewish Pioneers of South Africa," *Transactions (Jewish Historical Society of England)* 7 (1911–1914), 180–205.

CHAPTER 1

1. Charles Chapman, *A Voyage from Southampton to Cape Town and Back, In the Union Company's Mail Steamer "Syria"* (London: George Berridge & Co., 1872), 90. Subsequent quotes in this paragraph are from this edition.
2. Boyle, *To the Cape for Diamonds*, 48.
3. Boyle, 66; See also William J. Morton, "The South African Diamond Fields and a Journey to the Mines," *Journal of the American Geographical Society of New York* (April 30, 1878), 69; Williams, *The Diamond Mines of South Africa*, 187–190; "The Diamond Mines of the Cape," *Appletons' Journal of Literature, Science and Art* (January 16, 1875), 78–81.
4. This number increased to 50,000 people by the end of 1871, approximately 20,000 of whom were white and 30,000 were black. For more on the demographic history of the diamond fields, see Worger, *South Africa's City of Diamonds*; Turrell, *Capital and Labour*.
5. George Beet, *Grand Old Days of the Diamond Fields: Memories of Past Times with the Diggers of Diamondia* (Cape Town: M. Miller, 1931), 12.
6. "The Diamond Fields," *Cape Argus* (November 5, 1870), 3. See also an editorial from *The Diamond Fields* (November 5, 1870), 3. Charles Payton, a correspondent from the popular British magazine *The Field*, noted "men of numerous nationalities, of every grade in the social scale, and every type of character and manners. A large proportion of the diggers are Cape colonists, and Natalians, then come the Dutch Boers, both of whom have, of course, facilities for trying their luck at the diggings at little expense, owing to the small cost of the journey. Then come Englishmen, Australians, and Americans, the former in very large and continually increasing numbers. A good many Germans, with a sprinkling of Frenchmen, Italians, and Spaniards, are also to be found among the diggers." Payton, *The Diamond Diggings of South Africa*, 104. James Anthony Froude estimated in 1874 that "in the midst of them a hundred or so keen-eyed Jewish merchants" could be found. See James Anthony Froude, *Two Lectures on South Africa* (London: Longmans, Green and Co., 1880). The Xhosa, Cape Malays (of Muslim and Indonesian descent), Zulu, and Pedi refer to ethnic and cultural groups living in Southern Africa.
7. Chapman, *A Voyage from Southampton to Cape Town and Back*, 123, 145; Williams, *The Diamond Mines of South Africa*, 189–200; Matthews, *Incwadi Yami*. Matthews achieved notoriety for unethical medical conduct during the 1884–1885 smallpox epidemic, when he refused to confirm the disease out of fear of upsetting the diamond mines' labor supply. See I. R. Phimister, "Historians and the Big Hole: Kimberley's Historiography Reviewed," *South African Historical Journal* 20 (1988), 105–113.
8. K., *The Diamond Fields of South Africa: With Notes of Journey There and Homeward, and Some Things about Diamonds and Other Jewels* (New York: American News Company, 1872), 89; "Latest Finds Reported at the Diamond Fields," *Port Elizabeth Telegraph* (May 26, 1871), 3.
9. Edward Stanford, *The South African Diamond Fields, Extracted from Cape and Other Newspapers, with an Introduction and Explanatory Preface by a Colonist* (London: E. Stanford, 1870), 40; "From the Diamond Field," *The Natal Witness: Agricultural and Commercial Advertiser* 25: 1647 (November 4, 1870), 3.
10. *Berliner Missions Berichte*, 1876, p. 112. Quoted in Turrell, *Capital and Labour*, 201.
11. Cape Archives Depot: Griqualand West (GLW) 55, From Inspector of Claims, Wright to J. B. Currey (October 1, 1874).

12. For more on black Africans and claim ownership, see I. B. Sutton, "The Diggers' Revolt in Griqualand West, 1875," *International Journal of African Historical Studies* 12: 1 (1979), 40–61; Turrell, "The 1875 Black Flag Revolt"; F. Johnstone, *Class, Race and Gold: A Study of Class Relations and Racial Discrimination in South Africa* (London: Routledge, 1976); Worger, *South African's City of Diamonds*; Turrell, *Capital and Labour*; J. M. Smalberger, "IDB and the Mining Compound System in the 1880s," *South African Journal of Economics* 42: 4 (1974), 398–414; Smalberger, "The Role of the Diamond Industry in the Development of the Pass-Law System in South Africa," *Interdisciplinary Journal of African Historical Studies* 9 (1976). I. R. Phimister, in a review of Turrell's and Worger's work, maintained that the De Beers and Kimberley Central companies closely cooperated in order to control and discriminate against black workers in the 1880s and 1890s, the historical details of which have been deliberately expunged from corporate memory. Phimister, "Historians and the Big Hole," 106.
13. Gustav Saron and Louis Hotz, *The Jews in South Africa: A History* (Oxford: Oxford University Press, 1955), 44. According to Saron and Hotz, there may have been 4,000 Jews in the country in 1880. By 1891 this number had grown to some 10,000. In 1899 there were about 24,000 Jews, out of a total white population of 850,000. The 1904 census listed 19,537 Jews in the whole Cape Colony, or 3.37 percent of the white population. Of these, 8,114 lived in Cape Town proper, and about 3,000 in the suburbs.
14. For more on the early digging communities, see Mendel Kaplan, *Jewish Roots in the South African Economy* (Cape Town: C. Struik Publishers, 1986); Brian Roberts, *Kimberley: Turbulent City* (Cape Town: D. Philip, 1976); Worger, *South Africa's City of Diamonds*, 10–12; Boyle, *To the Cape for Diamonds*, chapter 6; F. Algar, *The Diamond Fields: With Notes on the Cape Colony and Natal* (London: Clement's Lane, 1872), 43–52.
15. Colin Newbury, *The Diamond Ring: Business, Politics, and Precious Stones in South Africa, 1867–1945* (Oxford: Clarendon Press, 1989), 18. For more on the nineteenth-century South African economy, see D. Hobart Houghton and Jenifer Dagut, eds., *Source Material on the South African Economy, Vol. 1: 1860–1899* (London: Oxford University Press, 1972).
16. "Bloemfontein," *Cape Argus* (August 27, 1870), 2. The founder and chief editor of this Cape Town newspaper, commonly known as *The Argus*, was Saul Solomon (1817–1892), who first published it in 1857. It exists to this day.
17. *The Diamond Field* 1: 1 (April 27, 1871), 1. Meyers advertised on the front page: "First storekeeper on the Diamond Fields. Joel Myers, the Iron Store," *The Diamond Field* 1: 17 (August 17, 1871), 1.
18. "Diamond-Fields," *Cape Argus* (November 12, 1870), 3.
19. *The Diamond Field* 1: 19 (August 31, 1871), 6.
20. See advertisement on the front page of the *Grahamstown Journal* (October 20 and 27, 1842), 1. The ad reads: "Messrs. Mosenthal Brothers, having lately arrived from Europe, with an assorted and valuable cargo of general merchandise, will open a mercantile and shipping house at Port Elizabeth, on the arrival of the 'Sara Crisp' at that Port. Having made arrangements in England, and being well acquainted with the frontier trade, they will be enabled to offer their goods on favourable terms." Over time the list of items became so long, and the Mosenthal name sufficiently well known, that advertisements in the 1850s and 1960s just mentioned "merchandise." For more on the Mosenthal family, see Dolores Fleischer and Angela Caccia, *Merchant Pioneers: The House of Mosenthal*

(Johannesburg: Jonathan Ball Publishers, 1983). Julius Mosenthal became the first Jew to be elected to the Cape legislative Assembly in 1858.
21. Louis Hermann, *A History of the Jews in South Africa, From the Earliest Times to 1895* (Westport, CT: Greenwood Press, 1935), 15. Mosenthal & Co. also supported Alphonse Levy, a gun and general merchant, who in 1875 owned property worth 10,000 pounds. They supplied him with goods and credit on a 6-month basis. Like other large Port Elizabeth merchants, such as L. Lippert and Company, D. Blaine and Co, and A. C. Stewart and Co, Mosenthals exemplified the dominant trend of supporting trading constituents in Kimberley.
22. "Life at the Diggings. No. 6," *Cape Argus* 15: 2215 (April 25, 1871): 4; *Cape Argus* 15: 2168 (January 3, 1871): 2.
23. Kaplan, *Jewish Roots in the South African Economy*, 47.
24. Kimberlite pipes are underground carrot-shaped chimneys, formed through the high-pressure volcanic eruption of kimberlite magma. These pipes contain the highest concentrations of precious and semiprecious gemstones.
25. Williams, *The Diamond Mines of South Africa*, 265. See also Harry Raymond, *B. I. Barnato: A Memoir* (New York: E. P. Dutton and Co., 1898), 29; William Charles Scully, *Reminiscences of a South African Pioneer* (London: Unwin, 1913). Harris's first windfall came not from diamonds, but from a lucky game of roulette played in a Kimberley bar. He won £1,400 in an hour. See Martin Meredith, *Diamonds, Gold, and War* (London: Simon & Schuster, 2007), 52.
26. Saron and Hotz, *The Jews in South Africa*; Doughty, *Early Diamond Days*, 119. Newbury, *The Diamond Ring*, 24. Payton, *The Diamond Diggings of South Africa*, 116: "Like most diamond buyers, Mr. Unger affects rather a loud and dashing style of dress, such as a velvet jacket, whit cord or buckskin breeches, and long tight-fitting well-polished boots, adorned with glittering spurs. A handsome courier bag is slung to his side."
27. *Jewish Chronicle* (1895), quoted in Eric Rosenthal, "On the Diamond Fields," in Saron and Hotz, *The Jews in South* Africa, 109.
28. Williams, *The Diamond Mines of South Africa*, 268; Stefan Kanfer, *The Last Empire: De Beers, Diamonds, and the World* (New York: Farrar, Strauss & Giroux, 1993), 54.
29. Joel Rabinowitz wrote in the 1895 edition of the *Jewish Chronicle* that Lewis and Marks "had a large wooden store erected, and took it up to the fields, being their own carriers taking with them at the same time a quantity of goods, then opened the store, doing a roaring trade. They, however, discovered, by their shrewdness, that it would pay them better to relinquish that kind of business, and entered the diamond trade. They gained the confidence of the diggers, with whom they did a very profitable business. They also commended buying claims and working them. . . . Both Messrs. Lewis and Marks had brothers who came out to them." See Rabinowitz, *Jewish Chronicle* (June 28, 1895), 11; "The Jews in South Africa," *Jewish Chronicle* (August 25, 1906), 21.
30. Barnato is quoted in Harry Raymond, *B. I. Barnato*, 17. For more on Barney Barnato, see Edgar Bernstein, "Jews in South African Public Life," in Leon Feldberg, ed., *South African Jewry* (Johannesburg: Fieldhill Publishing), 89–117; Stanley Jackson, *The Great Barnato* (London: Heinemann, 1970); G. Wheatcroft, *The Randlords: The Men Who Made South Africa* (London: Weidenfeld & Nicolson, 1985); Newbury, *The Diamond Ring*.
31. *The Diamond Field* 1: 1 (October 13, 1870) and 1: 1 (April 27, 1871), 4. These early editions are available at the National Library of South Africa in Cape Town.

32. Payton, *The Diamond Diggings of South Africa*, 120; Rosenthal, "On the Diamond Fields," 108; Doughty, *Early Diamond Days*, 59; Emil Holub, *Seven Years in South Africa: Travels, Researches, and Hunting Adventures between the Diamond Fields and the Zambesi (1872–1879)*, trans. Ellen E. Frewer (London: Sampson Low, Marston, Searle & Rivington, 1881), 72–73.
33. *Eastern Province Herald* (September 28, 1869), 1. South African Public Library.
34. Stanford, *The South African Diamond Fields*, 29. "By 1876," writes Robert Turrell, "Kimberley had become the largest commodity market for coastal merchants and as the value of diamond exports surpassed that of wool, they added diamonds to their trade." Turrell, "The 1875 Black Flag Revolt," 215. See also Standard Bank Archive, Inspection Report (Port Elizabeth), July 31, 1876, f 613; Inspection Report (Dutoitspan), November 17, 1873; Inspection Report (Kimberley) June 23, 1875, f 86; September 1, 1876, f 187; *Diamond News* 8 (December 1874).
35. *Diamond News and Vaal Advertiser* 1: 3 (November 3, 1870), 4; *Natal Witness: Agricultural and Commercial Advertiser* 25 (August 26, 1870), 3.
36. *The Diamond Field* 1:1 (April 27, 1871), 4.
37. "The Diamond Mines," *Cape Almanac* (1886), 457. The proprietor of Dorstfontein, Adriaan van Wyk, for example, initially charged diggers 7s.6d. for the right to mine each claim "for as long as the paper on which the receipt was written held together," but he sold the property soon after the rush began in earnest. Adriaan van Wyk is quoted in Newbury, *The Diamond Ring*, 12.
38. Fébé Van Niekerk, ed., *Knights of the Shovel: From the Original Typescript Manuscript*, A History of the Diamond Fields *by George Beet* (Kimberley: Africana Library, 1996), 19; Payton, *The Diamond Diggings of South Africa*, 116–120; "Great Discoveries of Diamonds," *Cape Argus* (August 4, 1870), 3.
39. Fleischer and Caccia, *Merchant Pioneers*, 216.
40. Kaplan, *Jewish Roots in the South African Economy*, 49; Turrell, *Capital and Labour*, 2. Louis Hond was bought out of the Hopetown Company and became an independent buyer. After he was arrested for illicit diamond dealing, the subject of chapter 5, he returned to the Netherlands.
41. *The Diamond News* (June 25, 1874), 2. Turrell calculates that in Kimberley alone, 34 general merchants supplied 133 canteen keepers and 258 storekeepers, rapidly making Kimberley the largest market town in South Africa. Turrell, *Capital and Labour*, 60.
42. Colin Newbury, "Technology, Capital and Consolidation: The Performance of De Beers Mining Company Limited, 1880–1889," *Business History Review* 61: 2 (Spring 1987), 6.
43. An Outsider, "Our Probable Future," *The Cape Monthly Magazine* 6: 31 (January 1873), 1.
44. Trollope, *South Africa*, Vol. 2, 195.
45. *The Emigrants' Guide to South Africa, Including Cape Colony, the Diamond Fields, Bechuanaland Transvaal, the Goldfields, Natal, the Orange Free State, and the Territories of the British South Africa Co. Containing a Mass of Useful and Valuable Information, With Map* (London: A. White & Co., 1896), 34; K., *The Diamond Fields of South Africa*, 12, 46.
46. Payton, *The Diamond Diggings of South Africa*, 61.
47. In 1865, when the first official census was taken, the Cape Town municipal population stood at 28,400, with a small preponderance of females. Whites, at 15,100, slightly outnumbered "Other" at 12,400, with 628 "Hottentots" and 274 "Kaffirs" making up the rest. The great majority were locally born, with only 4,600 from

Europe and 536 born "elsewhere." Although the single largest component was in the age group 21–39 (9,000), this was a young city with 9,700 under the age of 14. Only 1,700 were over the age of 55. See Nigel Worden, Elizabeth van Heyningen, and Vivian Bickford-Smith, *Cape Town: The Making of a City* (Cape Town: New Africa Books, 2012), 177.
48. Payton, *The Diamond Diggings of South Africa*, 61. See also Doughty, *Early Diamond Days*, 23.
49. Boyle, *To the Cape for Diamonds*, 60.
50. Payton, *The Diamond Diggings of South Africa*, 64.
51. Chapman, *A Voyage from Southampton to Cape Town and Back*, 91.
52. Doughty adds that in the early 1870s the "kings of the road" were the new American horse-drawn coaches, which had been rendered superfluous by the building the Trans-Pacific Railway, and which had been shipped across the Atlantic by Cobb and Co., with a capital of 10,000 pounds to start a twice-weekly journey from Port Elizabeth to the diamond fields. These coaches carried passengers and luggage to their destination in five and a half days, for which they charged twelve pounds. Doughty, *Early Diamond Days*, 31. On Scotch-carts and spider wagons, see Chapman, *A Voyage from Southampton to Cape Town and Back,* 119. Richard Murray mentioned in his South African Reminiscences that in 1870 and early 1871, "from sixty to eighty ferry boats plied for hire on the river and were going to and fro from dawn to midnight." *South African Reminiscences* (Cape Town: J. C. Juta & Co., 1894), 236.
53. Geoff Shandler, "Diamonds of Neptune," *American Scholar* 70: 4 (2001), 88. Women were part of the early digging scene, but their numbers were small. See Maureen Rall, *Petticoat Pioneers: The History of the Pioneer Women Who Lived on the Diamond Fields in the Early Years* (Kimberley: Kimberley Africana Library, 2002). A scholarly analysis of Jewish and non-Jewish women in the international diamond industry has yet to be made.
54. In July 1873, Colesberg Kopje, also known as New Rush, received its current name Kimberley, after the British Secretary of State for the Colonies, Lord Kimberley. The Secretary insisted that towns and cities in the colonies receive "decent and intelligible names. His Lordship declined to be in any way connected with such a vulgarism as New Rush." For details, see Brian Roberts, *Kimberley: Turbulent City* (Kimberley: D. Philip, 1976), 115–117.
55. David Harris is quoted in Doughty, *Early Diamond Days*, 46.
56. Williams, *The Diamond Mines of South Africa*, 104–105, 189.
57. Dean Williams, *The Times* (September 29, 1870). Williams is quoted in Stanford, *The South African Diamond Fields*, 18.
58. Gwayi Tyamzashe, "Life at the Diamond Fields," *Kaffir Express/Isigidimi* (August 1874), reprinted in Francis Wilson and Dominique Perrot, eds., *Outlook on a Century: South Africa 1870–1970* (Lovedale, South Africa: Lovedale Press, 1972), 19–21. Tyamzashe was a Xhosa convert to Christianity, who came to Kimberley to engage in missionary work. He described the diamond fields and its diversity in the bilingual missionary journal *Kaffir Express/Isigidimi*.
59. Murray, *South African Reminiscences*, 108.
60. Richard P. Impey, "Another Correspondent's Letter" (Vaal River, July 15, 1870), in J. G. Steytler, *The Diamond Fields of South Africa: With a Map of the Country and Full Particulars of the Roads, Prices of Necessaries etc.* (Cape Town: Saul Solomon, 1870), 20.

61. "At present operations have been carried on at the diamond fields in the most primitive manner," in Steytler, vi.
62. Morton, "To South Africa for Diamonds!"
63. "Letters from the Fields: A Thousand Diggers at Work" (Pniel, July 11, 1870), in Steytler, *The Diamond Fields of South Africa*, 8. Louis Hond left Amsterdam for Cape Town in 1863.
64. "Perseverance Rewarded. A Gem of 23 Carats Found. Good Order on the Diggings" (*Klipdrift*, July 15, 1870), Steytler, *The Diamond Fields of South Africa*, 12. For a few years after arriving in Cape Town, Louis Hond lived at 33 Hout Street among small tradesmen and was listed in the municipal registry as a "lapidary." The *Grahamstown Journal*, in an editorial about the 1867 Eureka diamond find, stated that he was "a professional diamond polisher of 22 years European experience, an exhibitor at the Paris Exhibition, and the holder of a certificate from the Mayor of Amsterdam." *Grahamstown Journal* (April 22, 1867). Marian Robertson, *Diamond Fever: South African Diamond History, 1866–9, from Primary Sources* (New York: Oxford University Press, 1974), 41.
65. Matthews, *Incwadi Yami*, 199; Payton, *The Diamond Diggings of South Africa*, 5; Chapman, *A Voyage from Southampton to Cape Town*, 142.
66. *Diamond News* 2 (July 22, 1871), 1.
67. *The Diamond Field* 1: 3 (May 11, 1871), 3.
68. The *Natal Mercury* is quoted in Rosenthal, "On the Diamond Fields," 108.
69. Williams, *The Diamond Mines of South Africa*, 161–163.
70. This incident is described in a letter, "Pniel Diamond Fields," which appeared in the *Herald* on August 8, 1870, and was reprinted in "Colesberg," *Cape Argus* (August 27, 1870), 2.
71. Louis Herrman, "Cape Jewry before 1870," in Saron and Hotz, *The Jews in South Africa*, 27; Milton Shain, "'Vant to Puy a Vaatch': The Smous and Pioneer Trader in South African Jewish Historiography," *Jewish Affairs* 57: 3 (2002), 39–46; Louis Hotz, "South Africa's Economic Development," in Leon Feldberg, ed., *South African Jewry* (Johannesburg: Fieldhill Publishing, 1968), 51–69; Fleischer and Caccia, *Merchant Pioneers*, 74. Eric Rosenthal, "Jews in South African Trade and Commerce," in Leon Feldberg, ed., *South African Jewry 1965* (Johannesburg: Fieldhill Publishing, 1965), 141–153.
72. Louis Cohen, *Reminiscences of Kimberley* (London: Bennett & Co., 1911), 18. The practice of *kopje-walloping* was allowed to continue until the middle of 1876, when the following advertisement appeared among the notices published in the *Government Gazette*: "His Excellency the Administrator directs to be notified for general information that from and after this date the practice known as kopje-walloping, or otherwise the purchasing of diamonds in places other than the offices of Licensed Bankers or Diamond Dealers, will be strictly prosecuted by the police, who have received orders, etc. Offenders under the Section relating thereto are liable to a penalty, upon conviction, of not less than 100 pounds, and to the forfeiture of the License." See John Angove, *In the Early Days: The Reminiscences of Pioneer Life on the South African Diamond Fields* (Kimberley: Handel House, 1910), 64.
73. *The Diamond Field* 1: 20 (September 7, 1871), 1.
74. "Life at the Diggings. No. 1: Trade, Stores, and Stocks," *Cape Argus* 15: 2204 (March 28, 1871), 4. Payton, *The Diamond Diggings of South Africa*, 116.
75. "The Diamond-Fields" (December 13, 1870), 3. Charles Du Val, who penned *With a Show through Southern Africa* in 1882, described Rothschild and Goodchild

as "Diamond-Fields knights of the hammer . . . . the principal members of the 'going! Going! gone! Fraternity' whose advertising was characterized by 'brilliant colouring and perfervid imaginative powers.'" He described Rothschild as "a man of cultivated intelligence and accomplishments." See Du Val, *With a Show through Southern Africa and Personal Reminiscences of the Transvaal War* (London: Tinsley Brothers, 1882), 87.

76. *Eastern Province Herald* (September 28, 1869), 1.
77. George Beet quoted in Rosenthal, "On the Diamond Fields," 108. See also advertisements in *The Cape Times and Daily Advertiser* 1: 63 (June 1876), 1: "Goodchild & Rothschild, Auctioneers, Land, Law & General Agents, Diamond Fields, Kimberley. . . . Advances made upon goods coming in for sale, and account sales rendered, accompanied with a draft on the Oriental Bank, Cape Town, the post following the sale."
78. Payton, *The Diamond Diggings of South Africa*, 132.
79. Payton, 120.
80. The *Times* (February 1, 1872); Payton, 121. Newbury, *The Diamond Ring*, 24: From one account of Cape and London auctions, it seems that biweekly sales at Cape Town of the larger stones fetched 2–5 pounds per carat, plus a margin of 1–2 pounds overseas. Colonial Office Confidential Print, African 89 (1876), 38; *The Diamond Field* (January 20, 1875).
81. Trollope, *South Africa*, 195. In 1876, reported Trollope, the registered export of diamonds from Kimberley amounted in value to 1,414,590 British pounds and reached 773 pounds avoirdupois in weight.
82. Boyle, *To the Cape for Diamonds*, 272.
83. Boyle, 272, 373; Doughty, *Early Diamond Days*, 152.
84. John Blades Currey, "Half a Century in South Africa," chapter 17: "A Story of a South African Diamond Robbery," (1870), no pagination. J. B. Currey Collection, South African Public Library MSB 140, box 5.
85. Cape Archives: GLW "Letters from the Colonial Office," Colonial Secretary, June 6, 1872; July 8, 1872.
86. "Another Mail Robbery," *The Diamond Field* 2: 67 (August 1, 1872), 3.
87. Morton, "To South Africa for Diamonds!," 667. Brokers thus found buyers for a seller's merchandise, receiving a commission for his services.
88. Cohen, *Reminiscences*, 215–216.
89. Renée Rose Shield, *Diamond Stories: Enduring Change on 47th Street* (Ithaca: Cornell University Press, 2002).
90. "Orange Free State Mission," *Quarterly Papers* 18 (1872), 9.
91. Morton, "The South African Diamond Fields," 73; Payton, *The Diamond Diggings of South Africa*, 23. The 1873 *Cape Almanac*: "[W]e have 25 bakers, 51 butchers, 140 diamond dealers, 8 apothecaries, 26 auctioneers, 21 wholesale wine and spirit dealers, 68 wholesale warehousemen, 135 retail shopkeepers, 10 gunpowder and 458 retail wine and spirit licenses. Total 942 licenses . . . . The number of claims registered by the respective Inspectors was, at Dutoitspan and Bultfontein (including 40 to 50 coloured people) 1,198."
92. Matthews, *Incwadi Yami*, 99, 189: "So numerous were the wires that the mine seemed a yawning pit over which some Titanic spider had woven its web, while the noise of the wires was as loud as the din of the traffic in Cheapside or the Strand, the rattle of the machinery in a Lancashire factory, or, to be more imaginative, the roar of angry waves buffeting a rock-bound coast." Gardner Williams described the scene as a beehive in *The Diamond Mines of South Africa*, 197. For

the "great canvas city" reference, see Angove, *In the Early Days*, 33. The German E. Lippert, giving a public lecture in Hamburg in 1877, described Kimberley as a "Weltwunder," one of the wonders of the world: "Die Diamantfelder Süd-Afrika's," *Mitteilungen der Geographischen Gesellschaft in Hamburg* II (L. Friederichsen & Co., 1878), 328.

93. Robert Turrell estimates that 50–80,000 Africans went to and left Kimberley each year between 1871 and 1875, mostly Pedi, Tsonga, and South Sotho. Already deeply involved in migrant labor prior to 1870—many Africans worked on farms and public works of the Cape Colony—they went to work in the Kimberley mines to earn money for cattle or ploughs to improve their farming. Others mined to earn guns on the instructions of chiefs and elders, which became more pressing when white settlement on African lands increased. They commonly worked between three and six months in the mines, after which they purchased commodities and left. Africans, states Turrell, made up nearly 90 percent of the mines' labor force, peaking at 30,000 during the boom periods (1878–1881; 1886–1890). For more on African migrant labor on the diamond fields, see Robert Vicat Turrell, "Diamonds and Migrant Labour in South Africa, 1869–1910," *History Today* 36: 5 (1986), n.p.; Turrell, *Capital and Labour*; A. J. A. Janse, "A History of Diamond Sources in Africa, Part I," *Gems and Gemology* 31: 4 (Winter 1995), 228–255, 237; Robert Ross, *A Concise History of South Africa* (Cambridge: Cambridge University Press, 1999), 55–58. For demographic data on Jews in South Africa, see Milton Shain and Richard Mendelsohn, *The Jews in South Africa: An Illustrated History* (Johannesburg: Jonathan Ball Publishing, 2009), 25. The majority of Jews, argue Shain and Mendelsohn, still resided in the Cape Colony, where they made up a paltry 0.23% of the entire white population. Cape Town (169), Port Elizabeth (123), Graaff-Reinet (36), Grahamstown (25), and Victoria West (22) were the only centers in the Colony with significant concentrations of Jews.

94. Advertisements listed under the heading "The Diamond Trade," *The Diamond Fields Advertiser and Commercial Guide* (May 18, 1878), 4.

95. Lionel Phillips, who first worked as a diamond sorter, recalled that initially "there was a panic among the claim-holders when [blue ground] was struck, as it was suspected to be the bottom of the mine. On striking it men frequently covered up the ominous exposure hastily and rushed to town to sell their claims." Only later did they discover blue ground contained even richer carbon deposits than the yellow soil above it. Lionel Phillips, *Some Reminiscences of South Africa* (London: Hutchinson & Co., 1924), 25. Lower oxides of iron cause the bluish color of the soil.

96. A windlass is a device designed to haul heavy weights, consisting of a barrel and wooden frame, a horizontal cylinder, cable or rope, and a crank.

97. Theodore Reunert, *Diamonds and Gold in South Africa* (Cape Town: J. C. Juta & Co., 1893), 27.

98. John Blades Currey, "Half a Century in South Africa," J. B. Currey Collection, South African Public Library MSB 140: Box 5 (no page numbers). For more on new innovations in diamond mining, see Newbury, "Technology"; Bennet H. Brough, "The Mining Industries of South Africa, As Shown at the Kimberley Exhibition," *Journal of the Society of the Arts* (January 20, 1893), 166–176; S. H. Ball, "The Diamond and the Diamond Industry," *Transactions of the Royal Canadian Institute* 18: 2 (University of Toronto Press, 1932), 251–269.

99. Payton estimated that preliminary expenses for a digger coming from Europe amounted to 160 pounds, which included his voyage, journey to the diamond fields, tools, etc. He estimates that for six months on the fields, a digger required

the sum of 270 pounds to make a fair start at the diggings. See Payton, *The Diamond Diggings of South Africa*, 42.

100. Morton, "The South African Diamond Fields," 80; Reunert, *Diamonds and Gold in South Africa*, 80. The term "Kaffir" means "unbeliever" in Arabic and became a disparaging label for all Africans.
101. "Half a Century in and out of South Africa, 1864–1919," unpublished manuscript, Cape Archives KAB: A540 Lewis Mitchell Collection, Box 29, n.p.
102. *Diamond Field* (January 7, 1874). For a detailed description of the mining process, see "The South African Diamond Field," *Jeweller and Metalworker* (January 15, 1881), 15–16.
103. Standard Bank Archives, Letter Book V, General Manager to London Office (January 7, 1875), n.p. See also Henry Mitchell, *Diamonds and Gold of South Africa* (London: Mathieson & Son, 1888), 5–6; Holub, *Seven Years in South Africa*, 69–70.
104. For more on the relationship between colonial banks and diamond diggers, see Turrell, "The 1875 Black Flag Revolt on the Kimberley Diamond Fields," 226–228. "Every lawyer on the Fields," explains Turrell, "had money on loan to diggers. Attorneys J. J. G. Rhodes and L. P. Ford formed the Kimberley Loan Company in 1873 with a capital of 12,000 pounds, which returned a dividend of sixty percent per annum. The auctioneer A. A. Rothschild had 5,000 pounds invested in his business and a similar sum earning interest from diggers." See also Newbury, "Technology, Capital, and Consolidation," 28.
105. "The Diamond Diggings," *The Mining Magazine and Review: A Monthly Record of Mining, Smelting, Quarrying, and Engineering. Vol. I* (London: Henry S. King & Co., 1872), 372.
106. Port Elizabeth Chamber of Commerce, *Reports of the Committee for the Year 1875* (Port Elizabeth, 1875), 8, 16, 26.
107. "Griqualand West," *Cape Almanac* (1874), 58a–66a.
108. Morton, "To South Africa for Diamonds!," 563. Turrell explains that banks became more lenient in the 1880s: "Diamond merchants, in particular, depended on the banks for credit and a whole range of commercial services. Rough stones were, for the most part, sent to London through the post by the banks. They were insured by either the banks or the shippers. Merchants drew bills on their London firms, and local banks advanced money in Kimberley for the purchase of diamonds. Often advances were made before diamonds were delivered to the banks. As the invoice value of diamonds exported varied against the fluctuating prices in London, the banks took a margin of safety on its advance from 10 percent to as much as 40 percent; the banks would seldom advance more than 27,000 pounds against an invoice value of 30,000. However, selected customers were allowed to negotiate bills against diamonds of equal value. For example, in 1883 Barnet Lewis was authorized to pass drafts on his London firm for up to 31,000 pounds at any one time and the security was a fixed deposit of the same value held at the Kimberley branch of the Standard Bank. Once a month or every 6 weeks Lewis shipped a parcel of diamonds. His normal practice was to take his parcel sorted into different packets to the Standard manager. Then, Lewis weighed each packet and the manager checked their value against the detailed invoice. The parcel was then placed in a strong tin box, sealed with Lewis' seal and sent off to the London office of the Standard Bank. Once there the diamonds were given up when the draft had been accepted by Lewis' London firm." Turrell, *Capital and Labour*, 76.

109. *Diamond News* (June 23, 1874), 3.
110. Fleisher and Caccia, *Merchant Pioneers*, 215.
111. Barnato spoke at the first annual meeting of the De Beers Consolidated Mining Company in 1890. His full speech is included in Raymond's *B. I. Barnato*, 51–74.
112. Henning Albrecht, *Alfred Beit, The Hamburg Diamond King* (Hamburg: Hamburgische Wissenschaftliche Stiftung, 2012), 22. Ludwig returned to Hamburg to continue to manage the company after his father's death, his two brothers remaining in South Africa.
113. The journalist Frank Harris (1856–1931) interviewed Beit and quotes him in his memoir *My Life and Loves*, Vol. 4 (New York: Frank Harris Publishing Co., 1925), 749.
114. Julius Wernher in a letter dated January 22, 1880, addressed to his parents, quoted in Raleigh Trevelyan, *Grand Dukes and Diamonds: The Wernhers of Luton Hoo* (London: Faber and Faber, 2012).
115. Jules Porgès withdrew from the business in December 1889, after which Werner, Beit & Co. took over as the successor company. See Albrecht, *Alfred Beit*, 37; Williams, *The Diamond Mines of South Africa*, 289; Turrell, *Capital and Labour on the Kimberley Diamond Fields*, 212.
116. SBA, Letter Book ix, London Office to General Manager (October 12, 1876), 234.
117. "South African Affairs," *Cape Times* (January 10, 1879), 3; Angove, *In the Early Days*, 199: "South Africa, which may be styled the 'Cinderella of the British Colonial family,' was generally ignored by the rest of the Empire. She, however, like Cinderella, eventually eclipsed her sisters in the brilliancy of her wealth." *The Cape Monthly Magazine* had expressed similar sentiments in 1871, when it claimed that "[a]ccording to Downing-street, the Cape Colony is an expensive luxury, pretty and lively, but very extravagant in her demands for protection and always in hot water with her neighbors. She produces comparatively little, manufactures next to nothing, and is too lazy to work the soil of which she has plenty and to spare. . . . England regards us as a bit of a nuisance." See "Our Noble Selves!," *The Cape Monthly Magazine* 2: 7 (January, 1871), 4.
118. *Diamond News* (April 24, 1877), 2.
119. Fleischer, *Merchant Pioneers*, 219–220; Worger, *South Africa's City of Diamonds*, 45.
120. George Kilgour (Kimberley manager of the London and SA Exploration Company) to the London secretary, July 29, 1880, quoted in Worger, 44.
121. Newbury, "Technology, Capital, and Consolidation," 7; Meredith, *Diamonds, Gold, and War*, 111; Reunert, *Diamonds and Gold in South Africa*, 39: "Speculative mania took possession of the public, and mining scrip [sic] was regarded as a sure passport to wealth. . . . The eagerness to be 'in the swim' silenced every prompting of prudence; clerks threw up their situations, merchants left their stores, and prof. men their duties, to hang about street corners and dabble in stocks, of the real value of which they were generally profoundly ignorant . . . the bubble burst. For the next 3–4 years, investors were as hard to convince of the value of our mines, as they had previously been recklessly eager to buy into them . . . 'share mania,' which developed out of a phase of rapid mining company formation. The majority of private companies and small holdings in the mines were put into joint-stock mining companies. . . . 15 of the 71 companies formed in 1881 were incorporated in London and Paris, and these 15 accounted for one-third of the total nominal capital of the mines."

122. Colin Newbury, "Cecil Rhodes, De Beers and Mining Finance in South Africa: The Business of Entrepreneurship and Imperialism," in Raymond E. Dumett, ed., *Mining Tycoons in the Age of Empire, 1870–1945: Entrepreneurship, High Finance, Politics, and Territorial Expansion* (London: Ashgate, 2009), 92; Colin Newbury, "The Origin and Function of the London Diamond Syndicate," *Business History* 29: 1 (1987), 6; Newbury, "Technology." *The Diamond Fields' Times* reported, "[t]he diamond merchant's importance to the Fields has never been appreciated as it ought to have been. . . . The licensed diamond dealer is as essential to the well-being of the Fields as is the diamond digger. . . . When there is an active diamond trade here the produce of the mines are transformed into money which circulates through every channel of trade in the Fields, and every one residing here gets some of it. The baker, the butcher, the shoemaker, the builder, the joiner and the merchant all find their businesses thriving, and they in their turn spend again with other people, and so the whole community prospers." *The Diamond Fields' Times* (October 20, 1884), 3–4.

123. Rhodes's first success on the diamond fields originated from a water pumping contract that he and his partner, Charles Dunnell Rudd, signed in 1873. They imported a twelve-horse-power Ransome and Sims engine and a Blake's steam pump from the London branch of Rudd & Co. to help pump the mines dry. Rhodes used the revenue from this venture to invest in De Beers claims. Turrell notes that the brilliance of this enterprise lay not merely in the absolute necessity of the machinery in deep-level mining, but also in its ability to regulate the value of claims: "Submerged claims sold cheaply on the market and gained remission of rates and license fees. They possessed a dormant value which erupted in the late 1870s as the water was extracted. With a steady income from the water contract, Rhodes . . . bought claims in potentially the richest ground in the mines, which formed the reservoir of their pumping operations." See Robert Vicat Turrell, "Rhodes, De Beers, and Monopoly," *Journal of Imperial and Commonwealth History* 10: 3 (1982), 318; Raymond E. Dumett, ed., *Mining Tycoons in the Age of Empire, 1870–1945: Entrepreneurship, High Finance, Politics and Territorial Expansion* (Burlington: Ashgate, 2009); Stanley Chapman, *The Rise of Merchant Banking* (London: Routledge, 2006). Colin Newbury has shown that Rhodes, as a member of the Cape Parliament, was effective in promoting legislation that was favorable to diamond companies, most notably in ensuring that the burden of taxation was kept low. Rhodes was successful, he argues, in the sphere of "political entrepreneurship," curtailing the power of the Cape Government over the diamond fields of the Northern Cape. Instead, diamond mining companies exercised almost complete control over both local government at Kimberley and the distribution of minerals, with little regulation or interference by the state. Not until 1904 did the Cape Government apply a tax to diamond companies. Newbury, *The Diamond Ring*, 63, 149. The reference of Rhodes to "the Napoleon of the diamond world" originates from "Diamond Cutting: Its Great Growth in the Last Twenty-Five Years," *The Atlanta Constitution* (November 10, 1895), 5.

124. Archives of N. M. Rothschild & Sons, London, BAL 109/26, E. L. De Crano to Rothschild (November 23, 1887).

125. "Production Statistics of the De Beers DMC," *The Statist* (June 9, 1899), 651. See also Turrell, *Capital and Labour*, 237–239. The dividends for De Beers Mining Company were 12 percent in 1886, 16 percent in 1887, and 25 percent in 1888. These growing numbers resulted from improvements in the value of "blue" and the reduction in expenses. In 1881, blue had only yielded 7/10ths of a carat per

load and in 1882, only 8/10ths carat, while the working expenses had amounted to 13s.2d. per load, so that in that year it had cost 16s.6d. to produce a carat of diamonds. In 1887, the average yield was 1.15 carats per load and the cost of production 8s.2d. per load, equivalent to 7s.2d. per carat, so that in those five years the yield had improved over 40 percent and the cost of production had been reduced nearly 40 percent. Reunert, *Diamonds and Gold in South Africa*, 43.

126. "Appendix: Exports and Imports of the Cape Colony Increased by the Export of Diamonds, 1869–1888," in Max Bauer, *Precious Stones* (London: Charles Griffin & Co., 1904), 236; A. Michielsen, *De diamant-economie. Waarde, prijs en conjunctuur* (Antwerp: Christelijke Belgische Diamantbewerkerscentrale, 1955), 125; Turrell, "Rhodes, De Beers, and Monopoly." The 1884 *Cape Almanac* reported, "The three banks in Kimberley give returns of diamonds shipped by them during the last four months of 1882, amounting to 603,569 carats. Through the Kimberley Post Office, 1,666 lbs. weight of diamonds, incl. packages, were transmitted during 1882, but the Inspector of Mines has not been able to learn what amount went through the Dutoitspan Post Office for the same period. Thirty per cent as tare is usually allowed off the weight of these packages sent per post. 2,240 carats go to the pound weight, so that the total weight in diamonds transmitted through the Kimberley Post office during last year appears to have been 2,602,880 carats." See "Imports and Exports," *Cape Almanac* (1884), 62.

127. "Nine Months Cape Exports," *Cape Almanac* (1890), 148–149: "Colonial Produce Exported from the Cape Colony in 1888 and 1889: Precious Stones: Diamonds: 3,005,174 carats at a value of £3,296,818 (1888) and 2,352,821 carats at a value of £3,136,889 (1889). Total exported between January and September: £6,339,914 (1888) and £6,788,039 (1889)."

128. Turrell, "Rhodes, De Beers, and Monopoly," 320.

129. The principal accepting houses handling De Beers and Central issues were N. M. Rothschild & Sons; T. Henry Schroder & Co.; Mosenthal, Sons & Co.; Kleinwort, Sons & Co.; Jules Porgès & Co.; Hardy Nathan & Son; and R. Raphael & Sons.

130. Barnato is quoted in Raymond's *B. I. Barnato*, 70. Raymond interviewed Barnato for a South African newspaper, although it's not clear if or where this interview appeared.

131. One long-term implication of company centralization was the gravitational shift from South African to European shareholders. While in 1885 very few De Beers shares sold in London or on the Continent—receiving capital instead from local investors—five years later European shareholders held the bulk of its capital and they consequently collected dividends that otherwise would have been distributed to South African entrepreneurs and funneled into the local economy. Theodore Reunert provides the following figures for dividends and debenture payments in 1891: Dividends paid in the Colony £300,000 and paid in Europe £588,000; Interest on debentures paid in the Colony £3,000 and paid in Europe £253,000. See Reunert, *Diamonds and Gold*, 63. This financial drain caused a drop in the circulation of money in the Kimberley community, leaving a formerly bustling town a shadow of its former self by the turn of the century.

132. Williams, *The Diamond Mines of South Africa*, 512.

133. Brough, "The Mining Industries of South Africa, As Shown at the Kimberley Exhibition," 172.

134. Angove, *In the Early Days*, 123.

135. Angove, 127. Charles Allen expanded on this point. Electricity proved instrumental in lighting mining shafts and tunnels. Electric bells and telephones

connected depositing floors, underground level mines, and work offices, improving the speed of communication. See Allen, *Diamond Mining in the Kimberley Field and the Mechanical Equipment of the Kimberley Diamond Mines* (New York: John R. Dunlap, 1903), 11–12.

136. For more on racial discrimination in the mining industry, see Charles van Onselen, *New Babylon, New Nineveh: Everyday Life on the Witwatersrand, 1886–1914* (Johannesburg: J. Ball Publishers, 2001). For the difference in wages between black and white minters, see the *Statistical Register of the Colony of the Cape of Good Hope for the Year 1893* (Cape Town: Richards & Sons, 1894), 239–240.

137. William Worger notes that "changes in claim holding and technology in the mid1870s produced a white work force. Before 1876, with production in the hands of small claim holders, all wage labor in the mines had been done by black workers. Each claim holder, perhaps assisted by one or two partners, or working someone else's claims on shares, had supervised his own work force of ten to twenty black laborers. White men rarely sold their labor. Their services were generally not required since black labor was cheaper, and most supervisory functions could be performed by the diggers themselves. But the growth of larger units of production, and the increasing sophistication of machine workings, encourage the growth of two new elements in the mine work force: white supervisory workers and white skilled miners and artisans—a direct result of the expansion of the scale of production." Worger, *South Africa's City of Diamonds*, 148. For a detailed description of "Laws on Digging for, and Dealing in, Precious Metals and Precious Stones in the South African Republic" (1887), see Mitchell, *Diamonds and Gold of South Africa*, 57–84. Leonard Thompson observed that "arrangements in Kimberley foreshadowed later refinements of urban segregation, labor control, and all-male hostels for migrant black workers." See "Diamonds, Gold, and British Imperialism, 1870–1910," in *A History of South Africa* (New Haven, CT: Yale University Press, 2000), 110–153.

138. Shain and Mendelsohn, *The Jews in South Africa*, 46; Gideon Shimoni, *Community and Conscience; The Jews in Apartheid South Africa* (Hanover: Brandeis University Press, 2003), 131.

139. Louis Cohen referred to Kimberley as "Diamondopolis" in his *Reminiscences*, 18.

140. *Diamond News* (October 1881), 1. Rosenthal, "On the Diamond Fields," 120.

141. Adam Mendelsohn, *The Rag Race: How Jews Sewed Their Way to Success in America and the British Empire* (New York: New York University Press, 2014), 14.

142. For a detailed account of this event, see Roberts, *The Diamond Magnates*, 117–125; 139–152.

143. The house of Rothschild concerned itself mainly with loans to governments and public bodies. However, in the 1890s it became heavily involved in diamond and gold mining on the Rand. When Alfred Beit and Julius Wernher floated Rand Mines in February 1893, R. were allotted 27,000 of the 100,000 shares. See Niall Ferguson, *The World's Banker: The History of the House of Rothschild* (London: Weidenfeld & Nicolson, 1998), 877–892.

144. Sander L. Gilman and Milton Shain have made this point in *Jewries at the Frontier: Accommodation, Identity, Conflict* (Urbana: University of Illinois Press, 1999), Introduction.

CHAPTER 2

1. Currey, "Half a Century in South Africa," Chapter 17.

2. "Another Mail Robbery," *Diamond Field* 2: 67 (August 1, 1872), 3; Cape Archives, Cape Town: GLW: Letters from the Colonial Office, Vol. 28 (June 6, 1872), n.p.; "Foreign and Colonial News," *Illustrated London News* 61: 1725 (September 28, 1872), 294.
3. George McCall Theal, *History of South Africa since September 1795. Volume 5: The Cape Colony and Natal to 1872, Griqualand West to 1880* (London: Swan Sonnenschein, 1910), 272–273.
4. Theal, *History of South Africa*, 272.
5. Cape Archives: GLW: Letters from the Colonial Office, Vol. 28 (July 18, 1872), n.p.
6. Diamond miners, for example, purchased aerial ropeways from Commans & Co. of 52 Gracechurch Street, London, and portable steam and mining engines from Ransomes, Sims and Jefferies Ltd, of Orwell Works, Ipswich. See Ivor Herbert, *The Diamond Diggers: South Africa 1866 to the 1970s* (London: Tom Stacey, 1972), 79.
7. National Archives, London: "Importation of Diamonds and Other Precious Stones: Customs Procedures," CUST 33/404 (1858).
8. Danielle Kinsey, "Imperial Splendor: Diamonds, Commodity Chains, and Consumer Culture in Nineteenth-Century Britain" (PhD Dissertation, University of Illinois at Urbana-Champaign, 2010), 185; Turrell, *Capital and Labour*, 76–77. For close connections between diamond merchants and banks, see "Loewenthal and Goldsmith," *The Diamond News* (Kimberley, September 11, 1872), 1.
9. "South African Diamonds," *Jeweller and Metalworker* (September 15, 1877), 141.
10. "Of South African Diamonds," *Jeweller and Metalworker* (October 15, 1881), 194. Theodore Reunert reported, "[t]he weight of diamonds sent through the Kimberley Post Office in 1884 was 1,801 lbs (gross) and in 1885 it was 1,830 lbs. Forty per cent must be deducted from these weights for weight of packages, leaving respectively 1,080 and 1,100 lbs. as the net weight of diamonds shipped each year, equivalent to 2,385,000 and 2,430,000 weight in carats." See Reunert, *Diamonds and Gold in South Africa*, 212.
11. The *Times* (February 1, 1872): "The largest sale by auction of these gems that has yet been known in this country, was held yesterday at the rooms of Messrs. Debenham, Storr, and Sons. The auction comprised upwards of one thousand carats of cut brilliants and rough diamonds as found. . . . The total realized by the sale was about 9,730 pounds." See also auction coverage in the *Diamond News* (September 11, 1872), 2; "Auctioneers and Peddlers," *Jeweller and Metalworker* (November 15, 1882), 217; Payton, *The Diamond Diggings of South Africa*, 124.
12. There are too many articles on the diamond discovery and the developing diamond fields to list here, although note 26 in chapter 1 provides a small collection. Already in 1872, *The Graphic* stated that "[a]n immense deal has been written about the South African diamond fields, and therefore we are anxious not to bore our readers." See "The South African Diamond Fields," *The Graphic* (June 22, 1872), 575.
13. Rachel Lichtenstein, *Diamond Street: The Secret History of Hatton Garden* (London: Penguin, 2013).
14. For company addresses, see G. Eugene Harfield, *A Commercial Directory of the Jews of the United Kingdom* (London: Hewlett and Pierce, 1894). The Directory lists names and addresses of London diamond merchants, located primarily at Hatton Garden and Holborn Viaduct, but also of jewelers, brokers, diamond mounters, dealers, and "manufacturers of diamond scales and all other requisites for the diamond trade."
15. Anthony Hocking, *Oppenheimer and Son* (New York: McGraw-Hill, 1973), 29.

16. Godehard Lenzen, *The History of Diamond Production and the Diamond Trade* (London: Barrie & Jenkins, 1970), 166; Russell Shor, *Connections: A Profile of Diamond People and Their History* (Antwerp: World Federation of Diamond Bourses, 1993), 29; Newbury, "Technology, Capital, and Consolidation."
17. See also Williams, *The Diamond Mines of South Africa*, 516.
18. van Agtmaal, "Het Diamantvak in Amsterdam," 118; "The Diamond Cartel," *Yale Law Journal* 56: 8 (1947), 1404–1411. "Purchasers cannot exercise the normal power of selection which exists in a competitive market. The cartel justifies this type of selling on the grounds that producers cannot profitably carry out mining operations for a particular type of diamond and must be assured of a market for the entire run-of-the-mine production.... [T]he diamond cartel holds a monopoly in an industry which produces a substance essential to many American industrial processes today. It is a monopoly of long-standing, with the rigidity of a system now half a century old—a solidly knit structure of ownership, control, contractual relationship, and trade practices. Such a system of control has been able to impose the burden of high, fixed prices upon the American industrial diamond consumers because they have been without any bargaining power to force a change in the arbitrary methods of marketing." De Loos, in 1890, stated that the price of rough rose from 18 to 42 shillings per carat within an eleven-month time span, leading to higher retail prices and a drastic decline in sales. D. de Loos, *Diamant en edele metalen, Vol. 1* (Haarlem: De Erven Loosjes, 1890), 69.
19. Henri Polak, *De strijd der diamantbewerkers* (Amsterdam: S. L. van Looy, 1896), 21. Italics in the original.
20. Polak, 20.
21. ANDB Archief, International Institute of Social History, Amsterdam, Inv. Nr. 3077.17: Wernher, Beit & Co., London, 1895.
22. "No Slump in Diamonds," *New York Times* (June 10, 1900), 16; "Diamonds to Be Dearer," *New York Times* (August 17, 1889), 8; "Dear London Diamonds: Reasons Given for the Recent Great Advance; The Combination That Has Cut Down Production," *New York Times* (January 12, 1890), 14.
23. "Lordly Lords of Diamonds: You Take What the Syndicate Offers at Its Price," *The Sun* (December 3, 1909), 5.
24. Leopold Stern, Our Diamond Cutters Excel," *New York Times* (August 6, 1906), 7. Stern was born in Monzingen, Germany, in 1848 to Nathan Stern and Regina Ullman Stern. Nathan Stern, employed in the diamond business, emigrated to America in the early 1860s. In 1871, at the height of the South African diamond rush, they settled in New York City, where Nathan, Leopold, and Isidore started Stern Brothers & Co., one of the first diamond-cutting establishments in the city. The *New York Times* credited Stern with introducing diamond cutting on a commercial scale in New York, the topic of chapter 4. "Leopold Stern Dies at the Age of 80," *New York Times* (December 30, 1928), 20.
25. "Diamond Mines May Fail and the Price of Gems Go Up," *Atlanta Constitution* (October 1, 1899), B4.
26. Hocking, *Oppenheimer and Son*, 26; Kanfer, *The Last Empire*, 153; Jade Davenport, *Digging Deep: A History of Mining in South Africa* (Johannesburg: Jonathan Ball Publishers, 2013).
27. Chapman, *Merchant Enterprise in Britain*, 130; Youssef Cassis, "Jewish entrepreneurs in England, c.1850--c.1950," in Werner E. Mosse and Hans Pohl, eds., *Jüdische Unternehmer in Deutschland im 19. und 20. Jahrhundert*

(Stuttgart: Franz Steiner Verlag, 1992), 24–35; Yogev, *Diamonds and Coral*; Israel, *European Jewry in the Age of Mercantilism*.
28. Hocking, *Oppenheimer and Son*, 15.
29. Simmel, *The Philosophy of Money*; Siegel, *The Mazzel Ritual*, 52. Tulips serve as a useful example. During the seventeenth-century Dutch Golden Age, the tulip, first imported from the Ottoman Empire, became a coveted luxury item. As Dutch growers developed different varieties, the flower's fashionability soared. A single Viceroy bulb, displayed in the 1637 catalog *Verzameling van een Meenigte Tulipaanen* (known in English as *The Tulip Book*) sold for more than 3,000 florins, ten times the annual salary of a craftsman. Fortunes were made and lost during the *tulpenmanie* (tulip craze) of the 1630s, when contract trading in bulbs reached extraordinary heights. Creators of the *Semper Augustus*, famous to this day for being the most expensive tulip ever sold at 5,500 florins (approximately $100,000), received an offer of twelve acres of land, inspiring the British journalist, Charles Mackay, to title his book *Extraordinary Popular Delusions and the Madness of Crowds*. Although the speculative bubble burst, tulips would become the fourth leading export product of the Netherlands, wildly popular among consumers at home and abroad. See Charles Mackay, *Extraordinary Delusions and the Madness of Crowds* (London: Richard Bentley, 1841).
30. Ed Caesar recently made a similar point about the appeal of diamonds in the *New Yorker*: "Although the market appears to be a paradox—an abundant resource that relies on the illusion of scarcity—it depends on a deep truth about human desire. We prize diamonds because others prize them." See "The Rock," *New Yorker* (February 3, 2020), 35.
31. "Precious stones," stated a female spectator at the Great Exhibition of 1851, "enable us to realize in our minds the wildest wonders of an Arabian tale." See "A Lady's Glance at the Great Exhibition, No. III," *ILN* 19: 512 (August 23, 1851), 242.
32. H. Trueman Wood, *Reports on the Colonial Sections of the Exhibition: Issued under the Supervision of the Council of the Society of Arts* (London: William Clowes & Sons, 1887), 39. The mineral wealth of the Colony was summarized by a revised, corrected, and extensively researched geological map, which was to be followed by an explanatory textbook issued in time for the Exhibition in London. From the preliminary report of the subcommittee for Minerals dated March 31, 1885: Cape Archives, Cape Town: Archive of the Secretary to the Commission for the Colonial and Indian Exhibition (CIE). For an excellent dissertation on the Exhibition, see Dipti Bhagat, "Buying More Than a Diamond: South Africa and the Colonial and Indian Exhibition, 1886" (Doctoral Dissertation, Victoria & Albert Museum/Royal College of Art, 1996), 58.
33. For more on performativity at Colonial Exhibits, see Dipti Bhagat, "The Poetics of Belonging: Exhibitions and the Performance of White South African Identity, 1886–1936" (PhD Dissertation, University of London, 2002), 18.
34. Danielle C. Kinsey, "Koh-i-Noor: Empire, Diamonds, and the Performance of British Material Culture," *Journal of British Studies* 48: 2 (2009), 391–419; Paul Young, "'Carbon, Mere Carbon': The Kohinoor, the Crystal Palace, and the Mission to Make Sense of British India," *Nineteenth-Century Contexts* 29: 4 (2007), 343–358; David Brewster, "The Diamond—Its History, Properties, and Origin," *North British Review* 18 (November 1852), 186–234; Nevil Storey-Maskelyne, "On the Koh-i-Noor Diamond," unpublished manuscript, Story-Maskelyne Papers, Natural History Museum Archives: DF5001/415, page 15. For contemporary pieces on the diamond see, among others, "The Koh-i-Noor Diamond," *ILN* (May 26, 1849),

332; "The Koh-i-Noor," *ILN* (December 23, 1848), 397; "The Great Eastern Nave—The Koh-i-Noor; and Precious Stones in the Crystal Palace, *Illustrated Exhibitor*, no. 1 (June 7, 1851), 19–20; and no. 6 (July 12, 1851), 93–95; "The Gems," *ILN* 18 (May 17, 1851), 426–428; "The Great Indian Diamond," *ILN* (July 27, 1852), 7.
35. Lady Login, the wife of the East India Company director, is quoted in Kinsey, "Koh-i-Noor," 403.
36. "The Opening of the Great Exhibition," *ILN* (May 2, 1851), 5; "The Great Exhibition," *ILN* (May 3, 1851), 5.
37. "The Front Row of the Shilling Gallery," *Punch Magazine* 21 (July 5, 1851), 11; "A Lady's Glance at the Great Exhibition, No. III," 242; "The Koh-i-noor Cut and Come Again," *Punch Magazine* 23 (August 1852), 54–55.
38. "The Chemistry of the Great Exhibition," *ILN* 19: 505 (July 26, 1851), 131.
39. "The Cutting of the Koh-i-Noor," *ILN* (July 19, 1852), 8; "The Great Indian Diamond," *ILN* (July 27, 1852), 7; "The Re-Cutting of the Koh-i-Noor," *ILN* (August 28, 1852); "The Recutting of the Koh-i-noor," *National Magazine* 1: 5 (November 1852), 443–444; James Tennant, "On the Recutting of the Koh-i-noor Diamond," Report of the 24th Meeting of the British Association for the Advancement of Science (Liverpool, September 1854), 75–76. Meijer Coster was the son of Moses Elias Coster, who had founded the diamond manufacturing company M.E. Coster at the Korte Houtstraat in Amsterdam. It became one of the most successful diamond-cutting and -polishing firms in the world and exists to this day.
40. "Re-Cutting of the Koh-i-Noor," *ILN* 21: 570 (July 24, 1852), 54; "The Koh-i-Noor," *ILN* 21: 579 (September 18, 1852), 213.
41. "The Recutting of the Koh-i-noor," *National Magazine* 1: 5 (November 1852), 443–444. Queen Victoria wore the stone in a brooch and a circlet. After she died in 1901, the Kohinoor was set in the Crown of Queen Alexandra, wife of Edward VII. It was transferred to the Crown of Queen Mary in 1911, and finally to the Crown of Queen Elizabeth (later known as the Queen Mother) in 1937 for her coronation as Queen consort.
42. "A Ramble through the Cape of Good Hope Court," *ILN* 89: 2478 (October 16, 1886), 414.
43. The Colonial and Indian Exhibition held 81 sessions of conference that included discussions such as the colonies' natural products, agriculture, and mining. Bhagat, "Buying More Than a Diamond," 64.
44. Bhagat, "Buying More Than a Diamond," 64.
45. "Preliminary Report of the Sub-Committee for Minerals," dated March 31, 1885. Cape Archives: Archive of the Secretary to the Commission for the Colonial and Indian Exhibition (CIE).
46. *Colonial and Indian Exhibition, 1886: Official Catalogue* (London: William Clowes and Sons, 1886), 305. Diamonds in the rough and matrix were exhibited by The French Diamond Mining Company, Kimberley, De Beer's DMC, Phoenix DMC, French and D'Esterre DMC. See also *The Westminster Review* (July 1886), 46.
47. Bhagat, "Buying More Than a Diamond," 55. Early European travelers used the derogatory term "Kaffir," meaning "unbeliever," to refer to black Africans. See Herbert, *The Diamond Diggers*, 24.
48. Frank Cundall, ed., *Reminiscences of the Colonial and Indian Exhibition* (London: William Clowes, 1886), 25.
49. The Exhibition venue operated an emigration office on the premises. For a detailed layout of the exhibition, see Cundall, *Reminiscences of the Colonial and Indian Exhibition*, 3. F. Pennfather presented a lecture on the premises, titled "The

Empire: A Field for Emigration," encouraging emigration as the best viable option for an ever-growing British population. *Colonial and Indian Exhibition, 1886*, pamphlet in the Cape Archives: BP 12, Acc. No. 140.

50. *Colonial & Indian Exhibition Daily Programme* (London: William Clowes and Sons, 1886), ii. The washing and sorting machinery at the Exhibition had been lent to the Commission by Messrs. Davey, Paxman, and Co. See J.C.D., "The Colonial and Indian Exhibition: Cape of Good Hope," *Illustrated Naval and Military Magazine* 5 (London: W. H. Allen & Co., 1886), 413.
51. Wood, *Reports on the Colonial Sections of the Exhibition*, 43.
52. Sidney Cowper, "Report of the Secretary to the Executive Commissioner for the Cape Colony at the Colonial and Indian Exhibition, 1886," presented to the Governor of the Cape Colony, 1887, published as an annexure to the Votes and Proceedings of the House of Assembly, Cape Town, No. G 53–87.
53. J.C.D., "The Colonial and Indian Exhibition," 413–418. On theft at the Exhibit, see "Colonial and Indian Exhibition: Cape of Good Hope," *ILN* 89: 2478 (October 16, 1886), 412: "Examining the large and excellent model of the Bultfontein Diamond Mine, in Griqualand West, one learns with regret from Mr. Cowper that the miniature engines have been 'conveyed' by certain kleptomaniacal members of the British public, but there is yet plenty to interest one in scanning the spider's-weblike appearance of the huge pit with the aerial hauling-gear, the depositing floors, and washing-gear of the miners. This capital model adds eloquent force to the fact that 'the daily output of one hauling-gear approaches 750 loads of 16 cubic feet.'"
54. *Colonial & Indian Exhibition Daily Programme* (London: William Clowes and Sons, 1886): "The diamond-cutting and polishing is carried on daily, from 10.30 to 1.0 p.m., from 2.0 to 6.0 p.m., and 6.45 to 8.0 p.m."
55. Danielle Kinsey explains that "[b]eginning in 1862, the Albert Coster diamond-cutting firm's diamond-cutting and diamond-setting demonstrations, usually in the Dutch sections of the exhibition, were staples of world's fairs. . . . Coster's displays became more and more elaborate, peaking at the Amsterdam International Colonial in 1883 where an entire building was devoted to demonstrating diamond cutting and trade." Kinsey, "Imperial Splendor," 324.
56. "No-More a Secret Art," *Washington Post* (February 2, 1896), 10; "The English Diamond Industry," *Jeweller and Metalworker* (September 15, 1882), 175–176: "The English diamond industry, although unsurpassed for excellence, is not yet equal in extent to that of Amsterdam. The cutting and polishing of diamonds has, for at least a couple of centuries, been an art exclusively practiced by Jews, who tenaciously guarded the secrets of the craft, and refused to work in the presence of strangers." See also "Diamonds Art a Secret: Process of Cutting the Stones Is Jealously Guarded," *Washington Post* (October 22, 1905), 4. "The difficulty in the way of developing a British diamond-cutting industry," stated the *Post*, "is that of teaching the British workman an art which the present diamond cutters keep very secret. The Antwerp factories, it may be added, are principally conducted by Jews, as are those of Amsterdam." "The English Diamond Industry," *Diamond News and West Griqualand Gazette* (October 19, 1882), 3.
57. "Colonial and Indian Exhibition: Cape of Good Hope," 416.
58. Interestingly, Dipti Bhagat noted that the official Exhibition Guide, contrary to the popular press, lacked any mention of indigenous peoples. Excluding their presence and identity, she argued, "served to deny the non-European nature of the colony." Bhagat, "Buying More Than a Diamond," 67. See also Sadiah Qureshi,

Peoples on Parade: Exhibitions, Empire, and Anthropology in Nineteenth-Century Britain (Chicago: Chicago University Press, 2011).
59. From the report of the sub-committee for Manufactures, dated Feb 8, 1885; Cape Archives: Archive of the Secretary to the Commission for the Colonial and Indian Exhibition (CIE) 2423, No. 43/8, 1886.
60. "Diamonds at the Paris Exhibition," *Scientific American* 61: 18 (November 2, 1889), 277.
61. De Loos, *Diamant en edele metalen*, 67.
62. See, among others, advertisements in *ILN* (October 1886), 65; *The Times* (June 23, 1897), 8.
63. "Precious Stones by Prof. Henry A. Miers," *Jeweller & Metalworker* (September 1, 1896), 850.
64. [No title], *Jewish Chronicle* (September 27, 1889), 7. Jenna Weissman Joselit recently argued that the American Jewish press expressed equal enthusiasm and delight at the prominence of Jews in the diamond trade, especially in South Africa and Holland. Jenna Weissman Joselit, "Cut Gems: How Jews Brought Diamonds from South Africa to Amsterdam to Midtown Manhattan," *Tablet Magazine* (January 23, 2020), https://www.tabletmag.com/sections/community/articles/cut-gems
65. From a Correspondent, "The Cape Colony," *Jewish Chronicle* (July 3, 1891), 6.
66. The Anglo-Jewish Association (AJA), founded in 1871 and inspired by the Alliance Israélite Universelle in Paris, was an organization that promoted Jewish social, legal, and intellectual advancement at home and abroad. Jacob Waley served as its first president. By 1900, it had thirty-six branches, fourteen of which operated in the British colonies.
67. "Lectures to Jewish Working Men, *Jewish Chronicle* (January 6, 1871), 5. The non-Jewish press covered Bergtheil's lecture as well. See, for instance, J. Bergtheil, "The Diamond Fields of the Cape," *Mechanics Magazine* (January 13, 1871), 28–29.
68. The Golden Jubilee of Queen Victoria was celebrated on June 20, 1887, on the occasion of the fiftieth anniversary of Victoria's accession to the throne, in June 1837. The celebration included a banquet to which fifty members of Europe's royalty were invited.
69. "The Queen's Jubilee," *Jewish Chronicle* (June 25, 1886), 10–11.
70. In attendance were, among others, the presidents of the Society Antiquaries, Archeological Institute, Anthropological Institute, the Palestine Exploration Fund, Society of Biblical Archeology, and the Royal Historical Society. "The Proposed Jewish Exhibition," *Jewish Chronicle* (May 21, 1886), 5. "A meeting to promote the holding of an Anglo-J. Historical Exhibition was held at the residence of Mr. F. D. Mocatta on Sunday last. There were present: Mr. F. D. Mocatta, in the Chair; the Revs. Dr. H. Adler, Morris Joseph, and A. Lowy; Dr. Asher, Dr. Friedlander, Major Goldsmid; Messrs. Alfred L. Cohen, Israel Davis, Lewis Emanuel, Hyman Montagu, S. Montagu, M. P., and Lucien Wolf.
71. Heinrich Graetz's address was published in *The Jewish Chronicle*: "Lecture before Anglo-Jewish Exhibition," *Jewish Chronicle* (June 24, 1887), and later published under the title *Historic Parallels in Jewish History: A Discourse Delivered at the Anglo-Jewish Historical Exhibition, 16th June, 1887* (London: Wertheimer, Lea & Co., 1887). For more on the foundation of the Jewish Historical Society of England, see Stephen Massil, "The Foundation of the Jewish Historical Society of England, 1893," *Jewish Historical Studies* 33 (1993), 225–238. The exhibition planted the seed that sprouted the JHSE, founded in 1893, still in existence today.

72. F. D. Mocatta, "Report to the Members of the General Committee of the Anglo-Jewish Historical Exhibition," *Catalogue of the Anglo-Jewish Historical Exhibition, Royal Albert Hall, London, 1887*, compiled by Lucien Wolf and Joseph Jacobs (London: F. Haes, 1888), 211; "Notes of the Week," *Jewish Chronicle* (May 21, 1886), 5.
73. "Kimberley Diamond-Fields Synagogue," in *Catalogue of Anglo-Jewish Historical Exhibition, 1887* (London: William Clowes, 1887), 16.
74. John MacKenzie, *Imperialism and Popular Culture* (Manchester: Manchester University Press, 1986); Sarah Cheang, "Selling China: Class, Gender, and Orientalism at the Department Store," *Journal of Design History* 20: 1 (Spring 2007), 1–16.
75. Joanna de Groot, "Metropolitan Desires and Colonial Connections: Reflections on Consumption and Empire," in Catharine Hall and Sonya Rose, eds., *At Home with the Empire: Metropolitan Culture and the Imperial World* (New York: Cambridge University Press, 2007), 166–190; Susie L. Steinbach, *Understanding the Victorians: Politics, Culture and Society in Nineteenth-Century Britain* (London: Routledge, 2012); David Cannadine, *Ornamentalism: How The British Saw Their Empire* (New York: Oxford University Press, 2001); Alan Kidd and David Nicholls, eds., *Gender, Civic Culture and Consumerism: Middle-Class Identity in Britain, 1800–1940* (Manchester: Manchester University Press, 1999); Thomas Richards, *Commodity Culture of Victorian England: Advertising and Spectacle, 1851–1914* (Stanford: Stanford University Press, 1990).
76. "Utilitarianism and Art," *Jeweller and Metalworker* (October 15, 1874), 255–256.
77. "The Jewelry Trade in 1877," *Jeweller and Metalworker* (January 1, 1878), 194–195.
78. The art historian Marcia Pointon argues jewelry was to women what land was to men, and the normative union of controlling interests in property and currency spoke to a gendered symmetry in maintaining imperial-national health. Marcia Pointon, *Brilliant Effects: A Cultural History of Gem Stones and Jewellery* (London: Paul Mellon Centre BA, 2010); Jennie Batchelor and Cora Kaplan, *Women and Material Culture, 1660–1830* (London: Palgrave Macmillan, 2007), 63.
79. "Madame Tussaud's Exhibition," *Observer* (June 9 1889), 7; "The Female Beauty Gallery," *Jeweller and Metalworker* (February 15, 1880), 40; "An Exhibition of Diamonds," *Jeweller and Metalworker* (April 15, 1881), 71; "The Princess of Wales Presents at South Kensington," *Jeweller and Metalworker* (July 1, 1876), 291.
80. "Representative Windows," *Watchmaker, Jeweller, and Silversmith* (February 1, 1893), 155; *The Times* (April 20, 1885), 9; "Great Exhibition of Gems," *Watchmaker, Jeweller, and Silversmith* (October 1, 1895), 606; "Jewelers' Shop Windows," *Jeweller and Metalworker* (May 15, 1877), 73. For more on Victorian culture, see Erika Rappaport, *Shopping for Pleasure: Women in the Making of London's West End* (Princeton: Princeton University Press, 2001);John Plotz, *Portable Property: Victorian Culture on the Move* (Princeton: Princeton University Press, 2008).
81. Edward Bulwer Lytton, *The Siamese Twins, A Satirical Tale of the Times*, Book I (London: H. Colburn and R. Bentley, 1831), 50. Lytton is quoted in Steinbach, *Understanding Victorians*, 113.
82. See, among others, *Fashionable London* (April 27, 1892), 5; (May 4, 1892), 68–70; (May 11, 1892), 83–84; (June 4, 1892), 148; (June 11, 1892), 162; (July 15, 1892), 248.

CHAPTER 3

1. Boudien de Vries, "De joodse elite in Amsterdam, 1850–1900: Oude en nieuwe rijkdom," in Hetty Berg, ed., *De gelykstaat der Joden: Inburgering van een minderheid* (Amsterdam: Joods Historisch Museum, 1996), 82.
2. "Personal tax" was assessed according to a person's "evidence of well-being and prosperity," which included the combined value of a family's home interior, domestic servants, horses, and the like. In addition, the state required business owners to pay an annual patent tax, based on the type of business and the number of employees. In Amsterdam, up to 1887, those men who paid more than fl. 112 in combined annual taxes gained the right to vote. Between 1853 and 1887, the Amsterdam electorate consisted of 4,000–5,000 men, approximately 14 percent of the adult male working population. By the mid-1880s, 17.6 percent of the electorate were Jews, a sharp increase from 8.6 percent thirty years earlier. It points not merely to the growth of a new Jewish elite, but also to the overrepresentation of Jews in the electorate as they constituted approximately 11 percent of the total Amsterdam population. For more on the Dutch electorate, see Boudien de Vries, *Electoraat en elite: Sociale structuur en sociale mobiliteit in Amsterdam, 1850–1895* (Amsterdam: De Bataafsche Leeuw, 1986); Wiel, *Van Rapenburgerstraat naar Amerika*, 20.
3. Salvador Bloemgarten, "De emancipatie van het joodse proletariat," in *De gelykstaat der Joden*, 98.
4. Polak, *De strijd der diamantbewerkers*, 3.
5. According to the Dutch historian Karin Hofmeester, approximately 1,532 eastern European Jewish immigrants settled permanently in Amsterdam between 1880 and 1914. While London, Paris, Antwerp, and New York attracted large numbers of Jewish émigrés, Amsterdam remained predominantly a temporary stop for most travelers. For more statistical data, see Karin Hofmeester, *Van Talmoed tot Statuut: Joodse arbeiders en arbeidersbewegingen in Amsterdam, Londen en Parijs, 1880–1914* (Amsterdam: Stichting Beheer IISG, 1990), 16, 120–128. For a detailed analysis of Belgium's diamond industry, see Veerle Vanden Daelen, *Laten we hun lied verder zingen. De heropbouw van de joodse gemeenschap in Antwerpen na de Tweede Wereldoorlog, 1944–1960* (Amsterdam: University of Amsterdam Press, 2008); Erik Laureys, *Meesters van het diamant: De Belgische diamantsector tijdens het Nazibewind* (Tielt: Lannoo, 2005); Iris Kockelberg, Jan Walgrave, and Eddy Vleeschdrager, eds., *The Brilliant Story of Antwerp Diamonds* (Antwerp: MIM, 1992); Martine Vermandere, *Adamastos: 100 jaar Algemene Diamantbewerkersbond van België* (Antwerp: Archief en Museum van de Socialistische Arbeidersbeweging, 1995).
6. A large variety of popular magazines, scientific journals, and daily newspapers in Great Britain and the United States featured articles and advertisements about the international diamond trade, the manufacturing process in Amsterdam, and contemporary fashion in jewelry, including the *New York Times*, the *Scientific American*, the *Illustrated London News*, the *Jewish Chronicle*, the *Jewish Messenger*, the *Washington Post*, the *Times*, *Punch*, and *The Graphic*.
7. Kinsey, "Imperial Splendor," ii.
8. Attics were preferred over other rooms as skylights offered the best lighting. Occupants often replaced roof tiles with glass panels to maximize natural light. See "Diamantnijverheid IV," *Nieuws van de Dag*, no. 6198 (April 21, 1890), 5; "Diamantnijverheid," *Nieuws van de Dag*, no. 6204 (April 28, 1890), 2.

9. Samuel Coronel, Sr., "De diamantwerkers te Amsterdam: Een sociale studie," *De Economist* 14 (1865): 77–78; M. Barents, *De Diamantslijperij Maatschappij te Amsterdam, 1845–1920* (Amsterdam: M. Barents, 1920), 17; Theo van Tijn, "Geschiedenis van de Amsterdamse diamanthandel en –nijverheid, 1845–1897," *Tijdschrift voor Geschiedenis* 87: 1 (1974), 19. Karin Hofmeester states that between 1822 and 1855, Amsterdam counted between seven and nine diamond factories that used horse power, offering employment to approximately 300–400 people. See Hofmeester, *Een schitterende erfenis*, 20.

10. "Annual Rapport of the Chamber of Commerce: Factories in Amsterdam, 1863–1865," Gemeente Archief Amsterdam [Amsterdam Municipal Archive, hereafter cited as GAA], #5287:421–422 Archief van de Kamer van Koophandel en Fabrieken voor Amsterdam, p. 129; Theo van Tijn, *Twintig jaren Amsterdam* (Amsterdam: Scheltema & Holkema, 1965), 91.

11. M. Barents, *Het onderling Diamantslijpers Weduwen- en Weezenfonds (1848–1916). Een stuk maatschappelijk werk uit de negentiende eeuw* (Amsterdam: M. Barents, 1927), 31.

12. In Dutch, the word "juwelier" has two meanings, namely that of a shop owner who sells jewelry and that of a merchant who purchases rough stones from suppliers, outsourcing them to factory workers and selling the finished product to retailers. The latter meaning applies here.

13. "De diamantbewerkers-beweging," *Algemeen Handelsblad* 67, no. 20626 (November 14, 1894), 1. For a detailed description of the manufacturing process, see "Karakterschets: Henri Polak," *De Hollandsche Revue* 5: 5 (May 24, 1900), 309–334; "Diamond Cutting—A New Industry in New York," *Scientific American: A Weekly Journal of Practical Information, Art, Science, Mechanics, Chemistry, and Manufactures* 29: 14 (October 4, 1873), 214–216; "Diamond Cutting By Hand and Machine," *Scientific American* 65: 3 (July 18, 1891), 31–32.

14. Alicia Oltuski, *Precious Objects: A Story of Diamonds, Family, and a Way of Life* (New York: Scribner, 2001), 58.

15. The newspaper *Nieuws van de Dag* [Daily News] featured a series of articles on diamond manufacturing in 1890. For a detailed description on polishing, see "Diamantnijverheid I," *Nieuws van de Dag*, no. 6189 (April 10, 1890), 1.

16. Coronel, "De diamantwerkers te Amsterdam," 101.

17. Wietske Van Agtmaal, "Het diamantvak in Amsterdam: Van oudsher een joodse negotie," in Hetty Berg et al., eds., *Venter, fabriqueur, fabrikant: Joodse ondernemers en ondernemingen in Nederland, 1796–1940* (Amsterdam: Joods Historisch Museum, 1994), 116. An 1890 edition of the *Nieuws van de Dag* reported that the *Diamantslijperij Maatschappij* finished approximately 17,000 carats for a total value of fl. 10,000,000 in 1865. The company consisted of 53 shareholders, 46 of whom were Jewish. Nearly all lived in Amsterdam, except for Eduard Zadok Dresden and Levy Joseph Posno, who resided in London and Paris respectively. Jacob Joseph Posno serves as company president and Jonas Ephraim Dresden as vice-president. See "Diamantnijverheid," *Nieuws van de Dag*, no. 6204 (28 April, 1890), 5.

18. "Statuten van de Diamantslijperij-Maatschappij," *Bijvoegsel tot de Nederlandsche Staats-Courant*, no. 84 (April 9, 1845); "Naamloze Vennootschappen," *Nederlandsche Staats-Courant*, no. 178 (July 30, 1853).

19. J. C. H. Blom and J. J. Cahen, "Jewish Netherlanders, Netherlands Jews, and Jews in the Netherlands," in J. C. H. Blom, R. G. Fuks-Mansfeld, and I. Schöffer, eds., *The History of the Jews in the Netherlands* (Oxford: The Littman Library of Jewish

Civilization, 2007), 237. In the 1860s, the Jewish population averaged around 30,000, a number that doubled to nearly 60,000 by the end of the century.
20. Carolus Reijnders, *Van "Joodse Natiën" tot Joodse Nederlanders: Een onderzoek naar getto- en assimilatie-verschijnselen tussen 1600 en 1942* (Amsterdam: Joko, 1969), 80.
21. Louis M. Hermans, *Krotten en Sloppen: Een onderzoek naar den woningtoestand te Amsterdam, ingesteld in opdracht van den Amsterdamsche Bestuurdersbond* (Amsterdam: S. L. van Looy, 1901). Hermans, a writer and politician, conducted municipal research into the living conditions of the poor in the 1890s. He concluded that "population density in the Jewish Quarter [was] more than seven times higher than elsewhere in the city, and in 1896, the number of residences infested with contagious diseases [was] 14 times higher for measles and 13,5 higher for scarlet fever in the Jewish neighborhood than anywhere else in the city."
22. According to the demographer E. Boekman, the Jewish population of Amsterdam consisted in 1869 of 29,952 people (11.3 percent of the city population and 44 percent of the total number of Jews in Holland). In 1879 the number reached 40,318 (12.7 and 49.3 percent respectively); in 1889 54,479 (13.3 and 55.97 percent); in 1899 59,065 (11.5 percent of the city and 56.4 percent of Jews in Holland); and in 1909 60,970 (10.7 and 59.6 percent). See Emanuel Boekman, *Demografie van de Joden in Nederland* (Amsterdam: Hertzberger, 1936); Blom et al., *The History of the Jews in the Netherlands*, 237.
23. Salvador Bloemgarten, "De emancipatie van het joodse proletariat," in Hetty Berg, ed., *De gelykstaat der Joden: Inburgering van een minderheid* (Amsterdam: Joods Historisch Museum, 1996), 103.
24. The weekly newspaper *De Diamant* blamed the combination of adolescence and spending money for the "vulgarities" and "indecencies" exhibited by Jewish and non-Jewish diamond workers in factories and social establishments. One polisher named J. Loopuit confessed that "the large majority of [his] colleagues are unruly people uninterested in any kind of improvement," while another blamed their "bad reputation" and "lack of morality" on the desire "to go anywhere they can make noise." See "De Diamantnijverheid voor de Enquête," *Nieuws van de Dag*, no. 6967 (October 17, 1892), 5; Theo van Tijn and M. G. Emeis, *Amsterdam en diamant, 1845–1897* (Amsterdam: A. van Moppes, 1976), 67.
25. Marien van der Heijden and Wietske van Agtmaal, eds., *Henri Polak: Grondlegger van de moderne vakbeweging, 1868–1943* (Amsterdam: Nationaal Vakbondsmuseum, 1991), 21.
26. Ludo Abicht, *Geschiedenis van de joden van de Lage Landen* (Amsterdam: Meulenhoff, 2006), 197.
27. Heertje, *De Diamantbewerkers van Amsterdam*, 31.
28. Barents, *De Diamantslijperij Maatschappij*, 57; van Tijn and Emeis, *Amsterdam en diamant*, 61. In the May 1874, edition of the *Daily News*, the Diamantslijperij-Maatschappij reported that cutters averaged fl. 80 to fl. 95, while assistants earned fl. 25 to fl. 36 per week. See "Diamantnijverheid VI," *Nieuws van de Dag*, no. 6216 (May 12, 1890), 4.
29. F. van der Wal, *De oudste vakbond van ons land, 1866–1916:. Ontstaan en vijftigjarige werkzaamheid van den Algemeenen Nederlandsche Typografenbond* (Nijmegen: Bondsvergadering, 1916), 26–27; Peter Tammes, "'Hack, Pack, Sack': Occupational Structure, Status, and Mobility of Jews in Amsterdam, 1851–1941," *Journal of Interdisciplinary History* 43: 1 (2012), 1–26.
30. For more on Andries van Wezel, see Wiel, *Van Rapenburgerstraat naar Amerika*.

31. *De Diamant: Internationaal wekelijks nieuwsblad voor de belangen van het diamantvak* 3: 142 (October 20, 1886); also 5: 214 (March 9, 1888); and 7: 319 (March 14, 1890): International Institute for Social History, Amsterdam, #PMPM269 and #ZF17631.
32. Quoted in Lenzen, *The History of Diamond Production*, 132; Thorstein Veblen, *The Theory of the Leisure Class: An Economic Study of Institutions* (New York: Macmillan, 1899).
33. "The Diamond Industry," *Current Literature* 26: 1 (July 1899), 83.
34. On Simmel, see Marcia Pointon, *Brilliant Effects: A Cultural History of Gem Stones and Jewellery* (New Haven, CT: Yale University Press, 2010); Kurt H. Wolff, ed., *The Sociology of Georg Simmel* (New York: The Free Press, 1950). For more on women and modern consumer cultures, see among others, Kathy L. Peiss, "American Women and the Making of Modern Consumer Culture," *Journal for MultiMedia History* 1: 1 (1998); Rappaport, *Shopping for Pleasure*); Judith Walkowitz, *City of Dreadful Delight: Narratives of Sexual Danger in Later-Victorian London* (Chicago: Chicago University Press, 1992); Thomas Richards, *The Commodity Culture of Victorian England: Advertising and Spectacle, 1851–1914* (Stanford: Stanford University Press, 1990); Alan Kidd and Daid Nicholls, eds., *Gender, Civic Culture, and Consumerism: Middle-Class Identity in Britain, 1800–1940* (Manchester: Manchester University Press, 1999); Catherine Hall and Sonya O. Rose, *At Home with the Empire* (Cambridge University Press, 2006).
35. Heertje, *De Diamantbewerkers van Amsterdam*, 32; "Karakterschets: Henri Polak," *De Hollandsche Revue*, 317.
36. "Foreign News," *Jewish Messenger* (May 23, 1873), 2.
37. A. L. van Minden, "Verslag ter gelegenheid van het 10-jarig bestaan der Vereeniging," in *Gedenkboek uitgegeven door de Vereeniging Beurs voor den Diamanthandel* (Amsterdam: Vereeniging Beurs voor den Diamanthandel, 1919), 9.
38. The painter Salomon "Sal" Meijer, born into a family of diamond workers, is quoted in Roelie Meijer and Peter Engelsman, *Vier eeuwen diamant: Amsterdam, Antwerpen, London* (Hoorn: Uniepers, 1986), 99.
39. For full entry of the almanac, see Simone Lipschitz, *De Amsterdamse Diamantbeurs* (Amsterdam: Stadsuitgeverij Amsterdam, 1990), 41–44.
40. The board of directors of the Diamantslijperij-Maatschappij Company reported in 1873 that "workers are trading on their own nowadays and constitute a most serious competition." See "Annual Rapport of the Chamber of Commerce: Factories in Amsterdam, 1873," GAA #5287: 372 Archief van de Kamer van Koophandel en Fabrieken voor Amsterdam, p. 82. See also *De Diamant* 2: 71 (June 10, 1885); "Diamantnijverheid VII," *Nieuws van de Dag*, no. 6221 (May 19, 1890), 8.
41. Heertje, *De Diamantbewerkers van Amsterdam*, 196. The brothers Israël, Marcus, and Hartog Boas are a good example of this entrepreneurship. Putting together all of their resources, the Boas brothers started a new firm, first at Nieuwe Keizersgracht and later, in 1879, after bursting at the seams, at Uilenburgerstraat 173. This monumental building, which exists to this day, was the largest diamond factory in the world. A crew of 357 polishers, 122 assistants, and 142 apprentices processed an average of 10,000 carats per week.
42. The Association for the Diamond Exchange had its roots in the *Centrale Diamanthandels Bond*, or Central Diamond Trade Association, founded in 1881 by a small group of Jewish entrepreneurs. By 1886, it consisted of 800 members. Due to internal disagreements, the Association split in 1889 and most of its

members established the Diamond Exchange, formally recognized by royal decree in 1890. See van Tijn, "Geschiedenis van de Amsterdamse Diamanthandel –en nijverheid," 36.
43. Lipschitz, *De Amsterdamse Diamantbeurs*, 47. The Association for the Diamond Exchange consisted mostly of self-employed "eigenwerkmakers" who started their careers on the factory floor as apprentices, quickly climbing the professional ladder. Long-established, elite families running the *Diamant Maatschappij* remained unaffiliated with the Exchange and continued to meet clients separately at a private residence at Nieuwe Heerengracht no. 49.
44. Siegfried van Praag, "The Diamond Exchange When I Was a Boy." Van Praag is quoted in Lipschitz, *De Amsterdamse Diamantbeurs*, 29.
45. "New Diamond Bourse in Amsterdam," *Jewish Chronicle* (September 22, 1911), 15. The *Chronicle* reported that the new building "was opened with great ceremony . . . a center worthy of its importance has been established for the diamond trade." It was "a day of great significance for the economic progress of the diamond merchants in Amsterdam, and especially for a large proportion of the Jewish population." The newspaper added that the Exchange "will be closed on Saturday, as will also be the Post Office, located in the building, and will be opened on Sundays. The first telegram despatched from the Post Office was one of homage to the Queen. The imposing structure, which cost 50,000 pounds, is situated near the old Jewish quarter, and close to the State Railway Station. The entire arrangements are as practical as they pleasing to the eye."
46. "De Amsterdamsche diamantnijverheid: Ontwikkeling en tegenwoordige toestand," *Het Nieuws van den Dag*, no. 48, Vierde Blad (February 27, 1930), 3.
47. Dutch writer Herman Heijermans titled his well-known novel *Amsterdam Diamantstad* (Amsterdam: S. L. van Looy, 1904).
48. The founders of the Amsterdam Bank included, among others, Lippmann Rosenthal & Co, Wertheim & Gompertz, Frederik Salomon van Nierop, and Becker & Fuld, all of whom were Amsterdam Jewish bankers. For a history of the Amsterdam Bank, see S. Brouwer, *De Amsterdamsche Bank, 1871–1946* (Amsterdam: De Amsterdamsche Bank, 1946). For more on van Nierop, see A. S. Rijxman, "Mr. Frederik Salomon van Nierop, 1844–1924," in I. J. Brugmans and W. J. Wieringa, eds., *Bedrijf en samenleving: Economisch-historische studies over Nederland in de negentiende en twintigste eeuw* (Alphen aan de Rijn: Samsom, 1967), 137–155. For more on the involvement of Dutch Jews and industrial investments, see Huibert Schijf and Michiel Wagenaar, "De joodse bourgeoisie in Amsterdam, 1796–1914," in Huibert Schijf and Edward van Voolen, eds., *Gedurfd verzamelen: Van Chagall to Mondriaan* (Amsterdam: Joods Historisch Museum, 2010), 26–39; Joost Jonker, *Merchants, Bankers, Middlemen: The Amsterdam Money Market during the First Half of the Nineteenth Century* (Amsterdam: NEHA, 1996).
49. One municipal council member recalled in a public meeting that "the Amsterdam Bank used to accept assort-ments of polished stones in exchange for advanced loans so merchants could purchase rough." See J. van der Velden, "Gemeenteraad van Amsterdam," *Gemeenteblad* 2 (February 27, 1907): 346. See also "Naamlooze Vennootschap," *Algemeen Handelsblad* 59, no. 17607 (December 19, 1885); "Incasso-Bank Amsterdam," *Algemeen Handelsblad* 69, no. 21164 (May 8, 1896); "Diamantnijverheid VII," *Nieuws van de Dag*, no. 6221 (May 19, 1890), 8.
50. Abraham Salomon Rijxman, *A. C. Wertheim, 1832–1897: Een bijdrage tot zijn levensgeschiedenis* (Amsterdam: Keesing, 1961), 128; S. Brouwer, *De Amsterdamsche Bank*, 75. For more on ethnic economic networks, see Yogev, *Diamonds and Coral*;

David de Vries, *Diamonds and War: State, Capital, and Labor in British-Ruled Palestine* (New York: Berghahn Books, 2010), Introduction.
51. van Tijn, "Geschiedenis van de Amsterdamse Diamanthandel –en nijverheid," 45.
52. Huibert Schijf, "A. C. Wertheim: Portret van een Joods Bankier," *Groniek* 115 (1991), 30.
53. *Nieuw Israëlitisch Weekblad*, no. 31 (February 21, 1873), 3. The company was owned by J. W. Bottenheim.
54. S. Brouwer concluded that the Amsterdam Bank's "relationships and connections to the diamond trade developed intra muros, while it continuously strengthened ties to economic life in the Netherlands and abroad." See Brouwer, *De Amsterdamsche Bank*, 75.
55. Kees Bruin, *Een herenwereld ontleed: Over Amsterdamse oude en nieuwe elites in de tweede helft van de negentiende eeuw* (Amsterdam: Sociologisch Instituut, Universiteit van Amsterdam, 1980), 42–43; Brouwer, *De Amsterdamsche Bank*, 74; Schijf and Wagenaar, "De Joodse Bourgeoisie in Amsterdam, 1796–1914."
56. Lippman and Rosenthal, for example, together with banking firms De Hirsch and Bisschoffsheim, helped found the *Algemene Maatschappij voor Handel en Industry* (the General Company for Trade and Industry) in 1862, whose new director was also the president of the National Chamber of Commerce. While the company folded in the early 1870s, it did establish the longer-lasting Dutch-Indies Trade Bank and the Dutch-Indies Railroad Company. For a more comprehensive discussion of the ties between banking firms and industrial companies, see Huibert Schijf, *Netwerken van een financieel-ecnomische elite: Personele verbindingen in het Nederlandse bedrijfsleven aan het eind van de negentiende eeuw* (Amsterdam: Het Spinhuis, 1993); Boudien de Vries, *From Pedlars to Textile Barons: The Economic Development of a Jewish Minority Group in the Netherlands* (Amsterdam: North Holland, 1990).
57. According to de Vries, two-thirds of the new Jewish electorate in 1884 worked in the diamond industry. See de Vries, "De joodse elite in Amsterdam, 1850–1900," 84.
58. Bruin, *Een herenwereld ontleed*, 43.
59. For more on the *Handwerkers Vriendenkring*, see Rijxman, "Mr. Frederik Salomon van Nierop," 260.
60. Theo van Tijn, *Twintig jaren Amsterdam. De maatschappelijke ontwikkeling van de hoofdstad, van de jaren '50 der vorige eeuw tot 1876* (Amsterdam: Scheltema & Holkema, 1965), 234. The three largest firms in the Syndicate, who made up 58% of the market distribution of rough stones, were also major shareholders of De Beers Co., intricately linking the two into an unrivaled monopoly.
61. For more on the history of De Beers, see among others Kanfer, *The Last Empire*; Shield, *Diamond Stories*; Peter Carstens, *In the Company of Diamonds: De Beers, Kleinzee, and the Control of a Town* (Athens: Ohio University Press, 2001); Janine Roberts, *Glitter and Greed: The Secret World of the Diamond Empire* (New York: Disinformation, 2003); Robert Vicat Turrell, "Capital, Class, and Monopoly: The Kimberley Diamond Fields" (PhD Dissertation, University of London, 1982).
62. "Nijverheid te Amsterdam: Het verslag der Kamer van Koophandel," *Algemeen Handelsblad* 71, no. 21941 (June 26, 1898), 1.
63. "De werkloosheid onder de diamantbewerkers," *Algemeen Handelsblad* 67, no. 20397 (March 29, 1894), 1.
64. "Karakterschets: Henri Polak," *De Hollandsche Revue* 5:5 (May 24, 1900), 311–312.

65. Van Tijn concludes that the lack of financial reserves on the part of Amsterdam merchants, as well as the lack of cooperation, contributed to the "structural weakness" of the Dutch diamond industry, compounded in 1889 by a serious slump in American demand. See van Tijn, "Geschiedenis van de Amsterdamse diamanthandel en –nijverheid," 161. See also "Diamantnijverheid I," *Nieuws van de Dag*, no. 6189 (10 April, 1890), 1.
66. "Amsterdam," *Jeweller and Metalworker* (December 15, 1890), 388.
67. "The Diamond Industry," *Current Literature* 26: 1 (July, 1899), 83. "Dear London Diamonds," *New York Times* (January 12, 1890), 14 [On amalgamation]: "For the shareholders, as well as the dealer and merchants who hold stocks of diamonds, whether in the rough or finished state, or who bought on a rising market, the combination has been a very good thing; but, like all such trade arrangements, the pinch is felt somewhere. In this instance thousands of the Amsterdam diamond cutters have been thrown out of employment."
68. van Tijn, "Geschiedenis van de Amsterdamse diamanthandel en –nijverheid," 46.
69. "De werkstaking in het diamantvak," *Algemeen Handelsblad* 67, no. 20623 (November 11, 1894), 2.
70. *Enquête betreffende werking en uitbreiding der wet van 19 September 1874 en naar den toestand van fabrieken en werkplaatsen* (Sneek: H. Pijttersen, 1887); Coronel, "De diamantbewerkers te Amsterdam."
71. Wiel, *Van Rapenburgerstraat naar Amerika*, 28. According to the 1889 *enquête*, 62 percent of the working population of Amsterdam, a little over 70,000 people, belonged to the proletariat, a 5 percent increase from 1850 (p. xx introduction). See also van Tijn, "Geschiedenis van de Amsterdamse diamanthandel en – nijverheid," 47.
72. Heertje, *De diamantbewerkers van Amsterdam*, 57.
73. Meijer and Engelsman, *Vier eeuwen diamant*, 101.
74. Jacques Giele, ed., *De Arbeidsenquête van 1887: Een Kwaad Leven. Deel I: Amsterdam* (Culemborg: Uitgeverij Link, 1981), 149.
75. Giele, 98. Emphasis in the original.
76. In 1866, Jewish diamond polishers founded the *Diamantslijpers-Vereeniging*, a small union that consisted of 240 members by the end of the decade and that Salvador Bloemgarten referred to as a union *in statu nascendi*. While it achieved some small, short-term successes, this organization—together with others set up by cleavers and cutters—disintegrated in the 1870s. Bloemgarten, "De emancipatie van het joodse proletariaat," 99.
77. In 1893, moderate members in favor of parliamentary reform split from the SDB and founded the Social-Democratic Labor Party (SDAP), in which Jewish diamond workers such as Henri Polak, Dolf de Levita, and Jos Loopuit became influential figures. This new organization, neither orange nor red, contributed to the politicization of Amsterdam Jewry.
78. Karin Hofmeester, "'Als ik niet voor mijzelf ben . . .' De verhouding tussen joodse arbeiders en de arbeiderbeweging in Amsterdam, Londen en Parijs, 1870–1914" (PhD Dissertation, University of Amsterdam, 1999), 62.
79. For statistics on the age of diamond workers, see van Tijn, "Geschiedenis van de Amsterdamse diamanthandel en –nijverheid," Deel II, 184.
80. Herman Kuijper, *De Algemeene Nederlandsche Diamantbewerkersbond te Amsterdam: Feiten, cijfers en verrichtingen uit zijn geschiedenis* (Amsterdam: Uitgave ANDB, 1896), 21.

81. For more on Henri Polak, see van der Heijden and van Agtmaal, *Henri Polak*); Salvador Bloemgarten, *Henri Polak: Sociaal Democraat, 1868–1943* (The Hague: Sdu Uitgevers, 1996); Bloemgarten, "Henri Polak: A Jew and a Dutchman," in J. Michman, ed., *Dutch Jewish History I: Proceedings of the Symposium on the History of the Jews in the Netherlands* (Jerusalem: Tel-Aviv University, 1984), 261–278; Jaap Meijer, "Henri Polak: Rebbe der diamantbewerkers," *De Vrije Katheder* 5 (1946), 556–557; Evelien Gans, *De kleine verschillen die het leven uitmaken. Een historische studie naar joodse social-democraten en socialistische-zionisten in Nederland* (Amsterdam: Vassalluci, 2002).
82. See, for example, "Gemengd nieuws," *De Standaard*, no. 6958 (November 10, 1894), 2; M. W. C., "De loonbeweging in het diamantvak," *Algemeen Handelsblad* 67, no. 20626 (November 14, 1894), 7; "De werkstaking," *Nieuws van de Dag*, no. 7606 (November 9, 1894), 2–3; "Werkstaking onder brillantslijpers" and "De loonsbeweging onder de diamantbewerkers," *De Telegraaf* 2, no. 675 (November 7, 1894), 2; no. 676 (November 8, 1894), 2; no. 679 (November 11, 1894), 2.
83. Meijer and Engelsman, *Vier eeuwen diamant*, 103; Van Agtmaal, "Het diamantvak in Amsterdam," 124.
84. The ANDB statutes stated specifically that it "aimed for the material and moral improvement of diamond workers, setting aside all religious, political, and additional unrelated matters." See *Weekblad ANDB* (January 31, 1896). There were, however, three small diamond unions based on religious affiliation: the Catholic St. Eduardis, the Protestant Patrimonium, and the Jewish Betsalel unions, all of which catered toward religious workers and which generally cooperated with the ANDB. In 1903, Betsalel counted 170 members, while the ANDB's membership list topped 7,500. For more on these religious labor unions, see C. A. van der Velde, *De A.N.D.B: Een overzicht van zijn ontstaan, zijne ontwikkeling, en zijne beteekenis* (Amsterdam: Algemeene Nederlandsche Diamantbewerkersbond, 1925).
85. Blom et al., *The History of the Jews in the Netherlands*, 262.
86. This statement was made by Adriaan H. Gerhard in September 1893. Gerhard, a non-Jewish school principal and the son of a tailor, would become one of the main political leaders of the Social-Democratic Labor Party; he was elected Member of Parliament in 1913. For his address, see "Werkloosheid in het diamantvak," *Nieuws van de Dag*, no. 7249 (September 15, 1893): 2; "Diamantbewerkers," *Algemeen Handelsblad* 66, no. 20206 (September 15, 1893), 3.
87. See, for example, C. W. Breukelaar, "Streven naar Verbetering," *Weekblad ANDB* (February 8, 1895); H. Kuijper, "Anti-semitisme," *Weekblad ANDB* (September 27, 1895): International Institute for Social History, Amsterdam # ZF 17294. Heertje, 81.
88. *De Hollandsche Revue*, 326.
89. Bloemgarten, *Henri Polak*, 320.
90. Fritz de Jong, "Van ruw tot geslepen: De culturele betekenis van de Algemene Nederlandse Diamantbewerkers Bond in de geschiedenis van Amsterdam," at the sixtieth anniversary of the ANDB (November 17, 1954). International Institute of Social History: #Bro N 793, p. 14.
91. Van der Heijden and van Agtmaal, *Henri Polak*, 21.
92. The Hollandsche Revue, which spoke of the "evolution" of Amsterdam diamond workers, maintained that "over three-quarters of adults taking classes at 'Our House' [a Toynbee Hall-type settlement, founded in Amsterdam in 1892, that practiced strict political and religious impartiality in its aim to educate the working class] were diamond workers. . . . Indeed, the members of the Diamond

Workers' Union generally belong to the most cultivated people in the profession and in today's labor movement." This is most certainly not a sentiment that a popular, non-Jewish magazine would have publicly advertised before the 1890s. See "Karakterschets: Henri Polak," *De Hollandsche Revue*, 334.

93. ANDB Brochure, "Henri Polak (1868–1943)," published by available at the ANDB Building Amsterdam.
94. Henri Polak, *Weekblad ANDB* (March 5, 1901).
95. Henri Polak, *Weekblad ANDB* (December 6, 1905). See also Heertje, *De diamantbewerkers van Amsterdam*, 120.
96. Judith Frishman and Hetty Berg, eds., *Dutch Jewry in a Cultural Maelstrom, 1880–1940* (Amsterdam: Aksant, 2007).
97. *Report of the Secretary of the Interior; Being Part of the Message and Documents Communicated to the Two Houses of Congress at the Beginning of the Second Session of the Fifty-Fourth Congress*, Vol. 4, Part 3 (Washington, DC: Government Printing Office, 1896), 900.
98. Archive 00210, Inventory No. 3054.8: Oppenheimer, E., Kimberley (Zuid-Africa), Amsterdam, Bad Homburg (May 21, 1909), International Institute for Social History, Amsterdam.
99. Archive 00210, Inventory Nr. 3054.8: Oppenheimer, E., Letter dated July 12, 1909. N.p.
100. "Diamond Cutting in South Africa," IISG Archive 00210, Inventory Nr. 3054.8: Oppenheimer, E., unknown date but most likely June 1909. Oppenheimer thanks Polak for the report in a letter dated July 26, 1909. Subsequent quotations in this paragraph are from their correspondence.
101. The American Department of the Interior, in a 1906 geological survey, confirmed that "it is not likely that diamond cutters could be attracted from their homes in their native lands unless they were offered greatly increased salaries over what would be required to offset the increased cost of living in South Africa." See "Notes on the Diamond Industry," *Mineral Resources of the United States, Calendar Year 1906* (Washington, DC: Government Printing Office, 1907), 1224–1225.
102. Quoted in Van Agtmaal, "Het diamantvak in Amsterdam," 126.
103. "Joodsche toestanden in Amerika," *Nieuw Israëlitisch Weekblad* 30: 22 (November 23, 1894), 2; "Diamantbewerkers uit Amerika," *De Nieuwe Amsterdammer: Dagblad voor Nederland* 1: 1 (January 14, 1896), 2; "Nederlandsche diamantbewerkers in New York," *De Telegraaf* 3: 1070 (December 7, 1895), 1; "Are Diamond Cutters Exempt? The Question of Their Right to Come to This Country Under Contract to be Argued Tomorrow in Washington," *New York Times* (December 21, 1894), 13; "The Case of the Diamond Cutters," *Washington Post* (March 30, 1895), 6; Frank G. Carpenter, "Precious Stones of Africa Taken by United States," *Atlanta Constitution* (October 11, 1908), 5.
104. J. C. H. Blom and J. J. Cahen contend that by 1930, Dutch Jews were disproportionally represented among doctors, lawyers, dentists, and economists, although the majority of the labor force remained concentrated in commerce. See "Jewish Netherlanders, Netherlands Jews, and Jews in the Netherlands, 1870–1940," 245.
105. Historians have almost exclusively situated the origins of Jewish labor movements in eastern European and in Yiddish-speaking immigrant communities, treating London and New York as extensions. Jonathan Frankel, among others, contends that modern Jewish political culture "came into being

in Vilna, Minsk, Bialystok, the East End of London, and the Lower East Side of New York. Its lingua franca was Yiddish; its economic base, the clothing industry and the sweat shop; its politics, the running dispute and constant interaction between socialist internationalism and Jewish nationalism; its organizational expression, the Yiddish press, the public meeting, the trade union, the ideologically committed party, and (where relevant) the armed self-defense unit." Lloyd Gartner, too, argued that "[i]t is possible to view the Jewish labor movement as one whole; from its origins in Eastern European Jewry it spread to western Europe and overseas, to North and South America." Amsterdam Jews and the ANDB remain curiously absent from this literature on Jewish labor. The translated work of Karin Hofmeester is a clear and welcome exception, as is Nancy Green's 1998 edited volume, *Jewish Workers in the Modern Diaspora*. Hofmeester suggests that the origins of the Jewish labor movement lie not merely in eastern Europe, among Yiddish-speaking socialists who exported their political activism to London and New York by means of emigration. Native Dutch Jews were similarly vital to Jewish unionization and politicization. See Karin Hofmeester, *Jewish Worker and the Labour Movement: A Comparative Study of Amsterdam, London, and Paris, 1870–1914* (London: Routledge, 2004); Jonathan Frankel, *Prophecy and Politics: Socialism, Nationalism, and the Russian Jews, 1862–1917* (Cambridge: Cambridge University Press, 1981), 3; Lloyd P. Gartner, "The Jewish Labor Movement in Great Britain and the United States," in Tamar Manor-Friedman, ed., *Workers and Revolutionaries: The Jewish Labor Movement* (Tel Aviv: Beth Hatefutsoth, The Nahum Goldmann Museum of the Jewish Diaspora, 1994), 93; Nancy Green, ed., *Jewish Workers in the Modern Diaspora* (Berkeley: University of California Press, 1998); Tony Michels, *A Fire in Their Hearts: Yiddish Socialists in New York* (Cambridge, MA: Harvard University Press, 2005).

CHAPTER 4

1. "De Hollandsche diamantwerkers in Amerika," *De Telegraaf* 1: 42 (February 11, 1893), 1.
2. "Stern and the Contract Law: He Explains the Arrival of the Kalf Brothers at Ellis Island," *The World* (November 8, 1892), 5; "Detained at Ellis Island," *The Evening World* (November 8, 1892), 4, and (November 9, 1892), 4.
3. "De Hollandsche diamantwerkers in Amerika," *De Telegraaf*, 1.
4. "Stern and the Contract Law," *The World*.
5. Gompers, born of Dutch-Sephardic parents in London, came to the United States as a teenager in the midst of the Civil War. "No figure," concluded John H. M. Laslett, "has been more important in the development of the American labor movement than Samuel Gompers." John H. M. Laslett, "Samuel Gompers and the Rise of American Business Unionism," in Melvyn Dubofsky and Warren Van Tine, eds., *Labor Leaders in America* (Urbana-Champaign: University of Illinois Press, 1987), 62–88. For more on Gompers, see Stuart B. Kaufman, *Samuel Gompers and the Origins of the American Federation of Labor, 1848–1896* (Westport: Greenwood Press, 1973); Harold C. Livesay, *Samuel Gompers and Organized Labor in America* (Boston: Little, Brown and Company, 1978); Bernard Mandel, *Samuel Gompers: A Biography* (Yellow Springs: Antioch Press, 1963); Stuart Kaufman, Peter J. Albert, and Grace Palladino, eds., *The Samuel Gompers Papers*, Vols. 1–13 (Urbana-Champaign: University of Illinois Press, 2013); Paul Buhle, *Taking Care of Business: Samuel Gompers, George Meany, Lane Kirkland, and the Tragedy of American Labor* (New York: Monthly Review

Press, 1999). For more on the Jewish labor movement in America, see Howard Sachar, *A History of the Jews in America* (New York: Knopf Doubleday Publishing, 1993); Melech Epstein, *Jewish Labor in the USA: An Industrial, Political, and Cultural History of the Jewish Labor Movement* (New York: Ktav, 1969); Philip Sheldon Foner, *History of the Labor Movement in the United States* (New York: International Publishers, 1947–1981); Ezra Mendelsohn, ed., *Essential Papers on Jews and the Left* (New York: New York University Press, 1997); Tony Michels, *A Fire in Their Hearts: Yiddish Socialists in New York* (Cambridge, MA: Harvard University Press, 2005); Daniel Soyer, *A Coat of Many Colors: Immigration, Globalism, and Reform in the New York Garment Industry* (New York: Fordham University Press, 2005); Elias Tcherikower, *The Early Jewish Labor Movement in the United States*, trans. Aaron Antonovsky (New York: YIVO, 1961).

6. "De Hollandsche diamantwerkers in Amerika," *De Telegraaf* (February 11, 1893), 1.
7. Heertje, *De Diamantbewerkers van Amsterdam*, 178.
8. "Diamond Cutters Protest Allegations That the Contract Labor Law Is Violated," *The World* (January 19, 1893), 7. "Among the imported diamond workers now employed in the Stern establishment are these: Joseph and David Kalf, Bakker, Saks, Witmond, Gajet, Bromet, Vrooman, van Gelder, Maykeis [sic], Slieman, Bendix, Heertje, van Praag, and Beer."
9. "Another Batch of Diamond Workers Come to these Shores," *Jewelers' Circular and Horological Review* 29: 17 (November 21, 1894), 14. This journal will be referred to as *JCHR* from here forward. See also "Diamond Cutters Coming Here," *Glens Falls Daily Times* (November 21, 1894), 3; "Diamond Cutters Not Sent Back," *New York Times* (November 15, 1894), 9. A few weeks before the Hudmacher brothers arrived, three siblings named Zilver disembarked from the steamer *Veendam*, with fifteen cutters in tow. They brought letters of credit, "announcing their intention of setting up business in Brooklyn. Soon came 25 other cutters, no doubt to be employed by the Zilver brothers, though the authorities failed to find evidences of the contract." See "The Diamond Cutters," *Zion's Herald* (August 15, 1894), 480; "More Diamond Cutters Detained," *New York Times* (July 29, 1894), 17.
10. "Another Batch of Diamond Workers Come to these Shores," 14.
11. See also "Joodsche toestanden in Amerika," *Nieuw Israëlitisch Weekblad* 30: 22 (November 23, 1894), 2; "Diamantbewerkers uit Amerika," *De Nieuwe Amsterdammer: Dagblad voor Nederland* 1: 1 (January 14, 1896), 2; "Nederlandsche diamantbewerkers in New York," *De Telegraaf* 3: 1070 (December 7, 1895), 1; "Are Diamond Cutters EXEMPT? The Question of Their Right to Come to This Country under Contract to be Argued Tomorrow in Washington," *New York Times* (December 21, 1894), 13; "The Case of the Diamond Cutters," *Washington Post* (March 30, 1895), 5.
12. H. Witmondt, letter addressed to Henri Polak (Brooklyn, July 17, 1896): International Institute for Social History, Archive No. 00210: Algemene Nederlandse Diamantbewerkers Bond [ANDB], Inv. Nr. 3078.13: American Correspondence Files. "Diamantbewerkers in Amerika," *Algemeen Handelsblad* 68: 20754 (March 23, 1895), 3.
13. Wiel, *Van Rapenburgstraat naar Amerika*, 164; Swierenga, *The Forerunners*, 114.
14. *JCHR* 30: 7 (March 20, 1895), 12–13. The *Brooklyn Daily Eagle* stated that Kryn & Wouters were merchants from Antwerp, although others emphasize their Dutch origins. "How Diamonds Are Cut," *Brooklyn Daily Eagle* (March 31, 1895), 11.

15. "Expansion of the Diamond Cutting Industry in America," *American Economist* (December 28, 1894), 312. The same piece appeared in *JCHR* 29: 17 (November 21, 1894), 8–11. A report by the secretary of the interior estimated the value of imported rough diamonds at $3,329,545 in 1895, although this included precious stones other than diamonds. See "Diamonds," in *Report of the Secretary of the Interior*, 926.
16. Douglas B. Sterrett, "Precious Stones," in *Mineral Resources of the United States: Department of the Interior, United States Geological Survey* (Washington, DC: Government Printing Office, 1907), 1226.
17. "Seventeenth Annual Report of the United States Geological Survey, Part III: Mineral Resources," in *Report of the Secretary of the Interior*, 925–926. One Dutch factory owner lamented in 1895 that Amsterdam "had lost its best customer." See B., "Iets over de werkstaking der diamantbewerkers," *Algemeen Handelsblad* 68: 20895 (August 13, 1895), 3; "Effect of Increased Duty on Cut Diamonds," *JCHR* 29: 8 (September 26, 1894), 32.
18. "Expansion of the Diamond Cutting Industry in America," 312.
19. *First Annual Industrial Directory of New York State* (Albany: New York State Department of Labor, 1912), 199: Register of Factories: Lapidary Work.
20. *Nieuwe Rotterdamsche Courant* (February 1912), quoted in Jabob van Hinte, *Netherlanders in America: A Study of Emigration And Settlement in the Nineteenth and Twentieth Centuries in the United States of America* (Grand Rapids, MI: Baker Book House, 1985), 838.
21. Glenn Klein, *Faceting History: Cutting Diamonds and Colored Stones* (Bloomington: Xlibris, 2005), 72.
22. Quoted in Shor, *Connections*, 48.
23. For more on the diamond trade in the early modern period, see, among others, Yogev, *Diamonds and Coral*; Vannesté, *Global Trade and Commercial Networks*.
24. Samuel Meyer Isaacs, *Jewish Messenger*, quoted in Swieringa, *The Forerunners*, 113. That Isaacs, editor of the *Jewish Messenger* from 1867 to 1878, was born in Friesland may have contributed to his praise of Dutch enterprise.
25. Hinte, *Netherlanders in America*, 837. Hermann is also mentioned in the *Scientific American*: "Diamond Cutting By Hand and Machine," *Scientific American* 65: 3 (July 18, 1891), 31–32. Sadie Battles set the precedent for women specializing in the craft of diamond cutting, a topic that remains virtually unexplored in secondary historical literature.
26. "The Diamond in America: Where the Gems Comes From, Who Buys Them and What They Are Worth," *Washington Post* (October 17, 1880), 3.
27. George F. Kunz, "Development of Diamond-Cutting," *Current Literature* 19: 2 (February 1896), 146–148. This piece also appeared as "Diamond Cutting: Its Great Growth in the Last Twenty-Five Years," *Atlanta Constitution* (November 10, 1895), 5. Harry A. Mount repeated this point in 1920: "[I]n establishing an American cutting industry some difficulty was encountered," he stated in the *Scientific American*, "not only in finding competent workmen, but in getting buyers 'on the list.' The process of getting 'on the list' is a long and tedious one, sometimes requiring fifteen or twenty years of persistent effort on the part of an individual. And so not only were the diamonds and the workmen imported from Europe, but the buyers of rough stones had to be imported, too. It is because of this fact that many of the important New York diamond merchants even today are descendants of Dutch families and can trace a lineage of diamond merchants through a century or more." Harry A. Mount, "Our Diamond Industry: How the United States Has

Become the Greatest Buyer of Diamonds in the World," *Scientific American* 123: 25 (December 18, 1920), 623–624.
28. "American banks," stated a 1896 report of the Secretary of the Interior, "do not make advances on uncut diamonds as do the English and Dutch banks, which make loans on the rough stones, knowing that the cutting enhances the value of the material on which advances are made." See "Diamonds," *Report of the Secretary of the Interior*, 900.
29. "An Amsterdam Industry Transferred to New York," *JCHR* 29: 5 (September 5, 1894), 22.
30. "Een belangrijk jubileum in de diamantnijverheid," *Nieuwe Rotterdamsche Courant* 81: 233 (August 23, 1924), 2. Van Dam also opened a company firm in Antwerp in 1899. His Amsterdam factory, employing 500 diamond workers, moved to the Ruysdaelstraat in 1906.
31. "An Amsterdam Industry Transferred to New York," *JCHR* 29: 5 (September 5, 1894), 22.
32. "Diamond Importers Protest against an Increased Tariff on Precious Stones," *JCHR* 27: 19 (December 6, 1893), 10–11.
33. *Bulletin No. 54, Part I: Committee on Finance, United States Senate. Replies to Tariff Inquiries* (Washington, DC: Government Printing Office, July 10, 1894), 72.
34. "The Duty on Precious Stones," *JCHR* 27: 19 (December 6, 1893), 13.
35. "Debate in the House on the Taxation of Diamonds and Precious Stones," *JCHR* 27: 27 (January 31, 1894), 11. It appeared initially that the petition was successful. The JCHR reported the following week that "it cannot but prove a matter of congratulations and relief that the arguments of the importers of precious stones against the original propositions in the Wilson Tariff Bill . . . have met with a speedy appreciation in Congress" and that the "agitation of the importers has borne fruit." But this victory appears to have been short-lived because the discussion resumed in January 1894. See *JCHR* 27: 19 (December 13, 1893), 13.
36. "Debate in the House on the Taxation of Diamonds and Precious Stones," 12.
37. "Debate in the House on the Taxation of Diamonds and Precious Stones," 12.
38. "Open Letter to the Hon. Amos J. Cummings," *JCHR* 27: 27 (January 31, 1894), 12. Meyer D. Rothschild's import company stood at 41–43 Maiden Lane, New York.
39. St. George, "Among the South African Diamond Mines," *JCHR* 29: 2 (August 15, 1894), 18.
40. "De Diamanthandel," *Algemeen Handelsblad* no. 67: 20379 (March 10, 1894), 1.
41. "The Tariff Bill Passed," *JCHR* 29: 2 (August 15, 1894), 36.
42. Monroe Engelsman, "Views on the Diamond Tariff from an American in Holland," *JCHR* 30: 15 (June 12, 1895), 8–10.
43. "Effect of Increased Duty on Cut Diamonds," *JCHR* 29: 8 (September 26, 1894), 32; "Consul Downes on the Diamond Industry of Amsterdam," *JCHR* 29: 22 (December 26, 1894), 9; "Affects the Diamond Industry: Increased Tariff Causes Withdrawal of American Patronage from Amsterdam," *Washington Post* (September 23, 1894), 5.
44. Engelsman, "Views on the Diamond Tariff from an American in Holland," 10.
45. "Diamond Cutters Coming Here," *Glens Falls Daily Times* (November 21, 1894), 3. The Arnstein Bros., among others, who started as a diamond importing company in 1886, opened a cutting workshop on 45 John Street in 1894. See "Expansion of the Diamond Cutting Industry in America," 18.
46. "Diamond Cutters Coming Here," 3.

47. "Is Diamond Cutting a New Industry in America?," *JCHR* 29: 20 (December 12, 1894), 25; "Importation of Diamond Cutters: The Special Board of Inquiry Begins Its Investigation," *New York Times* (December 8, 1894), 4.
48. The 1885 Alien Contract Labor Law, also known as the Foran Act, prohibited any company or individual from bringing unskilled immigrants into the United States to work under contract. The law made exceptions for foreigners recruited to do domestic service, skilled workers needed to help establish a new trade or industry, professional artists, lecturers, and actors.
49. For more on small Jewish labor unions, see Bernard Weinstein, *The Jewish Unions in America: Pages of History and Memories* [1929], trans. Maurice Wolfthal (Cambridge, UK: Open Book Publishers, 2018).
50. "The labor unions, it is said, are behind the fight against the importation of cutters." See "Is Diamond Cutting a New Industry in America?," *JCHR* 29 (December 12, 1894), 25.
51. "Is it a New Industry?," *Washington Post* (December 21, 1894), 9. "The Diamond Cutters' Association of New York, composed of Americans, are naturally opposed to so many foreign diamond cutters coming into this country, as their advent will have a tendency to lower the sale of wages."
52. "Diamond Cutting Is Not a New Industry in the U.S.," *JCHR* 30: 7 (March 20, 1895), 13.
53. "Are Diamond Cutters Exempt?," 13.
54. "Many Laborers Concerned: Question of Admitting Diamond Cutters Aimed at the Treasury," *Washington Post* (December 23, 1894), 3.
55. "Diamonds and Street Bands Are Keeping the Immigration Commissioner Hustling," *Brooklyn Daily Eagle* 55: 76 (March 18, 1895), 1; "Diamond Cutting on a Large Scale," *New York Times* (March 21, 1895), 14.
56. "To Detain Diamond Cutters: Information Lodged That a Number Are to Arrive from Antwerp," *The Sun* (March 17, 1895), 8; "Looking for Diamond Cutters," *New York Times* (March 17, 1895), 8.
57. *JCHR* 30: 7 (March 20, 1895), 12–13.
58. "Diamond Cutters," *The World* (March 15, 1895), 2. See also "A Large Party of Foreign Diamond Workers Start for New York," *JCHR* 30: 7 (March 20, 1895), 12–13.
59. A. Samuel, "Letter to the Editor," *The World* (March 16, 1895), 5.
60. W. H. Allen, Immigration Restriction League No. 1, Brooklyn, "To Keep the Diamond Cutters Out," *The World* (March 19, 1895), 4; "Diamond Cutting on a Large Scale," *The New York Times* (March 21, 1895), 14; "They Must Go Back," *The Washington Post* (March 22, 1895), 6.
61. For a full reading of the decision, see John G. Carlisle, Secretary of the Treasury, *Synopsis of the Decisions of the Treasury Department and the Board of the U.S. General Appraisers on the Construction of the Tariff, Navigation, and Other Laws, For the Year Ending December, 1895* (Washington, DC: Government Printing Office, 1896), 216–218; "Diamond Cutting Is Not a New Industry in the U.S.," 13; "Treasury Department Decides That They Cannot Come Here under Contract," *New York Herald* (March 17, 1895), 5; "Foreign Diamond Cutters Cannot Come In," *Washington Post* (March 17, 1895), 4.
62. "Diamantbewerkers in Amerika," *Algemeen Handelsblad* 68: 20754 (March 23, 1895), 3; "Diamantbewerkers in Amerika," *Algemeen Handelsblad* 68: 20755 (March 24, 1895), 2.

63. "Smuggling in the Cutters," *Brooklyn Daily Eagle* 55: 80 (March 22, 1895), 1; "Diamond Cutting on a Large Scale," 14.
64. "Smuggling in the Cutters," 1. The subtitle to this article reads: "Bright men with money to be admitted, the others to be sent back."
65. "Diamond Cutters Must Go Back," *Washington Post* (March 22, 1895), 6; "Sixty-Two Diamond Cutters Going Back," *Washington Post* (March 23, 1895), 1; "Diamond Cutters Must Be Deported," *New York Times* (April 10, 1895), 1; "The Former Decision of the Board of Inquiry Sustained," *JCHR* 30: 10 (April 10, 1895), 17; "Diamond Cutter Decision Sustained," *Washington Post* (April 8, 1895), 9.
66. "The Case of the Diamond Cutters," *Washington Post* (March 30, 1895), 6.
67. Samuel Gompers, leader of the AFL, is a good example. Even though an immigrant himself, he professed nativism without restraint, opposing free immigration. See Ehud Manor, *Forward: The Jewish Daily Forward (Forverts) Newspaper. Immigrants, Socialism and Jewish Politics in New York, 1890-1917* (Brighton, UK: Sussex Academic Press, 2009), 29; Charles Leinenweber, "The American Socialist Party and 'New' Immigrants," *Science and Society* 32: 1 (Winter 1968), 3; Arthur Mann, "Attitudes and Policies on Immigration: An Opportunity for Revision," *AJHS* 46: (1957), 298-299; Irwin Yellowitz, "Jewish Immigrants and the American Labor Movement, 1900-1920," *American Jewish History* 71 (December 1981), 188-217.
68. "Bureau Nonsense Called In," *Washington Post* (March 27, 1895), 6.
69. "Diamond Cutters May Enter," *Chicago Daily Tribune* (January 23, 1909), 5.
70. "Alien Workers to Return: Deported Diamond Polishers Said to Be Coming Back Again," *The World* (May 15, 1895), 7; "The Employment of Diamond Workers," *JCHR* 30: 1 (March 20, 1895), 15.
71. D. De Sola Mendes, Letter written to Henri Polak: International Institute of Social History (IISH), Archief No. 00210: ANDB; Inv. Nr. 3050.7: Mendes & Co. Cutting Factory, New York (May 10, 1895).
72. "Diamantbewerkers in Amerika," *Algemeen Handelsblad* 68: 20754 (March 23, 1895), 3.
73. "How Diamonds Are Cut," *Brooklyn Daily Eagle* (March 31, 1895), 11.
74. Albert Ulmann, *Maiden Lane: The Story of a Single Street* (New York: Maiden Lane Historical Society, 1931), 64.
75. *Wilson's Business Directory of New York City, 1865-1866* (New York: John F. Trow, 1865), 130; *Wilson's Business Directory of New York City, 1874-1875* (New York: John F. Trow, 1875), 181-182. In 1877, there were 62. See *Rand's New York City Business Directory* (New York: W. Heugh & Co., 1877), 105.
76. *The Trow Business Directory of New York City* (formerly *Wilson's*), Vol. 48 (New York: The Trow Directory, Printing and Bookbinding Company, 1895), 296-298.
77. *Real Estate Record and Builders' Guide* 53: 1366 (May 19, 1894), 801.
78. Advertisement for the "Diamond Exchange Building," *JCHR* 27: 24 (January 10, 1894), 10.
79. *New Amsterdam Gazette* 584 (1883), 3; *Illustrated New York: The Metropolis of Today* (New York: International Publishing Company, 1888), 191; Marinus Gerardus Emeis, *A. van Moppes & Zoon, 1809-1959* (Amsterdam: N.V. Diamant Industrie A. van Moppes & Zoon, 1959).
80. "New York Notes," *JCHR* 23: 6 (September 9, 1891), 30.
81. "New York Notes," *JCHR* 30: 1 (March 20, 1895), 16.
82. Advertisement Henry Fera, *JCHR* 30: 3 (February 20, 1895), 8.

83. "New Diamond Cutting Works in New York," *JCHR* 26: 2 (February 8, 1893), 32-b. See also an advertisement by Stern Bros. & Co. in *JCHR* 29: 18 (November 28, 1894), 39. Chaim Even-Zohar (online): "In 1876, Henry Fera established a small plant employing 15–20 workers; followed by Herman Levy and Tiffany (the latter to support its jewelry dpt in NY's Union Square. . . . In 1882, E. L. Enrich set up a plant that operated some 25 wheels; this was the first plant where most cutters were already U.S. natives. What is clear from the development of the U.S. diamond business is that all its early founders—and most importantly the workers and trainers—came mostly from Amsterdam and Antwerp. Fera was born in 1842 in Altoona, Germany and came to the U.S. in 1858 on the Austria from Hamburg, which burned in mid-ocean on her next trip, Sept. 13, 1858. He first settled in Chicago, as a clerk. Volunteered during the Civil War. In 1868 he entered the employ of Henry Greenbaum & Co., bankers, with whom he came to NY. Went into business from himself as an importer of diamonds in 1871. First office on Maiden Lane and he began the cutting of diamonds in 1874. He's crossed the ocean 108 times."

84. "Stern Bros. & Co., Cutters and Importers of Diamonds," *JCHR* 26: 2 (February 8, 1893), 32–b.

85. *Brooklyn Daily Eagle* (March 31, 1895), 11; "Expansion of the Diamond Cutting Industry in America," 19; "An Amsterdam Industry Transferred to New York," *JCHR* 29: 5 (September 5, 1894), 22; "Expansion of the Diamond Cutting Industry in America, part II," 12–13.

86. Advertisement in *JCHR* 29: 18 (November 28, 1894), 37.

87. *First Annual Industrial Directory of New York State* (New York State Department of Labor, 1913), 199: Register of Factories: Lapidary Work, Product manufactured: diamond cutting and polishing. See also *JCHR* 29: 2 (August 15, 1894), 18; *Trow Business Directory of New York City, 1892* (New York: Trow, 1892). Andrew Heinze's research shows that jewelry shops equally clustered in Maiden Lane. By 1892, the area counted 138 watch and jewelry shops, and "136 diamond shops were doing business in or next to the Jewish district of lower Manhattan." Andrew R. Heinze, *Adapting to Abundance: Jewish Immigrants, Mass Consumption, and the Search for American Identity* (New York: Columbia University Press, 1990), 187.

88. "The Diamond in America," 3; "Diamond Cutting by Hand and Machine," *Scientific American* 65: 3 (July 18, 1891), 31–32.

89. Bertram Reinitz, "Diamond Curb Is Still Active," *New York Times* (September 30, 1928), 138.

90. Harry A. Mount, "Diamond Dealers of the Curb and Dim-Lit Auction Rooms," *New York Times* (November 7, 1920), 48. Mount writes: "Many of them have offices or desk rooms in nearby buildings and deals which are actually negotiated on the curb are closed there. These traders do very little, if any, dealing with the public. Among the big diamond houses in Maiden Lane you can hear tales of lambs who went to the diamond curb to buy their stones and who were promptly and efficiently sheared. As a rule, the traders deal only among themselves." A different version of this article appeared in the *Scientific American*. "Our Diamond Industry," 614, 623–624.

91. "The Diamond Curb Is Still Active," 138.

92. Quoted in Christopher Gray, "An Unshowy Setting for Gems," *New York Times* (August 29, 2008), https://www.nytimes.com/2008/08/31/realestate/31scap.html. See also Jenna Joselit Weissman, "Cut Gems: How Jews brought diamonds from South Africa to Amsterdam to midtown Manhattan," *Tablet Magazine*

(January 23, 2020), https://www.tabletmag.com/sections/community/articles/cut-gems.
93. "Diamonds," *Report of the Secretary of the Interior* (1896), 900. The report estimated that approximately 500 diamond workers lived and worked in New York, including 10 cleavers, 370 polishers, 50 cutters, and 70 setters.
94. *Handbook of American Trade-Unions. Bulletin of the United States Bureau of Labor Statistics*, no. 506 (US Department of Labor, 1929), 203. Why the history of American diamond unions has been largely ignored is a mystery. Weinstein's *The Jewish Unions in America* discusses even the smallest of labor unions, such as the Seltzer Workers' Union of New York, the Raincoat Workers' Union, and the Theater Ushers and Bill-Posters' Union, yet missing are the diamond workers. The Department of Labor's *Handbook of American Trade Unions* lists the DWPU in 1929 under the heading "small craft unions," along with the International Broom and Whisk Makers' Union, United Powder and High Explosive Workers of America, and the American Wire Weavers' Protective Association.
95. Van der Wiel, *Van Rapenburgstraat naar Amerika*, 165; *Twelfth Annual Report of the Bureau of Statistics of Labor of the State of New York for the Year 1894* (Albany: James B. Lyon, 1895), 51.
96. "Diamond Workers in Amsterdam on Strike," *JCHR* 29: 2 (August 15, 1894), 18.
97. *JCHR* 29: 16 (November 14, 1894), 18.
98. "Strike of the Diamond Cutters of New York," *JCHR* 29: 18 (November 28, 1894), 36.
99. "Diamond Workers Out," *The World* (November 23, 1894), 3; "Strike of the Diamond Cutters," 36.
100. "The Diamond Polishers Organize the Diamond Workers' Union," *JCHR* 29: 19 (December 5, 1894), 23.
101. "From the World of Labor," *Evening World* (December 3, 1894), 8; "Diamond Polishers on Strike," *The Sun* 62, no. 90 (November 29, 1894), 1.
102. "The Strike of the Diamond Polishers and Setters Ended," *JCRH* (December 12, 1894), 16.
103. "Brooklyn News Notes," *New York Daily Tribune* (October 20, 1895), 20.
104. "Fifty Diamond Workers Go Out on Strike," *Philadelphia Inquirer* (October 17, 1895), 2.
105. "Diamond Workers Go on Strike," *New York Herald* (October 19, 1895), 7. Zilver, stated this article, believed "this strike to be international. He learned that 1,200 men had struck in Amsterdam." While Zilver knew about the general strike among diamond workers in Holland, he underestimated the numbers and its success.
106. "Diamond Workers Migrate Again," *The World* (November 21, 1895), 3; "Diamond Workers Sail Away," *The Sun* (November 21, 1895), 3; "City Jottings," *New York Herald* (November 21, 1895), 6.
107. This passenger steamer, the SS *St. Louis*, is different from the MS *St. Louis* that carried over 900 Jewish refugees from Germany to Cuba in 1939, forced to sail back to Europe after passengers were denied entry.
108. "Diamond Workers Migrate Again," 3; "Are Going Back to Holland," *New York Times* (November 21, 1895), 9.
109. Letter addressed to Henry Polak, dated December 10, 1895: IISH Archive No. 00210: ANDB Inv. Nr. 3032.15: United Diamond Workers Union.
110. "Diamantbewerkers uit America," *De Nieuwe Amsterdammer* 1 (January 14, 1896), 2.

111. International Institute for Social History, Amsterdam: Archief No. 00210: ANDB, Inv. Nr. 3032.15: United Diamond Workers Union, December 10, 1895.
112. "One Hundred Diamond Setters Strike," *The Sun* (April 8, 1899), 5: "A strike of 10 diamond setters is in progress in the shop of Kern & Waters [Kryn & Wouters], in Brooklyn, for an increase in wages. The strikers belong to the International Diamond Workers' Union, which has its headquarters in Amsterdam. As soon as the strike was declared the branch in NY assessed its members fifty percent of their wages for the strikers. The NY branch reported yesterday that it has turned over to the strikers the sum of $800 so far. The strikers are also receiving financial support from the International Union." Various Notes," *Evening Post* (August 31, 1904), 8; "New Deal in Diamond Cutting," *The Sun* (February 13, 1905), 2; "Diamond Polishers Strike; Want above $50 a Week," *Evening Telegram* (March 10, 1905), 1; "Diamond Polishers Go to Work Today," *New York Herald* (March 30, 1905), 8.
113. For correspondence on strikes in New York, see IISH Archief No. 00210: ANDB, Inv. Nr. 3001.3: Abonnees Weekblad ANDB Brooklyn, New York (1900–1901); Inv. Nr. 3032.14: S. Moscoviter, United Diamond Verstellers Union of America, December 27, 1901; Inv. Nr. 3032.13: United Diamond Polishers Union, Brooklyn; Inv. Nr. 3080.7: N. Zwart, November 20, 1900; Inv. Nr. 3060.12: Jacob J. van Rijn, Brooklyn, December 13, 1898.
114. IISH Archief Nr. 00210: ANDB; Inv. Nr. 3032.13: Diamond Polishers' Protective Union, Brooklyn, July 1904. Jacques Benjamin, also on the board of the DPPU, added that Polak should also lecture American diamond workers on "how to behave" as responsible union members, something Polak was known for in Amsterdam. See Inv. Nr. 3013.30: A. Jacques Benjamin, Diamond Polishers' Protective Union of American, October 31, 1903. For other small unions, see Inv. Nr. 3032.12: United Diamond Cutters of America, Brooklyn; Inv. Nr. 3049.5: Machine Diamond Cutters Union of America; Inv. Nr. 3032.14: United Diamond Verstellers [Setters'] Union of America. The historians Annie Polland and Daniel Soyer have argued that "[t]hroughout the 1880s and 1890s, Jewish workers had gained a reputation for waging spectacular strikes, only to let their unions dissipate once moments of acute conflict had ended." What happened with American diamond unions thus seems to have been part of a larger pattern. This changed after the founding the of International Ladies' Garment Workers' Union in 1900 and the United Hebrew Trades, both of which mobilized tens of thousands of members by the early twentieth century. See Annie Polland and Daniel Soyer, eds, *Emerging Metropolis: New York Jews in the Age of Immigration, 1840–1920* (New York: New York University Press, 2012), 188; Hadassa Kosak, *Cultures of Opposition: Jewish Immigrant Workers, New York City, 1881–1905* (Albany: SUNY Press, 2000); Moses Rischin, *The Promised City: New York's Jews, 1870–1914* (Cambridge, MA: Harvard University Press, 1962).
115. IISH Archief Nr. 00210: ANDB: Inv. Nr. 3032.12: United Diamond Cutters of America, Brooklyn, December 15, 1898. N. Zwarts, who wrote Polak on a regular basis, complained about the lack of leadership among diamond workers in New York: IISH Archief 00210: ANDB; Inv. Nr. 3080.7: letter dated December 30, 1900.
116. IISH Archief Nr. 00210: ANDB; Inv. Nr. 3080.9: N. Zwart, "Fellow Workmen!," June 1901.
117. N. Zwart, the Secretary of the DPPU, February 9, 1901, Letter to Henri Polak: International Institute for Social History, Amsterdam: Archief Nr.

00210: ANDB; Inv. Nr. 30380.7. For other complaints about Polak's silence, see Inv. Nr. 3080.8: N. Zwart, October 27, 1901; Inv. Nr. 3060.13: Jacob J. van Rijn, March 23, 1900; Inv. Nr. 3032.14: S. Moscoviter, December 27, 1901.
118. "Revival in the Diamond Trade," *New York Times* (July 31, 1897), 12.
119. "The Tariff on Diamonds," *The Sun* (April 25, 1897), 9.
120. Tariff Hearings before the Committee on Ways and Means, vol. 2. Fifty-fourth Congress, second session; House of Representatives, Doc. No. 338 (Washington: Gvt Printing Office, 1897), 1885–1899. Minutes of the Tariff Hearings: January 11, 1897.
121. "Diamond Industry's Growth: Importation of Stones into the United States Has Increased at the Rate of $1,000,000 Worth a Year during Each Year of Past Decade," *New York Times* (March 1, 1903), 34; "Proposed Dutch Tariff: American Export Trade Watching Bill in Holland House," *New York Times* (March 20, 1904), 15.
122. Mount, "Our Diamond Industry," 623; Albert A. Hopkins, "The Art of Cutting Diamonds," *Scientific American* 134: 3 (March 1926), 177.
123. Swieringa, *The Forerunners*, 115.
124. William Leach, *Land of Desire: Merchants, Power, and the Rise of a New American Culture* (New York: Pantheon, 1993), introduction 3–12; Roland Marchand, *Advertising the American Dream: Making Way for Modernity* (Berkeley: University of California Press, 1985); Susan Strasser, *Satisfaction Guaranteed: The Making of the American Mass Market* (New York: Pantheon, 1989); Lawrence Glickman, ed., *Consumer Society in American History: A Reader* (Ithaca: Cornell University Press, 1999); Richard S. Tedlow, *New and Improved: The Story of Mass Marketing in America* (New York: Basic, 1990); Kathy L. Peiss, "American Women and the Making of Modern Consumer Culture" (lecture delivered at the State University of New York, Albany, March 26, 1998).
125. "The Wonder of Precious Stones," *JCHR* 29: 22 (December 26, 1894), 21.
126. "Diamonds on Credit" Advertisements in *Puck* 52: 1327 (1902), 13; 54: 1359 (November 25, 1903), 11; *The Ladies' Home Journal* 19: 12 (November 1902), 56; 21: 1 (December 1903), 55; *Life* (June 1, 1905), 45; *Harper's Bazaar* 36: 6 (June 1902), 32; 39: 3 (March 1905), 49. Other merchandise could be purchased on credit in the second half of the nineteenth-century, including sewing machines, furniture, and pianos. For more on this new practice, see Heinze, *Adapting to Abundance*.
127. "Diamonds—The Ensigns of Prosperity," *National Magazine* 31: 3 (December 1900), 344–345.
128. See the obituary for Samuel Loftis, "S. T. A. Loftis Buried," *Jewelers' Circular* 81: 2 (August 11, 1920), 89.
129. Leach, *Land of Desire*, 23; Polland and Soyer, *Emerging Metropolis*, 42–43; Robert Hendrickson, *The Grand Emporiums: The Illustrated History of America's Great Department Stores* (New York: Stein and Day, 1979). Macy's was the first large retail store to merchandize kosher foods. Nancy F. Koehn, "Consumerism and Consumption," in Morton Keller, ed., *Encyclopedia of the United States in the Nineteenth Century*, (New York: Charles Scribner's Sons, 2000). For an excellent analysis of department stores in nineteenth-century Germany, see Paul Lerner, *The Consuming Temple: Jews, Department Stores, and the Consumer Revolution in Germany, 1880–1940* (Ithaca: Cornell University Press, 2015).
130. Frederic J. Haskin, "Diamonds," *Washington Post* (April 29, 1910), 10.

131. "Extravagance in Diamonds: The Higher the Price the More Eagerly Women Covet Them—Fall Styles in Jewelry," *Washington Post* (November 19, 1905), 2. "They wear no large, flashy pieces of jewelry for the reason that such designs look ridiculous with a plain toilet. . . . That is why our best diamonds don't all go to the very rich. It is a sign of the times, too, that the women—and men, too—just as they desire the best in paintings, the finest in bric-a-brac, rugs and tapestries. Yes, the public taste in diamonds becomes more highly cultivated every year."
132. Frank G. Carpenter, "Precious Stones of Africa Taken by United States," *Atlanta Constitution* (October 11, 1908), 5. For more on De Beers advertisement see Edward Epstein, *The Diamond Invention* (New York: Random House, 1982).
133. For an analysis of the De Beers' successful ad campaign, see among others Uri Friedman, "How an Ad Campaign Invented the Diamond Engagement Ring," *The Atlantic* (February 13, 2015); Edward Jay Epstein, "Have You Ever Tried to Sell a Diamond?," *The Atlantic* (February 1, 1982), no page numbers.
134. Sarah Brentworth, "Diamonds," *The Chautauquan: A Weekly Newsmagazine* (August 1896), 23–26. The *JCHR* reported in 1893: "If any evidence of the popularity of diamonds were needed, it would be sufficient to say that on the opening night of the opera season at the Metropolitan Opera House, New York, it was figured that $29,000,000 worth of jewels was displayed by the persons in the auditorium." *JCHR* 27: 21 (December 20, 1893), 13; "Diamonds Worth Millions Purchased by Americans," *Atlanta Constitution* (July 10, 1903), 3.

CHAPTER 5

1. "Jumped into the Sea," *Ann Arbor Argus* (June 18, 1897). The officer jumping in after Barnato was William Tarrant Clifford, who received £1,000 from the Joel family for his efforts to save Barnato. For Solly Joel's testimony, see "The Death of Mr. Barnato," *Cardigan Observer* (June 27, 1897), 4.
2. W. Coxwell served as coroner. See David Green, "1897: A Diamond Magnate Drowns under Mysterious Circumstances," *Haaretz* (June 13, 2015). Podcast: https://www.haaretz.com/jewish/.premium-1897-diamond-magnate-drowns-in-odd-circumstances-1.5371501.
3. "Barney Barnato's Suicide," *New York Times* (June 16, 1897), 3; "Jumped into the Sea," *Ann Arbor Argus* (June 18, 1897), 3.
4. For a recent literary analysis of Victorian diamonds, see Adrienne Munich, *Empire of Diamonds: Victorian Gems in Imperial Setting* (Charlottesville: University of Virginia Press, 2020).
5. Collins, *The Moonstone*, 3.
6. Anthony Trollope, *The Eustace Diamonds* (London: Chapman and Hall, 1873). Similar characters can be found in *Mr. Scarborough's Family* (Hamburg: Karl Grädener and J.F. Richter, 1883), 131–132. Arthur Conan Doyle, *The Sign of Four*; Robert Louis Stevenson, "The Raja's Diamond" (1878); George Eliot, *Daniel Doronda*; Louise Vescelius-Sheldon, *An I.D.B. in South Africa* (New York: John W. Lovell, 1888); J. R. Couper, *Mixed Humanity: A Story of Camp Life in South Africa* (Cape Town: J. C. Juta, 1892).
7. Collins, *The Moonstone*, 314. For an analysis on Collins's use of Jewish characters, see Andrew Gasson and William Baker, "Forgotten Terrain: Wilkie Collins's Jewish Explorations," *Jewish Historical Studies* 48: 1 (2017), 177–199.
8. H. Rider Haggard, *King Solomon's Mines* (1885), 222–223, 225.

9. For more on Haggard, see Heidi Kaufman, "*King Solomon's Mines*? African Jewry, British Imperialism, and H. Rider Haggard's Diamonds," *Victorian Literature and Culture* 33 (2005), 517–539. Kaufman argues that Haggard's fantasy novel participated "in a system of signs, values, and hierarchies that enables him to write white, Christian, English identity into perpetual supremacy." See also Wendy R. Katz, *Rider Haggard and the Fiction of Empire: Critical Study of British Imperial Fiction* (Cambridge: Cambridge University Press, 1987); William Minter, *King Solomon's Mines Revisited: Western Interests and the Burdened History of Southern Africa* (New York: Basic, 1986); Tom Pocock, *Rider Haggard and the Lost Empire* (London: Weidenfeld and Nicolson, 1993); Lindy Stiebel, *Imagining Africa: Landscape in H. Rider Haggard's African Romances* (Westport: Greenwood, 2001).

10. There is a sizable body of scholarship on colonialism and nineteenth-century fiction. Of particular interest here is Cora Kaplan, "Imagining Empire: History, Fantasy and Literature," in Hall and Rose, eds, *At Home with the Empire*, 191–211; Steinbach, *Understanding the Victorians*. For diamonds appearing in poetry, see, for example, Gerard Manley Hopkins, "That Nature Is a Heraclitean Fire and of the Comfort of the Resurrection" (1888) and Lord Tennyson, *Idylls of the King* (1859–1885).

11. Couper, *Mixed Humanity*, 25; Isabel Hofmeyr, "The Mining Novel in South African Literature: 1870–1920," *English in Africa* 5: 2 (September 1978), 1–16.

12. W. T. Eady, *I.D.B. or the Adventures of Solomon Davis on the Diamond Fields and Elsewhere* (London: Chapman and Hall, 1887), 7; Rev. A. A. Green, "The Jew in Fiction," *American Israelite* (January 6, 1898), 1.

13. John Burns, a member of the Labor Party: "The Trail of the Financial Serpent Is over This War from Beginning to End." *Parliamentary Debates*, Fourth Series, vol. 78 (February 6, 1900), col. 785. See also K. D. Brown, *John Burns* (London: Royal Historical Society Studies in History, 1977), 92–93.

14. *Justice* (October 7, 1899), 4–5; J. W. Auld, "The Liberal Pro-Boers," *Journal of British Studies* (1975), 106–107; Claire Hirshfield, "The British Left and the 'Jewish Conspiracy': A Case Study of Modern Anti-Semitism," *Jewish Social Studies* (1981), 98–99.

15. David Feldman, "Jews and the British Empire c.1900," *History Workshop Journal* 63: 1 (2007), 70–89; Claire Hirschfield, "The Anglo-Boer War and the Issue of Jewish Culpability," *Journal of Contemporary History* 15: 4 (1980), 619–631.

16. *Justice* (January 4, 1896); (April 25, 1896).

17. *Justice* (September 30, 1899); (October 14, 1899); *Reynolds's Newspaper* (February 13, 1898); (November 12, 1899); J. A. Hobson, "Capitalism and Imperialism in South Africa," *Contemporary Review* 79 (1900), 4–5.

18. *The Owl*, no. 4 (January 31, 1902). For more on *The Owl* and anti-Semitic depictions of Jews in South Africa, see among others Milton Shain, *Jewry and Cape Society: The Origins and Activities of the Jewish Board of Deputies for the Cape Colony* (Cape Town: Historical Publication Society, 1983); M. Shain, *The Roots of Antisemitism in South Africa* (Charlottesville: University of Virginia Press, 1994).

19. John X. Merriman is quoted in Milton Shain, "The Foundations of Antisemitism in South Africa Images of the Jew, c. 1870–1930" (PhD Dissertation, University of Cape Town, 1990), 152; later published as *The Roots of Antisemitism in South Africa*. Anti-Jewish hostility, Shain reminds us, should be understood in the context of economic and social dislocation, particularly of rural farmers: "Rapid industrialization and its by-product urbanization contribut[ed] to white poverty, a

subject regularly debated after 1890. The penetration of the Jewish middleman into the agrarian and urban economy enabled him to serve as a convenient explanation for the plight of the uprooted. With such a high proportion of Jewish immigrants to the Cape colony, the reasons for the complicated relationship between anti-alienism and antisemitism become obvious."

20. W. J. H., "Diamonds and Vulgarity: Pointed Observations from the Branch," *New York Times* (July 31, 1887), 9.
21. Gideon Shimony explains that "Kaffir eating houses" catered to African diamond and gold miners. The wait-staff were known as *kaffireatniks*, a derogatory term used to describe East-European Jewish immigrants who had white skin but served food to Africans. Their subservient role to black workers and lack of economic standing in the community called into question their whiteness. See Gideon Shimony, *Community and Conscience: The Jews in Apartheid South Africa* (Hanover: Brandeis University Press, 2003), 6.
22. Angove, *In the Early Days*, 67; Turrell, *Capital and Labour on the Kimberley Diamond Fields*, 175.
23. Cohen, *Reminiscences*, 147; Hall, *Petticoat Pioneers*.
24. Cohen, *Reminiscences*, 148. Sammy Marks, son of a Russian-Jewish tailor and future director of the diamond company Lewis and Marks, estimated that as much as one-third of the white population on the fields engaged in illicit trading, and that theft was rampant throughout the work force. See Richard Mendelsohn, *Sammy Marks: The Uncrowned King of the Transvaal* (Athens: Ohio University Press, 1991), 17.
25. George F. Kunz, "Diamond Mining in South Africa," *Scientific American* 71: 13 (September 29, 1894), 204. Cohen, *Reminiscences*, 160: "Many a time at prayers in the shul I have seen a pious and fervent worshiper get the tip, and hurriedly forsake his exhortations ostensibly to wash his hands, and return smilingly to devotional duties with a merry glint in his eye, and a goniva in his mouth—which happy event, by means of an esoterical wink, he transmitted to his partner, who forthwith celebrated the blessed occasion by increased and louder orisons and sundry tremendous thumpings on the left breast. It was all magnificent, but hardly prayer. The other congregationalists quite realised what had happened, and between their prayers, which were fervent supplications to Heaven to be all reunited in Jerusalem next year (wild horses could not have dragged one of them to that unsavory, though highly historical, place), would murmur, with agitated eyebrows, to each other, 'Jacob's got a motza puddin',' and wonder about its color and its size."
26. Cohen, 165; Herbert, *The Diamond Diggers*; George F. Kunz, "Fashions in Precious Stones," *North American Review* 147: 380 (1888), 52; Kunz, "Diamonds and the Diamond-Fields," *Appleton's Physical Geography* (1887), no pagination. For a dramatic story on diamonds smuggled inside an anaconda, see "The Diamond Smugglers of New York," *New York Press* (1902). "Diamonds smuggled in the breast hair of a newfoundlander dog," *Jeweller & Metalworker* (June 1, 1886), 188.
27. "The Governor of Cape Colony and the Jews," *Jewish Chronicle* (August 8, 1873), 312.
28. See "The Governor of the Cape Colony and the Jews," *Jewish Chronicle* (August 15, 1873), 336. For a defense of Barkly, see the *Diamond News* (September 11, 1872), 2–3.
29. Sydney Mendelssohn, "Journalism (!) Extraordinary," *Diamond News and Griqualand Gazette* (March 1, 1883), 3.

30. Standard Bank Archive, Johannesburg, South Africa: Henry Files, correspondence L. Michell to General Manager (April 17, 1882). No pagination.
31. Matthews, *Incwadi Yami*, 227.
32. Matthews, 206.
33. Brian Roberts has systematically exposed Barnato Brother's involvement in IDB. See *The Diamond Magnates*, 139–152; Turrell, *Capital and Labour*, 195.
34. Gardner F. Williams explained that the Diamond Trade Act required each parcel of rough stones on the diamond fields to be described and registered. Every transaction, from the date of recovery to the final shipment from the Cape Colony, had to be recorded. The act also stipulated that anyone dealing in diamonds required a license, that record books of purchases and sales were subject to police inspection, and that violations would be judged in a Special Court. See Williams, *The Diamond Mines of South Africa*, 266.
35. Cape Archives, Cape Town, South Africa: Special Court, Vol. 512: Queen vs Isaac Joel (March/April 1884), f. 19.
36. Kunz, "Diamond Mining in South Africa," 204. The subsequent quote is also from this article.
37. William J. Morton, "To South Africa for Diamonds! Second Paper," *Scribner's Monthly* 16 (1878), 669; E. B. Biggar, "The Diamond-Mines of South Africa," *Lippincott's Magazine* (March 1881), 217–231; "Diamond Hunting: The Negro Diggers of the South African Diamond Syndicate," *Sacramento Daily Record-Union* (April 16, 1896), 6. For a discussion of the alleged partnership between Jews and African on the diamond fields, see Zine Magubane, *Bringing the Empire Home: Race, Class, and Gender in Britain and Colonial South Africa* (Chicago: Chicago University Press, 2003).
38. Matthews, *Incwadi Yami*, 415; "Notes from the Pan," *The Diamond News and Griqualand West Gazette* (September 26, 1882), 2. The correspondent maintained that "thieving by the native labourers [was] induced by the I.D.B. fraternity."
39. For more on closed compounds, see Turrell, *Capital and Labour*; Turrell, "Diamonds and Migrant Labour in South Africa"; Worger, *South Africa's City of Diamonds*.
40. Henry Knollys, "Diamond-Digging in South Africa," *Blackwood's Edinburgh Magazine* 150: 911 (September 1891), 317–333, 318.
41. Saron and Hotz, *The Jews in South Africa*; Shain, *Jewry and Cape Society*; Shimony, *Community and Conscience*; Gilman and Shain, *Jewries at the Frontier*; Shain and Mendelsohn, *The Jews in South Africa*; Milton Shain, Vivian Bickford-Smith, and Richard Mendelsohn, "Testing Cosmopolitan Tolerance: Port Jews in Cape Town during the Late Victorian and Edwardian Years," *Jewish Culture and History* 7: 1–2 (2004), 235–246. James Campbell states that a "substantial majority of the new arrivals—70% or more—hailed from greater Lithuania. The largest contingent came from the Kovno and its hinterlands, but substantial numbers also arrived from the districts of Vilna, Grodno, north Suwalki, and Vitebsk. Thousands more arrived from Poland, Latvia, Byelorussia, and as far afield as Odessa in the Ukraine. While some traveled to South Africa directly, most were transmigrants, who arrived after spending months or years elsewhere: in the East End of London, on New York's Lower East Side, in Germany." See James T. Campbell, "Beyond the Pale: Jewish Immigration and the South African Left," in Milton Shain, ed., *Memories, Realities, and Dreams: Aspects of the South African Jewish Experience* (Johannesburg: Jonathan Ball Publishers, 2002), 96–123.
42. Shain et al., "Testing Cosmopolitan Tolerance," 237.

43. Milton Shain, "Jewish Cultures, Identities and Contingencies: Reflections from the South African Experience," *European Review of History* 18: 1 (February 2011), 89–100.
44. "News from the Cape," *Jewish Chronicle* (November 10, 1875), 508.
45. Steinbach, *Understanding Victorians*; C. W. King, *The Natural History, Ancient and Modern of Precious Stones and Gems and of Precious Metals* (London: Bell and Daldy, 1865).
46. "Illicit Diamond Buying," *The Graphic* (October 13, 1883), 362; "Passing Notes," *Illustrated Police News* (May 2, 1885), 3; "The Great Diamond Trial," *Glasgow Herald* (November 12, 1886), 4; "The Diamond Fields of Kimberley," *Belfast Newsletter* (February 27, 1890), 3; "The Diamond Trade," *Birmingham Daily Post* (August 15 1893), 3; "Colonial Convict Life," *Glasgow Herald* (January 9, 1897); "A Diamond King," *Freeman's Journal* (October 9 1899), 6; "Alleged Illicit Diamond Buying," *Daily News* (March 28, 1900), 7; "Illicit Diamond Buying," *Liverpool Mercury* (April, 18 1900), 10; "Alleged Illicit Diamond Buying," *Reynold's Newspaper* (April 1, 1900), 2; "A Boer's Deal in Diamonds," *Newcastle Weekly Courant* (April 21, 1900), 3; "The Evil Genius of the Diamond Fields," *Aberdeen Weekly* (June 6, 1900), 2.
47. T.S. Eliot wrote the introduction to *The Moonstone* for a 1928 edition. See Collins, *The Moonstone*. Eliot had composed a highly anti-Semitic poem only a few years before, in 1920. In "Burbank with a Baedeker: Bleistein with a Cigar," Eliot equates Jews with rats, scurrying about with a "lusterless protrusive eye star[ing] from the protozoic slime." They were "money in furs."
48. Collins, *The Moonstone*, 2–3.
49. Plotz, *Portable Property*, 40; Ian Duncan, "The Moonstone, The Victorian Novel, and Imperialist Panic," *Modern Language Quarterly* 55 (September 1994), 297–300.
50. See, e.g., Cheyette, *Constructions of "The Jew" in English Literature and Society*); Anne Aresty Naman, *The Jew in the Victorian Novel: Some Relationships between Prejudice and Art* (New York: AMS Press, 1980); Anthony Julius, *Trials of the Diaspora: A History of Anti-Semitism in England* (Oxford: Oxford University Press, 2010), 148–241; Derek Cohen and Deborah Heller, eds., *Jewish Presence in English Literature* (Montreal: McGill-Queen's University Press, 1990); and Edgar Rosenberg's pioneering study, *From Shylock to Svengali: Jewish Stereotypes in English Fiction* (Stanford, CA: Stanford University Press, 1960), focused on stereotypes in literature.
51. Collins, *The Moonstone*, 41.
52. Collins, 80.
53. Pointon, *Rocks, Ice and Dirty Stones*, 196.
54. Judith R. Walkowitz, *City of Dreadful Delight: Narratives of Sexual Danger in Late-Victorian London* (Chicago: University of Chicago Press, 1992), 20.
55. James Greenwood, *Unsentimental Journeys: or, Byways of the Modern Babylon* (1867), Greenwood described the gemstone trade houses in Houndsditch as "black slum golcondas" populated by "beady-eyed and hawk-nosed" Jews.
56. *Uitenhage Times* (September 13, 1883). Quoted in Shain, *Jewry and Cape Society*, 4.
57. Shain, 4.
58. The *Cape Times*, referring to Jewish immigrants, spoke of a "disreputable-looking coterie of parasites of the social fabric, standing a little apart, conversing in a gibberish of mid-Europe, bare-legged, frowzy-headed, shifty eyed, and nervously sharp, ready to pounce upon the rough handed sons of the seas as they come to land," as the "keen-witted specimen of the lower species of the immigrant Hebrew

race in unvarnished guise and unreserved demeanour." To *Cape* editors, the "rapacious foreign Hebrew... never risks his own life or safety [but] pockets his profit, and so he prospers from day to day" (March 20, 1902).
59. Nina Morais, "Jewish Ostracism in America," *American Hebrew and Jewish Messenger* (August 19, 1881), 3. Morais's piece was originally published in the *North American Review* 122: 298 (September 1881), 265–275.
60. W. J. H., "Diamonds and Vulgarity: Pointed Observations from the Branch," *New York Times* (July 31, 1887), 9. Jewish ostentation remained a topic of debate for decades. In 1909, Simon Wolf lamented that "Jewish newspapers are again, as they have for many years, more or less crowded with editorials and communications on the subject of an exclusion of from summer hotels.... One loud Jew or Jewess in a hotel is enough to brand us all.... The Jewess who dresses in vulgar taste and comes to breakfast bedecked with diamonds galore, and who talks in broken vernacular, is naturally an object of aversion, and stands unfortunately as a type of the whole sex." See Simon Wolf, "Summer Hotels and Kindred Insanity," *American Israelite* (July 15, 1909), 4. For more on Jews in American cartoons, see Matthew Baigell, *The Implacable Urge to Defame: Cartoon Jews in the American Press, 1877–1935* (Syracuse, NY: Syracuse University Press, 2017).
61. "A New American Judaeophobe," *American Hebrew* (August 5, 1887), 194.
62. A Victorian writer commenting on female fashion stated: "[D]ress becomes a sort of symbolical language—a kind of personal glossary—a species of body phrenology, the study of which it would be madness to neglect ... every woman walks about with a placard on which her leading qualities are advertised." Quoted in Thad Logan's *The Victorian Parlour* (Cambridge: Cambridge University Press, 2001), 375–376.
63. Morais, "Jewish Ostracism in America," 3.
64. For more on American Jews and patterns of consumption, see Heinze, *Adapting to Abundance*; Gideon Reuveni and Nils Roemer, eds., *Longing, Belonging, and the Making of Jewish Consumer Culture* (Leiden: Brill, 2010); Jenna Weissman Joselit, *A Perfect Fit: Clothes, Character, and the Promise of America* (New York: Macmillan, 2001); Elizabeth Hafkin Pleck, *Celebrating the Family: Ethnicity, Consumer Culture, and Family Rituals* (Cambridge, MA: Harvard University Press, 2000); Marilyn Halter, *Shopping for Identity: The Marketing of Ethnicity* (New York: Schocken Books, 2000).
65. See the recent "Roundtable on Anti-Semitism in the Gilded Age and Progressive Era," *Journal of the Gilded Age and Progressive Era* 19: 3 (2020), 473–505; Naomi W. Cohen, "Antisemitism in the Gilded Age: The Jewish View," *Jewish Social Studies* 41 (1979), 187–210; Eric Goldstein, *The Price of Whiteness: Jews, Race, and American Identity* (Princeton: Princeton University Press, 2006); Beth Wenger, *The Jewish Americans: Three Centuries of Jewish Voices in America* (New York: Doubleday, 2007). For more on stereotyping of American Jewish women, see Riv-Ellen Prell, *Fighting to Become Americans: Jews, Gender, and the Anxiety of Assimilation* (Boston: Beacon Press, 1999); Paula E. Hyman, *Gender and Assimilation in Modern Jewish History: The Roles and Representations of Women* (Seattle: University of Washington Press, 1995).
66. Joselit, "Cut Gem."
67. "Immodest Apparel," *American Hebrew* (February 19, 1886), 20.
68. "Ladies' Column," *American Israelite* (October 5, 1899), 8.
69. FRIC, "Who Is Extravagant?," *Jewish Messenger* (February 7, 1868), 1.

70. "The Modern Midas," *American Israelite* (November 7, 1895), 5; "Barnato a Suicide," *New York Tribune* 57: 18,475 (June 15, 1897), 1.
71. "Stories of Barnato," *Morning News* (Savannah, GA, June 19, 1897), 6.
72. Williams, *The Diamond Mines of South Africa*, 274.
73. "Barnato a Suicide," 3.
74. *Philadelphia Inquirer* 136, no. 167 (June 16, 1897), 1.
75. "Barnato a Suicide," 1; "Barney Barnato," *The Chautauquan: A Weekly Newsmagazine* 25 (August 1897), 571; "Diamond King Suicides," *Evening Herald* (PA, June 15, 1897), 3; "The Suicide of Mr. Barnato," *London Daily News* (June 16, 1897), 7; "Death of Mr. Barney Barnato," *The Star* (June 17, 1897), 1; "Barnato," *Colonies and India* (June 19, 1897), 22; "The Death of Mr. Barney Barnato," *Lloyd's Weekly Newspaper* (June 20, 1897), 18; "Went Overboard," *Colorado Weekly Chieftain* (June 17, 1897), 5; "Barney Barnato's Suicide," *New York Times* (June 16, 1897), 3; "Kaffir King Barnato," *Morning Times* (June 16, 1897), 5.
76. "Suicide of Barney Barnato," *Reynolds's Newspaper* (June 20, 1897), 3; "Barney Barnato," *Reynolds's Newspaper* (June 20, 1897), 4.
77. *Jewish Messenger* (June 18, 1897), 4, no title; *Jewish Chronicle* (June 18, 1897), 16. The *American Israelite* had ameliorated this view by 1908, when it spoke of Barnato as being "himself a rough diamond [with] a good heart." See Maurice Brodsky, "A Barney Barnato Echo," *American Israelite* (January 2, 1908), 5.
78. John Burns, Labour MP for Battersea, stated during the Boer War that "[w]herever we examine, there is the financial Jew, operating, directing, inspiring the agencies that have led to this war.... The trail of the financial serpent is over this war from beginning to end." *Parliamentary Debates* (Commons), 78 (February 6, 1900), 789. See also Brown, *John Burns*, 92–93.

CONCLUSION

1. "Kroniek van Dr. Henri Polak," *Zaans Volksblad: Sociaal-Democratisch Dagblad* 1: 201 (October 8, 1938), 2.
2. Polak is quoted in Bloemgarten, *Henri Polak*, 632.
3. Bloemgarten, 633.
4. Kunz, "Precious Stones in North America."
5. *Verzuiling* refers to the "pillarization" of the Dutch religious, political, and social landscape that intensified in the second half of the nineteenth century, lasting until the 1960s. Roman Catholics, Protestants, Liberals, and Social Democrats gradually organized into distinct segments (pillars), each with their own social institutions, political party, schools, newspapers, unions, and recreational services. Dutch Jewry in many ways resembled these pillars, but it was both too small in number and too loyal to the Liberals to form a pillar of its own. Good observations of Dutch pillar divisions are offered by Joris van Eijnatten, in his introduction to *Liberty and Concord in the United Provinces: Religious Toleration and the Public in the Eighteenth-Century Netherlands* (Leiden: Brill, 2003); Harry Post, *Pillarization: An Analysis of Dutch and Belgian Society* (Aldershot: Avebury, 1989).
6. Diamond histories have consistently eclipsed the contributions made by women, not merely in the actual manufacturing process but also in organizing societies for cultural development (*ontwikkelingsclubs*), ANDB administration, and international congresses. In the Dutch context, Margree Schrevel's work has started to change this. See Margreet Schrevel, "Een stem in het kapittel: Diamantbewerkers organiseren zich," in Hofmeester, *Een schitterende erfenis*. The contributions of women in the international mineral industry is a topic that still needs to be mined.

7. Rall, *Petticoat Pioneers*; Ed Caesar, "The Woman Shaking Up the Diamond Industry," *New Yorker* (January 27, 2020), https://www.newyorker.com/magazine/2020/02/03/the-woman-shaking-up-the-diamond-industry.
8. Henri Polak, *Diary 1940–1942* (Netherlands Institute of War Documentation, Amsterdam #244: Europese Dagboeken en Egodocumenten, file 869: Henri Polak).
9. Jessica L. Ghilani, De Beers' "Fighting Diamonds": Recruiting American Consumers in World War II Advertising," *Journal of Communication Inquiry* 36: 3 (2012), 222–245.
10. "Cutting and Polishing Diamonds," and "Have Not the Space to Give," *Chicago Daily Tribune* (January 27, 1892): 10; "Diamond Mining at Jackson Park," *Chicago Daily Tribune* (March 11, 1893): 2; Kinsey, "Imperial Splendor," 336.
11. "Gems in the Dirt," *Chicago Daily Tribune* (May 28, 1893): 25; *The Official Directory of the World's Columbian Exposition, May 1st to October 30th, 1893* (Chicago: W. B. Conkey, 1893), 114.
12. "Diamond Mining at Jackson Park," 2.
13. *The Official Directory*, 114; "Gossip of the Exposition," *Jewelers' Circular and Horological Review* 26: 9 (March 29, 1893), 30; "Valley of Diamonds: How Bright Gems Are Extracted From the Soil of the Dark Continent," *Anaconda Standard*, December 22, 1895), 15.
14. Sarah Brentworth, "Diamonds," *The Chautauquan; A Weekly Newsmagazine* 23: 5 (August 1896): 629.
15. *Report of the Secretary of the Interior*, 898.
16. Fikile Portia Ndlovu-Mitchell, "The Growth and Development of South African Diamond Law: A Critical Analysis," *Commonwealth Law Bulletin* 39: 4 (2013), 675–701.
17. George Kunz, for example, noted in 1889 that only seven of sixteen diamond cutting firms in New York ran full-time, but that the others saw unemployment "between 14 and 240 days of the year, owing to inability to obtain rough material at a price at which it could be advantageously cut." Unable to secure rough diamonds, many companies could not afford to keep the mills spinning. The firms fully employed were generally the larger ones. See Kunz, "Precious Stones in North America," 37–38.
18. For "Fighting Diamonds" advertisements, see among others *New Yorker* (May 16, 1942), 3; "Invincible Diamonds," *New Yorker* (June 27, 1942), 3. On the 1942 "Diamond Raid," see Paul Post and Bies van Ede, *De diamantenroof: Hoe hoge Nazi's met diamanten uit België en Nederland naar Zuid-Amerika vluchtten* (Utrecht: Omniboek, 2016); Gerard Aalders, *Roof: De ontvreemding van joods bezit tijdens de Tweede Wereldoorlog* (Den Haag: Sdu Uitgevers, 1999), translated into *Nazi Looting: The Plunder of Dutch Jewry during the Second World War* (Oxford: Berg Publishers, 2004).
19. Meijer, "Henri Polak." Milly Polak, critically ill, died in Westerbork. Her fellow inmates were deported to Sobibor and Auschwitz.
20. "The Diamond Industry," *The Diamond News and Griqualand West Gazette* (October 19, 1882), 3. The newspaper referenced the *London Standard*, where the article first appeared.
21. *Scientific American: A Weekly Journal of Practical Information, Art, Science, Mechanics, Chemistry, and Manufacturers* 29: 14 (October 4, 1873), 215.
22. Hall and Rose, *At Home with the Empire*, 6; Alan Lester, *Imperial Networks: Creating Identities in Nineteenth-Century South Africa and Britain* (London: Routledge, 2001).

23. Standard Bank Archive, Inspection Report (Port Elizabeth): July 31, 1876, f 613; Inspection Report (Dutoitspan): November 17, 1873; Inspection Report (Kimberley): 23 June 1875, f 86; September 1, 1876, f 187; *Diamond News* (December 8, 1874).
24. Angove, *In the Early Days*, 123.
25. Morton, "The South African Diamond Fields," 75. An 1873 *Cape Almanac* report stated: "Licenses issued for the district of Pniel, including Dutoitspan and Bultfontein, for the six months ending June 30, 1872: we have 25 bakers, 51 butchers, 140 diamond dealers, 8 apothecaries, 26 auctioneers, 21 wholesale wine and spirit dealers, 68 wholesale warehousemen, 135 retail shopkeepers, 10 gunpowder and 458 retail wine and spirit licenses. Total 942 licenses." *Cape Almanac* (1873), 1, 198.
26. Trollope, *South Africa*, 200; *Statistical Register of the Colony of the Cape of Good Hope* (Cape Town: Government Printers, 1902), 8. The 1879 *Cape Almanac* reported that between 1860 and 1870 "[t]here was not any remarkable increase [in Cape exports], the value being declared at very little more than 2 1/2 million pounds sterling in 1871. Owing to the discovery of diamonds the value was augmented so rapidly that in the succeeding year more than 4 1/2 million is returned as the value of colonial produce sent beyond seas. Since 1872, the exports have always been returned as more than 5 million sterling, the maximum being attained in 1875, when it was £5,731,319. . . . Nearly the whole of the colonial exports are sent to the United Kingdom, which took from the Cape of Good Hope alone, in the year 1877, produce of which the declared value was 3,299,557 pounds." See "Section IV: Trade and Customs," *Cape Almanac* (1879), 218–246.
27. *Statistical Register of the Cape of Good Hope*, 218–219. See also *Reports on the Colonial Sections of the Exhibition*, 43.
28. Wallis Richard Cattelle, *The Diamond* (New York: John Lane Company, 1911), 32.
29. Cattelle, *The Diamond*, 37–38.
30. For more on commercial connections among (and between) Jews and non-Jews before the nineteenth century, see Francesca Trivellato, *The Familiarity of Strangers: The Sephardic Diaspora, Livorno, and Cross-Cultural Trade in the Early Modern Period* (New Haven: Yale University Press, 2009); Tijl Vanneste, "Unpaid Diamonds: Trust, Reputation, and the Merchant's Style in Eighteenth-Century Europe," *Shofar: An Interdisciplinary Journal of Jewish Studies* 38: 3 (Winter 2020), 13–45.
31. See, among others, Adam Mendelsohn, *The Rag Race: How Jews Sewed Their Way to Success in America and the British Empire* (New York: New York University Press, 2015); Michael R. Cohen, *Cotton Capitalists: American Jewish Entrepreneurship in the Reconstruction Era* (New York: New York University Press, 2017); Sarah Abrevaya Stein, *Plumes: Ostrich Feathers, Jews, and a Lost World of Global Commerce* (New Haven: Yale University Press, 2010).
32. "The Cape Colony," *Jewish Chronicle* (July 3, 1891), 5. "Of course Jews were settled in South Africa long before [the diamond discoveries]," stated a Cape Town correspondent, "extend[ing] their trading operations into what was in those days the Hinterland. . . . The commercial supremacy they established has remained unchallenged even unto the present day."
33. David Feldman made a similar point in his essay, "Jews and the British Empire, c.1900," *History Workshop Journal* 63: 1 (2007), 70–89.
34. "The Jews of South Africa," *Jewish Chronicle* (March 16, 1912): 40–41.
35. Henri Polak, *De strijd der diamantbewerkers* (Amsterdam: S. L. van Looy, 1896), 3.

BIBLIOGRAPHY

Aalders, Gerard. *Roof: De ontvreemding van joods bezit tijdens de Tweede Wereldoorlog.* The Hague: Sdu Uitgevers, 1999.
Abicht, Ludo. *De joden van Antwerpen*. Groningen: Hadewijch, 1993.
Abicht, Ludo. *Geschiedenis van de joden van de Lage Landen*. Amsterdam: Meulenhoff, 2006.
Adamson, Glenn, Giorgio Riello, and Sarah Teasley, eds. *Global Design History*. London and New York: Routledge, 2011.
Aerts, Remieg en Piet de Rooy. *Geschiedenis van Amsterdam, Deel III*. Nijmegen: Uitgeverij SUN, 2006.
Albrecht, Henning. *Alfred Beit: Hamburger und Diamantenkönig*. Hamburg: Hamburgische Wissenschaftliche Stiftung, 2012.
Alderman, Geoffrey, ed. *New Directions in Anglo-Jewish History*. Brookline: Academic Studies Press, 2010.
Algar, Frederic. *The Diamond Fields: With Notes on the Cape Colony and Natal.* London: Clement's Lane, 1872.
Allen, Charles V. *Diamond Mining in the Kimberley Field and the Mechanical Equipment of the Kimberley Diamond Mines*. New York: Dunlap, 1903.
Amatori, F., and G. Jones, eds, *Business History around the World*. Cambridge: Cambridge University Press, 2003.
Angove, John. *In the Early Days: The Reminiscences of Pioneer Life on the South African Diamond Fields*. London: Handel House, 1910.
Appadurai, Arjun, ed. *The Social Life of Things: Commodities in Cultural Perspective.* Cambridge: Cambridge University Press, 1986.
Arbel, Rachel, and Jacob Tamir. *The Jews of South Africa*. Tel Aviv: Beth Hatefutsoth, the Nahum Goldmann Museum of the Jewish Diaspora, 1983.
Ashmead, Edward. *Twenty-Five Years of Mining, 1880–1904: A Retrospective Review, with an Appendix Four Years Later, 1905–1908*. London: The Mining Journal, 1909.
Asscher, S. *Diamant, wonderlijk kristal*. Bussum: Fibula-Van Dishoeck, 1975.
Babe, Jerome L. *The South African Diamond Fields*. New York: David Wesley, 1872.
Baigell, Matthew. *The Implacable Urge to Defame: Cartoon Jews in the American Press, 1877–1935*. Syracuse: Syracuse University Press, 2017.
Bair, Jennifer. *Frontiers of Commodity Chain Research*. Stanford: Stanford University Press, 2009.
Bakker, Martha, Renee Kistemaker, Henk F. K. van Nierop, Wim Vroom, and Piet Witteman, eds. *Amsterdam in de tweede Gouden Eeuw*. Bussum: Thoth, 2000.
Baigell, Matthew. *The Implacable Urge to Defame: Cartoon Jews in the American Press, 1877–1935*. Syracuse: Syracuse University Press, 2017.

Ballantyne, Tony. *Moving Subjects: Gender, Mobility, and Intimacy in an Age of Global Empire*. Urbana-Champaign: University of Illinois Press, 2009.
Bancroft, Hubert Howe. *The Book of the Fair*. Chicago: The Bancroft Company, 1893.
Bar-Yosef, Eitan, and Nadia Valman, eds. *The Jew in Late-Victorian and Edwardian Culture: Between the East End and East Africa*. London: Palgrave Macmillan, 2009.
Barents, M. *De Diamantslijperij Maatschappij te Amsterdam, 1845–1920*. Amsterdam: M. Barents, 1920.
Barents, M. *Het onderling Diamantslijpers Weduwen- en Weezenfonds (1848–1916). Een stuk maatschappelijk werk uit de negentiende eeuw*. Amsterdam: M. Barents, 1927.
Batchelor, Jennie, and Cora Kaplan, eds. *Women and Material Culture, 1660–1830*. London: Palgrave Macmillan, 2007.
Bauer, Max. *Precious Stones*. London: Charles Griffin & Co., 1904.
Beckert, Sven. *Empire of Cotton: A Global History*. New York: Knopf, 2014.
Beet, George. *Grand Old Days of the Diamond Fields: Memories of Past Times with the Diggers of Diamondia*. Cape Town: M. Miller, 1931.
Beet, George, and Thomas Laurent Terpend. *The Romance and Reality of the Vaal diamond Diggings*. Kimberley: Diamond Fields Advertiser, 1917.
Belgrave, Dalrymple J. *Luck at the Diamond Fields*. London: Ward & Downey, 1887.
Benson, John, and Gareth Shaw. *The Evolution of Retail Systems, c. 1800–1914*. Leicester: Leicester University Press, 1992.
Berckelaer, L. van, I. Lipschutz, and Henri Polak. *Diamant in handel en nijverheid*. Antwerpen: De Sikkel, 1930.
Berg, Hetty, ed. *De gelykstaat der joden: Inburgering van een minderheid*. Amsterdam: Joods Historisch Museum, 1996.
Berg, Hetty, et al. *Venter, fabriqueur, fabrikant: Joodse ondernemers en ondernemingen in Nederland 1796–1940*. Amsterdam: Joods Historisch Museum, 1994.
Berg, Maxine. *Consumers and Luxury: Consumer Culture in Europe, 1650–1850*. Manchester: Manchester University Press, 1999.
Bergstein, Rachelle. *Brilliance and Fire: A Biography of Diamonds*. New York: Harper, 2016.
Berman, Mildred. "The Location of the Diamond-Cutting Industry." *Annals of the Association of American Geographers* 61: 2 (1971), 316–328.
Bhabha, Homi K. *The Location of Culture*. New York: Routledge, 1994.
Bhagat, Dipti. "Buying More Than a Diamond: South Africa and the Colonial and Indian Exhibition, 1886." PhD Dissertation, Royal College of Art/Victoria & Albert Museum, 1996.
Bhagat, Dipti. "The Poetics of Belonging: Exhibitions and the Performance of White South African Identity, 1886–1936." PhD Dissertation, University of London, 2002.
Bloemgarten, Salvador. *Henri Polak: Sociaal Democraat, 1868–1943*. Den Haag: SDU, 1993.
Blom, J. C. H., Renate G. Fuks-Mansfeld, and I. Schoffer, eds. *The History of the Jews in the Netherlands*. Oxford: The Littman Library of Jewish Civilization, 2007.
Boas, Henriëtte. "Jews and the Amsterdam Diamond Trade." *Studia Rosenthaliana* 26 (1992), 214–223.
Boekman, Emanuel. *Demografie van de Joden in Nederland*. Amsterdam: Hertzberger, 1936.
Bolotin, Norman, and Christine Laing, eds. *The World's Columbian Exposition: The Chicago World's Fair of 1893*. Urbana-Champaign: University of Illinois Press, 2002.
Bos, Dennis. *Waarachtige volksvrienden: De vroege socialistische beweging in Amsterdam 1848–1894*. Amsterdam: B. Bakker, 2001.

Boyle, Frederick. *To the Cape For Diamonds: A Story of Digging Experiences in South Africa*. London: Chapman and Hall, 1873.
Brown, K. D. *John Burns*. London: Royal Historical Society Studies in History, 1977.
Bruin, Kees. *Een herenwereld ontleed: Over Amsterdamse oude en nieuwe elites in de tweede helft van de negentiende eeuw*. Amsterdam: Sociologisch Instituut, Universiteit van Amsterdam, 1980.
Bryce, James. *Impressions of South Africa*. London: Macmillan and Co., 1897.
Buhle, Paul. *Taking Care of Business: Samuel Gompers, George Meany, Lane Kirkland, and the Tragedy of American Labor*. New York: Monthly Review Press, 1999.
Burton, Antoinette, ed. *After the Imperial Turn: Thinking With and Through the Nation*. Durham, NC: Duke University Press, 2003.
Cameron, Rondo E., "The Crédit Mobilier and the Economic Development of Europe." *Journal of Political Economy* 61: 6 (1953), 461–488.
Cañizares-Esguerra, J., and E. R. Seeman, eds. *The Atlantic in Global History, 1500–2000*. Upper Saddle River, NJ: Pearson Prentice Hall, 2007.
Cannadine, David. *Ornamentalism: How the British Saw Their Empire*. New York: Oxford University Press, 2001.
Carstens, Peter. *In the Company of Diamonds: De Beers, Kleinzee, and the Control of a Town*. Athens: Ohio University Press, 2001.
Cassis, Youssef. "Jewish Entrepreneurs in England, c.1850–c.1950." *Jüdische Unternehmer in Deutschland Im 19. Und 20. Jahrhundert*. Edited by Werner E. Mosse and Hans Pohl. Stuttgart: Franz Steiner Verlag, 1992. Pp. 24–35.
Cassis, Youssef, and Avraham Barkai. "Aspects of the Jewish Business Elite in Britain and Germany." *Two Nations: British and German Jews in Comparative Perspective*. Edited by Michael Brenner, Rainer Liedtke, and David Rechter. Tübingen: Mohr Siebeck, 1999. Pp. 279–290.
Cattelle, Wallis Richard. *The Diamond*. New York: John Lane Company, 1911.
Cesarani, David, ed. *Port Jews: Jewish Communities in Cosmopolitan Maritime Trading Centres, 1550–1950*. London: Routledge, 2002.
Chapman, Charles. *A Voyage from Southampton to Cape Town, in the Union Company's Mail Steamer "Syria."* London: George Berridge & Co., 1872.
Chapman, Stanley D. *Merchant Enterprise in Britain From the Industrial Revolution to World War I*. Cambridge: Cambridge University Press, 1992.
Chapman, Stanley D. *The Rise of Merchant Banking*. London: Allen & Unwin, 1984.
Cheyette, Bryan. *Constructions of "the Jew" in English Literature and Society: Racial Representations, 1875–1945*. Cambridge: Cambridge University Press, 1993.
Clark, Grahame. *Symbols of Excellence: Precious Materials as Expressions of Status*. Cambridge: Cambridge University Press, 1986.
Cohen, Deborah. *Household Gods: The British and Their Possessions*. New Haven: Yale University Press, 2009.
Cohen, Derek, and Deborah Heller, eds. *Jewish Presence in English Literature*. Montreal: McGill-Queen's University Press, 1990.
Cohen, Louis. *Reminiscences of Kimberley*. London: Bennett & Co., 1911.
Cohen, Michael R. *Cotton Capitalists: American Jewish Entrepreneurship in the Reconstruction Era*. New York: New York University Press, 2017.
Cohen, Naomi W. *Jews in Christian America: The Pursuit of Religious Equality*. New York: Oxford University Press, 1992.
Collins, Wilkie. *The Moonstone*. New York: Harper & Brothers, 1890.

Coombes, Annie E. *Reinventing Africa: Museums, Material Culture, and Popular Imagination in Late Victorian and Edwardian England*. New Haven: Yale University Press, 1994.

Coronel, S., Sr. "De Diamantwerkers Te Amsterdam." *De Economist* 14: 1 (1865), 73–106.

Cottrell, P. L. *Industrial Finance, 1830–1914: The Finance and Organization of English Manufacturing Industry*. London and New York: Methuen, 1980.

Couper, J. R. *Mixed Humanity: A Story of Camp Life in South Africa*. Cape Town: J. C. Juta, 1892.

Cowen, Charles. *The South African Exhibition, Port Elizabeth, 1885; Lectures, Prize and Other Essays, Jury Reports and Awards*. Cape Town: Argus, 1886.

Crookes, Sir William. *Diamonds*. New York: Harper & Brothers, 1909.

Cundall, Frank. *Reminiscences of the Colonial and Indian Exhibition*. London: William Clowes, 1886.

Daelen, Veerle Vanden. *Laten we hun lied verder zingen. De heropbouw van de joodse gemeenschap in Antwerpen na de Tweede Wereldoorlog, 1944–1960*. Amsterdam: University of Amsterdam Press, 2008.

Dash Moore, Deborah. *City of Promises: A History of the Jews of New York*. New York: New York University Press, 2012.

Davenport, Jade. *Digging Deep: A History of Mining in South Africa*. Johannesburg: Jonathan Ball Publishers, 2013.

De Launay, Louis. *Les diamants du Cap*. Paris: Librairie Polytechnique, Baudry & Co., 1897.

Deconinck, Youssef. *Diamantmigratie naar Antwerpen voor, tijdens en na de Kaapse Tijd. De Antwerpse diamantsector en zijn Amsterdamse migranten (1865–1880)*. Antwerpen: Universiteit Antwerpen, 2012.

Denucé, Jan. *Inleiding tot de geschiedenis van het diamantbedrijf te Antwerpen*. Antwerpen: De Batist, 1937.

Diner, Hasia R. *Roads Taken: The Great Jewish Migrations to the New World and the Peddlers Who Forged the Way*. New Haven: Yale University Press, 2015.

Doughty, Oswald. *Early Diamond Days: The Opening of the Diamond Fields of South Africa*. London: Longman, 1963.

Dubin, Lois. "Port Jews in the Atlantic World." *Jewish History* 20 (2006), 117–127.

Dubofsky, Melvyn, and Warren Van Tine, eds. *Labor Leaders in America*. Urbana-Champaign: University of Illinois Press, 1987.

Dumett, Raymond, ed. *Mining Tycoons in the Age of Empire, 1870–1945: Entrepreneurship, High Finance, Politics and Territorial Expansion*. London: Ashgate, 2009.

Eady, W. T. *I.D.B. or the Adventures of Solomon Davis on the Diamond Fields and Elsewhere*. London: Chapman and Hall, 1887.

Emeis, Marinus Gerardus. *A. van Moppes & Zoon: 1809–1959*. Amsterdam: N.V. Diamant Industrie A. van Moppes & Zoon, 1959.

Endelman, Todd M. "New Turns in Jewish Historiography?" *Jewish Quarterly Review* 103: 4 (2013), 589–598.

Epstein, Edward. *The Diamond Invention*. New York: Random House, 1982.

Epstein, Melech. *Jewish Labor in the USA: An Industrial, Political, and Cultural History of the Jewish Labor Movement*. New York: Ktav, 1969.

Erlich, Edward I., and Dan Hausel. *Diamond Deposits: Origin, Exploration, and History of Discovery*. Englewood, CO: Society for Mining, Metallurgy, and Exploration, 2002.

Even-Zohar, Chaim. *From Mine to Mistress: Corporate Strategies and Government Policies in the International Diamond Industry*. London: Mining Communications Ltd., 2002.
Feldberg, Leon. *South African Jewry 1965*. Johannesburg: Fieldhill Publishing Co., 1965.
Feldman, David. *Englishmen and Jews: Social Relations and Political Culture, 1840–1914*. New Haven: Yale University Press, 1994.
Feldman, David. "Jews and the British Empire c.1900." *History Workshop Journal* 63: 1 (2007), 70–89.
Feldman, David. *Structures and Transformations in Modern British History*. Cambridge: Cambridge University Press, 2011.
Feldman, Leybl. *Oudtshoorn, Jerusalem of Africa*. Johannesburg: Friends of the Library, University of the Witwatersrand, 1989.
Feldt, Jakob Egholm. *Transnationalism and the Jews: Culture, History and Prophecy*. New York: Rowman & Littlefield, 2016.
Ferguson, Niall. *The World's Banker: The History of the House of Rothschild*. London: Weidenfeld & Nicolson, 1998.
Finestein, I. *Jewish Society in Victorian England: Collected Essays*. Chicago: Vallentine Mitchell, 1993.
Fischer, E. J. "Economic Emancipation of Jews in Manufacturing and Service Industries in the Netherlands in the Nineteenth Century." *Studia Rosenthaliana* 30: 1 (1996), 57–66.
Fleischer, Dolores, and Angela Caccia. *Merchant Pioneers: The House of Mosenthal*. Johannesburg: J. Ball, 1983.
Foner, Philip S. *History of the Labor Movement in the United States*. New York: International Publishers, 1947–1981.
Fort, George Seymour. *Alfred Beit: A Study of the Man and His Work*. London: Nicholson & Watson, 1932.
Frankel, Jonathan. *Prophecy and Politics: Socialism, Nationalism, and the Russian Jews, 1862–1917*. Cambridge: Cambridge University Press, 1981.
Free, Lisa. "'Dirty Linen': Legacies of Empire in Wilkie Collins's The Moonstone." *Texas Studies in Literature and Language* 48: 4 (2006), 340–371.
Frishman, Judith, and Hetty Berg, eds. *Dutch Jewry in a Cultural Maelstrom, 1880–1940*. Amsterdam: Aksant, 2007.
Gans, M. H. *Juwelen en mensen: De geschiedenis van het bijou van 1400 tot 1900, voornamelijk naar Nederlandse bronnen*. Schiedam: Interbook International, 1979.
Gans, Evelien. *De kleine verschillen die het leven uitmaken. Een historische studie naar joodse social-democraten en socialistische-zionisten in Nederland*. Amsterdam: Vassalluci, 2002.
Gasson, Andrew, and William Baker. "Forgotten Terrain: Wilkie Collins's Jewish Explorations." *Jewish Historical Studies* 48: 1 (2017), 177–199.
Gereffi, Gary, and Miguel Korzeniewicz. *Commodity Chains and Global Capitalism*. Westport: Praeger, 1993.
Giele, Jacques. *De arbeidsenquête van 1887. Deel 1: Amsterdam*. Culemborg: Uitgeverij Link, 1981.
Gill, James. *The Emigrant's Guide to the South African Diamond Fields*. London: Sampson Low, Son, and Marston, 1870.
Gilman, Sander L., and Milton Shain, eds. *Jewries at the Frontier: Accommodation, Identity, Conflict*. Urbana-Champaign: University of Illinois Press, 1999.
Glickman, Lawrence, ed. *Consumer Society in American History: A Reader*. Ithaca: Cornell University Press, 1999.

Godley, Andrew. *Jewish Immigrant Entrepreneurship in New York and London 1880–1914*. London: Palgrave Macmillan, 2001.

Goldberg, Aleck. *Profile of a Community: South African Jewry*. Johannesburg: Rabbi Aloy Foundation Trust, 2002.

Goldman, Charles Sydney. *South African Mines: Their Position, Results, and Developments*. Johannesburg: Argus Printing and Publishing Company, 1896.

Goldstein, Eric. *The Price of Whiteness: Jews, Race, and American Identity*. Princeton, NJ: Princeton University Press, 2006.

Gompers, Samuel. *Seventy Years of Life and Labor: An Autobiography, Vol. II*. London: Hurst & Blackett, 1925.

Goodhart, C. A. E. *The Business of Banking, 1891–1914*. Aldershot: Gower Publishing Co., 1986.

Gray, J. L. *The Jew in the Economic Life of South Africa*. Johannesburg: The Society of Jews and Christians, publication No. 5, no date.

Green, Abigail. "The British Empire and the Jews." *Past and Present* 199: 1 (2008), 175–205.

Green, Timothy. "Buckets of Diamonds." *The British Empire* 29 (1972), 785–812.

Green, Timothy. *The World of Diamonds*. New York: Morrow, 1981.

Green, Nancy, ed. *Jewish Workers in the Modern Diaspora*. Berkeley: University of California Press, 1998.

Griffith, George Chetwynd. *Knaves of Diamonds: Being Tales of Mine and Vel'd*. London: C.A. Pearson, 1899.

Grynberg, Roman, and Letsema Mbayi. *The Global Diamond Industry: Economics and Development*. New York: Springer, 2015.

Haggard, H. Rider 1856–1925. *King Solomon's Mines*. Sahara Publisher Books, 1885.

Hall, Catherine. *Civilising Subjects: Colony and Metropole in the English Imagination, 1830–1867*. Chicago: University of Chicago Press, 2002.

Hall, Catherine, ed. *Cultures of Empire: A Reader: Colonizers in Britain and the Empire in the 19th and 20th Centuries*. London: Routledge, 2000.

Hall, Catherine, and Sonya O. Rose, eds. *At Home with the Empire: Metropolitan Culture and the Imperial World*. Cambridge: Cambridge University Press, 2007.

Heertje, Henri. *De Diamantbewerkers van Amsterdam, academisch proefschrift*. Amsterdam: D. B. Centen, 1936.

Heijden, Marien van der, and Wietske van Agtmaal. *Henri Polak: Grondlegger van de moderne vakbeweging 1868–1943*. Amsterdam: Nationaal Vakbondsmuseum, 1991.

Heijermans, Herman. *Diamantstad*. Amsterdam: S. L. van Looy, 1904.

Heinze, Andrew R. *Adapting to Abundance: Jewish Immigrants, Mass Consumption, and the Search for American Identity*. New York: Columbia University Press, 1990.

Hendrickson, Robert. *The Grand Emporiums: The Illustrated History of America's Great Department Stores*. New York: Stein and Day, 1979.

Hennelly, Mark M., Jr. "Detecting Collins' Diamond: From Serpentstone to Moonstone." *Nineteenth-Century Fiction* 39: 1 (June 1984), 25–47.

Herbert, Ivor. *The Diamond Diggers: South Africa 1866 to the 1970s*. London: Tom Stacey, 1971.

Herrman, Louis. *A History of the Jews in South Africa, from the Earliest Times to 1895*. Westport, CT: Greenwood Press, 1975.

Hermans, Louis M. *Krotten en Sloppen: Een onderzoek naar den woningtoestand te Amsterdam, ingesteld in opdracht van den Amsterdamsche Bestuurdersbond*. Amsterdam: S. L. van Looy, 1901.

Hertz, Joseph H. *The Jew in South Africa*. Johannesburg: The Central News Agency, 1905.

Higham, John. *Send These To Me: Immigrants in Urban America*. Baltimore: Johns Hopkins University Press, 1984.

Hinte, Jacob van. *Netherlanders in America: A Study of Emigration and Settlement in the Nineteenth and Twentieth Centuries in the United States of America*. Grand Rapids, MI: Baker Book House, 1985.

Hirshfield, Claire. "The Anglo-Boer War and the Issue of Jewish Culpability." *Journal of Contemporary History* 15: 4 (October 1980), 619–631.

Hocking, Anthoney. *Oppenheimer and Son*. New York: McGraw-Hill, 1973.

Hofmeester, Karin. *Van Talmoed tot Statuut: Joodse arbeiders en arbeidersbewegingen in Amsterdam, Londen en Parijs, 1880–1914*. Amsterdam: Stichting Beheer IISG, 1990.

Hofmeester, Karin, ed. *Een Schitterende Erfenis: 125 Jaar Nalatenschap van de Algemene Nederlandse Diamantbewerkersbond*. Zutphen: Walburg Pers, 2019.

Hofmeester, Karin. *Jewish Workers and the Labour Movement: A Comparative Study of Amsterdam, London and Paris 1870–1914*. London: Routledge, 2004.

Hofmeester, Karin. "Shifting Trajectories of Diamond Processing: From India to Europe and Back, from the Fifteenth Century to the Twentieth." *Journal of Global History* 8: 1 (March 2013), 25–49.

Holub, Emil. *Seven Years in South Africa: Travels, Researches, and Hunting Adventures Between the Diamond Fields and the Zambesi (1872–1879)*. Translated by Ellen E. Frewer, London: Sampson Low, Marston, Searle & Rivington, 1881.

Hoover, Chas. L. *Amsterdam Diamond Industry. Supplement of In- En Uitvoer: A Weekly of Commerce and Economics*. Amsterdam: Naamlooze venn. uitgevers-maatschappij Amsterdam, 1929.

Houghton, D. Hobart, and Jenifer Dagut, eds. *Source Material on the South African Economy, Vol. 1: 1860–1899*. London: Oxford University Press, 1972.

Israel, Jonathan I. *Diasporas within a Diaspora: Jews, Crypto-Jews and the World Maritime Empires, 1540–1740*. Leiden: Brill Publishers, 2002.

Israel, Jonathan I., and Salverda Reinier. *Dutch Jewry: Its History and Secular Culture (1500–2000)*. Leiden: Brill Publishers, 2002.

Jacobs, Henri, and Nicolas Chatrian. *Monographie du diamant*. Paris: Anvers, 1880.

Janse, A. J. A. "A History of Diamond Sources in Africa, Part I." *Gems and Gemology* 31: 4 (Winter 1995), 228–255.

Johnstone, F. *Class, Race and Gold: A Study of Class Relations and Racial Discrimination in South Africa*. London: Routledge, 1976.

Jones, George Chetwynd Griffith. *Knaves of Diamonds, Being Tales of Mine and Veld, Etc*. London: C. A. Pearson, 1899.

Jong, F. de. *Van Ruw Tot Geslepen. De Culturele Betekenis van de Alg. Ned. Diamantbewerkers Bond in de Geschiedenis van Amsterdam. Herdenkingsrede Ter Gelegenheid van Het 60-Jarig Bestaan*. Amsterdam: N.V.V., 1955.

Jonker, Joost. *Merchants, Bankers, Middlemen: The Amsterdam Money Market during the First Half of the Nineteenth Century*. Amsterdam: NEHA, 1996.

Julius, Anthony. *Trials of the Diaspora: A History of Anti-Semitism in England*. Oxford: Oxford University Press, 2010.

K. *The Diamond Fields of South Africa: With Notes of Journey There and Homeward, and Some Things about Diamonds and Other Jewels*. New York: American News Company, 1872.

Kagan, Richard L., and Philip D. Morgan, eds. *Atlantic Diasporas: Jews, Conversos, and Crypto-Jews in the Age of Mercantilism, 1500–1800*. Baltimore: Johns Hopkins University Press, 2009.

Kahn, Ava K., and Adam D. Mendelsohn, eds. *Transnational Traditions: New Perspectives on American Jewish History*. Detroit: Wayne State University Press, 2014.

Kalmar, Ivan, and Derek Penslar, eds. *Orientalism and the Jews*. Waltham: Brandeis University Press, 2004.

Kanfer, Stefan. *The Last Empire: De Beers, Diamonds, and the World*. New York: Farrar, Strauss & Giroux, 1993.

Kaplan, Mendel. *Jewish Roots in the South African Economy*. Cape Town: C. Struik Publishers, 1986.

Kaplan, Mendel, and Marian Robertson. *Founders and Followers: Johannesburg Jewry, 1887–1915*. Cape Town: Vlaeberg Publishers, 1991.

Karp, Jonathan. "It's the Economy, Shmendrick! An 'Economic Turn' in Jewish Studies?" *AJS Perspectives* (Fall 2009), 8–11.

Karp, Jonathan. *The Politics of Jewish Commerce: Economic Thought and Emancipation in Europe, 1638–1848*. Cambridge: Cambridge University Press, 2008.

Katz, Ethan B., Lisa Moses Leff, and Maud Mandel, eds. *Colonialism and the Jews*. Bloomington: Indiana University Press, 2017.

Katz, Wendy R. *Rider Haggard and the Fiction of Empire: Critical Study of British Imperial Fiction*. Cambridge: Cambridge University Press, 1987.

Kaufman, Heidi. "King Solomon's Mines? African Jewry, British Imperialism, and H. Rider Haggard's Diamonds." *Victorian Literature and Culture* 33 (2005), 517–539.

Kaufman, Stuart B. *Samuel Gompers and the Origins of the American Federation of Labor, 1848–1896*. Westport: Greenwood Press, 1973.

Kaufman, Stuart, Peter J. Albert, and Grace Palladino, eds. *The Samuel Gompers Papers*, Vols. 1–13. Urbana-Champaign: University of Illinois Press, 2013.

Kershen, Anne J. *Trade Unionism amongst the Jewish Tailoring Workers of London, 1872–1915*. London: London Museum of Jewish Life, 1988.

Kidd, Alan, and David Nicholls, editors. *Gender, Civic Culture and Consumerism: Middle-Class Identity in Britain, 1800–1940*. Manchester: Manchester University Press, 1999.

Kinsey, Danielle. "Imperial Splendor: Diamonds, Commodity Chains, and Consumer Culture in Nineteenth-Century Britain." PhD Dissertation, University of Illinois, Urbana-Champaign, 2010.

Kinsey, Danielle. "Koh-i-Noor: Empire, Diamonds, and the Performance of British Material Culture." *Journal of British Studies* 48: 2 (2009), 391–419.

Klein, Glenn. *Faceting History: Cutting Diamonds and Colored Stones*. Bloomington: Xlibris, 2005.

Knollys, Henry. "Diamond-Digging in South Africa." *Blackwood's Edinburgh Magazine* 150: 911 (1891), 317–333.

Knotter, Ad. *Economische transformatie en stedelijke arbeidsmarkt: Amsterdam in de tweede helft van de negentiende eeuw*. Zwolle: Waanders, 1991.

Kobrin, Rebecca, and Adam Teller, editors. *Purchasing Power: The Economics of Modern Jewish History*. Philadelphia: University of Pennsylvania Press, 2015.

Kobrin, Rebecca, ed. *Chosen Capital: The Jewish Encounter with American Capitalism*. New Brunswick: Rutgers University Press, 2012.

Kockelbergh, Iris, Eddy Vleeschdrager, and Jan Walgrave, eds. *The Brilliant Story of Antwerp Diamonds*. Antwerp: MIM, 1992.

Koskoff, David E. *The Diamond World*. New York: Harper & Row, 1981.

Kuijper, Herman. *De Algemeene Nederlandsche Diamantbewerkersbond te Amsterdam: Feiten, cijfers en verrichtingen uit zijn geschiedenis*. Amsterdam: Uitgave ANDB, 1896.
Laidlaw, Zoe. *Colonial Connections, 1815–1845: Patronage, The Information Revolution, and Colonial Government*. Manchester: Manchester University Press, 2005.
Lambert, David. *Colonial Lives across the British Empire: Imperial Careering in the Long Nineteenth Century*. Cambridge: Cambridge University Press, 2006.
Laslett, John H. M. "Samuel Gompers and the Rise of American Business Unionism." In *Labor Leaders in America*. Urbana-Champaign: University of Illinois Press, 1987. Pp. 62–88.
Laureys, Erik. *Meesters van het diamant: De Belgische diamantsector tijdens het Nazibewind*. Tielt: Lannoo, 2005.
Leach, William. *Land of Desire: Merchants, Power, and the Rise of a New American Culture*. New York: Vintage Books, 1994.
Legrand, Jacques. *Cut in Antwerp: Antwerpen, wereldcentrum voor diamant*. Amsterdam: VNU Books International, 1982.
Lenzen, Godehard. *The History of Diamond Production and the Diamond Trade*. London: Barrie & Jenkins, 1970.
Lerner, Paul. *The Consuming Temple: Jews, Department Stores, and the Consumer Revolution in Germany, 1880–1940*. Ithaca: Cornell University Press, 2015.
Lester, Alan. *Imperial Networks: Creating Identities in Nineteenth-Century South Africa and Britain*. London: Routledge, 2001.
Levin, Nora. *While Messiah Tarried: Jewish Socialist Movements, 1871–1917*. New York: Schocken Books, 1977.
Leviticus, Felix, and Henri Polak. *Geïllustreerde encyclopaedie der diamantnijverheid*. Haarlem: De Erven F. Bohn, 1908.
Lewinsohn, Richard. *Barney Barnato: From Whitechapel Clown to Diamond King*. New York: E. P. Dutton, 1938.
Lichtenstein, Rachel. *Diamond Street—The Secret History of Hatton Garden*. London: Penguin, 2013.
Lindley, Augustus F. *Adamantia*. London: Collingridge, 1873.
Lipschitz, Simone. *De Amsterdamse Diamantbeurs / The Amsterdam Diamond Exchange*. Amsterdam: Stadsuitgeverij Amsterdam, 1990.
Livesay, Harold. *Samuel Gompers and Organized Labor in America*. Boston: Little, Brown and Company, 1978.
Loos, D. de, *Diamant en edele metalen*. Vol. 1. Haarlem: De Erven Loosjes, 1890.
Luwel, Luc. *Antwerpen: Ongeslepen diamant*. Gent: Scoop, 2000.
MacKenzie, John. *Imperialism and Popular Culture*. Manchester: Manchester University Press, 1986.
Magee, Gary B., and Andrew S. Thompson. *Empire and Globalisation: Networks of People, Good and Capital in the British World, c. 1850–1914*. Cambridge: Cambridge University Press, 2010.
Magubane, Zine. *Bringing the Empire Home: Race, Class, and Gender in Britain and Colonial South Africa*. Chicago: Chicago University Press, 2003.
Maillard, Robert, ed. *Diamonds: Myth, Magic and Reality*. New York: Crown Publishers, 1988.
Mandel, Bernard. *Samuel Gompers: A Biography*. Yellow Springs: Antioch Press, 1963.
Manor, Ehud. *Forward: The Jewish Daily Forward (Forverts) Newspaper. Immigrants, Socialism and Jewish Politics in New York, 1890–1917*. Brighton, UK: Sussex Academic Press, 2009.

Manor-Friedman, Tamar, ed. *Workers and Revolutionaries: The Jewish Labor Movement*. Tel Aviv: Beth Hatefutsoth, The Nahum Goldmann Museum of the Jewish Diaspora, 1994.

Mantzaris, Evangelos A. "Jewish Trade Unions in Cape Town, South Africa, 1903–1907: A Socio-Historical Study." *Jewish Social Studies* 49: 3/4 (1987), 251–264.

Marchand, Roland. *Advertising the American Dream: Making Way for Modernity*. Berkeley: University of California Press, 1985.

Markovitz, Stefanie. "Form Things: Looking at Genre through Victorian Diamonds." *Victorian Studies* 52: 4 (2010), 591–619.

Massil, William I., et al. *Immigrant Furniture Workers in London 1881–1939: And the Jewish Contribution to the Furniture Trade*. London: Jewish Museum, 1997.

Matthews, Josiah Wright. *Incwadi Yami, Or, Twenty Years' Personal Experience in South Africa*. New York: Rogers and Sherwood, 1887.

Mattie, Erik. *World's Fairs*. New York: Princeton Architectural Press, 1998.

McCabe, I. B., G. Harlaftis, and I. P. Minoglou, eds. *Diaspora Entrepreneurial Networks—Four Centuries of History*. Oxford: Berg, 2005.

Mendelsohn, Adam. *The Rag Race: How Jews Sewed Their Way to Success in America and the British Empire*. New York: New York University Press, 2015.

Mendelsohn, Ezra, ed. *Essential Papers on Jews and the Left*. New York: New York University Press, 1997.

Mendelsohn, Richard. *The Jews in South Africa: An Illustrated History*. Johannesburg: Jonathan Ball, 2008.

Mendelsohn, Richard. *Sammy Marks: The Uncrowned King of the Transvaal*. Athens: Ohio University Press, 1991.

Mercier, Vincent. *Prins Diamant: Het tragische verval van een wereldimperium*. Antwerp: Van Halewyck, 2013.

Meredith, Martin. *Diamonds, Gold, and War*. London: Simon & Schuster, 2007.

Metz, Daniel. *Diamantgracht: Het joodse hart van een typisch Amsterdamse industrie*. Zutphen: Walburg Pers, 2022.

Michels, Tony. *A Fire in Their Hearts: Yiddish Socialists in New York*. Cambridge, MA: Harvard University Press, 2005.

Michielsen, A. *De diamanteconomie: Waarde, prijs en conjunctuur*. Antwerp: Christelijke Belgische Diamantbewerkerscentrale, 1955.

Michman, J., ed. *Dutch Jewish History I: Proceedings of the Symposium on the History of the Jews in the Netherlands*. Jerusalem: Tel-Aviv University, 1984.

Meijer, Roelie, and Peter Engelsman. *Vier eeuwen diamant: Amsterdam, Antwerpen, London*. Hoorn: Uniepers, 1986.

Minter, William. *King Solomon's Mines Revisited: Western Interests and the Burdened History of Southern Africa*. New York: Basic Books, 1986.

Mitchell, Henry. *Diamonds and Gold of South Africa*. London: Mathieson & Son, 1888.

Morris, Ruth. *Belgravia: A London Magazine and Representations of Jewish Characters and Jewish Culture 1866–1880*. London: Academica Press, 2015.

Morton, William J. *The South African Diamond Fields, and a Journey to the Mines*. New York: American Geographical Society, 1877.

Mosse, Werner E., and Hans Pohl, eds. *Jüdische Unternehmer in Deutschland im 19. und 20. Jahrhundert*. Stuttgart: Franz Steiner Verlag, 1992.

Mount, Harry A. "Our Diamond Industry: How the United States Has Become the Greatest Buyer of Diamonds in the World." *Scientific American* 123: 25 (December 1920), 614, 623–624.

Muller, Jerzy Z. *Capitalism and the Jews*. Princeton: Princeton University Press, 2010.

Munich, Adrienne. *Empire of Diamonds: Victorian Gems in Imperial Setting*. Charlottesville: University of Virginia Press, 2020.
Murray, Richard William. *South African Reminiscences*. Cape Town: J. C. Juta & Co., 1894.
Naman, Anne Aresty. *The Jew in the Victorian Novel: Some Relationships between Prejudice and Art*. New York: AMS Press, 1980.
Newbury, Colin. *The Diamond Ring: Business, Politics, and Precious Stones in South Africa, 1867–1947*. Oxford: Clarendon Press, 1989.
Newbury, Colin. "The Origins and Function of the London Diamond Syndicate, 1889–1914." *Business History* 29: 1 (1987), 5–26.
Newbury, Colin. "Technology, Capital, and Consolidation: The Performance of De Beers Mining Company Limited, 1880–1889." *Business History Review* 61: 1 (1987), 1–42.
Niekerk, Febe van, ed. *Knights of the Shovel: From the Original Typescript Manuscript, A History of the Diamond Fields by George Beet, Febe Van Niekerk and Diamond Fields Pioneers' Association (1996)*. Cape Town: Kimberley Africana Library, 1996.
Oltuski, Alicia. *Precious Objects: A Story of Diamonds, Family, and a Way of Life*. New York: Scribner, 2011.
Onselen, Charles van. *New Babylon New Nineveh: Everyday Life on the Witwatersrand, 1886–1914*. Johannesburg: Jonathan Ball Publishers, 2001.
Onselen, Charles van. *The Cowboy Capitalist: John Hays Hammond, the American West, and the Jameson Raid in South Africa*. Charlottesville: University of Virginia Press, 2018.
Payton, Charles Alfred. *The Diamond Diggings of South Africa: A Personal and Practical Account*. London: Horace Cox, 1872.
Phillips, Lionel. *Some Reminiscences*. London: Hutchinson & Company, 1924.
Phimister, I. R. "Historians and the Big Hole: Kimberley's Historiography Reviewed." *Suid-Afrikaanse Historiese Joernaal* 20: 1 (1988), 105–113.
Plotz, John. *Portable Property: Victorian Culture on the Move*. Princeton: Princeton University Press, 2008.
Pointon, Marcia. *Brilliant Effects: A Cultural History of Gem Stones and Jewellery*. London: Paul Mellon Centre BA, 2010.
Pointon, Marcia. *Rocks, Ice and Dirty Stones: Diamond Histories*. London: Reaktion Books, 2017.
Polak, Henri. *De Strijd Der Diamantbewerkers*. Amsterdam: S. L. van Looy 1896.
Polland, Annie, and Daniel Soyer, eds, *Emerging Metropolis: New York Jews in the Age of Immigration, 1840–1920*. New York: New York University Press, 2012.
Pollins, Harold. *Economic History of the Jews in England*. London: Associated University Presses, 1982.
Post, Paul, and Bies van Ede. *De diamantenroof: Hoe hoge Nazi's met diamanten uit België en Nederland nsar Zuid-Amerika vluchtten*. Utrecht: Omniboek, 2016.
Pratt, Mary Louise. *Imperial Eyes: Travel Writing and Transculturation*. London: Routledge, 2007.
Prell, Riv-Ellen. *Fighting to Become Americans: Assimilation and the Trouble between Jewish Women and Jewish Men*. Boston: Beacon Press, 1999.
Qureshi, Sadiah. *Peoples on Parade: Exhibitions, Empire, and Anthropology in Nineteenth-Century Britain*. Chicago: University of Chicago Press, 2011.
Rall, Maureen. *Petticoat Pioneers: The History of the Pioneer Women Who Lived on the Diamond Fields in the Early Years*. Kimberley: Kimberley Africana Library, 2002.

Rappaport, Erika. *Shopping for Pleasure: Women in the Making of London's West End.* Princeton: Princeton University Press, 2001.
Raymond, Harry. *B. I. Barnato: A Memoir.* London: Isbister and Company, 1897.
Reijnders, Carolus. *Van "Joodse Natiën" tot Joodse Nederlanders: Een onderzoek naar getto- en assimilatie-verschijnselen tussen 1600 en 1942.* Amsterdam: Joko, 1969.
Reunert, Theodore. *Diamonds and Gold in South Africa.* Johannesburg: J. C. Juta & Co., 1893.
Reuveni, Gideon, and Sarah Wobick-Segev, eds. *The Economy in Jewish History: New Perspectives on the Interrelationship between Ethnicity and Economic Life.* New York: Berghahn, 2010.
Reuveni, Gideon, and Nils Roemer, eds. *Longing, Belonging, and the Making of Jewish Consumer Culture.* Institute of Jewish Studies in Judaica 11. Leiden: Brill, 2010.
Richards, Thomas. *The Commodity Culture of Victorian England: Advertising and Spectacle, 1851–1914.* Stanford: Stanford University Press, 1991.
Richman, Barak. *Stateless Commerce: Cambridge: The Diamond Network and the Persistence of Relational Exchange.* Cambridge, MA: Harvard University Press, 2017.
Rijxman, A. S. *A. C. Wertheim, 1832–1897: Een bijdrage tot zijn levensgeschiedenis.* Amsterdam: Keesing, 1961.
Rijxman, A. S. "Mr. Frederik Salomon van Nierop, 1844–1924." In I. J. Brugmans and W. J. Wieringa, eds. *Bedrijf en samenleving: Economisch-historische studies over Nederland in de negentiende en twintigste eeuw.* Alphen aan de Rijn: Samsom, 1967.
Rischin, Moses. *The Promised City: New York's Jews, 1870–1914.* Cambridge, MA: Harvard University Press, 1962.
Roberts, Brian. *Kimberley: Turbulent City.* Cape Town: D. Philip, 1976.
Roberts, Janine. *Glitter and Greed: The Secret World of the Diamond Empire.* New York: Disinformation, 2003.
Robertson, Marian. *Diamond Fever: South African Diamond History 1866–69.* Oxford: Oxford University Press, 1974.
Robertson, Marian. "Investing Talent in the Witwatersrand: Jewish Traders, Craftsmen and Small Entrepreneurs." *Founders and Followers: Johannesburg Jewry 1887–1915.* Edited by Mendel Kaplan and Marian Robertson. Cape Town: Vlaeberg Publishers, 1991. Pp. 115–132.
Rosenberg, Edgar. *From Shylock to Svengali: Jewish Stereotypes in English Fiction.* Stanford: Stanford University Press, 1960.
Ross, Robert. *A Concise History of South Africa.* Cambridge: Cambridge University Press, 1999.
Ross, Robert. *Beyond the Pale: Essays on the History of Colonial South Africa.* Lebanon, NH: University Press of New England, 1993.
Rotberg, Robert I., and Miles F. Shore. *The Founder: Cecil Rhodes and the Pursuit of Power.* Oxford: Oxford University Press, 1988.
Rozen, M., ed. *Homelands and Diasporas: Greeks, Jews and Their Migrations.* London: I. B. Tauris & Co, 2008.
Rydell, Robert W. *All the World's a Fair: Visions of Empire at American International Expositions, 1876–1916.* Chicago: University of Chicago Press, 1987.
Rydell, Robert W. *World of Fairs: The Century-of-Progress Expositions.* Chicago: University of Chicago Press, 1993.
Sachar, Howard. *A History of the Jews in America.* New York: Knopf Doubleday Publishing, 1993.
Saerens, Lieven. *Vreemdelingen in een wereldstad: Een geschiedenis van Antwerpen en zijn joodse bevolking (1880–1944).* Tielt: Lannoo, 2000.

Saks, David. *South African Jewry: A Contemporary Portrait.* Jerusalem: Institute of the World Jewish Congress, 2003.

Saron, Gustav, and Louis Hotz. *The Jews in South Africa: A History.* Oxford: Oxford University Press, 1955.

Sattaur, Jen. "Commodities, Ownership, and the Eustace Diamonds: The Value of Femininity." *Victorian Literature and Culture* 38: 1 (2010), 39–52.

Schijf, Huibert. *Netwerken van een financieel-economische elite. Personele verbindingen in het Nederlandse bedrijfsleven aan het eind van de negentiende eeuw.* Amsterdam: Het Spinhuis, 1993.

Schijf, Huibert, and Michiel Wagenaar. "De joodse bourgeoisie in Amsterdam, 1796–1914." In *Gedurfd Verzamelen: Van Chagall tot Mondriaan.* Edited by H. Schijf en E. van Voolen. Amsterdam: Joods Historisch Museum, 2010. Pp. 26–39.

Schlugleit, Dora. *Geschiedenis van Het Antwerpsche Diamantslijpersambacht (1582–1797).* Antwerpen: Guillaume, 1935.

Schmidt, Ephraim. *Geschiedenis van de Joden in Antwerpen.* Antwerpen: Ontwikkeling, 1963.

Schöffer, I. "The Jews in the Netherlands: The Position of a Minority through Three Centuries." *Studia Rosenthaliana* 15 (1981), 85–100.

Scully, William Charles. *Reminiscences of a South African Pioneer.* London: Unwin, 1913.

Shain, Milton. "Diamonds, Pogroms and Undesirables: Anti-Alienism and Legislation in the Cape Colony, 1890–1906." *South African Historical Journal* 12: 1 (1980), 13–28.

Shain, Milton. *Jewry and Cape Society: The Origins and Activities of the Jewish Board of Deputies for the Cape Colony.* Cape Town: Historical Publication Society, 1983.

Shain, Milton. *The Roots of Antisemitism in South Africa.* Charlottesville: University of Virginia Press, 1994.

Shain, Milton. *Memories, Realities and Dreams: Aspects of the South African Jewish Experience.* Johannesburg: Jonathan Ball Publishers, 2002.

Shain, Milton. "'Vant to Puy a Vaatch': The 'Smous' and Pioneer Trader in South African Jewish Historiography." *Jewish Affairs* 57: 3 (2002), 39–46.

Shain, Milton, and Richard Mendelsohn. *The Jews in South Africa: An Illustrated History.* Johannesburg: Jonathan Ball Publishing, 2009.

Shield, Renée Rose. *Diamond Stories: Enduring Change on 47th Street.* Ithaca: Cornell University Press, 2002.

Shimony, Gideon. *Community and Conscience: The Jews in Apartheid South Africa.* Waltham: Brandeis University Press, 2003.

Shor, Russell. *Connections: A Profile of Diamond People and Their History.* Antwerp: World Federation of Diamond Bourses, 1993.

Sieborger, Rob. *The Recruitment and Organisation of African Labour for the Kimberley Diamond Mines, 1871–1888.* MA Thesis, Rhodes University, 1975.

Siegel, Dina. *The Mazzel Ritual: Culture, Customs and Crime in the Diamond Trade.* New York: Springer, 2009.

Smalberger, John. "I.D.B. and the Mining Compound System in the 1880s." *South African Journal of Economics* 42: 4 (1974), 398–414.

Smith, Alfred H. *A Short Sketch of the African Diamond Mines.* New York: Alfred H. Smith, 1881.

Soyer, Daniel. *A Coat of Many Colors: Immigration, Globalism, and Reform in the New York Garment Industry.* New York: Fordham University Press, 2005.

Stein, Sara Abrevaya. *Plumes: Ostrich Feathers, Jews, and a Lost World of Global Commerce.* New Haven: Yale University Press, 2010.

Steinbach, Susie L. *Understanding the Victorians: Politics, Culture and Society in Nineteenth-Century Britain*. London: Routledge, 2012.

Steytler, J. G. *The Diamond Fields of South Africa: With a Map of the Country and Full Particulars as to Roads, Prices of Necessaries, &c.* Cape Town: Saul Solomon & Co., 1870.

Stiebel, Lindy. *Imagining Africa: Landscape in H. Rider Haggard's African Romances*. Westport: Greenwood, 2001.

Strasser, Susan. *Satisfaction Guaranteed: The Making of the American Mass Market*. New York: Pantheon, 1989.

Streeter, Edwin W., *The Great Diamonds of the World: Their History and Romance*. London: G. Bell & Sons, 1882.

Streeter, Edwin W. *Precious Stones and Gems, Their History, Sources and Characteristics*. London, G. Bell & Sons, 1892.

Streeter, Patrick. *Streeter of Bond Street*. London: Matching Press, 1993.

Sutton, I. B. "The Diggers' Revolt in Griqualand West, 1875." *International Journal of African Historical Studies* 12: 1 (1979), 40–61.

Swierenga, Robert P. *The Forerunners: Dutch Jewry in the North American Diaspora*. Detroit: Wayne State University Press, 1994.

Tcherikower, Elias. *The Early Jewish Labor Movement in the United States*. Transl. Aaron Antonovsky. New York: YIVO, 1961.

Tedlow, Richard S. *New and Improved: The Story of Mass Marketing in America*. New York: Basic, 1990.

Thompson, Leonard. *A History of South Africa*. New Haven: Yale University Press, 2000.

Tijn, Theo van. "De Algemeene Nederlandsche Diamantbewerkersbond (ANDB). Een Succes En Zijn Verklaring." *BMGN—Low Countries Historical Review* 88: 3 (1973), 403–418.

Tijn, Theo van. *Twintig jaren Amsterdam*. Amsterdam: Scheltema & Holkema, 1965.

Tijn, Theo van, and M. G. Emeis. *Amsterdam en diamant 1845–1897*. Amsterdam: A. van Moppes, 1976.

Tolansky, S. *The History and Use of the Diamond*. London: Shenval Press, 1962.

Trivellato, Francesca. *The Familiarity of Strangers: The Sephardic Diaspora, Livorno, and Cross-Cultural Trade in the Early Modern Period*. New Haven: Yale University Press, 2009.

Trivellato, Francesca. *The Promise and Peril of Credit: What a Forgotten Legend about Jews and Finance Tells Us about the Making of European Commercial Society*. Princeton: Princeton University Press, 2019.

Trollope, Anthony. *South Africa: In Two Volumes*. London: Chapman and Hall, 1878.

Turrell, Robert Vicat. "Diamonds and Migrant Labour in South Africa, 1869–1910." *History Today* 36: 5 (1986), 45–49.

Turrell, Robert Vicat. "The 1875 Black Flag Revolt on the Kimberley Diamond Fields." *Journal of Southern African Studies* 7: 2 (1981), 194–235.

Turrell, Robert Vicat. "Rhodes, De Beers, and Monopoly." *Journal of Imperial and Commonwealth History* 10: 3 (1982), 311–343.

Turrell, Robert Vicat. *Capital and Labour on the Kimberley Diamond Fields, 1871–1890*. Cambridge: Cambridge University Press, 1987.

Turrell, Robert Vicat, and Jean-Jacques Van Helten. "The Rothschilds, the Exploration Company and Mining Finance." *Business History* 28: 2 (1986), 181–205.

Ulmann, Albert. *Maiden Lane: The Story of a Single Street*. New York: Maiden Lane Historical Society, 1931.

Van Onselen, Charles. *Chibaro: African Mine Labour in Southern Rhodesia, 1900–1933.* London: Pluto Press, 1980.
Van Onselen, Charles. *The Cowboy Capitalist: John Hays Hammond, the American West, and the Jameson Raid in South Africa.* Charlottesville: University of Virginia Press, 2017.
Vanden Daelen, Veerle. *Laten we hun lied verder zingen. De heropbouw van de joodse gemeenschap in Antwerpen na de Tweede Wereldoorlog, 1944–1960.* Amsterdam: University of Amsterdam Press, 2008.
Vanneste, Tijl. *Global Trade and Commercial Networks: Eighteenth-Century Diamond Merchants.* London: Pickering & Chatto, 2011.
Velde, C. A. van der. *De A.N.D.B.: Een overzicht van zijn ontstaan, zijne ontwikkeling, en zijne beteekenis.* Amsterdam: Algemeene Nederlandsche Diamantbewerkersbond, 1925.
Vermandere, Martine. *Adamastos: 100 jaar Algemene Diamantbewerkersbond van België.* Gent: Archief en Museum van de Socialistische Arbeidersbeweging, 1995.
Visser, Joop, et al. *Nederlandse Ondernemers, 1850–1950: Amsterdam.* Zutphen: Walburg Pers, 2013.
Vleeschdrager, Eddy. *Diamonds: Reality and Passion.* Liège: Editions du Perron, 1997.
Vleeschdrager, Eddy. *Hardheid 10. Diamant Geschiedenis–Bewerking–Handel.* Deurne: MIM, 1995.
Vries, B. W. de. *From Pedlars to Textile Barons: The Economic Development of a Jewish Minority Group in the Netherlands.* Amsterdam: North Holland, 1989.
Vries, Boudien de. *Electoraat en elite: Sociale structuur en sociale mobiliteit in Amsterdam, 1850–1895.* Amsterdam: De Bataafsche Leeuw, 1986.
Vries, David de. *Diamonds and War: State, Capital, and Labor in British-Ruled Palestine.* New York: Berghahn Books, 2010.
Wagner, Percy Albert. *The Diamond Fields of Southern Africa.* Johannesburg: The Transvaal Leader, 1914.
Wal, F. van der. *De oudste vakbond van ons land, 1866–1916:. Ontstaan en vijftigjarige werkzaamheid van den Algemeenen Nederlandsche Typografenbond.* Nijmegen: Bondsvergadering, 1916.
Walkowitz, Judith R. *City of Dreadful Delight: Narratives of Sexual Danger in Late-Victorian London.* Chicago: University of Chicago Press, 1992.
Weissman Joselit, Jenna. "Cut Gems: How Jews Brought Diamonds from South Africa to Amsterdam to Midtown Manhattan." *Tablet Magazine* (online: January 23, 2020).
Weissman Joselit, Jenna. *A Perfect Fit: Clothes, Character, and the Promise of America.* New York: Macmillan, 2001.
Wenger, Beth. *The Jewish Americans: Three Centuries of Jewish Voices in America.* New York: Doubleday, 2007.
Westwood, Sallie. "'Diamond Time': Constructing Time, Constructing Markets in the Diamond Trade." *Time and Society* 11: 1 (2002), 25–38.
Wheatcroft, G. *The Randlords: The Men Who Made South Africa.* London: Weidenfeld & Nicolson, 1985.
Wiel, Rein van der. *Van Rapenburgerstraat naar Amerika: de levenstijd van diamantbewerker en kunstverzamelaar Andries van Wezel (1856–1921).* Zwolle: Waanders Uitgeverij, 2010.
Williams, Gardner F. *The Diamond Mines of South Africa.* New York: B. F. Buck, 1905.
Wilson, Kathleen, ed. *A New Imperial History: Culture, Identity, and Modernity in Britain and the Empire, 1660–1840.* Cambridge: Cambridge University Press, 2004.

Worden, Nigel, Elizabeth van Heyningen, and Vivian Bickford-Smith, eds. *Cape Town: The Making of a City*. Cape Town: New Africa Books, 2012.

Worger, William H. *South Africa's City of Diamonds: Mine Workers and Monopoly Capitalism in Kimberley, 1867–1895*. New Haven: Yale University Press, 1987.

Wye Milley, Henry James. "The Eustace Diamonds and The Moonstone." *Studies in Philology* 36: 4 (1939), 651–663.

Yogev, Gedalia. *Diamonds and Coral: Anglo-Dutch Jews and Eighteenth-Century Trade*. New York: Holmes & Meier, 1978.

INDEX

For the benefit of digital users, indexed terms that span two pages (e.g., 52–53) may, on occasion, appear on only one of those pages.

A. E. Daniels & Zoon diamond factory, 1–2
A. J. Groeneman & Co. (jewelers), 140–42
Abrahams, Alfred, 46–47
Abrahams, J. E., 50
Adamant Diamond Mining Company, 56–57
Adler, Hermann, 90–91
Adler, Moses, 139
Adler, Nathan, 31–32
African Diamond Mining Company, 56–57
African exclusion from mine ownership, 29, 191–92
African labor/laborers, 55–56, 171–72, 220n.93, 225n.137
Albert (Prince), 80–81
Albrecht, Henning, 206n.7
Albu, George, 32–33
Albu, Leopold, 32–33
Algemeen Handelsblad, 104
Algemeene Nederlandse Diamantbewerkersbond (General Dutch Diamond Workers Union/ANDB), 74–75, 103, 114–16, 119, 137–38, 148–50, 187, 188–89, 240n.84, 241–42n.105, 248n.83; factory conditions efforts, 96–98, 186; successes, 19–20, 116, 186, 187–88; wage increase efforts, 6, 186; *see also* Polak, Henri
Alien Contract Labor Law (1885), 133–34, 246n.48
Allen, Charles, 224–25n.135

American Federation of Labor, 122–23, 133–34, 147
Amsterdam Bank, 108–9, 237n.48, 238n.54
Amsterdam diamond trade, 9, 17–18, 100–1, 208n.25, 230n.56, 239n.65; factories, 234n.9, 236n.41; Jewish involvement, 96–99, 106–9, 112; modernizations, 8, 98–99; wages, 6, 100–1, 103–4, 110, 112–14, 115, 117–18, 119, 145–46, 235n.28
Amsterdam Impressionist School, 1
Anglo-Jewish Association (AJA), 90, 231n.66
Anglo-Jewish Historical Exhibition, 90–92
Ansel, Judith Levie, 1–2
antisemitism, 24, 79, 177–78; in England, 161, 181–82; in popular culture, 161–70, 256n.47; in South Africa, 163, 164–65, 177, 192, 253–54n.19, 254n.21, 256–57n.58, 257n.60; in United States, 133–34, 178, 180
Antwerp diamond trade, 6, 9, 18, 23–24, 39, 74, 118–19, 207n.14, 208n.25; buyers, 105, 106–7; Jewish involvement, 106–7, 230n.56; New York immigration, 135, 140, 243n.14, 248n.83
Arbeidsenquête, 112–13
Arnholz, Adolf, 30–31
Arnold, Adolph (Israel), 54–55
Arnold, Rosa, 54–55
Arnstein Bros. & Co. (jewelers), 133, 140–42, 146

Arnstein, E., 134–35
Association for the Diamond Exchange, 106, 236–37n.42, 237n.45
Association of Diamond Workers, 130
Atherstone, William Guybon, 10
Atkinson, Lewis, 84, 86–87

B. & L. Arons, 101
Baird, David, 82–83
bankers/financiers, 108–9; *see also* Amsterdam Bank; Becker & Fuld; De Hirsch & Bisschoffsheim; Hollander & Lehren; Lippmann & Rosenthal; Nierop, Frederik Salomon van; Wertheim & Gompertz; Wertheim, Abraham Carel
Barkly, Henry, 167–68
Barnato, Babe, 159
Barnato, Barney, 17, 34–35, 37–38, 58, 65–67, 70–71, 77, 159–61, 162–64, 165–66, 181–83, 197; Barnato Brothers, 17–18, 38–39, 56–57, 59–60, 61, 72–73, 169–70, 171–72, 175–76, 206n.7, 255n.33; De Beers Company, 24–25, 61, 222n.111; gold mining, 3–4, 67; Kimberly Central DMC/Kimberley mine, 24–25, 34–36, 53–54, 55–56, 61, 72, 76–77, 194, 198
Barnato, Fanny, 159, 175–76
Barnato, Harry (Isaacs), 53–54, 169
Barnato, Isaac (Jack), 56–57, 159
Barnato, Lilly, 159
Barnato, Woolf, 53–54, 56–57
Bass, Solomon, 134–35
Battles, Sadie, 127, 244n.25
Becker & Fuld, 108–9, 237n.48
Beet, George, 28–29
Beit, Alfred, 54–55, 59–60, 66, 67, 77–78, 163–64, 169, 198, 225n.143; Beit & Co., 17–18, 37–38, 54–55, 61; De Beers, 56–57, 58–59, 61; gold mining, 3–4, 67, 206n.7; in London, 72, 77–78, 165–66; in South Africa, 54–56; Wernher & Beit, 72–73, 75, 77
Beit, Eduard, 54–55
Beit, Ludwig, 54–55
Beit, Otto, 206n.7
Beit, Wilhelm, 54–55
Belgrace, Dalrymple J., 175–76
Benedict Brothers, 139

Bergtheil, Jonas, 90
Berlage, H. P., 187
Berlin Missionary Society, 44–45
Blaine & Co., 52–53
Board of Special Inquiry, 136
Boas & Co., 87, 236n.41
Boehm, Abraham, 139–40
Boer farmers, 14–16, 28–29, 31–32, 36–37, 42–43
Boer War, 93, 258n.78
Borneo diamond trade, 10–11
Boyle, Frederick, 28, 30–31, 41, 47–48
Brazilian diamond trade, 9–13, 17, 72
Breitmeyer, Ludwig, 58
Breitner, George Hendrik, 1
Brentworth, Sarah, 157
British empire, 9–10, 11–12, 24–25, 40–41, 81, 82–83, 88–89, 90–91, 222n.117
Browne, James, 139
Bruhl, David, 139
Bruyn, P. de, 127
Bultfontein Homestead Company, 56–57
Butler, James, II, 139

capitalism/capitalists, 115, 116; growth of, 22–23, 96–98, 104, 108–9, 180, 191–92; and imperialism, 23, 183, 210n.44; and Jews, 22–23, 24–25, 96–98; and anti–Semitism, 23, 61, 162–63, 164–65, 177–78; in South Africa, 55–56, 57
Carlisle, Charles S., 137
Castens, Emil, 56–57
Cattelle, Wallis Richard, 196–97
Central Labor Council, 122–23, 147
Central Mining Company of Dorstfontein, 56–57, 224n.129
Central Selling Organization, 61
Chamberlain, Neville, 185–86
Chapman, Charles, 27–28, 30–31, 41
Chester Billings & Sons, 75–76
Chicago Exposition, 190–91
Chicago World's Fair (1893), 87
Child Labor Law (Netherlands, 1874), 112
Citroen, Barend Roelof, 96, 105
Cockran, William Bourke, 129–30, 131
Coffee, Daniel, 128
Cohen, Adolpus, 45–46
Cohen, Louis, 33–34, 45–46, 167

Cohn, Richard, 139
Collins, Wilkie, 161–62, 174–75, 176–77
Colonial and Indian Exhibition (1886), 82–83, 85–86, 90–92, 229n.43, 229–30n.49
colonialism, 4–5, 84, 86–87
Commission on Immigration, 136
Compagnie Française des Mines Diamants du Cap de Bonne Esperance (French Company), 54–55, 58–60
Content, Betje Hijman, 95–96, 140
Coon, Lewis, 139–40
Coster, Meijer, 80, 81, 229n.39
Coster, Mozes Elias, 80–81, 85–86, 101, 229n.39
Couper, J. R., 162–63
credit jewelers, 153, 251n.126
Cummings, Amos J., 130–31
Currey, John Blades ("JB"), 69

D. Blaine & Co., 36
D. De Sola Mendes & Co. (jewelers), 124–25, 140–42
D. L. van Moppes & Co., 140
D. S. Granaat, 124–25, 150–51
Dam, Eduard van, 124–26, 129
Daniels & Zoon diamond factory, 104
Davidson, J., 112–13
de Beer, Diederik Arnoldus, 13
De Beers Consolidated Mines Company, 36–37, 74, 116, 121, 131–32, 164–65, 214n.12, 224n.129; directors, 56–57, 77–78; employees, 61–64; London Diamond Syndicate relationships, 74–77, 78, 121, 127–28, 131–32, 238n.60; marketing, 155–57, 189–91; mines/production, 13, 17–18, 19, 58–59, 63–64, 72–73, 74, 109–10; stock/shareholders, 37–38, 58–61, 223–24n.125; *see also* Barnato, Barney, De Beers Company; Rhodes, Cecil
de Beers, Johannes, 36–37
De Bruyn, P., 6–7
De Hirsch & Bisschoffsheim, 109
de Pass, Elias, 56–57
De Sola Mendes & Co., 146
Debenham, Storr, and Sons, 47, 71–72, 93
deep-level mining, 50–52, 194
department stores, 154
Diamant Handelsblad, 104

diamantkoopers (diamond buyers), 32–33, 35–37
Diamantslijperij–Maatschappij (Diamond Polishing Company), 101, 234n.17, 236n.40
Diamantslijpers–Vereeniging, 239n.76
diamond abundance/scarcity, 33–34, 59–60, 74, 79, 228n.30
diamond buyers, 14, 77–78, 105, 106; in Amsterdam, 5–6, 96, 100, 106–9, 132–33; London Diamond Syndicate relationship, 17–18, 74, 109–10; in New York, 75–76, 144; in South Africa, 32–33, 44, 45–49, 50, 54–55, 63–64, 67, 167
diamond cleavers/cutters, 9, 134–35; in Amsterdam, 59–60, 100–1, 103–4, 105, 110, 111, 112–13, 117, 122, 239n.67; in Boston, 126–27; in New York, 122–26, 127, 133–34, 137, 140, 145, 147–48, 243n.8, 244n.25, 248n.83, 249n.93, 259n.17; *see also* Battles, Sadie; Rose Cutters Union (RSSV)
Diamond Cutters Association (DCA), 145–46, 149–50
Diamond Cutters' Association of New York (DCA), 133–34, 246n.51
diamond dealers, in Amsterdam, 53–54, 96, 105, 106, 108–10, 192, 239n.67; in London, 16–17, 20–21, 37–38, 74, 111, 169–70, 183, 223n.122; in New York City, 5, 75–76, 127–28, 143, 144–45; popular culture depictions, 161–62, 175, 176–77, 183; in South Africa, 28–29, 32, 219n.91, 260n.25
diamond diggers/digging, 3–4, 5, 13, 20, 32–33, 48–49, 50–51, 61–63, 70, 78, 79–80, 90, 193–94, 213n.6, 217n.53, 220–21n.99, 221n.104, 223n.122; diamond bartering/selling, 32–33, 36–37, 42–44, 52–53; dry digging, 13, 41–42, 44, 50; economic opportunity, 28–29, 41–42, 50, 52–53, 56–57; Jewish diggers, 14–17, 29–30, 32; licensing fees, 37, 42–43, 44–45, 50, 216n.37; outfitters/suppliers to, 30–31, 32, 34–35, 51–52, 65, 215n.29; in rivers, 12–13, 77

Diamond Exchange Building (New York), 109, 139–40
Diamond Fields Conveyance Company, 41
Diamond Fields Transport Company, 41
Diamond Importers Committee (New York), 129–30, 131, 132
diamond merchants, 9, 13, 27–28, 52–54, 55–57, 58–60, 65–66, 221n.108; in London, xi, 10–11, 17, 36–37, 65, 72, 74, 100, 104, 110, 226n.14; in the Netherlands, 234n.12, 237n.45, 237n.49, 239n.65, 239n.67, 243n.14; in New York, 61–63, 129, 139–49, 244–45n.27; in South Africa, xii, 14–18, 30–31, 32–33, 35–39, 44–45, 47, 48, 53, 58, 63–64, 65, 67, 70, 74, 77–78, 89–90, 194, 213n.6, 215n.21, 216n.32, 216n.34, 216n.41, 223n.122; see also Barnato, Barney; Beit, Alfred; Dünkelsbühler, Anton; Emanuel, Harry; Lewis, Isaac; Lilienfeld, Leopold; Marks, Sammy; Mège, Charles; Unger, Moritz
diamond polishers, in Amsterdam, 9, 95–96, 100–1, 103–4, 105, 110, 111, 112–13, 122, 147, 239n.76; in Antwerp, 147; in Boston, 126–27; in New York, 6–7, 125–26, 127–28, 132–34, 140, 145, 147, 249n.93; wages, 103–4; see also *Diamantslijperij-Maatschappij* (Diamond Polishing Company)
Diamond Polishers' Protective Union of America (DPPU), 133–34, 145–46, 149–50
diamond prospectors, 9–10, 13, 14–16, 20, 23, 30–31, 32–33, 41–42, 44–45
diamond robberies, 69–70
Diamond Trade Act, 169, 255n.33
Diamond Verstellers Union of America, 149–50
Diamond Workers Union (London), 148–49
Diamond Workers Union (New York), 148–49
Diamond Workers' Protective Union of America (DWPU), 145, 151
diamondkoopers, 50

diamonds: cultural significance, 79–80, 92–93; social significance, 79–80, 92–93, 104–5, 152, 178, 252n.131, 252n.134
Dickens, Charles, 162–63, 175
Dieulafait, Louis, 174
Dingley Act (1897), 150–51
Dinkelspiel & Oppenheimer (jewelers), 138–39
Disselkoen, John, 140–42
Donald Curry & Company, 39–40
Downes, Edward, 123–24, 132–33
Dresden, Eduard Zadok, 101, 234n.17
Dresden, Jonas Ephraim, 101, 234n.17
Dribbel, Léon, 112–13
Dünkelsbühler, Anton, 36–37, 38–39, 48, 53–54, 56–58, 59, 61, 65–66; Adolph Mosenthal & Co., 17, 36, 53–54; A. Dünkelsbühler (firm), 17–18, 48, 61, 72–73, 76–104, 116–17; Consolidated (Gold) Mines Selection, 67, 76–77
Dunnell, Ebden & Co., 52–53
Dutch Diamond Workers' Union, 187
Dutch Federation of Unions (FNV), 96–98
Duyn, Flora van, 128
Duyn, Lena, 128
Duyn, Solomon van, 128

Eady, T. W., 20–21, 175–76
Eady, W. T., 162–63
Ebden, Alfred, 36–37
economic mobility, 95–98, 103–4, 172–73
Eduard van Dam & Co., 150–51
Edwin Streeter's (London jewelry store), 71–72, 88–89
eigenwerkmakers (independent workers), 106
Eisenmann Brothers (jewelers), 139
Eliot, T. S., 136, 246n.47
Emanuel, Harry, 10–11, 167–68, 174
Emanuel, Harry, 174
Engelsman, Monroe, 132–33
Ephrussi & Porgès, 77–78
Exposition Universelle (1889), 87

fascism, 185–86
Fera, Henry, 134–35, 139, 140–42, 248n.83

Fera, Jacques, 136–37
Ford & Wright's Diamond Cutting and Polishing Works, 84–86
Fry, John, 170
Furnas, Clifford C., 186

Gammius, Max, 54–55
Gelder, L. van, 136–37
Geo. W. Shiebler Co., 129
Gers, Minna, 31–32
Gers, Sara, 31–32
Giddy, R. W. H., 195
Goldschmidt, Louis, 46–47
Goldsmith & Frank, 129–30
Goldsmith & Weill (jewelers), 140–42
Gompers, Jacob, 122–23
Gompers, Samuel, 122–23, 242–43n.5, 247n.67
Goode, Fenimore C., 144–45
Gordon, Isidore, 32
Graetz, Heinrich, 91–92
Great Exhibition (1851), 80
Greenbaum, Samuel P., 124, 133, 134–35
Gregory, James R., 10–11, 12
Griffith, Arthur, 174
Griffith, George Chatwynd, 20–21, 162–63, 176–77
Griqua people (South Africa), 12–13, 29
Griqualand West DMC, 56–57
Groen, J. H., 6–7, 127
Guynet, Georges, 138–39

H. A. Groen & Brother (jewelers), 124–25, 140–42
Haggard, H. Rider, 162
Hall, Catherine, 4, 193–94
Hall, Owen, 165–66
Hamlin, Charles S., 134–35, 136, 137
Handwerkers Vriendenkring (Craftsmen Circle of Friends), 109
Harding, John William, 69–70
Hardy Nathan and Son, 224n.129
Harris, Daniel, 147
Harris, David, 32–33, 34–35, 77, 215n.25
Harrod's (London department store), 71–72
Hart, Benjamin, 45–46
Hart, H. B., 50
Hart, Henry, 32

Heertje, Henri, 103–4, 112
Hegt, Jacob Jacques, 148
Henle Brothers (jewelers), 139
Henry Dreyfus & Co., 129–30
Hermann, Isaac, 127, 139
Hertse, M., 136–37
Herz, Leopold, 58, 169
Hesselmeijer, XXX, 98–99
het vak (diamond business), 1–2, 6–7, 95–96
Hirschberg, Sigmund, 140–42
Hirschhorn, Fritz, 77
Hirsh, Oppenheimer & Freund (jewelers), 138–39
Hodenpyl, A. J. G., 129–30
Hoed, Abraham 134–35
Hogarth, William, 12–13
Hollander & Lehren, 108–9
Holman, William Steele, 130
Holocaust, 192–93
Holst, Henriette "Jet" Roland, 187
Holst, Richard Roland, 187
Hond, Louis, 12, 13, 36–37, 44, 45, 216n.40, 218n.64
Hope Diamond, 9
Hopetown Company (South Africa), 13
Howard (jeweler), 122
Hudmacher, J. A., 123–24, 134–35, 146–47, 243n.9
Hudmacher, Solomon, 124, 134–35, 146–47, 243n.9
Hudson, W. C., 174
Hunt & Roskell (jewelers), 12
Hunter, Andrew J., 130
Hyndman, Henry, 163–64

illegal diamond buying (IDB), 20–21, 167–68, 169–70, 171–72, 174, 181–82, 197, 255n.33
Immigration Restriction League (Brooklyn, NY), 135–36
imperialism, 162, 206n.4, 210n.44, 222n.117
Indian diamond trade, 9, 10–13, 17, 72; *see also* Kohinoor Diamond
Inland Transport Company, 27–28, 30–31, 41
Isaacs, Barnett; *see* Barnato, Barney
Isaacs, Samuel Meyer, 50, 244n.24

Israëls, Isaac, 1
Italiaander, Samuel, 128

J. Hoedenmakers, 124–25, 150–51
Jacob Saltzman & Co. (jewelers), 138–39
Jacobs, Erasmus, 10–11
Jacobs, Erasmus, 174–75
Jameson Raid, 159–60, 206n.6
Jewelers' League (1877), 139
Jewelers' Mercantile Agency (1873), 139
Jewelers' Safety Fund Society (1884), 139
Jewelers' Security Alliance (1883). 139
Jewish bankers/investors, 16–17, 36–37, 55–56
Jewish depictions, in fiction, 162–63, 175–77; in journalism, 166, 168, 175–76, 177, 183; in political cartoons & caricatures, 163, 164–66
Jewish history, affluence, 3–4, 21, 23; assimilation/integration, 3–4, 21; diasporic activity, 3–4, 23–24; imperialism, 3–5, 22–23, 24–25, 37; *see also* Amsterdam diamond trade, Jewish involvement; antisemitism; Antwerp diamond trade, Jewish involvement; London Diamond Syndicate, Jewish involvement; New York diamond trade, Jewish involvement; South African diamond trade, Jewish involvement
Jewish identity, 81, 86–87, 91–92, 93
Jewish immigration, 91–92, 93, 133–34, 172–73, 194, 195, 212n.58, 233n.5, 249n.107, 255n.41
Jewish poverty, 101–3, 109, 173, 235n.21
Jewish Studies, 22–23
Jitta, Josephus, 101, 108–9
Joel, Isaac, 169–70, 171–72
Joel, Solly, 159
Joel, Woolf, 170
Joseph Bros., 58
Joseph Mosenthal & Co., 37–38
Joseph, Morris, 90–91
Jules Porgès & Co., 36–37, 54–56, 59–60, 77–78, 224n.129

Kahn & Limburger (jewelers), 138–39
Kalf, David, 121–22, 123

Kalf, Joseph, 121–22, 123
Kalmar, Ivan, 4–5
Kann, Rudolph Hirsch, 54–55
Karsen, Eduard, 1
Keesing, Isidore, 186
Keet, B. B., 177
Keizer, Aaron, 126
Kimberley Diamond-Fields Synagogue, 91–92
Kleinwort, Sons & Co., 224n.129
Knollys, Henry, 171–72
Koch & Dreyfus (jewelers), 140–42
Kohinoor ("Mountain of Light") Diamond, 9, 80–81, 93, 154–55, 163, 174, 175, 180
Kollem, Eliaz van, 128
Konijn & Frank, 124–25
kopjewallopers (peddlers), 32–33, 36–37, 44–45, 218n.72
Kora people (South Africa), 12–13
Koranna people (South Africa), 14–16
Kossuth brothers, 32
Kryn & Wouters Bros., 123, 124–25, 140–42
Kryn, Henry, 135
Kryn, Jacques, 135
Kunz, George, 127–28

L. & A. Abrahams, 58, 72–73
L. And M. Kahn & Co., 149
L. Tannenbaum & Co. (jewelers), 140–42
labor laws (US), 121–22, 123, 124, 133, 134–35
labor movement, 6, 19; in Amsterdam, 96–98, 112–15, 119, 146, 239n.76, 240n.84, 240–41n.92, 241–42n.105, 249n.105; in New York, 122–23, 133–34, 136–37, 145–50, 242–43n.5, 249n.94, 250n.112, 250n.114; in South Africa, 116; *see also Algemeene Nederlandse Diamantbewerkersbond* (General Dutch Diamond Workers Union/ANDB); Alien Contract Labor Law (1885); American Federation of Labor; Central Labor Council; Child Labor Law (Netherlands, 1874); Diamond Polishers' Protective Union of America (DPPU); Diamond Verstellers Union of America; Diamond Workers Union (London);

Diamond Workers Union (New York); Diamond Workers' Protective Union of America (DWPU); Dutch Federation of Unions (FNV); United Diamond Cutters of America; United Diamond Workers (United Diamond Workers Bond of America); United Diamond Workers of Brooklyn
Lazarus, Betje, 188–89
Lazarus, Sophie, 188–89
Lee, Lawrence P., 134–35
Leopold Lippert & Co., 35–36
Levie, Salomon, 104
Levy, Alexander, 46–47
Levy, David, 30–31
Levy, Herman, 140–42, 146
Levy, Howard, 133
Levy, Joseph, 46–47
Lewis & Marks Co., 17, 37–38, 55–56, 59, 254n.24
Lewis, Barnett, 217n.54
Lewis, Isaac, 17, 32–33, 37–38, 54–56, 58, 59, 67, 215n.29
Lilienfeld Bros., 31–32, 35–36, 37, 38–39, 52–53
Lilienfeld, & Co., 52–53
Lilienfeld, Abraham, 31–32
Lilienfeld, Gustav, 31–32
Lilienfeld, Leopold, 3–4, 13–14, 36–38
Lilienfeld, Martin, 3–4, 13–14, 31–32, 37–38, 56–57, 58, 72
Lippert & Co., 54–55, 56–57
Lippert, Adele, 54–55
Lippert, David, 54–55
Lippmann & Rosenthal, 108–9, 237n.48
Litkie, V. A., 58
Loftis Brothers, 153–54
Loftis, Samuel T. A., 153
London and South African Exploration Company, 36–37, 53–54
London Diamond Syndicate, De Beers association, 76–77, 78, 109–10, 116, 121, 127–28, 131–32, 238n.60; Jewish involvement, 17–18, 76–77, 86–87, 161, 183, 197; labor relations, 19, 75, 117–18; market control, 17–18, 19–21, 61, 63–64, 72–73, 75–76, 109–10, 127–28; price controls, 74, 121; supply controls, 74–75, 77–78, 121

London Emigration Society, 173
Loopuit, Jozef, 112–13
Louis & Meir (jewelers), 138–39
Louis Dreyfus & Co., 52–53
Louis Strasburger & Co. (jewelers), 139
Lowenthal & Goldsmith, 45–46
Löwy, Albert, 90–91
Ludwig Nissen & Co. (jewelers), 129–30, 140–42
Lyon & Behrman (jewelers), 138–39
Lyon, Aaron, 168

Machine Diamond Cutters Union of America, 149–50
male privilege, 2
Marchand, Leon, 98–99, 101
Marcus, Morris, 45–46
Marks, Sammy, 17, 32–33, 37–38, 54–56, 58, 59, 67, 215n.29, 254n.24
Martin Lilienfeld & Co., 56–57, 61, 65, 72–73
Matthews, Josiah Wright, 20–21, 50, 57, 168–69, 170
McKinley Tariff (1890), 124–25, 128
Mège, Charles, 48, 54–55
Meijer, Andries, 149–50, 151
Meijer, Salomon "Sal," 106
Mendelssohn, Sidney, 168–69
Mendes Cutting Works, 133
Mendes, D. de Sola, 137–38, 146–47
Merriman, John X., 165–66
Metz, Jacques, 96, 101, 105
Meyer, Andries, 145
Mfengu people, 29
Mitchell, Lewis, 168–69
Mocatta, Ernest, 56–57
Mocatta, Frederic David, 90–91
Monnikendam, T., 136–37
Montagu, Hyman, 90–91
Moppes, D. L. Van, 140, 207n.19
Moppes, Hermanus van., 140
Morais, Nina, 178, 180–81
Morse, Crosby & Foss (jewelers), 125–26
Morse, Henry D., 126–27
Morton, William J., 48–49, 51–52, 53, 195
Mosenthal Bros., 31–32, 35–36, 214–15n.20
Mosenthal Sons & Co., 36–39, 45, 52–53, 72–73, 76, 209n.36, 214–15n.20

Index

Mosenthal, Adolph, 36–38, 209n.36; Adolph Mosenthal & Co., 12, 13–14, 17–18, 32, 36, 46–47, 52–54, 70–71, 227n.21; wool exportation, 3–4, 36
Mosenthal, Harry, 37–38, 54–55, 56–57, 58–59, 61, 77–78
Mosenthal, Hermann, 31–32
Mosenthal, Joseph, 31–32, 36–37, 72–73
Mosenthal, Julius, 31–32, 37
Mosenthal, Sons & Co., 224n.129
Moses, E. R., 45–46
Moulin, B. du, 101
Mount, Henry, 143–44
Mpondo people (South Africa), 14–16
Murray, Richard W., 42
Myers, Joel, 30–31, 32

N. M. Rothschild & Sons, 224n.129
N. W. Ayer & Co., 189–90
Natal Zulu people, 29
Nathan M. Rothschild & Son, 36–37
Nathan, Max, 139
National Socialism, 185–86
nativism, 20–21
Neustadt & Barnett (jewelers), 138–39
New York Diamond Company, 127
New York Diamond Cutters' Association, 136–37
New York diamond trade, 14, 122, 124, 127, 152, 154–57, 252n.134; buyers/importers, 129–30, 132–33; cutters/cleavers, 122, 123–26, 133–34, 137, 140–42, 147–48, 207n.19, 248n.83, 249n.93; dealers, 5, 6–7, 23, 127–28, 138–40, 143–24, 145, 153–54, 248n.90; Dutch influences, 142–43, 151, 211n.49, 244–45n.27; immigration issues, 135–38, 150, 243n.9; import duty effects, 6–7, 129–33, 137, 150–51; Jewish involvement, 39, 96–98, 114–15, 119, 124–25, 126, 129, 140–42, 227n.24, 241–42n.105; labor activism, 114–15, 117–19, 123, 133–34, 136–37, 145–50, 249n.94, 249n.105; labor recruitment, 6–7, 19–20; labor treatment, 19, 117–19, 123; London Diamond Syndicate relations, 75–76; polishers, 23–24, 121, 122, 123–25, 132–34, 135–36, 140–42, 145, 207n.19, 249n.93; *see also* Diamond Importers Committee (New York); labor movement, in New York; New York Diamond Cutters' Association
New York Jewelers' Association (1874), 139
New York Jewelers' Board of Trade (1855), 139
Ngqika people, 29
Niekerk, Schalk van, 12
Nierop, Frederik Salomon van, 108–9, 237n.48

Ochs brothers, 56–57, 58
Onnes, Menso Kamerlingh, 1
Oppenheimer Bros. & Co., 140
Oppenheimer Bros. & Veith, 129–30
Oppenheimer, August, 140
Oppenheimer, Bernard, 76, 77
Oppenheimer, Ernest, 76–77, 78, 116–19, 189–90, 191–92
Oppenheimer, Harry, 189–90
Oppenheimer, Henry, 139, 140–42
Oppenheimer, Louis, 76, 77
Oppenheimer, M. E., 140–42
Orion Diamond Mining Company, 56–57
Orlov Diamond, 9
Osterman, Jonas, 136–37

Paddon Bros., 58
Pais, Abraham, 128
Pais, Emanuel, 128
Pais, Jesaya, 128
Pais, Sophia, 128
Panic of 1893, 125
Payton, Charles, 45–46, 47, 213n.6, 220–21n.99
Pedi people, 50
Penslar, Derek, 4–5
Phillips, Lionel, 50–51, 165–66, 206n.6, 220n.95
Plooy, Cornelius Hendrik du, 13, 36–37
Polak, Eduard, 113
Polak, Hans, 185–86
Polak, Henri: 103, 115–16, 117–18, 119, 124, 137–38, 148–50, 187–88, 192–93, 197, 198, 239n.77, 250n.114; diamond polishing, 104, 116–17; and London Diamond Syndicate,

74–75, 117–18; National Socialism, 185–86, 189–90; strike leader/promoter, 75, 96–98, 114, 149; unemployment benefits activism, 74–75, 115, 119; wage activism, 114, 115, 119; *see also Algemeene Nederlandse Diamantbewerkersbond (General Dutch Diamond Workers Union/ANDB)*
Polak, Milly, 185–86, 259n.19
Polak, Moses, 96–98
Polak-Feistl, Maria "Mitzi," 185, 186
Pollack, Charlotte, 77
Pollack, Joseph, 77
Pollack, Mary Lina "May," 77
Porgès, Jules (Yehuda), 54–56, 58, 61, 77–78, 222n.115
Porgès, Théodore, 77–78
Posno, Charles J., 56–57, 59–60
Posno, I. M., 98–99
Posno, J. M., 45–46
Posno, Jacob Joseph, 101
Posno, L. J., 101, 234n.17
Posno, M. J., 58
Praag, Siegfried Van, 106
Pratt, Mary Louise, 14–16
Prescott Bank (London), 53–54

R. Raphael & Sons, 224n.129
Reed, Thomas, 130–31
Rhodes, Cecil, 24–25, 58–61, 76–77, 131–32, 223n.123
Rijn, Meyer van, 128
Rischin, Moses, 207n.15
Robert Garrard & Co., 80–81
Robinson, Joseph B., 58–59
Rose Cutters Union (RSSV), 188–89
Rose, Sonya, 193–94
Rosenfeld & Co., 58
Rothschild house, 225n.143
Rothschild, Alfred Augustus, 35–36, 46–47,
Rothschild, Meyer D., 129–30, 131, 140
Rothschild, Nathan, 58–61, 218–19n.75
Royal Society for the Encouragement of Arts, Manufactures, and Commerce, 80
Rudd, Charles Dunnell, 223n.123

S. Konijn, 150–51
Samuels, A., 135–36

Sanders & Bruhl Manufacturing Co., 124–25, 133
Sarphati, Samuel, 6, 107–8
Saunders, John, 139
Schaffer and Hahn (jewelers), 139
Schellenger, Gilbert A., 139–40
Schultz, Wilhelm, 32, 36
Sebag-Montefiore, Joseph, 56–57
security concerns, 48–49
Seeligsohn, 30–31
Seligman brothers, 140
Senner, Joseph H., 123–24, 133, 136
Sheldon, Louise Vesalius, 174
Simmel, Georg, 78–79, 104–5
Singh, Duleep, 80
Smit, Marianna, 96–98
Smith & Hedges (jewelers), 139
Social Democratic Bond (SDB), 113
Society for Child Nourishment (Amsterdam), 109
Society for Public Housing (Amsterdam), 109
Sonnenberg, Ikey, 36
South African diamond trade, 9–12, 14–16, 81–82, 103–4, 109–10, 139, 209n.30, 210n.42, 213n.4, 213n.6, 214n.12, 219–20n.92, 222n.121; Barkly (formerly Klipdrift) camp, 12–13, 30–31, 32, 41–42, 47–48; Bultfontein farm/mine, 13, 83; Bultfontein settlement, 13, 29, 32, 50, 219n.91, 230n.53; Cape Commission, 83, 84, 85–86; Colesberg Kopje (Kimberley) mine, 13, 36–37, 41–42, 50, 55–56, 83, 96–98, 101, 220n.93, 224n.126, 226n.10; Dorstfontein mine, 13, 216n.37; Dutoitspan farm/mine, 13, 29, 36–37, 41–42, 50; Dutoitspan settlement, 13, 46–48, 219n.91, 224n.126; Hebron camp, 12–13, 41–42; Jewish involvement, 29–31, 32–36; Kimberley settlement, 47–48, 131–32, 195–96, 216n.34, 216n.41, 217n.54, 219–20n.92, 221n.108; New Rush settlement, 13, 29, 32, 47–48, 49, 50; Pniel camp, 12–13, 30–31, 32, 41–42; Subcommittee for Minerals in Kimberley, 83, 86–87
Spaulding (jeweler), 122
Special Board of Inquiry (US), 133

Speyer, Bertha, 128
Speyer, Gerrit, 128
Spielmann, Isidore, 90–91
Standard (Diamond) Company, 58–59
Standard Bank of South Africa, 53–54, 55–56
Star of Africa Diamond, 12, 13–14
steam power, 98–99, 126–27, 205n.1
Stern Brothers & Company (jewelers), 121–22, 123, 124, 133, 140–42, 145–47, 149, 227n.24
Stern, Isidore, 75–76, 227n.24
Stern, Leopold, 75–76, 122–23, 129–30, 134–35, 137–38, 146–47, 227n.24
Stern, Nathan, 227n.24
Stern, Regina Ullman, 227n.24
Street, Edward, 71–72
Streeter, Edwin, 174
Stump, H., 134–35, 136
Swierenga, Robert P., 6–7

T. Henry Schroder & Co., 224n.129
tariffs, 125, 129, 130–33; *see also* Wilson–Gorman Act (1894)
Tas, Louis (Levie), 140
Tas, Salomon Levie, 95–96, 98–100, 101–75, 140
Taylor, Deems, 186
Tennant, James, 80–81
Tiffany & Co., 122, 126–27, 129–30
Tlhaping people (South Africa), 12–13, 14–16
Trade Union Congress, 163–64
Treue, Wilhelm, 104
Trollope, Anthony, 11–12, 47–48, 161–62, 176–77, 196
Tsonga people, 50
Turrell, Robert Vicat, 12–13, 59–60, 220n.93, 221n.104, 221n.108

U.S. Immigration Bureau, 133–35, 136–37
Unger, Moritz, 44–45, 215n.26
United Diamond Cutters of America, 149–50, 250n.115
United Diamond Workers (United Diamond Workers Bond of America), 149–50

United Diamond Workers of Brooklyn, 145–46, 147
United Diamond Workers, 19

Van Dam & Co., 148
Van Moppes & Son, 6–7
Van Wezel & Co., 150–51
Veith, Gustave, 140
Veith, Henry, 140
Vescelius-Sheldon, Louise, 162–63
Victoria (Queen), 80, 81, 84–85, 90–91, 229n.40, 231n.68
Voorzanger, Benjamin, 128
Voorzanger, Levie Benjamin, 80–81
Vries, J. de,, 150–51
Vriesland, H., 122–23

Walkowitz, Judith, 176–77
Wallach & Schiele (jewelers), 133, 140–42, 146–47
Walter, J., 58
Webb, Henry Barlow, 13, 36–37, 56–57
Weening, Jacob, 128
Weinberg, Isaac, 139
Wernher, Julius, 54–55, 56–57, 77–78
Wertheim & Gompertz, 108–9, 237n.48
Wertheim, Abraham Carel, 108–9
Wezel, Andries van, 1–4, 5–6, 8, 23–24, 104, 109–10, 119; in Belgium, 6–7; London connections, 5–6, 17–18, 19; in New York, 6–7, 23–24
Wezel, Hartog van, 1–2, 6
Wezel, Joachim van, 1–2, 6–7, 124–26, 129
Wezel, Juda van, 1–2
Wezel, Katherine van, 129
Wezel, Louisa van, 129
Wezel, Marcus van, 1–2, 6–7, 124–26, 129
Wezel, S. L. van, 149
Wezel, Salomon Levie van, 1–2, 129
white labor, 225n.137
whiteness, 87–88, 180, 207n.11, 254n.21
Williams, Gardner F., 11–12, 41–42, 59–60, 61–63, 182, 255n.33
Wilson–Gorman Act (1894), 6–7, 124–25, 128, 131–33, 135, 137–38, 148–49, 150–51

Wodehouse, John (Lord Kimberley), 49, 167–68
Wodehouse, Philip, 10
Wolf, Lucien, 90–91
Wood, H. Trueman, 84
wool trade, 3–4, 9–10, 31–32, 208n.27
Woolf, Lewis, 167
Wouters Bros., 135

Xhosa people, 29

Zangwill, Israel, 24
Zilver Bros., 124–25, 128, 133, 140–42, 146–47, 149, 150–51, 243n.9
Zilver, Arie, 125–26, 128–29
Zilver, Joseph, 147–48
Zulu people, 50
Zutphen, Jan van, 114–15, 187–88
Zwart, M. H., 136–37